HARDPRESS

ISBN: 9781290757744

Published by:
HardPress Publishing
8345 NW 66TH ST #2561
MIAMI FL 33166-2626

Email: info@hardpress.net
Web: http://www.hardpress.net

A
COUNTING-HOUSE DICTIONARY

Ballantyne Press
BALLANTYNE, HANSON AND CO., EDINBURGH
CHANDOS STREET, LONDON

A COUNTING-HOUSE DICTIONARY

CONTAINING AN

EXPLANATION OF THE TECHNICAL TERMS

USED BY

MERCHANTS AND BANKERS

IN

The Money Market and on the Stock Exchange

WITH A

MINUTE DESCRIPTION OF THE COINS

ON WHICH

THE EXCHANGES OF THE WORLD ARE BASED

AND IN TERMS OF WHICH PRICES ARE QUOTED

BY

RICHARD BITHELL, B.Sc., Ph.D.

FELLOW OF THE INSTITUTE OF BANKERS

SECOND EDITION, REVISED

LONDON

GEORGE ROUTLEDGE AND SONS

Broadway, Ludgate Hill

GLASGOW AND NEW YORK

137.80

6

PREFACE.

In compiling the present Dictionary, the author has been guided by the following rules :—

I. To exclude all words found in ordinary dictionaries, used in the same sense by bankers and merchants as by the public.

II. To insert, as far as possible, all technical words used by bankers and merchants, but which are not used by others, except in connection with banking and mercantile affairs.

III. To include all such words as are used in a vague sense in colloquial speech, but which have a restricted and technical meaning when employed in economic science.

IV. All the principal moneys of account, the coins on which the exchanges are based, their weight and fineness, have been described with great minuteness. These descriptions are founded mainly on the information furnished by the reports of the Monetary Conference which met during the Paris Exposition of 1878, and on the tables, since drawn up by M. Sudre, *Chef des Bureaux de l'Administration des Monnaies*, and published in the *Annuaire par le Bureau des Longitudes for* 1879, 1880, 1881.

In carrying out his scheme, the author has been assisted by the advice and information of several gentlemen experienced in City affairs. Some of them have kindly read the articles bearing on topics with which they are specially familiar, and have furnished suggestions and improvements, since embodied in the respective articles.

In a work like the following it is obvious that its value must depend very largely on the care and assiduity exercised in the examination of writers and experts in the subjects treated of. A list of the works consulted, and from which definitions have been extracted, is given on page vii. It has not been found practicable, nor was it needful, that the name of every author quoted should be appended to each quotation. The constant repetition of names would have occupied so much space, and would have so encumbered the letter-press, as to embarrass rather than enlighten the reader. To the writings of the late Mr. Walter Bagehot, Mr. H. D. MacLeod, Professor Leone Levi, Professor Stanley Jevons, Professor Bonamy Price, and some others, the author is greatly indebted. These works contain the latest revision of the ideas of mercantile men on banking and mercantile topics, and the definitions which their writings afford are of the utmost value. Where writers of eminence have expressed themselves in language somewhat at variance from that of others, an exception has been made in respect of quotation, and the writer's name has been appended to the words quoted.

Although the primary object of the author has been to produce a handbook of reference for persons engaged in mercantile pursuits, he has never lost sight of a secondary object, which he deemed of scarcely less importance, namely, the presentation of the subjects treated of in such a form as should be intelligible to that large number of readers who, not being professionally engaged in mercantile pursuits, are often at a loss to understand the drift of banking and commercial reports, or of financial treatises, owing to the frequent use of technical terms, which, although clear enough to the initiated, convey to those whose vocations run in a different line, at least a vague, and sometimes a totally erroneous, impression. This, it is hoped, will be accepted as a sufficient reason for the introduction of some words which might have been thought too simple to need explanation. Experience has shown that writers, out of respect to their readers, are apt to assume a more varied knowledge than the latter would like to lay claim to, and the compliment is one, which is rarely very cordially accepted.

A glance at some of the articles contained in this work, will show that a somewhat unusual feature (in books of this description) has been introduced. The history and origin of the words have been traced out in many instances, and in others indications have been given as to the direction in which inquirers may look for further results. Owing to the spread of education, researches of this nature have great attraction for those who combine with the exigences of business a love of intellectual pursuits. Nevertheless, all these portions, which may be called the *philological*, as distinguished from the *commercial*, parts of the work, are printed in a smaller and more compact type; so that any one—if such a one can be found—who takes no interest in discussions of this kind, may pass them over, and confine his attention to what is, after all, the main purport of each article.

LIST

OF

PRINCIPAL AUTHORS CONSULTED.

Anderson—History of Commerce.

Bankers—Journal of the Institute of.

Bagehot, Walter—Lombard Street: A Description of the Money Market.

Bastiat, M. Frederic—Essays on Political Economy.

Beaufoy, Henry B. H.—London Traders', Tavern and Coffee House Tokens.

Blackstone—Commentaries on the Laws of England.

Brooke, Richard, F.S.A.—The Office and Practice of a Notary in England. Edited by Professor Leone Levi.

Browne, W. A., LL.D.—Money, Weights, and Measures of all Nations.

Cairnes, Prof. J. E.—Leading Principles of Political Economy.

" " Logical Method of Political Economy.

Churchwardens' Accompts of St. Margaret's, Westminster.

Coin Book, The—Published by J. B. Lippincott, Philadelphia. (Compiler not named.)

Cunningham, David—Conditions of Social Well-being.

Fawcett, Prof. Henry, M.P.—Political Economy.

Fenn—Compendium of the English and Foreign Funds.

Flügel, Dr. J. C.—Commercial Dictionary.

Francis—History of the Bank of England.

" Historyof the Stock Exchange.

Gilbart, James William, F.R.S.—Treatise on Banking.

" " " Logic of Banking.

Goschen, J. G., M.P.—Theory of Foreign Exchanges.

Ham, George D.—Revenue and Mercantile Vade-Mecum.

Hankey, Thomson, M.P.—Principles of Banking.

HEAD, BARCLAY—Ancient Systems of Weight as applied to Money. (Journal of the Institute of Bankers.)

JEVONS, PROF. STANLEY, M.A.—Money.

" " " Theory of Political Economy.

JUSTINIAN—Institutes of. Edited by Thomas Collett Sandars, M.A.

LAWSON, WILLIAM JOHN—History of Banking.

LIPPINCOTT—The Coin Book, published at Philadelphia.

LIVERPOOL, EARL OF—Treatise on the Coins of the Realm.

LEVI, PROF. LEONE—Work and Pay.

" " Manual of Mercantile Law.

LUBBOCK, SIR JOHN, M.P.—Inaugural Address at the Institute of Bankers.

MACLEOD, HENRY DUNNING, M.A.—Theory and Practice of Banking

" " " The Elements of Banking.

" " " Economics for Beginners.

MADDISON, E. C.—On the Stock Exchange.

MARSHALL, ALFRED, and MARY PALEY—Economics of Industry.

MARTIN and TRUBNER—The Current Gold Coins of all Countries.

MARTIN, FREDERICK—History of Lloyd's, and of Marine Insurance in Great Britain.

MERREY, WALTER—Remarks on the Coinage of England, 1789.

MILL, JOHN STUART—Principles of Political Economy.

PRICE, PROF. BONAMY.—Chapters on Practical Political Economy.

RUDING—Annals of the Coinage.

SANDARS, THOMAS COLLETT, M.A.—Institutes of Justinian.

SEYD, ERNEST—Bullion and Foreign Exchanges Theoretically and Practically Considered; followed by a Defence of the Double Valuation, with Special Reference to the proposed System of Universal Coinage.

SIDGWICK, HENRY, M.A.—What is Money? (Contemporary Review, April, 1879.)

STEPHEN, JAMES, LL.D.—Blackstone's Commentaries on the Laws of England.

TATE, WILLIAM—Counting House Guide.

" " The Modern Cambist: A Guide to the Foreign Exchanges.

WALKER, F. A.—Money.

WOOLSEY, THEODORE D.—Introduction to International Law.

ANNUAIRE PAR LE BUREAU DES LONGITUDES, 1879—81.

BRITISH ALMANAC AND COMPANION, 1880.

GLOSSARIUM AD SCRIPTORES MEDIÆ ET INFIMÆ LATINITATIS. DU CANGE.

McCULLOCH'S DICTIONARY OF COMMERCE.

COUNTING HOUSE DICTIONARY.

A

A, occurs in several contractions.
A/c, account.
@ for the Latin *ad* at, or to.
A/d, after date.
A/s, account sales.
A/o, account of.

Abassi or **Abassis.** (*a*) A Persian silver coin valued at four Persian shahis. It weighs 2·08 grammes, ·900 fine, and is worth about 4*d.* sterling.

(*b*) The silver 20 copeck piece circulating in Russia. It weighs 4·079 grammes, but is only ·500 fine: worth 45 French centimes, or 4¼*d.* sterling.

Abatement. From the Latin, *batuo*, to beat, to strike; French, *battre*, to beat; *abattre*, to beat down: whence *abatement*, which signifies primarily a beating down, but is variously applied so as to convey at different times the senses of diminution, deduction, deficiency, &c.

In Commerce, *Abatement* signifies a deduction from a quoted price or value. These deductions are sometimes systematic, and fixed by the usages of particular trades; in other cases, a deduction is made in respect to a special bargain, and the phrase then used is "3 per cent. off" or "5 per cent. off" as the case may be. The most important form of *abatement* is that which occurs in the price lists of certain manufacturers, the quotations of which sometimes remain unaltered from year to year in order to avoid revision and reprinting; and the variation of price arising from fluctuations in demand and supply is indicated, by the abatement allowed, and which is announced by a trade circular from time to time as occasion may require.

Abra. A silver coin formerly in use in Poland, value about 1*s.* English.

Abrasion of Coins. Latin, *ab*, from; *radere*, to scrape or scratch.

By *abrasion*, is meant the ordinary and necessary wear and tear of coins, and is thus distinguished from *defacement*, which may be the result of violence, either intentional or accidental. If a sove-

B

reign is reduced in weight to 122·50 grains or 7·93787 grammes, it ceases to be a legal tender, and if anyone has such a sovereign offered to him in payment of a debt, he is required by the law to cut or deface the coin, when it becomes simply bullion, and the tenderer must bear the loss. If the justice of the proceeding be disputed, and the coin be found to be above the limit prescribed, the defacer must bear the loss. This injunction, however, is scarcely ever observed, except at the Bank of England, and some Government offices; it would be too irksome, and the more usual practice is, to avoid the use of sovereigns except in small quantities, and to make payments in Bank of England notes.

Abuquelp. A silver coin formerly in use in Egypt, value about 1*s*. 6*d*. sterling.

Acceptance. Latin, *ad*, to; *capio*, I take; *accipĕre*, to take to one's self; French, *accepter;* Italian, *accettare;* Spanish, *aceptar.*

To *accept* a Bill, signifies in full, to "accept the obligation of paying the Bill when it falls due." The Acceptor usually notifies his acceptance of a Bill by writing transversely across the face of it the word "Accepted" with the date at which it is payable, followed by his name, or that of the firm which he represents. An acceptance in this form is called *General.*

If, in addition to the above words, other words are added, making it payable at some particular house, for example, "payable at the Alliance Bank," the acceptance is then said to be *Special.*

If, further, the acceptor refuses to make himself responsible for more than a part of the sum stated on the Bill, say for £50, when the Bill was drawn for £100, he writes "Accepted for £50 only; or if he inserts any other alteration either in regard to time of payment, or the fulfilment of some condition, the Acceptance is said to be *Qualified.* (*See After Sight.*)

Acceptances. Bills accepted by a Banking or other commercial firm, and which take their place among the "liabilities" of the acceptors to the payees.

Acceptilation. From the Latin, *acceptilatio.* This word is not found in the works of classical writers, but was introduced into commercial language through the works of Justinian, and thus found its way into all the countries of Southern Europe. It is, however, still limited in its use to lawyers, the equivalent in English being "a release."

A Release from a debt or obligation. (*See Release.*)

Accommodation Bill. French, *accomoder;* Italian, *accomodare;* Spanish, *accomodar;* all from the Latin, *accomodare* (adcommodum), to adjust, to cause one thing to suit another, to do anything to oblige another.

To accommodate is to do anything to oblige, or for the convenience of another. Hence an "Accommodation Bill," is a bill drawn by one person and accepted by another for the convenience of the first. Accommodation Bills have a bad name among commercial men; and justly so, as they have been much abused. Not that there is anything in them essentially dishonest or fraudulent, but because the too frequent use of them opens the way for abuse. When a man of substance and good credit accepts a bill to oblige a friend who is in need of ready money, he simply gives his guarantee and becomes his surety for the amount of the Bill when it falls due. There is nothing fraudulent in this; but it facilitates the undue multiplication of Instruments of Credit, and often leads reckless individuals to engage in enterprises from which they would refrain if they could enter upon them only with cash in hand. A legitimate "Trade Bill" is an order for payment on account of "value received" or "goods shipped" or "services rendered" all of which phrases imply that means have been provided to meet the bill when it becomes due; and the necessity of providing these means before the bill is drawn, acts as a prevention to the undue multiplication of such bills. In the case of an *Accommodation Bill* no such check exists and hence the danger attending their use, and the ill odour in which they are held.

Account. Latin, *compretare*, to reckon or cast up; French, *compter*, to count, *compte*, an account; Italian, *conto*; German, *Rechnung*. (*See Capital Account; Profit and Loss Account; Revenue Account; Suspense Account.*)

In a colloquial sense, the word "account" is often used as the equivalent of "narrative" or "report." In mercantile practice its meaning is more restricted and is applied to formal statements of different kinds relating to goods, services, values, &c.

For **Account.** Bargains "for Account" are contracts made for settlement on the next settling day on the Stock Exchange and are thus distinguished from bargains "for money" which are settled immediately on being made.

Account Current. Latin, *curro*, I run; French, *compte courant*.

A running account; an account which is kept open and added to day by day, or from time to time, according to the nature of the business to which it refers. When the payments made or received are considerable, the balance for or against a customer is often of sufficient importance to admit of interest being paid or demanded on such balance, and an account current when properly kept exhibits all the additions and deductions thus made at the dates when they occur.

Account Sales. An abbreviation of the phrase "Account of the Sales" of goods. Such an account usually shows the charges for commission, porterage, &c., and the nett proceeds.

Acheson or **Ackeson.** A billon coin formerly used in Scotland, value about 8*d.* sterling, named from Atkinson, mint master. (*See Billon.*)

Ackie. A gold coin in use at Ashantee, value 5*s.* 4*d.*, English.

Action. From the Latin, *agere*, to do; and this again from the Greek, *αγειν*, to move. The German equivalent is *Prozess.*

An action is a legal process by which a right is enforced. There are two kinds of action recognized by jurists.

(*a*) Actions *in rem*, or Real Actions. In a real action the plaintiff claims, as against all the world, that a thing corporeal or incorporeal is his.

(*b*) Actions *in personam*, or against a *person*, in which a plaintiff claims that the defendant should give, do, or make good something to or for him.

Action de Jouissance. A French term corresponding to the German *Genuss-Actie*, and is usually rendered in English *Bonus Share.* Bonus Shares are issued to the holders of Railway or other companies' shares which have been drawn and paid off, and they entitle the holder to some further benefits either immediate or prospective notwithstanding the reimbursement and withdrawal of the original shares. They usually bear coupons and are thus distinguished from *Coupons* (or Certificates) *de Jouissance*, German *Genuss-Scheine*, which bear no interest, but simply entitle the holder to any future advantages which may accrue in respect to the shares which they replace. The Actions de Jouissance of the North of France Railways as well as those of the Lombardo-Venetian Railway, are examples well known in this country.

Active Bonds. Bonds bearing a fixed rate of interest payable in full, from the date of issue. (*See* PASSIVE *and* DEFERRED *Bonds.*) Consol Bonds, Russian Bonds, and indeed most bonds negotiable on the Stock Exchange are of this character.

Actuary. Latin, *actuarius*, from *ago, agere*, to act or to do. In classical times the term *actuarius* was applied to one who acted as an amanuensis, or short-hand writer; and also to one who kept domestic accounts, or managed the affairs of the household.

The duties of an actuary in modern times are of such a nature as to demand considerable ability, especially in performing the higher operations of Arithmetic and Algebra. The status and duties of an actuary in England will be best inferred from the following syllabus of subjects in which candidates are examined, if admitted previously to having filled any office of trust in connection with Life Insurance, Banking or other posts of a similar nature. The examinations are three in number, and are held at periods at least one year apart, and are as follows:—

MATRICULATION EXAMINATION—Vulgar Fractions; Decimal Fractions; Logarithms; Evolution; Equations, Simple and Quadratic; Series, Arithmetical and Geometrical; Permutations and Combinations; Binomial Theorem; Finite Differences; Geometry and First Four Books of Euclid.

SECOND YEAR'S EXAMINATION—Theory of Logarithms; Elements and Theory of Probabilities; Compound Interest and Annuities Certain; Tables of Mortality; Construction of Auxiliary Tables; Annuities and Assurances on Lives; Annuities and Assurances on Survivorships; Miscellaneous Questions.

THIRD YEAR'S EXAMINATION:—Life Assurance Finance: Construction and Graduation of Tables of Mortality; Existing Tables of Mortality, the mode of their Construction and their respective Merits; Methods of determining the Surplus in an Assurance Company, and of distributing it amongst the Assured. Legal Principles: Acts of Parliaments; Charters of Incorporation; Deeds of Settlement; Partnerships, Limited and Unlimited, Powers and Duties of Persons constituting them; Policy considered as a contract; Probates and Letters of Administration; Assignments; Personal Representatives; Bankruptcies. Statistics: Methods for the Arrangements and collection of Data; Tests of Accuracy; Preparation of Abstracts and Reports; General System of the Country's Finance; Funded and Unfunded Debt, and Fiscal Arrangements; Taxation. Currency, Banking, and Investment: Currency, Metallic and Paper; Nature of Banking—Bank of England, Private and Joint Stock Banks; Bills of Exchange; Comparative Value of Securities; High and Low Prices; Fluctuations in the Rate of Interest, &c.

Adha. A silver coin of Nepaul, equal to a quarter rupee, or about 5*d*. sterling. No longer in use.

Adlea. Tripoli. A billon coin issued in 1827, plated with gold, forced upon the people as the equivalent of a dollar, but now almost unknown.

Administration, Letters of. When a person dies without having made a Will—Intestate, as it is technically termed—it is necessary for his relatives to apply to the Probate Court (*see Probate*) for power to deal with his property and effects. The authority so to act is conveyed by a document called "Letters of Adminstration," and to obtain it the applicant must bring with him (or her) proof of the death of the deceased, and also some evidence that he (or she) is the proper person on whom the duties of administration devolve. Some useful suggestions to administrators are given under the art. "*Probate*," from a Report by Mr. Tidd Pratt, which apply equally to those who need Letters of Administration and those who need Grants of Probate.

The payment of duty on Letters of Administration, as well as on Grants of Probate (which are now assimilated) is effected by means of stamps, according to the following scale, which was communicated to the *Daily News*, March 26, 1880, by Lancelot C. Irons, Receiver of Wills, Probate Registry, Somerset House:—

Above the value of £100 and under £200, £2.

Of the value of	but under		Of the value of	but under	
£200	£300	... £4	£2,000	£3,000	... £62
300	400	... 6	3,000	4,000	... 88
400	500	... 9	4,000	5,000	... 113
500	600	... 11	5,000	6,000	... 140
600	800	... 15	6,000	7,000	... 165
800	1,000	... 22	7,000	8,000	... 190
1,000	1,500	... 30	8,000	9,000	... 215
1,500	2,000	... 40	9,000	10,000	... 240

Of the value of	but under		Of the value of	but under	
£10,000	£12,000 ...	£275	£120,000	£140,000 ...	£3,250
12,000	14,000 ...	325	140,000	160,000 ...	3,750
14,000	16,000 ...	375	160,000	180,000 ...	4,250
16,000	18,000 ...	425	180,000	200,000 ...	4,750
18,000	20,000 ...	475	200,000	250,000 ...	5,625
20,000	25,000 ...	565	250,000	300,000 ...	6,875
25,000	30,000 ...	690	300,000	350,000 ...	8,125
30,000	35,000 ...	815	350,000	400,000 ...	9,375
35,000	40,000 ...	940	400,000	500,000 ...	11,250
40,000	45,000 ...	1,065	500,000 and upwards, then in addition to the said duty of £11,250, for every full sum of £100,000 in excess of £500,000, and also for any fractional part of £100,000, so in excess		£2,500
45,000	50,000 ...	1,190			
50,000	60,000 ...	1,375			
60,000	70,000 ...	1,625			
70,000	80,000 ...	1,875			
80,000	90,000 ...	2,125			
90,000	100,000 ...	2,375			
100,000	120,000 ...	2,750			

In comparison with the old scale it will be seen that, so far as probates are concerned, the present scale is lighter for estates under £400.

For estates ranging from under £600 to under £2000, the scale is the same as the old probate scale. Above that amount (*i.e.*, from under £3,000 and upwards) the new duties are heavier for probates, but intestacies have an advantage until the figures under £18,000 are attained.

Advice. To **Advise.** The Latin, *visum*, from *videre*, to see, gave rise to Italian, *viso*; Old French, *vis*. *Visum mihi fuit*, it seemed to me; would be rendered in Old Italian, *fu viso a me;* Old French, *ce m'est vis.*—Diez.

"The erchbishop of Walys seide ys *avyse*
'Sire,' he seide, 'gef ther is any mon so wys
That beste red can thereof rede, Merlin that is.'"

To be *avised* or advised of a thing would thus be, to have notice of it, to be informed of it.

"Of werre and of bataile he was full avise."—*R. Brunne.*

Whence *advice* in the mercantile sense,—notice, news.

In colloquial speech "to advise," means to counsel, to recommend. In commercial language it signifies to warn, to give notice of, to inform. A "Letter of Advice" is consequently a letter giving information that some particular transaction has been effected, and it enables a correspondent or agent in a distant place to take account of that transaction, and to enter the necessary debits or credits in his books. It is a maxim in all good houses of business, that every transaction should be thus advised; for if this rule be neglected it invariably leads to errors which cause much subsequent trouble in their rectification.

Affidavit. From the Latin, *fides*, faith, truth, honesty: *fido, fidere*, to put trust in. In post-classical times was formed from the above the mediæval *affidare*, to pledge one's faith or honour to another. It was usual when pledging one's faith in a formal manner by means of a legal document to commence that document with engrossed letters, as "AFFIDAVIT N M, &c.," that is, "N. M. has pledged his faith, &c." From the conspicuous position of the word, all instruments of this kind were called "*Affidavits*" in conformity with the practice usual among lawyers; and thus what was formerly a verb in the third person, came to be used as a noun, in which sense alone it appears in the English language.

An affidavit is a legal document in which a party states upon oath that certain things are true, or certain things shall be done. Any one may make an affidavit, either in writing or by word of mouth, in which latter case it is called taking an oath, or swearing. In order that affidavits may have binding force in a court of law, it is usual, and indeed essential, that they be made before a mayor, magistrate, notary public, consul, or some public functionary. The person making the affidavit then signs it in the presence of witnesses, who attest the signature; after which it is sealed and signed by the consul or other authorized officer before whom it is made.

To **Affreight.** Dutch, *vragt*; German, *Fracht*; probably connected with the Latin *fero ferre*, to carry.

To hire a ship for the conveyance of goods or freight.

After Date. A phrase to be found on most Bills of Exchange; the date referred to is that at which the Bill is drawn, it is distinctly written at the head of the Bill, and fixes the period at which payment must be claimed by the Payee, or Holder.

After Sight. This phrase, when inserted in Bills of Exchange, signifies "after being presented for acceptance:" because the Drawee is assumed to have seen it for the first time when the Bill is thus presented. It follows therefore that when a bill is drawn payable "Three Months after sight," the payee, if he wishes for prompt payment should present it for acceptance as soon as possible after receiving it, and take care that the date is inserted on the face of it. Of course when the bill is payable "at sight," it may be presented for *acceptance* and *payment* at the same time.

Agio. Italian, *aggio*; German, *Agio*; French, *agio*; premium, surplus, difference. Littré connects it with the French *aise*, easy; Italian, *agio*, and some authors with *adagio*, with ease; but the connection is not clearly traced.

"Quel vantaggio, che si dà, o riceve per *aggiust*amento della valuta d'una moneta, a quella d'un altra, ovvero per barattare la moneta peggiore colla migliore."—*Vocabulario degli Accademici della Crusca.* (Some advantage, which one gives, or receives, by the adjustment of the value of one kind of money in that of another, or by the exchange of a depreciated coinage for a superior.)

This looks like a little play on the words *aggio* and *aggiustamento,* a kind of diversion of which old etymologists were rather fond.

This term though but little used in England is in common use among mercantile men on the Continent. It has several meanings as applied by them, amongst which the following are the most important.

(*a*). *Agio* primarily signifies the rate of exchange in the moneys of two nations. Thus the currency of Italy exchanges with that of England at rates varying from 25·15 francs to 25·50 francs for the pound sterling. This rate is called the *agio* between the two countries.

(*b*). In countries where a *silver* standard prevails, *gold* is used to make large payments, and according as gold is more or less abundant, a less or greater quantity of gold is given for a specified quantity of silver coin. The difference between the two metals thus exchanged is then called the *agio* on gold.

(*c*). In some countries possessing an inconvertible paper currency, the term *agio* is applied to the difference between the value of a note and coin of the same denomination. When used in this sense, it is identical with what in other countries is called a *premium*.

(*d*). In Hamburg, the term *Bank Agio* is used to signify the proportion between the *Bank Value* and the *Currency Value*. This Agio varies with the price of silver. (*See Bank Value.*)

(*e*). An allowance made in some countries for the wear and tear of coins, while the old standard of value and money of account is retained as at Amsterdam, Hamburg and other towns.

The term *agio* or *premium* is very frequently misapplied; but time and custom have so consecrated the misapplication, that nothing more can be done than simply to point it out, in order to prevent misapprehension on the part of those who use the term. When gold is said to be at a premium or agio as compared with silver or paper currency, it means that the silver or paper is depreciated or at a discount; for the gold in these cases is the standard of value, and the silver or paper variable. This customary use of the term prevails in the United States, in France, in Italy, in Austria, and in Russia: indeed in all countries where a paper currency has been adopted, or where a double standard of value is in use. In some of its applications the term is used in its proper sense, as in quoting the market value of stocks and shares. (*See Premium.*)

Ahmedî. A gold coin of Mysora (Hindustan), about 31*s*. to 32*s*. sterling, no longer in use.

Ahmulahs. Abyssinian salt money, various sizes, new, 20 to a dollar.

Akcheh. A Turkish silver coin, very small, value about one-third of the Para. Obsolete.

Akhter. A copper coin, value a quarter of the *pice* of Mysore.

Albus. A German copper coin, value twelve hellers, formerly used at Cassel, Cologne, &c.

Allonge. From the French, *allonger*, to lengthen: *allonge*, a piece, applied in commerce with the meaning of a piece attached to a document to lengthen it.

An *Allonge* is a slip of paper attached to a Bill in order to provide space for further indorsements, when the back of the Bill is already covered. It requires no stamp, as it is deemed a part of the original bill, which it is presumed is already stamped.

Allowance. Two distinct words, having a totally different origin, gradually assumed this one form in the English tongue.

I. From the Latin, *laudare*, to praise, approve, recommend, was formed *allaudare*, to praise one highly. These forms appear in the French as *louer* and *alouer*, with a similar meaning, and through the French it found its way into early English, as in Shakspeare, where it means *approval* or *sanction*.

> "You sent a large commission to conclude,
> Without the king's will or the States' *allowance*,
> A league between His Highness and Ferrara."

II. From the Latin, *locare*, to put, to place, was formed in post-classical times the compound *allocare*, to put into a place, to set apart for a purpose, to allot. These two words also appear in the French as *louer* and *allouer*, and being similar in spelling to the words above noted, became confounded in meaning, and when adopted in the English language, were used under one form, "allow" or "allowance," to express all the different ideas previously conveyed by distinct words, thus—

(*a*) Approval, as quoted by Richardson:

> "This is the sum of what I would have ye weigh,
> First, whether ye *allow* my whole devise
> And think it good for me, for them, for you,
> And if ye like it and *allow* it well."

(*b*) Permission. "I allowed him to walk in my garden whenever he chose."

(*c*) Authority, as in the passage above quoted from Shakspeare.

(*d*) Abatement. "In every twenty-five sheets an allowance of one sheet was made for damage, soiling," &c.

(*e*) Apportionment. "The sailors had a daily allowance of grog."

"And his allowance was a continual allowance given by the King, a daily rate for every day all his life."—2 Kings.

It is not improbable that certain other words contributed something towards the formation of our English "allow" and "allowance." The Anglo-Saxon *lyfan*, *alefan*, to permit, concede, or suffer, come very near to them in meaning, as exemplified in Goldsmith's "Deserted Village."

> "The ruin'd spendthrift, now no longer proud,
> Claimed kindred there, and had his claims *allowed*."

Allowance, in refinery, is a departure from the legal standard of fineness permitted by the State in consideration of the practical difficulty of securing the exact degree of fineness prescribed by law. The allowance is also made in respect of wear and tear. Two per mille is the allowance in the gold coinage of France, with respect both to weight and fineness. In England, two parts in one thousand are allowed for fineness, and 2-10ths of a grain in the sovereign for weight: so that a new sovereign which is supposed to weigh 123·274 grains would be within the *remedy* or allowance if it was found to weigh anything more than 123·074; other gold coins of which at the present time only half-sovereigns are in use, have a proportional allowance. In Russia, no allowance is made either for weight or fineness, and although it is impossible always to work to such a nicety, the gold imperials of Russia have a very high reputation, and are often remelted and coined by other countries, thus saving much of the expense of refining and mixing.

Alloy. From the Latin, *lex*, law; *ad legem*, according to law; French, *a loi*. "Unusquisque denarius cudatur et fiat *ad legem* undecim denariorum." —*Ducange*. (Every penny was coined and made according to law eleven pennies.) The accidental resemblance of the French verb *allier*, to blend, to mix, to blend together, has given rise to the prevalent error that it is the origin of the English *alloy*. But the words used in other languages for the mint term, corresponding to "alloy," all indicate a relationship to the word *lex*, the law, or rule, set up by authority for the regulation of the coinage.

"Monetam de auro et argento, et alio metallo, quocunque cunio, *allaia*, et taillia, prout sibi placuerit."

(Money of gold and silver, and other metal, of whatever coinage, *alloy*, and value, according as he pleases.)

Dated 1377. *Quoted by Rymer.*

In its most general sense, an alloy is a compound of any two or more metals. In economics, it signifies a compound of a cheap or base metal with a costly or precious one. In practice, the meaning of the term is yet more restricted, since it is applied not to the compound, but to the base metal in the compound: thus standard gold is said to be eleven-twelfths fine, and one-twelfth *alloy*. Gold is usually alloyed with silver or copper or both. Silver with copper only. This applies however to mints of good standing. In some countries, pewter, lead, and other base metals are used as alloys; if in large proportions the coins so produced are called *billon* coins. (*See Billon.*)

The object of alloying gold and silver is to render them somewhat harder than they are in their pure state. In a subordinate degree, the colour and tenacity of the metals are affected, but these are considerations of minor importance.

In the mining language of Spain, a modified form of the word is applied to the proportion of silver found mixed with certain ores, thus: "The extraction for the week was 750 cargoes of clean ore, average *ley* from nine to ten marks per monton."—*Times*, January 2nd, 1857.

Alsatia. A fanciful name formerly applied to the district of Whitefriars. It has lately been applied to the Stock Exchange. The reason for the modern application of the name is said to be that Whitefriars, was at one time a privileged place of sanctuary, and was frequently referred to by dramatists and others, as *Alsatia*, "It was the resort of libertines and rascals of every description, and here the corrupt practitioners of the law found a ready supply of affidavit men, or Knights of the post, as they were termed. The notorious noonday abuses committed here, and the riot in the reign of King Charles the Second, caused its suppression and clearance."—*Beaufoy's* "Tradesmen's Tokens." It was in allusion to these facts that one of our judges spoke of the questionable proceedings of the Stock Exchange as those of an *Alsatia;* and unfriendly outsiders have since that event been only too ready to fasten the odious cognomen on the institution.

Altmichlic. A silver coin used in Turkey value 3*d.* sterling, or sixty Turkish paras.

Amalgamation. *Amalgam*, a compound of quicksilver with some other metal. The origin of this word is a puzzle to philologists. It was used by the alchemists of the Middle Ages to denote a compound or alloy of quicksilver with any other metal. Many derivations have been suggested, but one of the most reasonable is that of the Greek αμαλος, soft, feeble, and γαμεω, to marry. *Amalgam* in this sense would mean a soft compound or alloy, and answers very well to the compound best known, in that early age of chemistry, of quicksilver and gold; which latter metal is easily dissolved by the former.

In commerce, amalgamation signifies the fusion of two or more companies, societies, or firms into one. Although amalgamation may, and sometimes does, take place in respect to private firms, it is had recourse to chiefly in regard to joint stock undertakings, such as Railway Companies, Insurance Societies, Joint Stock Banks, &c. As there is often a difficulty in fixing responsibility for the performance of outstanding contracts after amalgamation has been effected, special Acts of Parliament have been passed with the object of defining the responsibilities of the Amalgamated Companies, as well as that of the shareholders in companies which have thereby ceased to have an independent existence, and for further information on these points, the reader should refer to the Companies Clauses Consolidation Act, 1845, and the Life Assurance Companies Act, 1870.

Amortization. Greek, μορος, *moros;* Latin, *mors;* French, *mort*, death, decay, a wasting away.

Amortization, in finance usually signifies the gradual diminution of a debt, by paying it off in successive instalments. In some rare cases, amortizement is effected at a stroke by a single payment. (*See Sinking Fund.*) In England the term *amortization* is usually restricted to the extinction of a loan by means of a single payment, and the term Sinking Fund is commonly understood to mean the gradual disbursement of a loan in one of two ways:—

I. By setting apart a specified sum annually for the purpose, and determining by *drawing* or by *lot*, the bonds to be paid off, and by paying them off at par, that is, at their full nominal value. II. By expending such specified sum in the purchase of bonds at the market-price of the day. Both of these methods are practised extensively in London, the former being most in favour. The second method is open to grave objections, as it puts it in the power of dishonest borrowers to take advantage of low prices in the market, and offers a temptation to bring their own stocks into disrepute and to depress their price, by frightening timid holders into ruinous selling, when the borrowers come forward and buy them up.

Amount. From *mont*, a hill, was formed the adverb *amont*, upwards, and the verb *monter*, to rise, to ascend. Hence—

Amount is the total to which a number of charges rise up when added together.

Ancient Right Standard. The standard of fineness of English silver coin which has existed from time immemorial—namely, 11 oz. 2 dwts. of pure silver in the troy pound of 12 oz. The same degree of fineness is sometimes expressed as $\frac{222}{240}$ fine, and at others in conformity with the decimal notation as ·925 fine. All the recent silver coinage of England is of this degree of fineness.

Angel. A gold English coin value 6*s.* 8*d.*, bearing a figure of St. Michael and Dragon. This gold coin was first used in France, and was introduced into England in the reign of Edward IV. (1461—1483). It was then valued at 6*s.* 8*d.*, and fluctuated from that time till the reign of Charles I., when it was reckoned at 10*s.* It was 23 carats $3\frac{1}{2}$ grains fine. Shakspeare refers to it in the *Merchant of Venice* when he says, "They have in England a coin that bears the figure of an *Angel* stamped in gold," ii. 7. The angel here referred to was St. Michael slaying the Dragon.

Angelet. A gold English coin—the half angel, value 3*s.* 4*d.*

Angster. A copper coin, Swiss, value half a rappe, about $\frac{6}{123}$*d.*

Ankosee. Chinsoree, a rupee of silver, current in the Deccan.

Anna, or Ana. (*a*). The $\frac{1}{16}$ part of the Company's rupee. Owing to the depressed price of silver its metallic value is now (1881) not more than $\frac{4}{5}$ of what it was a few years since.

(*b.*) A silver coin in Hindoostan and Singapore sixteen to a rupee, value three half-pence.

Annuitant. One who receives an annuity. (*See next Article.*)

Annuity. Lat. *annus*, a year.

An annuity is a sum of money payable once a year. Hence, the Right to an Annuity is a right to demand this sum once a year. Legists distinguish between "the right to demand" a sum of money, and the "right to the sum of money," but this distinction though important in point of law, is of very little moment to the Annuitant.

The term *annuity* in England corresponds very closely to the term *Rente* as used on the Continent. Rente is a sum of money payable yearly. A bond or certificate entitling the holder to Rentes 20 francs, gives the holder a claim to 20 francs yearly, 10 francs every six months, or 5 francs every three months. French Rentes are paid in quarterly instalments; Austrian, Hungarian and Italian Rentes in half yearly instalments. In England Consolidated Annuities, or Bank Annuities are paid in half-yearly instalments. Metropolitan consolidated annuities are payable in quarterly instalments. But in all these cases the term Annuity or Rente is applied to the *yearly* sum, and not to the quarterly or half-yearly amounts.

Annulment. Latin, *ad*, to; *nullus*, no, none, nothing; *annullare–annihilo*, to reduce to nothing, to make of none effect.

This term is mostly used on the Continent as the equivalent of the English word "cancelling" or "cancelment." (*See Cancelling.*)

Ante-date. Latin, *ante*, before; *datum*, given (meaning, a given time).

To *antedate* a cheque or other writing is to inscribe upon it a date earlier than that on which the document is written. As *antedating* a document sometimes involves fraud, it is necessary for all who have the insertion of dates under their care, to see that there is nothing in their act which can be construed into a criminal offence. (*See Post Date.*)

Appraiser. French, *apprecier*, to value, to estimate; Italian, *apprezzare*; Spanish, *apreciar*, to set a price; all from the Latin, *ad*, and *pretium*, a price. The equivalent in German is *Schoetzer*.

Every person is deemed an *appraiser* who makes it his business or part of his business to make a valuation chargeable with stamp duty. A penalty of £50 is imposed on any person who acts as an *appraiser* without a license: but the penalty is not imposed on any servant or employé who in a single instance makes a valuation for the guidance and information of his employer, even though such servant has not taken out a license.

Appreciation. Latin, *ad*, to; *pretium*, value, price. French, *apprecier*, to value, to estimate.

(*a*) In ordinary speech, to *appreciate* means to set a value upon anything, to prize, to esteem, as in the phrases "I *appreciate* his friendship," "Wagner's style of music is too highly cultivated to be *appreciated* by the vulgar."

(*b*) In finance, this word has recently acquired a more strictly technical meaning, and is used in a sense as opposed to *depreciation*, especially in discussions relating to the "silver question." When one commodity exchanges for another in a pretty constant ratio, the value of each expressed in terms of the other is called its "normal value," and if from any cause one of these commodities is supplied in unusual abundance it becomes *depreciated* with respect to the other, that is, you have to give *more* of the superabundant commodity for the *same* quantity of that whose supply is unchanged. But when the converse takes place, and the supply of one of the two commodities is diminished, while the supply of the other remains unchanged, it then becomes *appreciated*. It should be observed also that when the rates of exchange between *two commodities only* is under consideration, the *depreciation* of the one always involves the *appreciation* of the other, as has been demonstrated very forcibly during the last few years by the fluctuations in the price of silver. In the days of Darius, we are told by Herodotus, gold was worth 13 times as much as an equal weight of silver; in modern days down to within the last ten years, it was worth about 15½ times as much: but since the demonetization of silver by Germany, and partly also in consequence of the large supplies from the American mines, gold has been worth 20 times its weight in silver. Hence the value of gold as measured in silver is said to be *appreciated*—that is, its value or price has been *added to*; and this marks the distinction between the technical and conventional use of the word. In the latter, it implies in a vague way the *setting a value* on a thing. In the former, an adding to its value as measured in some other thing.

Arbitrage. Arbitration. From the Latin, *arbitrari*, to judge, decide, to pass sentence, to give judgment: *arbiter*, a judge, an umpire, and primarily an eye-witness. But the origin of this word lies much further back in the history of language, and appears to be connected with the practice of the soothsayers, diviners, and lotsmen of primitive times. There was in the languages of Eastern Europe a root, *arp*, *arb*, *arv*, which is found in several words referring to the arts of divination and soothsaying, and which is still seen in the Finnish language; a language much more widely spread in former times than the present geographical limits of the country would suggest. Thus we have *arpa*, a lot, a divining-rod, or instrument of divination; *arpamies*, a diviner, an arbiter; *arpelen*, to decide by lot, to divine; *arwata*, to prophesy, to judge; *arwelo*, opinion, judgment. We find also in the Latin, *aruspex*, and its derivations, used with the same signification, and the Greek equivalent derived from ἱερος or ἱαρος, sacred, and σκοπος, a seer, one who has an insight into divine things. We have only to recollect how natural it is in the infancy of human thought to seek for guidance in doubtful matters from persons supposed to possess supernatural powers or superior knowledge, to convince ourselves how familiar the words and names used with reference to this sacred class and their occult arts must become on the lips of those who have recourse to them. This familiarity has two marked effects. It fixes the word in the common language of the people, and gets engrafted in their forms of speech, and secondly, by being constantly used, it gets modified, degraded, and worn down till all but the most slender traces of the original word remain.

In its original acceptation, *arbitration* signified the giving of an opinion according to the best of one's judgment, according to equity, and not necessarily according to law. This meaning is retained in the modern use of the phrase "Arbitration of Exchanges," not that there is much room for the play of the judgment in exchange operations, for when properly conducted both the data and the results are as intractable as those of a proposition in pure mathematics. Nevertheless as considerable experience and extended knowledge are required in the collection of the necessary data, the term *arbitration* or *arbitrage*, is by no means inappropriate. *Arbitrage* operations are applied not only to money and bullion, but perhaps even more largely to Foreign Bills of Exchange, and to merchandize bought in one country to be sold in another. These arbitrated rates are commonly called "Pars of Exchange." It is, therefore, important to note when this phrase is used, that an Arbitrated Par of Exchange, is a totally different thing from the Mint Par of Exchange. The Mint Par of Exchange expresses simply the sum of money in one country which contains an amount of fine metal equal to that in a given sum in another country. Thus the Mint Par of Exchange between England and France is £1=25·2215. (*See France.*)

Now take the following question. Suppose the 10 florin piece in Amsterdam to weigh 102 grains Troy, and gold in London to sell at 77*s*. 10½*d*. per oz. What is the Arbitrated Par of Exchange? In other words, what on the above conditions is the value of the pound sterling in Dutch florins? By Chain Rule.

How many florins = 20 shillings
If $77\frac{7}{8}$ = 480 grains Troy
102 = 10 florins

$$\frac{20 \times 480 \times 10}{102 \times 77\frac{7}{8}}$$

Multiplying both terms by 8.

$$\frac{20 \times 480 \times 80}{102 \times 623} = 12{\cdot}08\frac{1}{3}$$

Hence £1 = $12{\cdot}08\frac{1}{3}$ florins is the arbitrated Par of Exchange.

The following is an application of Arbitrage to the purchase and shipment of lead:

One Ton of lead @ £15 10/- less $2\frac{1}{2}$ % discount. Freight 32/6 per ton. Primage 10 % of freight. Insurance 20/-%. Exchange 3/$6\frac{3}{4}$ per dollar. What will it lay down at per picul in Hongkong? (1 picul = $133\frac{1}{3}$ lbs.)

	£	s.	d.
1 Ton of Lead @ £15 10/- per ton . .	15	10	0
Discount $2\frac{1}{2}$ %	0	7	9
	£15	2	3

CHARGES.

	£	s.	d.			
Freight at 32/6 per ton . .	1	12	6			
Primage 10 % on Freight .	0	3	3			
Insurance 20/- % . . .	0	3	1			
„ Policy . . .	0	0	3			
Commission 1 % . . .	0	3	1			
				2	2	2
				£17	4	5

Then by Chain Rule:—

How many dollars = 1 Picul
1 = $133\frac{1}{3}$ lbs.
2240 = 1 ton
1 = $344{\cdot}416\frac{2}{3}$ shillings (£17 4*s.* 5*d.*)
(3/$6\frac{3}{4}$) 3·56 = 1 dollar

Whence we get

$$\frac{133\frac{1}{3} \times 344{\cdot}416\frac{2}{3}}{2240 \times 3{\cdot}56} \text{ dollars}$$

or \$5·758, the price at which it will lay down in Hongkong.

The foregoing are examples of what is called *Simple Abitration*, in which two countries only are taken into account. But when a merchant has correspondents in several commercial centres, it often occurs that an advantage may be gained, by making a remittance, not in a direct, but in a circuitous, manner: and the calculation then becomes somewhat more complicated; the process being called *Compound Arbitration.* For fuller details, the reader may consult Tate's "Cambist," Ottomar Haupt's "London Arbitrageur," Seyd's "Bullion and Foreign Exchange."

The practice of Arbitration is also applied to the Weights and Measures of different countries; the object being to determine the relation between those of any two countries, either by direct comparison, or from their known relation to those of some third country.

Arbitrageur. This word, although French in form and sound, is not a recognised term in the French language, but has been introduced of late years as a convenient name for that class of persons who perform *arbitrage* operations or calculations of foreign exchange. There is no equivalent English term in use, the nearest being that of *cambist*, which is derived from the Italian. (*See Cambist, Arbitration, &c.*)

Articles of Association. A body of laws and rules drawn up for the government of Joint Stock Companies. The general principles on which Articles of Association are constructed are prescribed by the law of the land, and they form a rough model on which any given body of Articles may be drawn up; but the details are determined by the nature and objects of the Company itself. Every shareholder in a Joint Stock Company may demand a copy of its Articles of Association on payment of a nominal sum; or he may inspect a copy without charge at the offices of the company, any day within reasonable hours. (*See Memorandum of Association.*)

As. Greek, εις; in the Tarentine dialect, ας; Latin, *as*, one or unity: from which it may be inferred that it was the unit of value among some of the Greeks, and most of the Romans.

A Roman coin made of brass. In the time of Tullus Hostilius it was called the *As Libra, Libella, or Pondo*, because it actually weighed a pound or 12 *uncia* or ozs. After the first Punic war it was reduced to 2 ounces. After the second Punic war, to one ounce, and finally to half an ounce, in which state it continued to the reign of Vespasian. Its original stamp was that of a sheep, or sow, thus forming a collecting link between those primitive times when cattle constituted the medium of exchange, and those more civilized times when metals formed the currency.

Ashereh. A modern Egyptian silver coin, value ten paras, about one halfpenny.

Ashrafi. A gold coin of Persia, value 9*s.* sterling. There is also the treble Ashrafi, called the "Muhr-Ashrafi."

Ashruffy. A gold coin of Hindoostan, value 12*s.* 6*d.*

Aspar, Aspre, or Mina. A silver coin used in Turkey; 120 to a piastre, value about $\frac{1}{51}$*d.*

To Assay. *Ex* and *agere;* Latin, *exigere*, to examine, to prove by examination; "*annulis ferreis ad certum pondus exactis, pro nummo utentur:*" iron rings proved of a certain weight used as money.—*Cæsar.* Hence, *exagium*, a proof; *exagium solidi*, a proof shilling (literally, proof of a shilling). From *exagium* was formed the Italian *saggio*, a proof, trial, sample, taste of anything; *assaggiare*, to prove, try, taste; whence French, *essayer*, to try, and English, *assay, essay*, to try, to prove, to test.

"I have two boyes
Seeke Percy and thy selfe about the field:
But, seeing thou fall'st on me so luckily,
I will *assay* thee: so defend thy selfe."
Shakespeare, "First Part of King Henry IV." act. v. sc. 4.

An *assay* is a process in metallurgy consisting of two parts. The first part of the operation is conducted with a view to determine the simple metals of which a compound consists, and thus corresponds to what in Chemistry is called a *Qualitative Analysis*. The second operation is directed to the finding out of the actual proportions in which any one or more of those metals enters the compound, and corresponds to the Chemical process called *Quantitative Analysis.*

Asset. Commonly derived from French, *assez*, enough, and this again from the Latin, *ad*, to; *satis*, enough. There is, however, good reason for regarding these forms as nothing more than the proximate origin of the word, inasmuch as we find in several other tongues but slightly related to the Latin, words almost identical in meaning, and very similar in sound, all indicating the existence of some other root which they may claim as their common ancestor: for examples—Gaelic, *sioth, sith*, peace, reconciliation, satisfaction; Polish, *syt, sity*, satisfied, full; Bohemian, *sytiti*, to satisfy; Icelandic, *sætt, sætti*, reconciliation, content; German, *satt*, full, satisfied; Old English, *asseth, aseethe*, enough, sufficient, satisfaction; *assyth, sythe*, to make compensation.

"And if it suffice not for *asseth*."—*Piers Plowman.*

"And Pilat willing to make *aseeth* to the people left to them Barabbas."—*Wiclif*, Mark xv.

"And though on heapes that lie him by,
Yet never shall make his richesse
Asseth unto his greediness."
Chaucer, "Romaunt of the Rose."

Therefore I swore to the hows of Heli that the wickedness of his hows shall not be doon *asceth* before with slain sacrifices and giftis.—*Wiclif.* (In Vulgate *expietur.*)

In Stephen's "Blackstone," the following account of the origin of this word is given: An heir is liable, out of an estate taken by descent in fee simple, to be charged with the debts of the ancestor from whom it descended, "but only so far as he has taken in his character of heir, an estate of his ancestor *sufficient* (to some extent at least) to satisfy the debt: which *sufficient* estate is called in law *assets*, from the French word *assez* enough," or sufficient. The use of the word is now greatly extended, and is employed in mercantile affairs to signify property of any kind when applied as a set-off against liabilities, or for the satisfaction of certain demands.

Assignats. Latin, *assignare*, to allot, to assign.

French notes, first issued April 19th, 1790, by the Republican Government of that date. They were issued in such quantities as to become almost worthless, and hence the bad name they acquired at the time, and the ill odour which has attached to them ever since. They were so called because the confiscated estates of the Church were *assigned* to their redemption and withdrawal. The first issue amounted to 400,000,000 of francs, and was increased by degrees till 40,000,000,000 were afloat; shortly after which they ceased to have any value at all. Owing to this depreciation in France, and their bad reputation in some other countries, "dirty assignats" have mostly been looked upon as something intrinsically bad. In themselves they are convenient as a substitute for heavy coinages as those of silver and copper. They were even preferred to metal in Russia, when issued under Catherine II., in 1768, and circulated at a premium of ¼ per cent.

Assignee. Latin, *assigno*, from *ad* and *signare;* French, *assigner*, to allot, or allow.

The person or party to whom anything is assigned, or allotted: anyone appointed to discharge a given duty, as the distribution of a bankrupt's estate, or the care of a deceased person's property. The word takes its origin from the practice among the Romans of appointing persons to solemn duties under written instructions authenticated by a seal (*signum*).

Assurance and Insurance. Latin, *securus*, safe, from *cura* care, anxiety; whence *se* (=sine) *cura* without care, free from anxiety, and *insure* or *assure* to put one in a condition of safety, to free from anxiety: French, *assurer;* Italian, *assicurare;* Spanish, *asegurar.*

The word *assurance* or *insurance* as a mercantile term comes to us directly from the Lombards, and to a great extent its meaning covers the idea conveyed by the more ancient term in use among the Hanseatic traders, namely *bottomry*. (*See Bottomry*). In the use of the words *insurance* and *assurance*, no rule is discoverable, merchants applying one term or the other according to their fancy.

Attestation. From Latin, *testis*, a witness, *attestari*, to bear witness, to prove, to corroborate.

Attestation is the formal witnessing of the signature of a deed or declaration by some person authorized to perform that duty. Any person whatever may be employed to witness or attest the signature of another, but in the case of deeds, transfers or statutory declarations on which important issues may depend, it is more usual to employ a notary, or to make the attestation in presence of a magistrate, so that it may have recognized force in a court of law. The most usual and complete formula for an attestation is:—

> "Signed, sealed, and delivered by the said (Thomas Atkins) in the presence of ———"

If the declaration is not under seal, it is sufficient to say;—

> "Witness to the signature of the said (Thomas Atkins)."

Attine. A Polish silver coin, value 5*d.*

Attorney, Attorn, Attornment. Old Norman, *attourner*, to turn over, or transfer: *atorni*, one acting on behalf of another: whence the mediæval law Latin, *attornatus*, one put in the turn or place of another.

"Li *atorni* est ce qui pardevant justice est *atorni* pour aucun en Eschequier ou en Assize pour pour suivre et pour defendre sa droiture."
—*Fis Municipal Normannorum*, quoted by *Ducange*.

"The holy womā Susan held hir peace, and overcame hir enemies: for she defēded not hir self with reasoning of words, nor with speech of any *atturney*, but the holy womā hir self holding hir tongue, hir chastity spake for her."—*Instruction of a Christian Woman*, v. i. c. 12.

"I, by *attorney*, bless thee from thy mother."
Shakspeare, "Richard II."

An *Attorney* is one who is appointed by another to do something in his stead, and hence is equivalent to the French *procureur*.

To *Attorn* is to turn over to some one a right or duty properly belonging to another.

Attornment is the act of turning over or transferring a right or duty. (*See Power of Attorney.*)

The person who employs an attorney is called the principal, in French *mandant*, because it is by his mandate the attorney or procureur is authorized to act on his behalf.

Audit, Auditor. Latin, *audire*, to hear.

In the Middle Ages the Latin *audire* was used to denote the formal hearing of a case in a court of law: *audientia* was sometimes the court itself, at others the suit at law: to *give audience* was to give judgment, and the judge himself was called *Auditor*. In later days the name Auditor was applied to subordinate officers and notaries when appointed to hear and examine a case, and even to parties engaged to attest a deed. Although the word is still extensively used both in law and commerce, its meaning is almost entirely restricted to the examination and authentication of accounts, the process being called the *Audit*, and the party discharging the duty the *Auditor*.

Audit Office. A Government department whose duties cover most of the ground occupied by the Court of Exchequer and the Treasury: these latter control the Revenue and Expenditure of the nation in the interest *of Her Majesty's Executive:* but the Audit Office acts in the interest *of the Parliament and the people*, and is charged with the duty of seeing not only that revenue and expenditure are correctly recorded in the accounts, but also that they have been appropriated to the special objects, *and no other*, for which they were intended, and to which they were assigned by Parliament as the representative of the taxpayers.

Aught or Ought. Anglo-Saxon, *á-wiht*, something; Old High German, *eo-wiht;* Gothic, *waihts*, whence also the English, *whit*, a little thing, a jot.

Purists and grammarians have found this familiar word intractable. If they begin with *aught*, something, and add on the negative *n* for "nothing" they get *naught* which is commonly used as a contraction for "naughty." On the other hand if they begin with *nought* nothing, and cut off the initial *n* they get *ought*, a verb in constant use to express duty, or moral obligation. The result is that English literature abounds with examples which indicate the unsettled convictions of writers on this point,—*aught* and *ought* both being used at different times for "something:" *naught* and *nought* for "nothing."

The use of the word "ought" for a cipher (or 0) is of course a vulgar error arising from the transfer of the letter *n*. Instead of saying "a nought," people say "an ought;" just as the reptile which was formerly called "a nadder" (*German* Natter) is now called "an adder."

August D'or. A gold coin used in Saxony, value 16*s*. 3*d*.

Aureus. A Roman gold coin, value 16*s*. 8*d*.

Average. In law Latin, *averagium*. There are two different words, wholly distinct in origin and meaning denoted by the Latin *averagium*.

I. ——— A number of expressions are found in old law books, apparently derived from the (French, *avoir;* Latin, *habere*) to have, and denoting possession, having, or holding; we find *avers*, Latin *averia* for draught, cattle; and *averagium* is used to signify the work done for a lord by the *averia*, *avers*, or cattle of his tenant. Hence we read in Spelman, "Sciendum est quod unumquodque *averagium* æstivale fieri debit inter Hokday et gulam Augusti." (All summer *average* ought to be done between Hokday and the beginning of August.) This use of the term *averagium* is now obsolete, but it points clearly to a meaning altogether distinct from that in which it was subsequently used in connection with Marine Insurance.

II. *Average*, as used in Marine Insurance, has a totally different origin, and opinion is divided as to whether (*a*) it is to be found in terms used on the shores of the Baltic, or (*b*) in terms long used on the shores of the Mediterranean and in the Levant, or (*c*) whether certain words used in both districts, being somewhat similar in sound, became amalgamated and confounded in popular speech until all primary distinctions were obliterated.

With respect to the Baltic claims, it is to be observed that the present German word is *Haverei* or *Haverie*, and was used by the Hanseatic traders in the form of *Haferei*, *Haferie*, *Haverie*, *Haferey*, *Haverey*, or *Averey*. By the Germans it is derived from the Scandinavian *haf* or *hav*, the open sea, or from the German *Haff*, a sea, bay, or gulf.

With regard to the Mediterranean claims, there can be no doubt that a word somewhat similar in sound was used in very remote times. Santa Rosa and Marsh both agree in deriving the term from the Turkish *avania*, signifying aid, or help, a word much used in the Levant in the sense of a Government charge. Others think that the Arabic *awâr*, a defect, or flaw, is a more likely origin, as it is a purely technical term, and almost identical in meaning with the French *avarie*, damage by sea.

Reviewing all the evidence, it seems exceedingly probable that certain words were in use among seafaring men and merchants both in the Mediterranean and in the Baltic, and that owing to a vague similarity in sound and orthography they became confounded by the English and French, who derived many of their mercantile terms without prejudice from the Lombards and Venetians on the one hand, and from the Hanseatic traders on the other. Under those circumstances, it could hardly fail to happen that words similar in sound and signification would be adopted by them, and so modified as to suit the genius and habits of each language respectively. Hence the following forms:—

Avaris, decay of wares or merchandise, leakage of wines, charges of carriage, &c.—*Cotgrave.*

Avarie, "damage suffered by a vessel or goods from the departure to the return into port."—*Etym. Dictionary.*

Avariées, "damaged goods."—*Ibid.*

Haverei, "the money paid by those who received their goods safe, to indemnify those whose goods have been thrown overboard in a storm."—*Küttner.*

Averia. Italian. "Calculation and distribution of loss arising from goods thrown overboard."—*Altieri.*

Grosses avaries, "loss by tempest, shipwreck, capture, or ransom." —*Gattel.*

Menues avaries, "expenses incurred in entering or leaving port, harbour dues, tonnage, pilotage, &c.—*Ibid.*

S'avarier, "to suffer *averie*; to become damaged."

So early as the middle of the thirteenth century, we find in the Consulado del Mar, authority given to the notary to take pledges from every shipper for the value of "*lo nolit and les avaries*" (the freight and charges), and from that date onwards commercial and nautical language abounds in instances of the word or some modifications of it, as well as of the now recognized English form *average.*

The traders of the Hanseatic League were the first to introduce the practice of Marine Insurance into England, and it is therefore probable that they furnished the earliest term expressing the notion of "damage at sea." That the Lombards who followed them should adopt and soften the word is equally probable; when, owing to the wide extent of commercial operations, any term in use by them would be easily imposed upon those nations with whom they had intercourse. The form *averagium* in law Latin is clearly a mere adaptation of the English *average* to the grammatical requirements of the Latin language.

Average, signifying primarily "damage at sea," it gradually acquired more precise meanings as the requirements of commerce demanded. The following extracts show the modifications which had been established at the dates when they were written:—

In the "*Insurance Ordinances of Antwerp*," 1563, we read, "In order to ascertain the damage which shall appear by reason, and in consequence of the above mentioned jettisons, stranding, or cutting away for the effectual preservation of life, ship, and cargo, all the goods, whether lost or saved shall be valued together. . . . . and thus adding thereunto the value of the ship or the whole freight agreed for by the master . . . . all which being added together, everyone shall from the whole sum be rated, in *proportion* to the goods which he has lost, or which are saved, which estimation and calculation of such *averages* shall be made by masters of ships, and merchants experienced therein."

"*Insurance Ordinances of Middleburg*," 1600. "An action for the damage or decay of any ship or goods that are insured, generally called *average*, happened within a year and a half at farthest, if such *average* happened within the limits of Europe or Barbary," &c.—Here the original use of *average* for "damage by sea" is clearly brought out.

In Parok's "System of Marine Insurance," we read, "*Average* signifies a contribution to a general loss. Whatever the master of a ship in distress deliberately resolves to do for the preservation of the whole, in cutting away masts or cables, or in throwing goods overboard to lighten the vessel, is in all places permitted to be brought into a general or gross average, in which all who are concerned in ship, freight, or cargo, are to bear an equal, or proportionable part of the loss of what was so sacrificed for the common welfare, and it must be made good by the insurers, in such proportion as they have underwritten." Here we find the word employed to signify a compensation for the damage, and not the damage itself.

Mr. McWeskett in his "Complete Digest of the Theory, Laws, and Practice of Insurance," published in 1781, reverts again to the primitive meaning of the term.

"*Average*," says he, "means the accidents and misfortunes which happen to ships and their cargoes from the time of their lading and sailing till their return and unlading."

In the application of the law of average, two main distinctions have to be observed:—

I. Particular Average.
II. General Average.

Particular Average is a contribution to which the underwriters are liable for partial loss, damage, or destruction of property by perils of the sea, and any accidents against which insurance has been made, and which does not cover mere deterioration by ordinary wear and tear: as (1) where *part* of the goods are partly or *wholly* destroyed, or (2) where the *whole* of the goods are damaged, or *partly* destroyed. In either case the loss is estimated by deducting the sale value of the damaged goods, from the value they would possess in the market if sound. Both these values are determined by qualified agents, valuers, or brokers, and a proportional amount of the loss is made good by each of the parties responsible for the insurance,—namely, the underwriters.

General Average is distinguished from the former, by the circumstance that the loss by damage of particular goods is not borne exclusively by the underwriters for these goods, but by the owners of the whole ship, freight, and cargo. It only occurs therefore when any property on board, or belonging to the vessel, is thrown overboard or destroyed, in order to save the remainder or for the safety of the vessel itself. In such cases, those whose property is saved by the sacrifice of property belonging to others, are justly called upon to contribute their quota towards the compensation of those on whom the loss was inflicted.

In the phrase "Primage and Average accustomed," *Average* is a small charge levied proportionally on ship and cargo to cover expense of lights, pilotage, &c., and is quite different in meaning from Particular Average and General Average above described.

The use of the word *average* as an arithmetical term, signifying a mean proportional between two or more numbers, has completely overlaid and obscured in popular speech, the meaning attached to it in former times. The only connection between the two meanings consists in the idea of proportionality; for one of the senses in which it was used in Marine Insurance was that of the *proportion paid by each insurer*, and in another of the senses, the *proportion payable to each of the insured*. The connection, however, between the old primary meaning, and the modern derivative one, is very loose, and the *arithmetical* term "average" is best defined without reference to its derivation, as a number which may be substituted for each one of a series of numbers without altering their sum total.

Since ages, weights, and measures may all be expressed in numbers, it follows that the definitions of "average age" "average length," "average weight," and the like, come under the same law as that for simple numbers.

B

B, occurs in the following abbreviations:—

B/E, Bill of Exchange.
B/L, Bill of Lading.
B/P, Bill of Parcels, or Bills Payable.
B.P.B, Bank Post Bill.
B/S, Bill of Sale.

Baat or Bat. A Siamese silver coin, value 2*s.* 6*d.*, nut shaped; called also the *tical:* 5 *bats* are reckoned equal to 3 Mexican dollars. These when slightly worn may be taken at 4*s.* 2*d.* each, and this gives exactly 2*s.* 6*d.* for the Siamese *bat.*

Bache. A billon coin formerly used in Zurich, value 1¾*d.*

Backwardation. A barbarous term used on the Stock Exchange to denote the rate paid by speculative sellers of Stock for the privilege of carrying over or continuing a bargain, from one fortnightly account to another, instead of settling or closing it on the appointed day. When Stock is particularly scarce, and when there are speculative sales open for a large amount, and when there are, therefore, many operators desirous of carrying over sales, the terms for carrying over will be the payment of a percentage on sales instead of on purchases. The percentage in such cases is called a "backwardation." A backwardation is received by persons carrying over their purchases, and paid by those whose sales are carried over. The amount of the backwardation will vary, according to the scarcity of stock, and the amount of sales to be carried over. The terms for carrying over will be known two days before the "selling-day," when these transactions are arranged, and they will vary in a great measure according to the relative number and amount of the purchases and sales to be carried over, in addition to the circumstances already referred to. In other words, the state of the account to be settled—*i.e.*, whether sales or purchases have preponderated since the last settling-day—will in a great measure determine the rate of contango or backwardation. (Maddison).

Bagattino. A Venetian copper coin, value half a soldo; $\frac{1}{4}d$.

Bail. Bailment. From Latin, *bājulus*, a porter, carrier. It was also applied to one who carried children about, and afterwards to one who had care of children, and at length to those who had charge of persons and property generally. From *bājulus*, we have, Italian, *bailo*, *balivo*, and *bajulivus;* the French, *bail*, *bailli;* and the English, *bail*, *bailiff*. The expression "to give bail" implies that a person has made himself the custodian of another, and that he will produce him when required. From the Latin, *bajulare*, comes the French, *bailler*, to deliver, to bear, which is used in the sense of delivering or handing over a person or thing committed to one's charge.

Bailment is the delivery of goods to a person for some particular use or purpose. The delivery of goods to a carrier, or of property to an innkeeper, or of merchandise to a shipping agent or dock master, are all examples of *bailment*.

Bail has several different applications. In commerce, the principal are:—

I. To be *bail* for any one, that is, to stand as surety for him, and to engage to bring him forward when called for.

II. *Bail* is the amount stipulated, for which a surety will pledge himself, on behalf of the person who is to be called up for examination or trial.

III. The person himself who stands as surety for another is also called his *Bail*.

IV. To *bail*, is to deliver goods on trust, or to place property into the hands of another for safe keeping.

Bailiff. From Latin, *bājulus ;* Italian, *balivo*, *bajulivus*. Law Latin, *ballivus*.

A *Bailiff* is one to whom is committed the care of anything. Henry, of Flanders, on being made Regent of the Empire, issued a proclamation containing the phrase "Principes, barones et milites exercitus me imperii Ballivum elegerunt" (The princes, barons, and soldiers of the army have elected me Bailiff of the Empire). Between officers of this high rank, and the one who executes the writs of a sheriff, or the superintendent of a farm, there are many grades, but the ruling idea conveyed by the name is the same in all cases. It is simply one who has charge of some duty, or the custody of certain persons or things.

Baiocco. A Papal copper coin, value $\frac{1}{2}d$.

Baiochello. A Papal billon coin; single, value 1*d.*; double, value 2*d.*

Bais. A Burmese coin, value $1\frac{1}{2}d$. $\frac{1}{16}$ of a tical.

Bajoccho. A copper coin in the Roman States, about $\frac{1}{2}d$. English; now superseded by Italian system.

Bajoire. A Genevese silver coin, value 4*s.* 6*d.*

Bakri. A silver coin; the quarter rupee of Mysore.

Balance. From Latin, *lanx*, a dish or platter; and *bis*, two; whence *bilanx*, two dishes or pans used as a pair of scales. Italian, *bilancia;* Spanish, *balanza;* French, *balance.* The change from *i* to *a* in the first syllable is apparently a mere corruption, and cannot be otherwise satisfactorily accounted for.

The French, *bilan*, a balance sheet, or statement of an account, approaches very near to the original Latin *bilanx*, and indicates pretty clearly the connection between the ancient Latin and modern English form.

In banking accounts and commercial statements the word *balance* is a familiar term, but is used in a peculiar sense. It is, correctly speaking, the "difference" between the two sides of an account, in other words, it is the sum required to make the two sides equal, that is, to make the two sides *balance.* In the weekly report of the Bank of England, it is called "Rest," and the word "Balance" does not appear. In the French system of Book-keeping it is often called "Reste," but when so used it may generally be more accurately translated "difference" or "remainder."

Balance of Trade. A phrase used by economists to denote the difference between the *exports* from one country, and its *imports* from some other country, or all other countries. It is usually considered a sign of healthy trade when the exports of a country, however large, are balanced by its imports. On the other hand, it is thought, by some persons at least, that when the imports of a country exceeds the exports, such country must be living beyond its means, that it is consuming more than it produces, and shortly, that it is on the high road to impoverishment and ruin. As England has for the last ten years imported merchandize of greater value than that which it has exported, some timid thinkers have inferred that this country has entered on its downward path. It does not appear to have entered into the calculations of those thinkers, that if this country is being thus drained of wealth, some signs of depletion would be manifest in the condition of the people, and that the correctness of their forebodings might be tested by an appeal to the national statistics. Such an appeal, however, would show that, so far from the country being impoverished, it never possessed so large a mass of accumulated wealth, as during the last few years. Thus, *money* in the form of coin, which some people will continue to regard as a very important item of wealth, was never more abundant, nor was it ever so easy to replenish our stock of it, as it is now, by the simple expedient of raising the Bank Rate. *Land*, of course, cannot have diminished in quantity, and it has certainly increased in value. *House property* has enormously increased in quantity and value during the last ten years. The *food* of the people, though in some instances dearer, is in others cheaper, and, taking all together, is obtainable by the masses, of better quality and in greater abundance than in former times. *Clothing* is warmer and better made, and at no period of our history were the people better clad. The *savings* of the working classes have increased year by year for the last ten years, as is proved by the annual reports of the Savings' Banks. These facts do not indicate anything like impoverishment, still less ruin. Nevertheless, the unimpeachable truth remains, that English imports have for some years greatly exceeded the exports, and we are necessarily confronted by the question, How is this excess of imports paid for? For we may rely upon it, that our foreign cousins do not send us their cotton, hides, sugar, &c., without receiving an equivalent in return. We have seen above that we do not pay for them by drawing upon our stores of accumulated wealth; for that is increasing rather than diminishing year by year, and it is a problem well worthy of the attention of the curious, to determine by what means this payment is made.

In general terms, it may be said that the excess of imports over exports is paid for by the English people, in the form of *services* rendered, and which do not appear in the Returns of the Board of Trade. These services may be *past* services, embodied in different kinds of wealth, and paid for in the shape of interest on capital lent; or they may be services which are being rendered from day to day, and year to year, at the *present* time.

As an example of *past* services we may instance the loans by the English to Foreign States, and for which interest is sent to England. At a moderate estimate it may be said that at least twelve hundred millions (£1,200,000,000) have been thus contributed, and that interest on this sum must be sent to this country half-yearly in order to pay the dividends falling due. Reckoning 5 per cent. as the average rate of interest paid, this would require £60,000,000 to be sent to England every year; and as all, or nearly all, is sent in the form of merchandize, for which the producers draw Bills of Exchange, which Bills are negotiated in London, and are paid virtually by means of the coupons detached from Foreign Bonds; and further, since the merchandize appears in the list of imports, while the coupons do not appear in the list of exports, we hit at once on one item by means of which the excess of imports is paid for, and the balance between the two partially restored.

Then again, as an example of *present* services rendered to foreign nations, and which are not embodied in any report of exported wealth, take the "carrying trade" of Great Britain. All the sailors employed in navigating the ships, the tradesmen employed in victualling them, the builders in making them, the engineers in constructing their machinery, the purveyors of stores and clothing, are all rendering services to foreign nations which *do not appear* in any form of exported produce; but they have to be paid for to a great extent by foreign nations, and to that extent are actually paid by means of imported produce, and *this does appear* in the Trade Reports.

These examples might be multiplied. But sufficient has been said to indicate the nature of the problem, and the direction in which a solution may be looked for. Shortly, it may be thus stated: Given an excess of *imports into*, over the *exports from* England, what are the services rendered by England in compensation for that excess? (*See Mercantile System.*)

Ballot. From the French, *ballote*, a little ball.

The Ballot is a device for arriving at, or recording, decisions by means of a box called the "Ballot Box," and a number of balls, numbered, or coloured, or otherwise marked to suit the particular purpose to which they are to be applied. Two distinct and opposed objects are aimed at under different circumstances, when the ballot box is called into requisition :—

1. To arrive at a decision on any matter by an appeal to *pure chance.* Occasions often arise when it is desired to make a selection of persons or things so as to leave no room for the intrusion of prejudice, predilection, or error of judgment : as, for example, when three members of a committee, all presumed to be equally worthy, are called upon by the rules of a society to retire at the end of a year. In order to avoid favouritism or sinister influence, it is felt to be most fair to all parties to have recourse to the ballot. It is only necessary to put as many balls into the box as there are members of a committee, each being marked so as to indicate one member, and no other: the first three drawn, or the last three, or any other three according to agreement, to be the retiring members.

2. To enable the members of a society to satisfy their judgment, predilection, or prejudice, in such a way that it may not be known to any one but the individual who records his vote, in what way he voted. This method enables a voter to use his influence on behalf of a candidate without giving personal offence to other candidates, for whom perhaps the voter has great esteem, although choosing one for a special office in preference to them.

Of course there are many ways of conducting a ballot, and of marking the balls, so as to meet the exigencies of each particular case. But it may be worth while to describe one which is very useful in commercial practice, when a selection of two, or three, out of many, perhaps high, numbers have to be drawn. For this purpose as many boxes are provided as there are digits in the highest number—say 7860, which contains four digits. Each box contains 10 balls, numbered 0 1 2 3 4 5 6 7 8 9, except one for thousands, which should only contain 8, that is, all the numerals up to and including 7. If now the boxes be placed in a row, so that the left one stands for *thousands*, the next for *hundreds*, the next for *tens*, and the last for *units*, and one ball be taken from each box, it is evident that any number whatever between 1 and 7860 may perchance be drawn.

Suppose the 4 balls drawn to be figured thus :—

(0) (3) (9) (5)

then 395 is the number drawn. See also Art. *Drawing*.

Banco-Daler. Swedish paper-money issued by the National Bank, equivalent to about thirty-five cents.

Bani. The hundredth part of the Roumanian *ley*, which is the unit of value in Roumania. Since the *ley* is equal in weight and fineness to the French franc, the *bani* is the representative of the

French centime. A silver piece of 50 banis is struck: it weighs 2·500 grammes, ·835 fine, and is worth about 4¼*d.* in English.

Bank. From the German *Banck,* a mound or heap. It is a literal translation of the Italian, *monte,* a small hill, from the Latin, *mons.* The term *monte* originated in Venice in the twelfth century, when the city was at war with foes on every hand, and in great straits for want of money. A forced loan was raised from the inhabitants, and the proceeds being brought together formed a heap or hillock of money, and so gave rise to the name. The Germans, when they in later years formed a similar fund, followed their natural habit, and called it by a name derived from their own language, but meaning the same thing as the Italian *monte,* and that was *Banck.* But the Germans had over-run all the northern parts of Italy about this time, and had made their word, *Banck,* as familiar as its native origin, *monte;* only it was so modified as to suit the Italian language, and was called *Banco.* Now it happens that *banco* is the Italian for a bench, table, or counter, and as the bench or counter was a much more conspicuous object to the multitude than the heap, or mound, which was doubtless concealed in the vaults, the people generally very soon learnt to associate the name of *banco,* or bench, with the counter and not with the money. Hence appears to have arisen the popular notion that *bank* is derived from *banco,* the bench or table on which money-changers counted out their coins. Nor was this unreasonable, for the money-changer had from time immemorial been known by a name or names, all of which were derived from a word signifying a plank, table, counter, or *bench,* for either of which words *banco* might easily be substituted. Thus we have *mensarius,* a money-changer or banker, so named from the table, *mensa,* at which he stood, and which is thus referred to by Livy. "Quinque viri creati, quos *mensarios* ab dispensatione pecuniœ appellârunt." (Five men were appointed who were called *mensarii,* because they regulated the payment of the public funds.) Τραπεζα, *trapeza,* is a table, and is the word used for the tables of the money-changers in the temple, Mark xi. 15. Τραπεζιτης, *trapezites,* was one who kept such a table, a money-changer, a banker. The Latin form of the same, *trapezita,* was also used in the sense of money-changer or money-lender. It seems therefore highly probable that the word *bank,* like many other terms used in commerce, has a double origin, one traceable to classical times, and the other to the Teutonic dialects of Northern Europe.

The primary notion of a bank as derived from the practice of the Goldsmiths of Lombard Street, appears to have been that of a place for the safe custody of money and other valuable things of small bulk. But before the business had passed from the hands of the goldsmiths into those of the regular bankers, a way was seen by which the money might be made a source of profit without endangering its safety. Thus arose the practice of issuing goldsmiths' notes. (*See Goldsmiths' Notes*).

As banking is now conducted in England, a bank may be defined as an "agency for the exchange of commodities;" but the mechanism by means of which the exchange is effected is such that the commodities themselves never appear in connection with the operations of the Bank, nor is their existence often recognized. The exchange is effected by the creation of *instruments of credit* by means of which Bankers buy the money of their customers, or more frequently buy of them other instruments of credit. These instruments of credit consist mainly of bills of exchange, cheques, entries in the bank's books; but whatever the banker buys in the course of his business, whether money or paper, he always pays for it by means of credit. These instruments of credit may then be put into circulation, or otherwise employed in trade and manufacture so as to yield a profit, and this profit is the reward for the labour and skill employed in the business of banking.

Modern English Banking, which is a totally different thing from the ancient Banking System of Venice, and the Italian States, had a very humble origin. It may be traced to the ingenuity of the *trusty servants* and *care-takers* employed by merchants and traders in the troublous times immediately following the execution of Charles. These servants, on whom fell the responsibility of taking care of the money which their masters were all day long engaged in accumulating, took it to the Goldsmiths who had vaults and strong rooms for the safe custody of their wares. For the use of this money the Goldsmiths allowed the depositors 4*d*. per cent. for each day the money remained with them. Here was an advantage gained all round. The servants made the money entrusted to them more safe. The owners received interest on their unemployed cash, and the Goldsmiths made a profit by lending out the money entrusted to them. They almost immediately adopted the practice of discounting Bills, so that they had only to call themselves "Bankers," and both business and name corresponded to that of "Banker" in the modern English sense of the term.

Bank Annuities. Bank annuities is the legal name for what are now more commonly spoken of as the "Funds" or "Consols." The term Bank Annuities indicates pretty accurately their origin and their nature. They originated in a compact between the Government for the time being and the moneyed class among its subjects, in virtue of which compact it was agreed that everyone giving a certain sum to the Government, should receive from the National revenue, a fixed sum yearly (*i.e.*, an annuity) for ever. The sums thus collected from the subjects, when accumulated formed a "heap," a "monte," a "Banck," or, as we say a "Bank," and the annuities paid to those who contributed to this Bank were consequently called "Bank Annuities." The name is applied in all formal documents issued by the Bank of England and the National Debt Office, but by the people generally, the shorter term "Funds" or "Consols" is found more convenient.

Bank Dollar. A silver coin used in Hamburg. In England, the Spanish dollar, restamped and issued as a token by the Bank, in 1804.

Banker's Note. A Promissory Note given by a Banker to a customer promising to pay a given sum either on Demand or at a given date against sums standing to the credit of the customer at that Bank. It was the immediate successor of the old Goldsmith's note, and is now no longer in use.

Bank Note. A contraction of "Bank of England Note," and is thus distinguished from "Country Notes," the name applied in the City of London to Notes issued by all other banks in the United Kingdom.

Bank of Issue. A Bank of Issue is defined in law to be "any Joint Stock Banking Company lawfully issuing its own notes." No new Banks of Issue can now be formed. If any existing Bank of Issue becomes extinct, two-thirds the amount of notes it was authorized to issue is added to those authorized to be issued by the Bank of England. By the operation of this law, the Bank of England, which was at first authorized to issue only 14 millions of notes against Government and other securities, and to receive interest thereon, is now allowed to issue between 15 and 16 millions.

Bank Post Bills. Bills issued by the Bank of England, but not by any of its Branches, payable at *seven days* sight. They are *accepted* at the time they are drawn, so that they begin to run from that date. They form an exceedingly convenient and economical means of remitting sums above £10—the lowest sum drawn for—to any part of England. The money to be remitted is simply paid in at the Bank, and the applicant receives in return the Bank Post Bill, which he sends to the person whom he wishes to receive it. He pays nothing for the accommodation, the seven days interest being accepted by the Bank as a sufficient remuneration. Bank Post Bills originated in 1738 in consequence of the frequent robberies of the mail which had occurred for some time previous to this date, the object being "that in case of the mail being robbed, the proprietor might have time to give notice." The following is the form of a Bank Post Bill; the portions in capitals are printed: and fractional sums are written in at the time the Bill is applied for, as are also the names, here put in italics.

Bank of England Post Bill.

No. —— LONDON, —— 18—.

At seven days sight, I promise to pay this my Sola Bill of Exchange to *James Thornton*, or Order, ONE HUNDRED sterling value received of *Henry Green*.

For the Governor and Company of the Bank of England.

£ONE HUNDRED M—— N——

Bank Return. The Report issued by the Bank of England every Thursday afternoon, and which is looked for not only by City men, but by merchants and bankers all over the kingdom. It is a Report of the condition of the Bank set forth in such a way, as to show the amount of Bank notes in circulation, the stock of Bullion and Coin in reserve, and such other details as enable the experienced to judge of the state of the money market and its probable tendency in the immediate future. Since the passing of the "Bank Act of 1844" this Return has been drawn up in the form prescribed by Parliament, so as to separate the "Issue Department" from the "Banking Department." The *Old Form*, however, is easily compiled from the present one, and indeed is regularly published in the *Economist* newspaper for the information of those who prefer it in that shape. The following is the Bank Report for 22nd June, 1881.

BANK OF ENGLAND.

An Account pursuant to the Act 7th and 8th Victoria cap. 32, for the week ending on Wednesday, the 22nd day of June, 1881.

ISSUE DEPARTMENT.

Notes issued	£41,569,320	Government Debt ...	£11,015,100
		Other Securities......	4,734,900
		Gold coin & bullion..	25,819,320
		Silver bullion	...
	£41,569,320		£41,569,320

BANKING DEPARTMENT.

Proprietors' Capital.	£14,553,000	Government Securities	£14,907,127
Rest	3,080,785	Other Securities......	20,086,089
Public Deposits, including Exchequer Savings' Banks, Commissioners of National Debt, and dividend accounts...	8,358,928	Notes	15,153,595
Other Deposits	25,124,079	Gold and Silver coin	1,216,095
Seven-day and other bills....................	246,114		
	£51,362,906		£51,362,906

Dated June 23, 1881. FRANK MAY, Chief Cashier.

THE OLD FORM.

The above Bank accounts would, if made out in the old form, present the following results;—

Liabilities.		Assets.	
Circulation (including bank post bills)	£26,661,839	Securities	£36,190,216
Public deposits	8,358,928	Coin and Bullion ...	27,035,415
Private Deposits ...	25,124,079		
	£60,144,846		£63,225,631

The balance of Assets above Liabilities being £3,080,785 as stated in the above account under the head Rest.

The following explanation of the separate items in the above Report will probably be acceptable to those for whom this work is intended.

I. The Issue Department.

Notes Issued. This means that the Bank of England Notes circulating in the country, or held in reserve by the different Banks, amount to the sum indicated.

Government Debt. This is a Debt owing from the English Government to the Bank of England. It dates from the reign of William and Mary, 1694, when it was only £1,200,000, since which time several additions have been made to it till 1835, when it amounted to £11,015,100. From that time till the present it has appeared in the Report from week to week without alteration.

Other Securities. These are interest-bearing securities of a high class, and selected according to the judgment of the Directors; their value varies from time to time, but usually makes up with the foregoing item £15,000,000 or upwards. It is now £15,750,000.

Gold Coin and Bullion. These terms explain themselves. The amount varies materially from time to time, and it is an item on which the experts of the money market bestow great attention.

The last three items constitute the guarantee for the payment on presentation of every Bank note issued; that is to say, the Government is guarantee for £11,015,100; there are solid interest-bearing securities for £4,734,900, and there is standard metal for the remainder, whatever its amount.

II. The Banking Department.

Proprietors' Capital. This is what is called by other Joint Stock Companies "*Share Capital,*" and consists of the sums subscribed by the shareholders of the Bank in order to form a working capital. It is invested in securities of all kinds, including the above-named Government Debt, and the interest derived therefrom, forms one portion of the profits annually distributed among the shareholders.

Rest. The same thing, as in other accounts, would be called "balance" or "difference," and which usually appears in balance sheets as the last item on that side of the accounts, See *Rest*.

Public Deposits, &c. The Bank of England being the banking house of the nation, the national revenues are paid in there as fast as they are received by the collectors in all parts of the kingdom. Under this head are included moneys paid in on account of the Exchequer; the Savings' Banks; the Commissioners of the National Debt; the Inclosure Commissioners; the Paymaster-General; the Receiver-General of Customs; the Postmaster-General; the Receiver-General of Inland Revenue, &c., all of which are distinguished as Public Deposits, and kept separate from some other Government Accounts which fall under the next head.

Other Deposits. Under this head are included sundry sums paid into the credit of several Government offices, each of which keeps a separate account at the Bank, such as those of the Astronomer-Royal; the Master of the Mint; the Trinity House; and about twenty others. Besides these, the Joint Stock and Private Banks place their Reserves under the custody of the Bank of England for the sake of safety; while many wealthy merchants keep their ordinary banking account there, thus swelling this item to a degree which exceeds by far that of either of the others.

Seven Day and Other Bills. The meaning is, "Value given to the Bank in exchange for Bills issued." The seven-day bills are what we have described elsewhere as "*Bank Post Bills*," which see.

Passing to the other side of the account, we have, under four heads, the resources on which the Bank relies in order to meet the claims of its creditors whenever they are made.

Government Securities. Consisting of Consols, Exchequer Bills, Treasury Bonds, and, generally, securities for the due payment of which the Government is responsible, and the taxes of the nation are pledged.

Other Securities. Foreign Government Stocks, Railway Debentures, First Class Bills, and sundry negotiable instruments selected at the discretion of the Directors.

Notes. Bank of England Notes obtained from the Issue Department in exchange for gold coin and bullion.

Gold and Silver Coin. These, together with the Notes last mentioned, constitute the Banking Reserve, and is always maintained at a point which makes about one-third the total liabilities as shown on the-left hand side of the account.

But in making this comparison for commercial purposes, it is usual to take into account only the Deposits and Bills as "Liabilities," and the Notes and Coin as "Reserve," the other items being of little interest to the outside public.

As to the "Old Form" which, as above said, was the form in use previous to the passing of the Bank Act of 1844, and which some people prefer to the new one, while others like to have it presented to them for the sake of comparison with the earlier reports, the following explanations may be useful;—

Circulation. Found by adding together "Notes Issued" and Seven-day Bills," and then deducting the "Notes" forming part of the Banking Reserve, which from their mode of employment cannot form part of the *circulation.*

Public Deposits. Same as in Banking Department.

Private Deposits. Identical with "Other Deposits."

Securities. Add the "Government Debt" and "Other Securities" in the Issue Department, to the "Government Securities" and "Other Securities" in the Banking Department. Subtract "Proprietors' Capital."

Coin and Bullion. Equal to the sum of the same in both Departments.

Bankrupt. Littré derives this word from the Italian, *banca-rotta:* for the first half of the term, see *Bank.* *Rotta* is from *rotto;* French, *rompre,* and both these from the Latin, *rumpere*, to break; part. *ruptus*, broken. The long-received account of the origin of the term, though picturesque, is not well authenticated. It was long supposed that when a Venetian money-changer or banker became insolvent, the fact was proclaimed in the hearing of the people, and shown by the breaking-up of his *banco*, bench, or counter, in their presence. Another explanation is given by Blackstone, who says it may be derived from the French, *banque*, a bench; and *route*, a track; as "signifying that the bankrupt has removed his banque, leaving but a trace behind." A statute of Henry VIII. is directed against such "persons as *do make bankrupt*," which is a literal translation of the French idiom, "*qui font banque route*."

> "Poor *banckrout* conscience! where are those
> Rich houres but farmed to thee
> How carelessly I some did lose,
> And other to my lust dispose,
> As no rent day should be!"
>
> HABINGTON'S *Castara*, 1634-40.

In law a bankrupt differs from an ordinary debtor in the following particulars:—(*a*) his property is summarily seized for the benefit of all his creditors collectively; (*b*) his property is distributed among his creditors in general (instead of applying a portion of it to an individual complainant) and (*c*) the discharge of the debtor from future liability for debts then existing.

Bank Stock. The capital of the Banking Department of the Bank of England formed by the subscriptions of the proprietors, together with a surplus of the Profits which have been added from time to time. The capital at first amounted only to £1,200,000. It is now £14,553,000. It is quoted in the Stock Exchange Price List as "Bank Stock," and the price quoted is so much for £100 of Stock. Any amount of Bank Stock may be purchased which does not involve fractions of a penny. The rate of interest depends on the profits made by the Bank in the course of the year.

Bank Value. (*See Currency Value.*)

In Hamburg, Amsterdam, and some other towns, there existed previous to the establishment of our modern system of Banking, a species of Bank Credit, called also Bank Value, or Bank Money, terms still in use, and which originated in the exigences of those early stages of European Commerce. The towns above referred to were important centres of foreign trade, and coins of all sorts from different countries found their way there, and were presented in payment of accounts. As many of these coins were clipped, defaced, worn, and were in other respects of ill-defined value, disputes often arose between merchants as to how much a given heap of coins was to count for. To put an end to these disputes, and to facilitate business, it was agreed by the Magistrates of those cities, that a Bank of Deposit should be formed, and that all persons having coins to offer should bring them to the Bank, when they would be assayed and weighed, and a Bank Credit for their value entered in the books in favour of the customer. This Bank Credit, or Bank Money was in high esteem, since it was always exchangeable on demand for money of full weight and fineness; so that the terms Bank Credit, Bank Money, and Bank Value were used in a sense as commendatory in those days as the word *sterling* is with us. In Hamburg the superiority of Bank Value is still maintained, for whereas 3,608 grs. Troy of pure silver is coined into 35 marks current, it is in *mark banco* or Bank Value supposed to be coined into 27¾ marks. Hence, taking the proportion of gold and silver to be 15½ to 1, the mark banco or mark of Bank Value is 1*s.* 5·82*d.*, and the mark in Currency Value 1*s.* 2·13*d.* sterling.

Barbone. A Luccese silver coin, value 6*d.*

Bargain. The initial syllable *bar* in this word, and those immediately following, is supposed to be derived from an old root signifying noise, confusion, and has acquired the secondary meaning of contest, haggling, dispute, altercation, &c. In all the Romance languages and in many of the Teutonic, the same syllable is found, always conveying the same idea. Hence the old French, *barguigner*, to chaffer, to wrangle, haggle, &c., in the making of a bargain. Italian, *baruffa*, fray, dispute. Portuguese, *baralliar;* Spanish, *barajar*, to shuffle, entangle, or quarrel. Lithuanian, *barti*, to scold. Icelandic, *baratta*, strife, contest, and the old English, *bargane.*

A *Bargain* is at the present day pretty nearly what is implied by its etymology. It signifies a contract oral or written, agreed to after more or less effort on either side to obtain the most favourable terms.

Barratry, Barretry. Old French, *bareter*, to deceive, beguile; Spanish, *baratar*, to truck, to exchange; *barateria*, fraud, especially by the master of a ship. (*See also Bargain* and *Barter.*)

"Noble fathers, I am such a person whom ye knowe to have been a common *baratour* and thefe by a long space of yeares."—Elyot.

In commerce, *barratry* signifies damage done to a ship by the ship-master, through wilful neglect or with a deliberate design to commit a fraud upon the insurers.

Barratry also signified in law the practice of stirring up suits and quarrels for the purpose of involving the parties in litigation and mulcting them in the costs.

Barter. Like the word *bargain*, all the forms of this word indicate noisy contention, chaffering, haggling, and disputing. The old French, *bareter*, the Italian, *baratare*, and the Icelandic, *baratta*, with many other terms, convey the same notion.

"Al is dai, n' is ther no night
Ther n' is *baret*, nother strif."—Hickes.

"They run like Bedlam *barreters* into the street."—Hollingshead.

The practice of exchanging one commodity for another directly, without the intervention of money or other medium of exchange. In primitive times, and amongst uncultivated tribes in modern times, it was the regular way of effecting exchanges of goods. Under the name of *truck* (*see Truck System*) it is still practised in some remote districts in England, and even in the midst of our advanced civilization is sometimes had recourse to when two persons possess articles they do not want, and each one wants what the other possesses, as exchange is then made without the intervention of money. In order to facilitate this modernized form of Barter, one or two journals have been established, and the number of exchanges effected through the medium of these journals is said to be very great. As an example of what may be done by such an agency, a botanist having a microscope to spare wished to exchange it for a large garden-roller. One advertisement brought the two parties face to face, and the exchange was made much to the satisfaction of both. Had each article been sold to the second-hand dealers for cash, it is certain that the sum realized for each article would have been far from sufficient to purchase the other.

Batz. A Swiss copper coin, silvered (billon), value 1½*d.*, 10 rappen.

Batzen. A Swiss billon coin, 10 centimes, nearly one penny.

Bawbee. A copper coin formerly used in Scotland, and supposed to be a corruption of Bas Piece; value about one halfpenny.

Bear. This term as applied to a dealer on the Stock Exchange is a perfect specimen of pure slang. It is in constant use among brokers and jobbers, and yet no one is able to say when it first came into use, nor does any one appear able to assign a reason for its introduction. The meaning attached to it is purely conventional, and may have been first used by some individual in joke, in anger, or as an unmeaning cognomen.

A "*Bear*" is a dealer on the Stock Exchange who sells securities which he does not possess, with the hope of buying them back at a reduced price before the next fortnightly settling-day. It is needless to say that this hope is often frustrated, in which case he has to buy them back at a loss, and pay the difference. A dealer who sells securities, and delivers them, is not called a "bear" in Stock Exchange parlance, although his object may be like that of the Bear to make profit by buying them back when the price falls. Both "bearing" and "bulling" (*see Bull*), although pure speculation, are operations fully recognized by the committee of the Stock Exchange, and the rules for controlling them are enforced with rigour.

To Bearer. The phrase "To Bearer" as it appears on Bills or Cheques implies that the *Bearer* or *Holder* of Bill or Cheque has precisely the claims on the maker of it as the party specifically named. Without this addition, or that of the phrase "to Order" the instrument would not be negotiable; that is, the debt could not be transferred; or, if transferred, the transferree would not be able to sue the debtor in an English court of law. (*See To Order.*)

Bedidlik. An Egyptian gold coin = 100 piastres, or 4·97 United States dollars, or £1 0*s.* 5*d.* sterling.

Benda. An Ashantee gold coin, value £10 13*s.* 4*d.*

Bendiky. A gold coin used in Morocco, value about 9*s.*

Bes or Bessis. Roman piece of 8 unciae.

Beshlik. A Turkish billon coin, value five piastres, about 10*d.* nominal.

Bestic or Beslic. A Turkish silver coin, value 3*d.*

Betterness or **Worseness.** These two purely technical terms, are used in refinery to indicate the quantity of *alloy* to be taken from, or added to a piece of impure gold or silver to bring it to the condition of standard metal. (*See Standard.*)

In the "standarding" of Gold, every fragment operated on is supposed to be divided into 24 parts called *carats*. If such fragment on being assayed is found to contain 22 parts pure gold, and 2 parts alloy (which may be either silver or copper) it is said to be of the standard degree of fineness, and is called "Standard Gold." It is indifferently called 22 carats fine, $\frac{11}{12}$ fine, or ·9166 or ·916$\frac{2}{3}$ fine. If the assay shows that the fragment of gold contains 22$\frac{1}{2}$ parts of pure metal, and 1$\frac{1}{2}$ parts alloy, it is said to be $\frac{1}{2}$ carat better. A bar containing 21 parts pure metal and 3 parts alloy, is 1 carat worse. The carat is divided into 4 grains, and each grain into eighths of a grain; but the grain as thus used is as imaginary as the carat itself. This cumbersome method of expressing the betterness or worseness of bullion has no merit, but that of long use, and is now superseded by the decimal or Millièmes' system referred to below.

In the standarding of silver, the weight is estimated not in carats as above, but in *ounces* and *pennyweights*. Standard silver contains 11 ozs. 2 dwts. of pure metal in every 12 ounces, and 18 dwts. of alloy (which may be copper or other base metal), or what is the same thing 222 dwts. of fine silver and 18 dwts. of alloy. English silver has had this degree of fineness from time immemorial, and is called the "Ancient Right Standard." It may be expressed as $\frac{222}{240}$ fine, or ·925 fine. If the assay yields 219 dwts. of pure silver, and 21 dwts. alloy, it is called 3 dwts. Worse; 223$\frac{1}{2}$ dwts. pure silver, and 16$\frac{1}{2}$ alloy, 1$\frac{1}{2}$ dwts. Better. This method of recording the betterness and worseness is open to the same objection as that in use for gold, and hence the attempts of other nations to supplant it by a method more con venient and intelligible.

The method most in favour for reporting the fineness of bullion is called the Millièmes system, because every piece of metal operated upon is supposed to be divided into Millièmes or thousandth parts. When thus expressed it is easily understood in all parts of the world where the common arithmetical notation is known; besides which, all calculations are facilitated by its use. In France and America it is the official method; and in England it is now used for Gold, side by side with the old method for silver. The degrees of fineness are easily converted by an arithmetical process from one system to the other, as the following examples will show.

British Standard Gold is 22 carats or $\frac{11}{12}$ fine.

Therefore 12 : 11 : : 1000 : ·916$\frac{2}{3}$ fine.

Standard Silver is $\frac{222}{240}$ fine.

Therefore 240 : 222 : : 1000 : ·925 fine.

If Gold be reported 1 carat 1$\frac{3}{8}$ grains better—*i.e.*, 23 c. 1$\frac{3}{8}$ grs. in 24 c,—reducing to eighths of a grain, we have—

768 : 747 : : 1000 : ·973,

If Silver be reported $3\frac{1}{3}$ dwts. Worse—*i.e.*, $218\frac{1}{3}$ dwts. of fine silver in 240—we have—

$$240 : 218\tfrac{1}{3} :: 1000 : \cdot 910.$$

Bezant. Another name for the Byzantine gold ducat. There was also an old silver Byzantine coin in use from the fifth century A.D. Each was worth about 2*s.*, English.

Bezzo. A Venetian copper coin, value $\frac{1}{4}d.$

Bilateral or **Synallagmatic Contract.** (*See Contract.*)

Bill. (1) From the Latin, *bulla*, which originally meant a *bubble*, but was afterwards applied to small ornaments of bubble shape, as beads, &c.: afterwards to a *seal* which in ancient times had a similar form; then to a charter sealed with such a seal, and since the fifteenth century to Papal letters, or Bulls, exclusively. This is the origin of the term Bill as applied to all those instruments which were formerly authenticated with a seal, as Bills of Exchange mostly were, till within about a century ago.

(2) Norman French, *bille*, a billet, or piece of wood; Old English, *bylle* or *byll*. This is the origin of Bill as applied to those documents formerly represented by notched sticks, and notably Exchequer Bills.

Some old forms of Bills and Promissory Notes preserved at Child's Bank have the *seal* attached; others have none. This seems to indicate that somewhere about the year 1700 the practice of sealing was gradually discontinued.

In English commercial law the term Bill is applied to *orders to pay*, and is thus distinguished from Note. (*See Note.*)

Bill of Entry. "On the importation of any goods into the United Kingdom, and before the landing of the same, the importer is required to deliver to the Customs authorities a document declaring and describing his goods; this is termed "An Entry," or "Bill of Entry," and the particulars of such entry must correspond with the description given of the same goods and packages in the report of the ship, and in any certificate of origin, &c."—Ham's *Revenue and Mercantile Vade-Mecum.*

Bill of Exchange. A written order for the payment of a sum of money, to a certain person, and at a given date. A Bill of Exchange should always be addressed to the person who *owes the money*. If it is addressed to a person who simply holds the money on deposit, as a *Bailee, Trustee, Agent*, or *Servant*, it is called a Draft. (*See Draft.*) This legal distinction is not observed in commercial practice.

On examination of the appended Form of an Inland Bill, the following points will be noted:—

1st. Three names appear on the face of it. (*a.*) The Drawer, Benson & Co. (*b.*) The Drawee or Payer, Martin & Sons. (*c.*) The Payee, Harrison & Co. In every completed form of a Bill of Exchange the names of these three parties should appear.

2nd. The Sum to be paid, an essential part of every Bill.

3rd. Two dates—the one when it is drawn; the second implied by the phrase "Three months after date."

4th. The place at which it is drawn—namely, Manchester.

Bill of Exchange. Inland.

Manchester, Dec. 18th, 1878.

£720.

Three months after date please pay this Bill of Exchange to Messrs. Harrison & Co., *or Order, the Sum of Six Hundred and Twenty Pounds sterling for value received, and charge the same to my account.*

Benson & Co.

To Messrs. Martin & Sons, *London.*

Accepted
Payable 21st Mar., 1879, at the
ALLIANCE BANK, LONDON.
MARTIN AND SONS.

Pay to the Order of MR. ROBERT GREEN *for value received.*

HARRISON & CO.

Hull, Dec. 28, 1878.

Pay to the Order of CHEESMAN & SONS *value in account.*

ROBERT GREEN.

Birmingham, Jan. 6, 1879.

Pay MESSRS. ROBSON & CO. *or Order.*

CHEESMAN & SONS.

London, Jan, 18, 1879.

ROBSON & CO.

Feb. 1, 1879.

It has been decided that the phrase "for value received" is of no importance to the validity of a Bill or Promissory Note, but it is generally inserted.

Thus far, as to the Making or Drawing of the Bill. It should be presented by the holder for *Acceptance* without delay; because as soon as the Bill is accepted, he has the Acceptor's security as well as the Drawer's.

A Bill is said to be "accepted" by writing across the face of it the word "Accepted" and the signature of the Payer (or Drawee). This latter party then is called the Acceptor, and he is also responsible for the payment of the bill at the due date. In a full and complete acceptance the *due date* is inserted, as well as the *place* where it is payable, as in the form under consideration. The date here inserted includes the three "days of grace."

This Bill when properly stamped is now negotiable. It may be discounted at a Bank, or may pass from hand to hand by the process of Indorsement.

The Indorsements at the back of the example possess peculiarities which should be noted.

1st. By the first indorsement, Messrs. Harrison & Co. transfer their claim to Robert Green, and the phrase "for value received" is intended to show that it is a *bona fide* transaction, and that the indorsers have received either money or goods, or some other consideration from the indorsee.

2nd. The second indorsement shows that Robert Green has transferred his claim to Messrs. Cheesman & Sons. The phrase "value in account" indicates that the relative position of their accounts is such as to render some payment desirable from Mr. Robert Green to the firm of Cheesman & Sons.

3rd. The third indorsement is said to be "Incomplete." Cheesman & Sons transfer their Claim to Robson & Co., or Order without specifying or indicating the grounds on which the transfer is made.

4th. The fourth indorsement is called on "Indorsement in Blank," and renders the Bill payable to the holder, whoever he may be. (*See Foreign Bill.*)

Bill of Lading. A document handed to a shipper by a captain when goods are delivered to the latter for conveyance. Bills of Lading are negotiable instruments, and pass from hand to hand by indorsement in the same manner as Bills of Exchange. They are, however, quite different in their nature, in this respect, that no exchange is implied in the transaction. A Bill of Lading refers to certain goods, goes with those goods, and is of no value apart from them. It gives the holder a claim to those specific goods, and not merely to something of equal value, as a Bill of Exchange does. It can never exceed in quantity the property it represents, whereas a Bill of Exchange not only may, but mostly does, greatly exceed the coin it represents, simply because it does not carry with it a claim to any particular coin or money, but only a claim to money or coin of that value, at some given time, so that the same coin may discharge several Bills in succession. It follows that goods represented by a Bill of Lading, are of the nature of a *Depositum* as distinguished from a *Mutuum* (*which see*).

The form of a Bill of Lading is appended. Printed forms are always kept at the Stationers licensed to sell stamps. The words printed in Italics, are of course varied to suit each particular case. Those in Roman type are the same for all Bills of Lading.

Bill of Sale. A Bill of Sale is a document placed in the hands of a creditor as security for a loan or debt. It authorizes the creditor to sell the goods and chattels named therein, if the loan is not repaid or the debt liquidated at a specified time, and to reimburse himself out of the proceeds. But in order to prevent frauds on creditors by secret bills of sale, every Bill of Sale or a copy thereof, must be filed in the Court of Queen's Bench, within twenty-one days after it is made or given—otherwise it is "void to all intents and purposes."

Billon. *For Etymology see Bullion.*

A base coinage found in several countries, containing an excess of alloy. *Bas Billon* is the worst description of this sort of coinage. The *Billon or Bullion* was originally the place where gold and silver were brought to be assayed and coined. Hence when old coins were found to be light, or defaced, or debased, an old Act required that they should be brought to the Billon or Mint to be recoined—whence the proverbial expressions in Old French "porter au billon" and "mettre au billon" applied to things generally which require making up anew. Money which was so deteriorated was called "monnaie de billon," signifying money which must be sent to the Mint. From this expression came the old English "billon money," and more shortly billon, which some think corresponds in meaning to the Spanish *vellon*. For many years now the word *billon* has been used exclusively in the sense of base coin. (*See Vellon.*)

Bills for Acceptance. Bills sent to a merchant for him to get accepted. They are usually entered into a book called the "Bills for Acceptance Book," which records the number of the Bill and other particulars, with the name of the firm to whom it is sent for acceptance.

Bills Payable. Bills drawn on a merchant, and for the payment of which the merchant is responsible. They are entered into a book called the "Bills Payable Book."

Bills Receivable. Bills remitted to a merchant, by way of payment for merchandise, or for liquidation of a debt. They are entered in the "Bills Receivable Book."

Bimetallism. Latin *bis*, double or twice, and *metallum*, a metal.

The term *Bimetallism* is used to designate that system of currency which is based on a double standard as distinguished from that

Shipped in good Order and well conditioned by *Messrs. Shipley and Thornton* in and upon the good Steam Ship called the *Victoria Regia* whereof is Master for this present voyage *Capt. Williams* and now riding at Anchor in the *London Docks* and bound for *Cadiz.*

Mr. Carl Berg,
Cadiz.
Three Packages
numbered
1, 2, 3
respectively.

Three Packages

being marked and numbered as in the Margin and are to be delivered in the like good Order and well conditioned at the aforesaid Port of *Cadiz* the Act of God, the Queen's Enemies, Fire, Machinery, Boilers, Steam and all and every other dangers and Accidents of the Seas, Rivers, and Navigation of whatever nature or kind soever excepted unto *Mr. Carl Berg of Cadiz*

or to his ______ Assigns ______ Freight for the said Goods *being paid by the said Messrs. Shipley and Thornton*

with Primage and Average accustomed. In Witness whereof the Master or Purser of the said ship hath affirmed to 3 Bills of Lading all of this Tenor and Date the one of which Bills being accomplished the others to stand void.

Dated in *London, Sept. 20, 1878*

Weight and Contents unknown.

based on a single standard, and which is called *Mono-metallism.* (*See Double Standard.*)

Bisti. A Persian silver coin, value 2*d.*

Black Friday. Two days in the history of British commerce have received this gloomy cognomen. The first was in 1745, when Charles Edward the Pretender advanced from Scotland on his way towards London. It was when the news arrived that the rebels had reached Derby, which was on a Friday. "The gates of the city were shut. The train bands were placed on duty night and day. The guards were ordered out, The Tower was closed before its time. The shops were unopened; and no business was done excepting at the Bank."—FRANCIS's *History of the Bank of England.*

The second was on the day following that on which the celebrated firm of Overend, Gurney, and Co. closed their doors, in 1866, an event still fresh in the memory of every City man.

Blanc. A French silver coin, value 4*d.* The écu blanc, the French crown-piece, value about 4*s.* 6½*d.*

Blank Bill or Note. Bills are not always drawn payable to a payee named therein, nor even to Bearer. For example a Bill may be drawn in the following form:—

Jan. 7, 1881.

Please pay on demand the sum of Ten Pounds Fifteen Shillings.

HENRY WILSON.

To Mr. THOS. WHITE.

The following is a form of Promissory Note of the same kind.

Mar. 3, 1881.

I Promise to pay on Demand the sum of Twenty Pounds.

JAS. CLARKE.

Bills and Notes of this description are said to be drawn "in Blank:" or are called *Blank Bills* and *Blank Notes.*

Blank Credit. Bills drawn for convenience of trade, and to facilitate exchanges, but not representing at the time any actual settlement of indebtedness. Such bills are easily confounded with accommodation, bills which they much resemble. Indeed, they are too often used with a view of raising fictitious capital as accommodation paper is. Like this sort of paper, they may be used to serve a legitimate and useful purpose, but they ought to be carefully examined, and the increase of them jealously watched.

Blankeel. Morocco = 24 Flues = $\frac{23}{40}$*d.*

Blanquille. A silver coin used in Barbary, value, 2½*d.*

Bohmen or Bohemian. A silver coin used in Prague, value 3 kreutzers, or about 1¼*d.* English.

Bolivar. An alternative name for the venezolano (*which see*).

Boliviano or **Bolivian.** A name sometimes applied to the new Peso or dollar of Bolivia. It is of the same weight and fineness as the Five-franc piece. (*See Cinq Francs.*)

Bon. French, *bon*, good.

This adjective, signifying "good," is found on various documents, such as coupons, bills, &c. Thus "BON pour Cinquante Francs" (good for Fifty Francs) is found on Coupons attached to Italian Rentes. Treasury Bons, or *Bons du Trésor*, have sometimes on their face "BON *pour Mille Francs*" (good for a thousand francs), and so on for other values. Owing to the conspicuous position of the adjective "BON," documents of this kind have come to be called "Bons," in conformity with a custom widely prevalent among legal practitioners and commercial men of naming documents from conspicuous initial words. Unfortunately, however, the similarity of the word *Bon* with the English *Bond* has led many persons to confound one with the other. "Bond" is properly translated "*obligation*" in French, and usually contains on its face certain words which *bind* the subscribing party to pay a specified sum at a given date. But a *Bon* does not necessarily contain any words implying such obligation. Nevertheless, a "Bon" may become a "Bond" by the insertion of words declaring the sum named thereon, payable at a specified date, and by the signature of the party responsible for the payment. *Bons du Trésor*, Treasury Bonds, have usually this complete form, and to call them Treasury Bonds does not in this case involve any inaccuracy of language although the practice implies some confusion of ideas.

Bond. Anglo-Saxon, *bindan*, to bind; German, *binden*; Old Dutch, *bond*, a tie an agreement.

Anything which binds. In banking and commerce a written or printed document containing the terms and conditions by which a person, corporation, or company is bound. Hence the distinctive names, Government Bonds, State Bonds, City Bonds, Railway Bonds, Mortgage Bonds, &c. In financial affairs the most important features of a Bond are those which distinguish it from a Share or Share Certificate. A Share Certificate simply entitles a holder to a share in the profits of an undertaking, proportional to the amount of capital he has subscribed to it. If there are no profits he gets no return for his outlay. If there are large profits he gets a large return. But a Bondholder from the terms of his Bond claims interest thereon, before any profits are divided among the Shareholders, and the amount of that interest is almost invariably a fixed sum. Bonds are issued by trading companies for two opposite reasons. (*a.*) In the case of companies whose finances are in an embarrassed condition, with a view to increase their capital, and when from the nature of the case it would be difficult to induce ordinary shareholders to put additional money into the concern. (*b.*) In the case of companies whose prospects are promising, although further capital is temporarily needed. Under these circumstances shareholders object to having their future prospects infringed, by a permanent addition to their Capital, and bonds are issued bearing a low rate of interest, which interest is not increased however great the profits yielded by the undertaking. Railway bonds are regarded as among the best means of investment for persons unacquainted with business, owing to the regularity of the income derivable therefrom, and also owing to the generally good security on which they are based. (*See Active, Passive, Deferred* and *Preference Bonds.*)

Bonded Goods. Goods imported and placed in warehouses or vaults until duties are levied and paid on them. They are called "bonded" because the owner or importer signs a Bond *binding* him not to remove them until the customs or duties shall have been paid thereon.

Bon-Gros. A silver coin, formerly used at Hesse-Cassel, worth about 2*d.* English.

Bonus. A Latin word signifying "good."

Bonus is a name given to any exceptional advantage accruing to the shareholders of a company over and above the ordinary dividends paid. In every Joint Stock Company it is found expedient to keep a reserve out of the profits gained from year to year in order to meet any unforeseen demand that may arise. These reserves sometimes become larger than is necessary for the safety of the undertaking, and a portion is then distributed among the shareholders *pro rata*. Such a distribution is called a "Bonus," or "Cash Bonus."

Boo. (*See Itziboo.*)

Book Credits. Entries in the books of merchants and bankers to the credit of particular persons. By means of book credits the use of coin and notes is largely dispensed with, and it is estimated that the amount of wealth which changes hands through the agency of book credits is many times greater than that which circulates by the intervention of all the coin and bank-notes in the kingdom put together. This is easily understood when it is recollected that the enormous mass of transactions which are passed through the Clearing House, are balanced in many instances by a few small cheques without the use of a single coin. But the business of the Clearing House, large as it is, is only a small part of the business transacted by the merchants of the City of London and other centres of trade, most of which in like manner is settled by balancing the credits of one merchant against those of another with whom he deals.

Boom. An Americanism recently introduced into the vocabulary of the London money market, and said to owe its origin to the Dutch merchants on the other side of the Atlantic, in whose language *bomme* is a drum; *bommen*, to drum, to beat the drum. It is connected with the Welsh, *bwmp*, a hollow sound, and the Saxon, *bymian*, to blow a trumpet. In which words, says the "Imperial Dictionary," we see "the senses of *sounding*, *uttering the voice*, *swelling*, and *rushing forward* are connected."

A *Boom* as understood on the Stock Exchange is an outburst of speculation in some particular department of trade: thus giving rise to distinctive names, such as "railway boom" "gold boom" "mining boom," &c. Sometimes a *boom* takes the form of a speculation in agriculture; and an exodus of city men and labourers for the purpose of opening up a new district diverts capital and labour from markets which for the moment are overstocked with those commodities.

Borbi. An Egyptian copper coin, value 3 aspers, about $\frac{1}{16}d$.

Borjook. An Abyssinian glass coin. Three to a Kibear; worth about $\frac{1}{15}d$.

Bos. From the Greek, βους, *bous*, an ox.

The Greek didrachm, silver, with the figure of an ox on one side. Hence the name.

Bottom. Saxon, *Botm*, the lowest part of anything.

In marine affairs, a *bottom* signified originally the keel or hull of a ship, and subsequently was applied to the ship itself. Hence the proverb "To have all in one bottom," like "having all the eggs in one basket," signified the risking of everything in one venture. In Shakspeare's *Merchant of Venice* we have—

> "I thank my fortune for it,
> My ventures are not in one *bottom* trusted."

and in *Twelfth Night*,

> "With which such scathful grapple did he make
> With the most noble *bottom* of our fleet."

Bottomry. *Bödemerey*, so written in the "Recesous Hansæ" of Lubeck. *Bottomare*, *City Mercury*, 1680. *Bottomree*, Act 6 Geo. I.

Bottomry is defined (by Martin, *History of Lloyd's*) to be "the mortgage of a ship—*i.e.*, her bottom or hull—in such a manner that, if the ship be lost, the lender likewise loses the money he advanced on her: but that if she arrives safely at the port of destination, he not only gets back the loan, but receives in addition, a certain premium previously agreed on." The term is now to a great extent superseded by the modern phrase *Marine Insurance*.

Bottomry Bond. Although any policy of marine insurance may be, and often has been, loosely called a Bottomry Bond, the term is now more strictly applied to those contracts of Hypothecation which a shipmaster enters into when abroad, in order to raise money to enable him to prosecute his voyage, after being delayed, or his ship damaged by storms, &c. The master of the ship being at a distance from the *owners* of the ship and its cargo, he is compelled in order to protect their interests to use his own discretion as to whether he shall pledge the cargo as well as the ship for the purpose of raising the means of bringing both to port. When the ship alone is pledged the contract is called a *Bottomry Bond;* where ship and cargo both, a *Respondentia Bond.*

Bouhamstash. Tripoli = 15 paras; value in sterling about 1*d.*

Bounty. Latin, *bonitas*, goodness; used by Cicero with the sense of *advantage.* French, *bonté;* Italian, *bontà.* As a commercial term, however, the French equivalent is *prime* or premium.

A Bounty is a bonus or premium paid by certain Governments to manufacturers or merchants, by which the latter are enabled to export certain goods at a cheaper rate, and so undersell other countries. As the bounty thus paid by Government is always raised by taxing the people governed, commercial bounties are not looked on with favour by any but the few individuals who directly profit by them, and even these regard them as expedients to be dispensed with as quickly as the exigences of the case will allow.

Bourbe. Barbary money of account at Tunis, value half asper.

Bousebbatash. Tripoli = 7½ paras; nearly ½*d.*

Boutteteen. Tripoli, silver = 30 paras; nearly 2*d.*

Bovella. A Persian silver coin, value 16*s.*

Brabant Krone. The Brabant crown. An Austrian silver coin value 2 florins, 30 kreutzers, or nearly 4*s.* 6*d.* sterling.

Broad Piece. An English gold coin, value 20*s.* The monetary unit in the time of King James I.

Broker. The origin of this word, and the obsolete verb *to broke*, has been the subject of much discussion. Some have derived it from the Greek βρυχω, *bruchō*, to howl, to bellow, from the practice of hawkers and others who wish to call attention to the goods they have to sell. Others, again, derive it from the Saxon, *brucan*, to bear, to employ, to procure; and this derivation, as pointing to the office of middleman, or go-between, is not without considerable show of reason. The supposition that the word is a form of the verb *to break*, from the practice of broken-down men undertaking the duties of factors or brokers, is altogether fanciful; the word is so widely used in one or more of its forms as to indicate the prevalence of some ruling idea respecting the duties of this class of men. In Old French, brokers were called *broggans*, and their commission, *broggage.*

But it seems most likely that the name came to us originally from the shores of the Baltic, whence we have derived so many of our trade terms. There are many words—rather, perhaps, many forms of the same word—all bearing the signification of flaw, defect, damage, refuse, or deterioration, and the officer or agent who made it his business to examine goods and point out their defects took his name from the same word or words. Thus we have the Russian, *brak*, refuse; *brakovat*, to pick, to sort; *brakovanie*, inspection. rejection; Polish, *brak*, defect, refuse, want; *brakowac*, to pick. Dutch, *brack*, damaged, rejected; *brack goed*, damaged goods; Low German, *braken*, to garble, to try; *wraken*, to pronounce unsound, to reject; German, *wrack*, refuse, wreck; Old English, *wrack.*

"Leave not a *wrack* behind."—SHAKESPEARE.

Lithuanian, *brokus*, a fault, matter of blame; *brokoli*, to blame, to criticise. In several countries the name *braker*, *bracker*, or *wracker* is applied to a person employed to inspect goods, and reject those that are unsound, and in "St. Petersburgh the price of tallow is quoted with or without *brack*, the term *brack* signifying the official inspection of sworn *brackers* or sorters."—TOOKE'S *Catherine*, i. 38.

All these, and many more, examples, seem to point to some old root word, *brak* or *wrak*, signifying defect, flaw, or damage, from which was derived the noun *braker*, *bracker*, or *broker*, as the name of one whose special duty it was to examine, criticise, and sort goods according to the flaws or defects to be found in them. The Greek equivalent of our word "broker" was προξενητης, *proxenetes*, and the Latin, *proxeneta*, both of which signified a negotiator of purchases or sales, a factor, or middleman.

The duties of a broker when properly understood are of a highly responsible nature. Hence the business is much distributed, and as a consequence each class of broker confines his attention to one particular branch of the business, thus giving rise to the distinction of Stock broker, Bill broker, Tobacco broker, Ship broker, while some prefer the name of factor, as Corn factor, Cotton factor, &c.

The functions of a *Stock broker* are primarily those arising from the negotiation of the purchase or sale of stocks, bonds, shares, &c. On the English Stock Exchange, a broker is forbidden to enter into partnership with a "jobber" (*See Jobber*) and is bound in honour to do the best he can for his client or customer. It is his duty to take care that the bonds or documents he delivers to his client are perfect and in proper form, that they have the proper coupons attached, and that they are duly stamped, all of which matters are but imperfectly understood by the public generally, and to supplement whose imperfect knowledge, the professional broker is employed. The charge made for this service is so very moderate, that no one would attempt to do the work himself, unless under quite exceptional circumstances.

The duties of the *Bill broker* are perhaps more onerous than those of the Stock broker, for he not only has to look at the documents in which he deals, and see that they are regular in form, but he has to undertake the delicate and difficult task of finding out the commercial standing and personal character of the men whose names appear on bills as Acceptors or Indorsers, a matter clearly of the highest importance, since it is from the commercial reputation of these names that Bills derive their character as First, Second, or Third Class paper.

Brokers in all departments of trade are indispensable to those needing the services of a skilled agent, who from long practice and extensive knowledge is able to form a judgment of the goods in which he deals, or to point out defects and flaws, and to determine their value.

Brokerage. The remuneration paid to a Broker by a client, for buying or selling stocks, shares, merchandise, &c. In the purchase of Bills the brokerage is sometimes double, that is, is paid by buyer and seller. In Stock Exchange transactions it is single, the broker being bound in honour to do the best he can for his client, and to receive his commission solely from him. But should two clients appear at the same time, one wishing to buy and the other to sell the same Stock, there is no rule to prevent the broker from receiving brokerage from both, and if the turn of the market were divided between them, they would certainly have no cause for complaint.

Bronze. Italian, *bronzo;* Spanish, *bronce;* pan metal; *bronzare,* to brase, to copper.

A mixture of copper with tin or some white metal. By the Act of 1860, the bronze coinage of England consists of 95 parts of copper, 4 of tin, 1 of zinc. In France the proportions are the same.

Bubbles. Financial schemes resting on no solid foundation, which promise well for a time, and cause much money to change hands, till their rottenness is discovered, and the schemes collapse, involving their victims in irremediable loss and sometimes ruin. The South Sea Scheme, and John Law's Mississippi Bonds are historical examples. The popular notion that schemes of this kind were called *bubbles* from their hollowness and unsoundness is a complete inversion of the truth. The word "bubble" or "bobbel" meant formerly to deceive, to cheat, to confuse, and the familiar soap-bubble derived its name from its inflated and bulky appearance, and because when pricked it proved itself a hollow cheat.

Budgerook. Hindoostan money of account on the Malabar coast, 6 to a pice.

Budschu. A coin used in Algeria, value 1*s.* 5½*d.* English.

Bugne. A silver coin current in Loraine about A.D. 1511. Struck in Metz.

Bull. A dealer on the Stock Exchange who buys stocks or shares with the hope of selling them again at a profit. The process is considered to be a branch of pure speculation, as distinguished from that in which a dealer buys with the intention of taking up the stocks he contracts for, although the same hope may be the motive for dealing in both cases. If when the settling-day arrives the "Bull" finds that the price of his stock has fallen, he has to sell at the reduced price, and pay the "difference." The *bonâ-fide* dealer if similarly caught pays the price contracted for, and locks up the stock till better times come round. The "Bull" consequently can operate with a much less capital than the legitimate dealer, but his chances of profit are by no means so great. (*See Bear.*)

Bullion. There can be no doubt that the word *bullion, boillon,* or *billon,* was formerly applied to the *mint* or office where money was coined.

In the Statute 9 Edw. III., we read "that all persons shall be able safely *porter à les exchanges ou billon* and not elsewhere, silver in plate, silver vessels, and silver in every form except false money and counterfeit sterling" for the purpose of exchange. The above phrase given in Norman French was mistranslated in the English version, "shall safely bring to the exchanges bullion or silver in plate," &c., instead of "to the exchanges *or* bullion," and this gave rise to the notion that the word bullion in those statutes meant uncoined gold and silver.

In the 27th Edw. III., it is provided "que toutz marchauntz —puissent savement porter—plate d'argent, billettes d'or et tut autre maner d'or et toutz moneys d'or et d'argent *a nostre bullione ou a nous exchanges* que nous ferons ordeiner a nous dites estaples et ailleurs pernant illoegs money de notre coigne convenablement à la value." Here the expression "to our bullion or to our exchanges," leaves no doubt as to the meaning of bullion.

In the 4th Henry IV., another clause occurs which is perhaps still more definite. It provides "que la tierce partie de tout la monoie d'argent que sera porte à *la boillon* sera faite es mayles et ferlynges." (That the third part of all the silver money brought to the *bullion* shall be made into halfpence and farthings.) Here is a clear allusion to the "boillon" as a place for the coinage of money; and in several subsequent statutes it is used in precisely the same sense, and with such frequency as to leave no doubt that it bore the meaning of "*mint*," or place where money was coined.

The transfer of the name "bullion" or "billion" from the place where coins were struck to the metal itself arose from two causes. One was the mistranslation of the old Statute 9 Edw. III., above referred to; and as it was known to most people through the English version, the popular view was that bullion was identical in meaning with silver plate, debased coins, and crude metal of all kinds But a more efficient cause of the change was the common and almost proverbial use of the phrase "monnoie de billon" or "monnoie de boillon,"—phrases which would almost certainly be cut down, in mercantile speech to the last and most significant word—and which were always used in the sense of gold and silver, which had been melted, standarded, and coined. Old defaced coins, and base money, were also called "bullion money" or "billon money," and from that to simple "bullion," was an easy and almost inevitable step. (*See Billon.*)

The origin of the word "bullion" as applied to the mint, is commonly supposed to be the Latin *bulla*, a seal, because it was the place where the King's seal was impressed upon the coin made, or the ingots assayed; from the same root was formed also the modern Greek *βουλλουω*, *boullouo*, to seal, to stamp.

Buntagui. A gold coin used in Morocco, equal to about $2·00 or 8*s*. 4*d*. sterling.

Burse or **Bourse.** French, *bourse*, a purse or money-bag; Dutch, *beurs;* Italian, *bolgia* and *bolza*, a wallet; Spanish, *bolsa*, a bag or purse; German, *Börse:* all of which words are used to signify a place where exchanges are carried on.

In most continental countries, the term Bourse is applied to the building where exchanges are carried on, and more particularly to establishments corresponding to the London Stock Exchange.

Bushe. A copper coin used in Aix-la-Chapelle, value 4 hellers=2*d.*

Buying in. An operation sanctioned by the Rules of the Stock Exchange for the protection of dealers against loss from defaulters. When a broker purchases stock for delivery on a certain day, and the seller fails to deliver it by half-past two o'clock, the broker may force delivery by buying it in the market at the price then current, and if any loss is entailed, it must be paid by the seller. This process is called "buying in." For the converse operation, see *Selling Out.*

Byzants. Gold coins from Byzantine. much used in Anglo-Saxon times when gold was not regularly coined in England.

C

C, occurs in the following abbreviations:—

C/-, currency, or coupon.
C.F.I., cost, freight and insurance.
Cr., creditor.
Cum d/-, with dividend.

Cahaun. A silver coin used in Bengal, value 7½*d.* *Cahuse,* a quarter rupee.

Caïmé, Caïmés. Turkish paper currency. Paper money, which is nearly always at a discount, has reached a degree of depreciation in Turkey, greater than has been known in any instance in modern times. During the first quarter of the year 1879, five paper medjidies were reckoned equal to one of silver; in other words, silver was at a premium of 400 per cent. The gradual withdrawal of the forced paper currency is regarded by the friends of Turkey as the first condition essential to the restoration of order in Turkish finance.

In May, 1879, Caïmés were quoted at 620, for 100 silver piastres.

Caisse. A French word derived from the Latin, *capsa,* a box or chest.

Caisse has three different, but closely related, meanings in finance.

1. It signifies, like its Latin original, a chest or receptacle for anything, especially money.

2. It is applied to the money contained in the chest or box, and is thus synonymous with our *Cash.*

3. It is the official name of the building where moneys are kept, or rather which contains the chest in which the moneys belonging to a State, a Company, or Corporation are deposited. Just as our word Bank is applied to the building in which the "bank," or "heap" of money is placed.

Call. When the applicant for shares in a new Joint Stock Company (or for additional shares in an old one) has had a stated number allotted to him, he may or may not be required to pay up in full the value of those shares immediately; most commonly he is not required to pay up in full, but only a small fraction of his subscription at first, and other fractions as may be necessary for the carrying on of the undertaking. When this need arises, he is informed of it by the secretary of the company, and a demand is made for a stated sum per share on every share he holds. Such demand is known in commerce as a "call." The shareholder does not know till he is specially informed when these calls will be made, nor for what amount, nor whether he will ever be required to pay up the full nominal value of his share at all. A "call" thus differs from an "instalment" in all these respects. These latter are recorded on the scrip issued to the shareholder; their amount and due date are known from the first; and taken altogether, they cover every liability in respect of such share. Interest or profit payable on shares is always in proportion to the amount "called" up, and not on the nominal value of the shares.

For "*Put and Call*" see *Options*.

Cancelling or **Annulment.** Latin, *cancellare*, to make lattice-wise; from *cancelli*, bars or sticks placed across each other.

Hence to *cancel* means primarily to make strokes with a pen crossing each other like lattice work, which describes pretty accurately the way in which a sheet of writing would be destroyed or made of none effect. In its modern use, the word signifies generally to annul, rescind, or destroy, whatever instrument may be used for the purpose. Coupons are mostly cancelled by perforation; and ingenious machines have been constructed capable of perforating a hundred at a stroke. When bonds and certificates have to be cancelled, the labour is very great, unless some machine of this kind is employed.

The cancelling or annulment of Bonds, Coupons, Bills, and, in short, all commercial instruments which are not allowed to be re-issued, is a very important duty. For if a person pays them, and neglects to cancel them, and they are afterwards re-issued or negotiated, the person who neglects to cancel them, and the one who negotiates such an instrument, are each liable to a penalty of £50. And any person accepting such instrument is liable to a penalty of £20.

Candareen or **Candarine.** (*a*) The 100th part of the Chinese tael, value $\frac{94}{100}$ of an English penny.

(*b*) The 10th part of Japanese mace, value $\frac{3}{5}$ of an English penny.

Capellone. A silver coin of Modena, value 3*d*. English.

Capital. From Latin, *caput*, the head. The wealth of the people in former times consisted largely of kine and other animals, which were counted by the head, thus giving rise to the phrase so many "head of cattle," whence the mediæval Latin, *capitalia*, and the Norman-French, *capitale*, and modern French, *cheptal*, meaning the live stock of a landlord or farmer. From these words came the law term, *chattel*, and the modern name, *cattle*. As the wealth of the country in former times consisted mainly of cattle or *capitalia*, this term came at length to signify wealth generally, and was applied, in its modified form, capital, to any kind of wealth employed in the maintenance of labourers with a view to profit.

(*a*) *Money, Labour*, or *Instruments of Credit* expended with a view to Profit. This definition excludes all wealth expended in administering to the necessities of life, in luxury or in waste.

Capital is divided into Fixed Capital and Circulating Capital. *Fixed Capital* is wealth expended in land, houses, factories, mills, machinery, tools, and other things not intended to be exchanged or sold, but to be employed in the production of additional wealth. The term "fixed" is not absolute, but relative, as the wear and tear of all machinery necessitates constant repairs, and ultimate replacement.

Circulating Capital is that portion of wealth set aside for the reward of persons engaged in the different kinds of labour and service, without which the capital fixed in machinery, mills, tools, &c., would be unproductive. Capital employed in this way is replaced as soon as it is expended, the produce of the workman being an equivalent for the money paid to him, plus something in addition, which is to form the capitalist's profit. When this produce is sold, the capital returns to its owner, and he can employ it again and again in a similar way. Thus a constant circulation of the capital is kept up, and hence the distinctive name "*circulating*" as applied to that portion of wealth set apart for this purpose.

The line of demarcation between Fixed and Circulating Capital is so ill-defined that many writers object to the distinction. Nevertheless, there are some kinds of machinery and other works requiring a large outlay of capital, which cannot be replaced till after a considerable lapse of time, and the term "fixed" as expressing this idea is so well understood that it would be difficult to find a substitute for it which would answer the purpose as well. It should also be noted that when economists say that wealth consumed in administering to the necessities of life *is not capital*, they mean that portion which is expended in the enjoyment and maintenance of the Capitalist himself. To expend it in ministering to the needs and maintenance of labourers, is the very thing, the chief end, for which capital is required, as it is only by so employing it that profit can be made.

(*b*.) *Capital* is also the name often given to the principal sum in a loan as distinguished from the interest:—

"Semper renovabantur cartæ et usura quæ excrevit vertebatur in *catullum*."—*Cronica Joccelini.*

(The bills were always renewed, and the interest which had accrued was turned into capital.)

This quotation has the merit of showing at once the economical meaning of the word in those early days, and also of indicating its origin.

In theoretical investigations Capital is distinguished as Positive and Negative. Money and Credit are both treated as Capital in Economic problems; but money represents services already rendered, *work done*. Credit represents services to be rendered at a future time, *work to be done*. Hence money in its various forms is called Positive Capital. Credit and Instruments of Credit, Negative Capital. This distinction is of great importance to those who wish to prosecute the theory of economics under the guidance of such teachers as McLeod or Jevons.

Capital Account. An account of the capital subscribed to any trading concern, and of the manner in which it has been expended. In joint stock companies, it is of great importance that the "Capital Account" should be kept distinct from the "Revenue Account" in order that a proper check may be kept upon the proceedings of Directors and Committees.

Caragronch. A silver coin used in Modern Greece, value 5*s.* English.

Carat. (*a.*) Arabian, a small coin of very base silver used at Mocha.

(*b.*) The carat weight for gold, named from the red bean of Abyssinia, the fruit of the *Kuara.*

(*c.*) Carat is used in refinery to signify the 24th part of any given weight of metal; hence when a piece of gold is said to be 21½ carats fine, it means that 21½ parts out of 24 consists of fine gold and 2½ parts of alloy.

In an article by Agnes M. Clerke in *Fraser's Mag.*, June 1880, the following note on the "carat" is given :—The word "carat" is derived through the Arabic from κερατιον, the Greek name for the fruit of the Karob-tree, κερατεα, the beans of which, owing to their nearly invariable size, were long ago selected as a standard weight for gold, by the natives of West Africa. Their use (or rather we should suppose an equivalent weight) passed from thence to India, and was introduced from India by the Arabs. A carat is equal to 4 diamond grains, or to 3·17 grains Troy.

Cardecu. A corruption of the French *quart d'Ecu,* a silver coin, value one-fourth of the French *Ecu* or crown.

Carival. Bombay, value 12 pice, or 1½*d.*

Carl d'Or. A gold coin used in Brunswick, value 16*s.* 4*d.*

Carlino. (*a.*) An Italian silver coin, value 5*d.* Coined first in 1490, by King Charles VIII. of France.

(*b.*) A billon coin lately used in the Papal States, worth about 3¼*d.*

(*c.*) A gold coin used in Sardinia, value £1 18*s.* 10*d.*

Carlo. A Lombardy silver coin, value 5*s.*

Carolin. A new gold coin of Sweden, value 7*s.* 11*d.*

Caroline. A Swedish silver coin, value 1*s.* 6*d.*

Carolin d'Or. A gold coin used in Bavaria, value £1 0*s.* 8*d.*

Carolus. A gold coin of the time of Charles II., value 23*s.*

Carrying Over. "In the event of a speculative bargain being closed before the settling day, by a corresponding purchase or sale, the transaction is completed simply by the profit or loss being received or paid. If, however, the bargain still remains open when the settling day arrives, and if the operator does not wish to close it, it may be kept open for another account—that is, until the following settling day. The process by which this is arranged is called "carrying over." (Maddison.)

Case of Need. "To whom apply in case of need," and the shortened forms "To whom in case of need"—"To whom in need"—"When in need," are phrases often seen on Bills of Exchange. They always follow the name of some individual or of some firm, and they imply that in case of any irregularity requiring explanation, application is to be made to the individual or firm thus referred to. It sometimes occurs that Bills have a great number of indorsements upon them, and in the event of the failure of any indorser to meet his engagements, or if there be any irregularity in either indorsement (and especially if not honoured in the acceptance or payment) the holder of the Bill has a claim on the indorser from whom he received it, and this one again on the one preceding. A Bill might thus be sent from one indorser to another preceding, until it had been returned to every one before it reached the original Drawer and Acceptor. This would be attended with considerable expense, and what is sometimes worse, might cause serious inconvenience to the maker of the Bill. It is with a view to avoid both these evils, that the phrase "in case of need" is inserted on their face. By direct application to the party named, steps would at once be taken to save his own honour and that of his correspondent.

Cash or Le. (*a*) The $\frac{1}{1000}$ part of the Chinese *tael*, worth about $\frac{7}{100}$*d.*

(*b*) A copper coin used in Hong Kong, representing the $\frac{1}{1000}$ part of a Mexican dollar; called also the *mil.*

Cash. Latin, *capsa*, a box or chest. French, *caisse*, which originally meant the box, chest, or till in which money and other valuables were kept.

By a process common to all languages, the name was transferred from the thing containing, to the thing contained, and thus *caisse* came to signify *money*, or, as we now say, *cash;* just as in the New Testament, where it says "Judas had the *bag*," it is evident that the money it contained was what the disciples referred to; and again in many other places, following the Greek idiom, the word "house," is used to signify, as it could signify nothing else, "*the people who dwelt in it*," and who are said to have "feared God," to have "believed," and to have been "baptized."

In former times the term *cash* was applied to coined money chiefly; more recently Bank of England notes were treated as cash, but "country notes"—that is, the notes of provincial banks—were scarcely considered to be entitled to the dignity of the name. At the present time, however, the term has acquired a much more extended meaning, as every one in possession of a banker's pass-book may assure himself, for here may be seen country notes, bankers' cheques, and bank credits all put down as *Cash*. Generally, it would seem that documents of all kinds payable on demand, or that can immediately be converted into money, are spoken of and treated as *Cash*.

Cash Bonus. *See Bonus.*

Cash Credit. A Cash Credit is a sum of money recorded in the books of a banker and placed to the credit of a customer, against which, and to the extent of which, that customer may draw cheques or "orders to pay." An account of this kind would never be opened in favour of a customer unless some person of substance and of good repute would stand as surety for the amount; but in places where bankers find a difficulty in employing the whole of their deposits, they are glad to employ their funds in this way. This was notably the case in Scotland, and it is said by the use of Cash Credits the commercial prosperity of that country has been immensely enhanced. Poor persons of good character have been enabled by means of Cash Credit to set up in business, and by thrift to pay off the sums advanced to them, thus laying the foundation of an ample fortune, which has been realized by not a few. In London, Cash Credits are not recognized. In some English country towns where customers are personally well known to the bankers, the absence of Cash Credits is to some extent supplied by allowing the customer to *overdraw* his account. But here, as in the case of Scotland, everything depends on reputation, for assuredly neither banker nor guarantor would risk his property by advancing money to persons in whom they had not full confidence. Whatever sums are drawn against a Cash Credit, is debited to the customer together with interest on the sum from day to day. Hence, as Mr. McLeod observes, a Cash Credit is "simply a drawing account, created in favour of a customer, upon which he may operate in precisely the same manner as upon a common drawing account; paying interest in the debit, instead of receiving interest on the Credit. It is thus an inverse drawing account." These Credits are extremely useful to all persons in business, or commencing a profession which requires a certain amount of Capital.

Cash Note. An order to pay, drawn upon a Banker; the same as is now called a *Cheque*. The earliest form of *Cash Notes* known were drawn upon goldsmiths, and were more commonly known as "Goldsmiths' Notes," a term which originated in this wise. Previous to the year 1660, merchants, and others having gold or silver, which in those troublous times they found difficulty in protecting, placed it for safety in the Tower. In the reign of Charles I., however, the King himself seized upon the money and bullion there deposited, in order to meet his own necessities, and merchants were not likely after this to place their accumulations within his reach. At that time the only persons who kept any large portion of the precious metals in their possession were the Goldsmiths of Lombard Street, and they had secret strong rooms in which they placed their property, and over which they kept a vigilant watch. As there were at that period no banks established in London, these strong rooms became the receptacles of the gold and silver accumulated by the merchants and traders of the City, that were not wanted for immediate use. At first, the Goldsmiths paid no interest for money thus deposited with them; on the contrary, they received compensation for the care they took of the valuables committed to their custody. When merchants wanted to avail themselves of the use of their money, there were two ways, either one of which was adopted at the convenience of the depositor. (1) The depositor might write an order on the Goldsmiths to pay a given sum to a person therein named; this was a "Cash Note," and was the direct ancestor of the modern "*Cheque;*" or (2) The Goldsmith might write a note containing a "promise to pay" to anyone holding that note a specified sum. This was the immediate ancestor of our Promissory Note." When Banks were afterwards established, the forms used by the Goldsmiths were retained. Slight modifications were introduced from time to time, as the requirements of trade demanded, and with a view of giving greater definiteness to the language in which they were written; but in all the main features they retain the same form as that used by the Goldsmiths before the Banks of the City were set up.

To **Cashier.** From the Latin, *cassus*, useless, empty, unprofitable; from which was formed the mediæval Latin verb, *casso, cassere*, and thence the French, *casser*, to quash, annul, &c. In English it is variously written, to *cash*, to *casseer*, and now to *cashier*.

To *Cashier* signifies to annul, to render useless, to dismiss from service, to disband.

"Like an old servant now *cashiered* he lay."

Cataa Hamsee. A modern Egyptian coin, value five piastres, or 1*s.*

Cati. A Chinese coin, value 16 taels, or £5 6*s.* 8*d.* English. It is also called catty.

Catty or **Chang.** A Siamese coin, value 20 tamlungs, or £10. English.

Caution. Latin, *cautio*, from *caveo, cavēre*, to take care.

Caution in ordinary language signifies wariness, carefulness. But among the Latins it acquired a secondary meaning, equivalent to our word, *bond*, or *security*; and, through the Roman law books, the word has been handed down to us with the same signification, as in the phrase "caution money," which is money paid down as a pledge or security for the due discharge of a contract or obligation.

Cavallotto. A Genoese billon coin, value 2*d.*

Caveer. Arabian money of account at Mocha, 40 to a dollar, English value, 1¼*d.* Also called *cabeer*, or *carear*.

Cedola. Cedula. Latin, defective verb, *cedo*, give; Italian, *cedola;* Spanish, *cedula*.

This word is often found on foreign bonds, coupons, and promissory notes. Owing to the prominence of the word on some Government promissory notes, these latter are often called in the South American

Republics by the name of "Cedulas," and are quoted under that name in Lists of Prices. It means, literally, a thing to be given up. Hence, *Cedolas* are pieces of paper which are to be given up in exchange for a sum of money, or they may be simply orders for the payment of money. *Cedolas* are in circulation bearing both these interpretations.

On the coupons of the South Italian Railway Bonds, we find the words "Cedola pagibile il 1st April, 1879," literally Coupon payable the 1st of April, 1879.

On the Italian 5 °/₀ coupon is the phrase "Cedola per L. Cinquanta," literally "Coupon for Fifty Lire."

Cent. A contraction of the Latin, *centum*, a hundred; and also of *centesimus*, a hundredth part.

In the English and several other languages, the phrase *per cent.* or *pro cent.* is used as a contraction of *per centum*, as in the expressions "Five per Cent.," German "Fünf pro Cent." meaning literally "Five for a hundred."

Cent is also used as a contraction of *centesimus* and its derivatives, in many parts of the world. In all these cases it signifies a hundredth part, and is without meaning except in reference to the monetary unit of which it forms the hundredth part. This unit is always understood in each country, and is never expressed. It is, however, pretty clearly indicated in many cases by the modifications of the full word for which the contraction "*cent*" is substituted. (*See Centavo, Centena, Centesimo, Centime*, and *Centussis*.)

For the sake of brevity, the sign °/₀ is used for the words per cent.: as 5°/₀, 4½°/₀, for five, four and a-half per cent. respectively. Cents or Centimes and their equivalents are written simply as decimals of the unit of value. Thus seven and a quarter francs may be written F. 7·25, or as is sometimes done 7 francs 25 centimes. In the United States a slight variation of this practice occurs. Thus seven and a quarter dollars may be written \$7·25 or \$7· $\frac{25}{100}$, or \$7^{25}, or \$7·25 cents; all of which forms are frequent in American journals and commercial documents.

Cent. Latin, *centesimus*, a hundredth part.

(*a*) In the United States the name is applied to a small bronze coin, the hundredth part of a dollar. There are silver coins of 3 cents, 5 cents, and 10 cents, the last being called the *Dime*. The silver 3 cent coin weighs 11·52 grains; ·900 fine.

(*b*) The hundredth part of the dollar of Mauritus, value $\frac{23}{50}$ of a penny.

(*c*) The hundredth part of the Dutch guilder, value $\frac{1}{5}$ of a penny.

Centavo. (*a*) The $\frac{1}{100}$ part of the Chilian *peso*. Silver pieces of 50, 20, 10, and 5 centavos are struck. The two latter are called respectively the *decimo* and *half-decimo*.

(*b*) The $\frac{1}{100}$ part of the Mexican *peso* or *dollar;* value almost exactly ½*d*. English. Silver pieces of 50, 25, 10 and 5 centavos are struck.

(*c*) Generally the $\frac{1}{100}$ part of the unit of value, like *cent*.

Centena. The $\frac{1}{100}$ part of the Bolivian dollar: value $\frac{37}{100}$ of the English penny.

Centesimo. A small copper coin used in the Italian States, value $\frac{1}{100}$ of the lira; about $\frac{1}{12}$ of a penny.

Centime. A copper coin, 100 to a franc, used in France, Belgium, and the Ionian Islands; value $\frac{19}{200}$ of a penny. Bronze coins of one centime, two centimes, five centimes, and ten centimes are in circulation; and silver coins of twenty centimes and fifty centimes.

Centimo. The 100th part of the old Spanish real vellon, value $\frac{1}{4}d$.

Centussis. This Latin word signified 100 Roman asses (*see As*) and was equal to ten Roman deniers; a nomenclature which indicates that, in those early days, some idea of the importance of a decimal coinage had found its way among mercantile men. Owing to the extreme changes in the value of the As, it is now impossible to assign any single value to the *centussis* in terms of English money.

Certificate de Jouissance. Sometimes called *Coupon de Jouissance*, and corresponds to the German *Genuss-Schein*, and usually rendered into English *Bonus-Certificate*. Bonus-Certificates are issued to the holders of Railway and other Company's Shares, which have been drawn and paid off, and they entitle the holder to any prospective profits that may arise in respect of such shares. They do not bear interest coupons, and are thus distinguished from *Actions de Jouissance* (*which see*). The *Coupons de Jouissance* issued by the Italian Government on the reimbursement of Bonds of the Italian State Domain Loan are examples.

Chain Rule. An arithmetical rule much used in commercial calculations, consisting in the formation of a series of equations connected together and dependent each on the one preceding like links in a chain. The following example taken from "Tate's Guide," affords a good illustration of the method of applying the rule.

Find the par of Exchange established by the purchase of gold in London at 77*s*. 9*d*. per oz. standard fineness or $\frac{11}{12}$ fine, and the sale of it in Paris at the rate of $4\frac{1}{2}$ per mille premium upon the fixed price of 3437.77 per Kilogramme reckoned equal to 15,434 grains Troy.

The question is:

How many francs	=	20 shillings
if $77\frac{3}{4}$	=	1 oz. standard gold.
12	=	11 oz. fine.
1	=	480 grains Troy.
15,434	=	1 kilogramme.
1	=	3437·77 francs.
1000	=	$1004\frac{1}{2}$ with premium.

The answer is found by dividing the product of all the numbers on the right of the equations by the product of all the left. Thus

$$\frac{20 \times 11 \times 480 \times 3437{\cdot}77 \times 1004\frac{1}{2}}{77\frac{3}{4} \times 12 \times 15434 \times 1000}$$

By direct cancelling, this prolix expression may be at once reduced to

$$\frac{220 \times 40 \times 3437.77 \times 1{\cdot}004\frac{1}{2}}{77\frac{3}{4} \times 15434.}$$

When by multiplying and dividing we obtain the answer—

Fr. 25 33 cents.

It will be seen that the most important precautions to be observed in forming the chain of equations, are that the left member of each equation shall be of the same denomination as the right member of the preceding one, and that the equations shall be so constructed as to contain all the conditions expressed in the question. For further information on the application of the Chain Rule, the little work published by Effingham Wilson may be advantageously consulted.

Challie. From *chally*, the Cingalese for copper.

A small copper coin used in Ceylon, value half a farthing, English.

Channel Islands Currency. The currency of Guernsey, Jersey, Alderney and Sark is expressed in pounds, shillings, pence, and farthings, as in England. But each denomination is rather less in value than the corresponding English one; the English sovereign being equal to £1 1*s.* 8*d.* in the Channel Islands currency.

Chappee. The Rupee, when marked or *chopped,* used in the East Indies.

Charter Party. German, *Fracht Contract* or *Certa-Partie;* French, *chartre partie.*

A paper relating to a contract of which each party has a copy. It is a mercantile instrument, partly printed and partly written, sometimes sealed and sometimes unsealed, by which each party engages an *entire vessel,* for the purpose of exporting goods from this country, or of importing them from another. When the terms have been agreed on, and the document fully executed, the ship is said to be *chartered,* and the party by whom she is engaged is called the *charterer.* When instead of an entire ship, only a portion is required, a *Bill of Lading* is used, and the ship is called a *general* and not a *chartered* ship.

Chattels. From Latin, *caput,* the head, whence the forms *capitale, captale, catallum,* used at different times for cattle, which were counted by the head. In the French, these words took the form of *chaptel, cheptel,* and *chatel,* and were applied to every kind of moveable property.

"Juxta facultates suas et juxta *catalla* sua."—*Laws of Edward the Confessor.* (Together with his goods and his cattle.)

"Cum decimi omnium terrarum ac bonorum aliorum sive *catallorum.*" —*Ingulphus.* (With tithes of all the lands and other goods or *chattels.*) The frequent use of the "bona et catalla," as in this quotation appears to be the origin of our now familiar "goods and chattels." At first it seemed to mark a distinction between the movable goods on an estate, and the cattle thereon. But by constant repetition, the distinction between the two was lost, and the expression was retained in its entirety to denote personal as opposed to real property.

Under the phrase "*goods and chattels*" are included all movable property—articles that can accompany the person—as distinguished from land and houses which are fixed. In law, all incorporeal property, such as credits in a banker's books, copyright, &c., are reckoned as Chattels.

Chaye. A Persian silver coin, value about 6*d*. English.

Cheap Money, Dear Money. Money cannot be said to be either *cheap* or *dear* in the sense in which other commodities are so described, because the value of money when measured in money is always the same. Nevertheless, the phrases *Cheap Money* and *Dear Money* are in current use, but with a strictly technical meaning, and the meaning is, that money can be borrowed at one time at a low rate of interest, and at another at a high rate of interest, or, what is the same thing, the rate of discount is sometimes low and sometimes high.

Check. To check clerical work is to examine it a second time, or have it examined by a second person with a view to detect and correct errors that may have crept into such work through inadvertence.

Cheirographum. From the Greek, χειρ, *cheir*, the hand, and γραφω, *grapho*, I write.

A handwriting, note of hand, bond. This word seems to be the origin of the vague term much in use by men of business—*note of hand*—and includes almost every kind of document such as in modern times are more minutely classified as bills of exchange, promissory notes, I O U.'s, letters of credit, &c. Owing to its vagueness, it is not much used by accurate writers on economics in the present day, but as used by the Greeks and Romans, it had a clear and definite signification. In the early days of Greek and Roman commerce, an exchange or sale, or transfer of debt required the presence of the three parties to the transaction; the original creditor and debtor, as well as the new party to whom the debt was to be transferred. By the introduction of the *Cheirographum*, transactions were greatly simplified and facilitated; the terms of the transfer were reduced to writing, and it possessed the twofold advantage of being a record of the transaction which could be produced in a court of justice, and it enabled merchants to transfer a debt or obligation without the cumbrous ceremony of bringing the three parties together, as would often happen from great distances. Hence we find in Cicero.—*Quando vestræ cautiones infirmæ sunt, Græculam tibi misi cautionem cheirographi mei.* "Since your securities are not valid, I have sent you a Greek form of my cheirographum" (that is, I have sent my note of hand or promissory note in the Greek form). Transactions of this kind passed between Rome and Athens, and are spoken of as events of quite ordinary occurrence, and it is obvious that exchanges could not be effected with anything like the same facility, if the parties to the exchange were separated by distances so great as that between Rome and Athens, and had to be brought together, as was the custom before the use of the *Cheirographum.*

Cheque. An order for a sum of money drawn on a banker or other person, desiring him to pay any sum standing to his credit, (1) to some person named on the order, or (2) to bearer, or (3) to the person drawing the cheque. The cheque may be *open* or *crossed.* (*See Crossed Cheque.*) An *open* cheque is simply an uncrossed cheque, and the holder, on presenting it to the Bank, on which it is drawn, is entitled to receive in cash or Bank Notes the sum specified thereon, provided the drawer have funds at the Bank sufficient to meet it.

Cheque to Bearer. A Cheque to Bearer is so-called because the words "or Bearer" are inserted on its face. A cheque to Bearer may be either "crossed" or "open," and does not require the indorsement of the person in whose favour it is drawn. (*See to Bearer*).

Copy of Cheque to Bearer.

London, 3rd Jan. 1879.

To the ALLIANCE BANK, Bartholomew Lane.

Pay to Messrs. Williamson Bros. or Bearer, the sum of Seven hundred and Fifty pounds.

£750. THOS. FRANKLIN.

Cheque to Order. A Cheque having the words "or Order" printed or written on its face. A Cheque to Order must have the name of the person in whose favour it is drawn written on the back of it. (*See to Order.*)

Copy of Cheque to Order.

London, 16th Nov. 1878.

To UNION BANK, Prince's Street.

Pay to Mr. Henry Black or Order, the sum of Twenty-five Pounds, fifteen shillings.

£25 15*s.* WILLIAM POWELL.

Chequin. A gold coin used in Turkey, value 9*s.* 6*d.* English. (*See Sequin*).

Chida. A Hindu coin composed chiefly of tin. Two coins bear this name; one *round,* value about ½*d.*, and the other *octagonal,* value 2*d.*

Chose-in-Action. French, *chose,* a thing. (*See Action.*)

A term much used in commercial law, and is intended to denote the distinction between property or things in one's *possession,* and property or things in which one has a *right of action.* The owner of a Consol bond may have the property in his *possession,* but the dividend due upon it, is not in his possession. In the dividend he has a *chose-in-action*; in plain English he has a right to claim it in a court of law, if such a course should be necessary. Again, suppose I pay into my banker's a five-pound note; before it was paid in, it was a thing in my possession, but as soon as I have paid it in, and it is placed to my credit on the banker's books, I lose all property in the note itself, and have in return a *chose-in-action*—that is, the right to demand at any time I please, the sum of five sovereigns, or a five-pound note, or something of equal value. In the practice of banking, this distinction is of great importance, and the non-observance of it often leads to much confusion of language on the part of those who have failed to make the distinction.

Choustack. A Polish billon coin, value 2*d.*

Christian d'Or. A Danish gold coin, value 16*s.* 5*d.*, and is of the same value as the Frederick d'Or.

Christine. A Swedish silver coin, value 1*s.* 2*d.*

Chrysus. A Greek gold coin, equivalent to the stater. English value about £1 3*s.* (*See Stater.*)

Cincotesto or 5 Testoons. A Portuguese silver coin, worth 2*s.* $2\frac{3}{4}$*d.* sterling.

Cinq Francs. A French silver coin, value 3*s.* $11\frac{3}{4}$*d.* It is worth rather more than 5 single silver francs, in order to bring it up exactly to the gold 5-franc piece in value.

Cipher or Cypher. French, *chiffre;* Italian, *cifra;* both from the Arabic, *cifr*, which was represented in the Arabic notation, as well as in the modern Turkish, by a dot instead of the (0), which we use. The Arabic word is said to mean a *pip* or *seed*, and was used to denote "nought," or a blank in the decimal system of arithmetic. In course of time the term cipher was employed by the nations of Western Europe and of America to denote any of the numerals from 0 to 9 inclusive.

Cipher or *Cypher* in its modern applications has three different meanings:—

(*a.*) It signifies a numeral figure used in arithmetical operations, and especially the 0 or *nought.*

(*b.*) To "*cipher*" is to "work sums," to perform arithmetical operations.

(*c.*) To "*write in cypher*" is to write in a secret handwriting by means of signs which are understood only by those who possess the "key" or who have the skill to find it.

Circular Letter of Credit. A Letter of Credit addressed to several bankers or merchants residing in different places. These letters are issued for the accommodation of persons travelling, and who may wish to avoid carrying large sums of money about their person. Suppose a person travelling for business or pleasure, and expecting to pass through Paris, Frankfort, Berlin, Vienna, Rome, and Marseilles; and that he wished to have £500 at his disposal during his tour. He might purchase a Circular Letter in London for this amount, and have it addressed to some resident in each of those places. The firm in London issuing such letter would also advise their correspondent in each of those places, that the letter had been addressed to him, and requesting him to honour it; enclosing at the same time the *signature* of the person accredited. Of course, the sums paid by the different correspondents will be written down on the letter itself, and the receipt acknowledged and signed by the recipient. These sums must not exceed the amount specified in the letter: if they fall short of it, the difference will be paid on his arrival in London.

Circulating Medium. The same with Currency (*which see*). It is however desirable to observe, that *currency* is a property or quality of the *circulating medium* and not the medium itself, although in commerce the two terms are generally confounded. The term *circulating medium* is properly applied to money, bills, and bank notes, because these are the instruments by *means* of which the *circulation* of commodities is effected, and not because they *themselves circulate.*

Circulation. The work done by the Currency of a Country. It is frequently confounded with the currency itself, the two words being used as though they were synonymous. But they are not so. There may be a large amount of currency in a country, with a small circulation, and on the other hand a small amount of currency may be associated with a large circulation. Whenever the word circulation is intended to mean the same as currency, it is advisable to use the phrases "Coins in Circulation," "Notes in Circulation," &c.

The term *Circulation* has also a restricted meaning as employed in the weekly Bank Return of the Bank of England. By the Act of 1845 it is enacted "that all Bank Notes shall be deemed to be in *circulation* from the time the same shall have been issued from any banker, or any servant or agent of such banker, until the same shall have been actually returned to such banker, or some servant or agent of such banker." The meaning of the word is sometimes extended so as to include the notes held *in reserve* in the Banking Department of the Bank of England. This is incorrect. Although these notes have been given out by the Issue Department, they are not in circulation so long as they are held *in reserve* by the Banking Department. It is the practice of some writers to speak of the notes actually passing from hand to hand as the "*Active Circulation,*" while those held in reserve are called the "*Passive Circulation.*"

Ckirsh. The Egyptian Piastre, value $2\frac{1}{4}$*d.* English.

Claco. A copper coin nominally $\frac{1}{64}$ of the Mexican Dollar, worth about $\frac{3}{4}$*d.* English.

Clear, To. (*a.*) To pass through the Clearing House. (*See Clearing House.*)

(*b.*) *Clearance of Vessels.* By the Clearance of Vessels in port is meant the examination of them by authorized officers, and the issue of a certificate declaring that the requirements of Her Majesty's Commissioners of Customs have been complied with. The "Clearance Outwards" refers to vessels about to leave port; and the "Clearance Inwards" to vessels that have arrived, and discharged their cargo.

(c.) *Clearance of Goods.* A service undertaken by a shipping agent, and consists in performing for his customers certain duties which persons inexperienced in those matters would find very irksome and expensive to do for themselves, such as finding a suitable vessel, arranging and paying the cost of freight, passing through the Custom House, &c. Some agents undertake, in addition, the purchase of the goods which a customer wishes to send, and this they can often do, owing to their trade connections, more cheaply than the customer could do it on his own account.

Clearing House. A Clearing House is an institution set up by commercial men with a view to economize time and labour in the settlement of accounts. The system of "clearing" is applicable to many departments of trade, but only three establishments of this kind require notice here: the Bankers Clearing House, the Stock Exchange Clearing House, and the Railway Clearing House.

The *Banker's Clearing House* is a plain oblong room, with rows of desks in compartments round three sides, and down the middle. A small office for the two superintendents stands at one end. Each bank sends as many clerks to the house as may be requisite for the rapid completion of the work, and some banks have as many as six clerks. The cheques and bills to be presented by any one clearing banker, say the Alliance Bank, upon any other clearing banker, are entered at home in the "Out-clearing book," and are then sorted into twenty-five parcels, one of which is to be presented on each of the other clearing banks. On reaching the Clearing House, these parcels are distributed round the room to the desks of the clerks representing the several paying banks, who immediately begin to enter them in the "In-clearing books" in columns bearing at the head the name of the presenting bank. After being entered, the drafts are, as soon as possible, forwarded to the banking house for examination and entry in the bank books. Any cheques or bills refused payment are called "returns," and can generally be sent back to the Clearing House the same day, and entered again as a reverse claim by the bank dishonouring them on the banks which presented them. At the close of the day the Clerks of the Alliance Bank are able to add up the whole of the claims which have been made upon them by the other twenty-five banks, and they learn from the out-clearing book the amount of the claims which the Alliance Bank is making on other banks. The difference is the balance which the Alliance Bank has either to pay or receive as the case may be. These balances being communicated to the superintendents of the House, are by them inserted in a kind of balance sheet. When finally added up, the debtor and creditor sides of the sheet should exactly balance, because every penny to be received by one bank must be paid by another.

There are three clearings daily at the Lombard Street House.

The morning clearing opens on ordinary days at 10.30; drafts are received not later than 11, and the work must be closed at noon. The country clearing then begins, drafts being received until 12.30, and the clearing closed at 2.15. The heaviest clearing, however, is that of the afternoon, which begins at 2.30. The bustle and turmoil of the work grow to a climax at 4 o'clock, the runners rushing in with the last parcels of drafts, up to the moment when the door is finally closed. On the fourth day of each month, when the heaviest work occurs, the hours are extended, the House opening at 9 o'clock. —*Jevons.*

Stock Exchange Clearing House. The business of the Stock Exchange Clearing House is conducted very much on the same principle as the Bankers, with this difference, that in the Bankers' Clearing House, the officers have to deal with *Cheques* almost exclusively, and in that of the Stock Exchange with *Bonds* and *Shares.* Just as with the Bankers, only certain banks are admitted, so with the Stock Exchange only a restricted number of members are allowed to participate in its advantages, and only certain specified stocks or shares are passed through, or cleared. But the number of members admitted, and the number of stocks cleared are increased from time to time. The Stock Exchange Clearing House is a comparatively new institution, and it has been deemed advisable to proceed by slow degrees, so as to see how the system works. So far as present experience goes, it is considered to work well, and notwithstanding certain drawbacks, there appears to be a probability of its operations being extended. There are some stocks, such as Russian, Turkish, and Egyptian, which are bought and sold by a broker many times during the fortnight which elapses between one settling-day and the next following; but it often happens that the sales so nearly balance the purchases, that the difference between what he has to receive and what he has to deliver is very small indeed. And yet, notwithstanding, the smallness of this difference, it would be necessary for him (without the intermediation of the Clearing House) to deliver all that he has sold, and to receive all that he has bought. But with the assistance of the Clearing House, a broker is able to proceed as though he had only one member to deal with, and all bargains between members of the Clearing House are settled by simply passing on the "ticket day" (*See Ticket Day*), by eleven o'clock in the morning, a list of each stock, with the amount to take and deliver, and the names of the members in each case. If the list shows a balance to deliver, he delivers on the settling-day by eleven o'clock; if he has a balance to take up, he claims it from the Clearing House at the same time.

Railway Clearing House. The Railway Clearing House in Seymour Street, Euston Square, is a large establishment, designed to facilitate the settlement of accounts of Railway Companies having running powers over each other's lines. As its operations are not much mixed up with the business of banking and commerce, it calls for no further details here.

Clerical Error. A clerical error is one that may be made by a clerk or educated person, as distinguished from one that is made through ignorance or stupidity. In these days when the ability to read, write, and cast accounts, is almost universal, a clerical error is regarded as blameworthy as an error through ignorance, though the latter may expose its perpetrator to the greater ridicule.

Clerk. The genealogy of this familiar word is curious. Its remote ancestor is the Greek κληρος, *kleros*, which signified a "lot." As the drawing of lots was one of the most popular methods by means of which the ancient oracles arrived at their decisions, and by which the diviners conducted their divinations, both the thing and the name became thoroughly familiar to the Greek mind. It could scarcely fail with increase of intelligence that men should attach more importance to the skill and learning of the priests and diviners who conducted these mystic operations, and interpreted their results, than to the operations themselves; so that in course of time, the word κληρος came to be applied to the sacerdotal or priestly order, rather than the process over which they presided; and to consult the oracle, or to have recourse to divination, was neither more nor less than to seek the advice and instruction of the priests and diviners, and thus, the name being unchanged, it was transferred in thought to these agents, and that so persistently, till the whole priestly or sacerdotal body, as distinguished from the laity, were called the κληρος. Hence we have *clerus*, as the Latin form of the same word, and possessing the same meaning. From this we have *Clericus*, another Latin word derived from the last-named, and applied to any individual priest, clergyman, or officiator at the sacred rites. This word was used in the same sense for nearly a thousand years, and during that time found its way to France and Britain. For some time prior to the Norman conquest, whatever learning or science existed in these countries was monopolized by the clergy, and especially the knowledge and practice of *law;* the judges were selected from the higher orders of the clergy, "persons of wisdom and authority," says the *Grand Costumier*, "such as archbishops, bishops, canons of cathedrals, abbots and priors of the churches." All the inferior offices were filled by the lower clergy; and to them fell especially the labour of writing, copying, and similar duties. So universal was this rule, that at the time of the conquest, all work of this kind was done by the *clerici*, or as we say the clergy. Hence, *Clerc*, the Norman-French form of this word, which signified still a clergyman, although restricted in its application to the lower clergy; and finally *Clerk*, the Anglicised form of the same word, which continued to be used, with the same signification, till the arts of reading and writing became so widely diffused as to render clerical work as easy to the laity as to their sacred predecessors; when the title was given them simply in virtue of those accomplishments.

Dr. Mackay questions the correctness of the common opinion respecting the origin of this word, and thinks it ought to be referred to the Celtic tongue. He says "the origin of the Latin *clericus* lies in the Celtic languages, and in the religion of the Druids. It was the duty of the Bards to celebrate in poetical composition, which they recited to the music of the harp, the great deeds of heroes, and to preserve by these means the history of bygone times, and impress its lessons on the minds of their contemporaries. The name of their harp was *clar*, from whence came *clarach*, pertaining to the harp, and *clarsair*, a bard or harper, which ultimately came to designate the priest who took part in the musical celebrations of the fane or temple." (CHARLES MACKAY, in *Notes and Queries*.) Without admitting that this is the true origin of *clericus* or *clerk*, it seems exceedingly probable that both words may have been in extensive use, and that we have here a key to the twofold pronunciation of *clerk* and *clark* about which we often hear some people talk in a very positive manner.

Client. Latin, *cliens*, a dependant, one who looks to some powerful personage for protection or support.

In Roman law, a *client* was one who depended on some renowned orator for defence, and as this defence, was undertaken without fee or reward, except the honour and influence resulting from it, the position of a suitor was strictly that of a dependant. The fiction of working without hire is still kept up in our courts of law; the fees paid to counsellors and advocates being regarded as a simple gratuity or *honorarium*, for the receiving of which, says Blackstone, they "can maintain no action." It is only in recent times that the customers of a banker or broker have been called their *clients;* formerly they were called *customers*, but there is something of a professional ring about the name of *client*, which seems to make it more acceptable to certain persons, who like to feel themselves distinct from the class of tradesmen; a distinction which is regarded by them as one of some importance.

Cobang. Japanese, gold. (*See Kobang.*)

Codicil. Latin, *codicillus*, the diminutive of *caudex* or *codex*, which meant originally the trunk or body of a tree. It came afterwards to signify anything made of wood, and especially a *book*, which, before the invention of parchment, was made of wood, sometimes covered with wax, for the more convenient reception of the letters. The name was retained after the invention of parchment and paper, and applied to a scroll or volume, or the main portion of any piece of writing; just as the word pen (from the Latin, *penna;* German, *Feder*, a feather) continued in use when pens were made of steel instead of quills. From *codex*, we have *codicillus*, a small book, a letter, a billet, and especially a small portion appended to a will.

A codicil is a piece of writing appended to the main body of a will or testament, and is necessarily made after the will itself, and sometimes explains or even alters the will. In law, it is considered as forming a part of the will, and whenever it falls to a clerk or accountant to examine a will, equal care should be bestowed on the codicil or codicils appended. In the counting-house, however, neither wills nor codicils are often seen; Certificates of Probate (*which see*) usually furnishing the authority required for the discharge of his functions.

Coin. Old French, *coigner;* Italian, *cuniare;* Spanish, *cunar*, to wedge or to coin. Both Menage and Spelman derive these words from the Latin, *cuneus*, the iron wedge (punch or die), which, on being struck, impressed the device on pieces of money; but the word *cuneus*, or wedge, may have been applied to the money itself, as it was formerly common to use the word wedge in the sense of *bar*, *ingot*, or plate of metal, as in Joshua vii. 21. From *cuneus* comes the Spanish *cuna*, and French, *coin*. Muratori endeavours to show that the word is really derived from the Greek, εικιον, an image, whence the Latin, *iconiare*, in the sense of coining money.

Pieces of money having impressed upon them a device or legend, or both, by some recognized body, mostly the supreme government of the country. In Numismatics, everything about the shape, composition, and marking of a coin is of interest. In Economics, the points of chief importance are the fineness, and the weight. Other points, though not so important, should not, however, be lost sight of, and Professor Jevons enumerates four principal objects which should be aimed at in deciding upon the exact design for a coin :—

1. To prevent counterfeit.
2. To prevent fraudulent removal of metal from a coin.
3. To reduce the loss of metal by legitimate wear and tear.
4. To make the coin an artistic and historical monument of the State issuing it, and the people using it.

Collateral Security. Collaterals. From the Latin, *lătus, lateris*, a side, and *con*, with: whence *collateral*, side by side with anything.

Collateral Securities, often called for the sake of brevity Collaterals, are documents deposited with a creditor as additional security for a debt or loan. Of course, in all business transactions, the chief security of a creditor is the character and means of the person with whom he deals. But, as a protection against loss through bankruptcy or other misfortune, it is usual to require, especially in the case of loans, some additional or collateral security, which commonly takes the form of a deposit of Bills of Exchange, Bills of Lading, Bonds, Policies, or other objects of value. Stock so deposited is often said to be put in pawn, or to be pawned, but the formalities connected with the mere deposit of securities are less rigorous than those accompanying a pawn, and the laws relating to them are different.

Collect, To. To collect a Bill, Note, or Draft, is to present it for payment as agent for the holder.

To collect coupons implies the additional work of listing and presenting them. Hence it will be seen that the term "To Collect" is used in a purely technical sense, since none of the above things said to be collected, are ever collected, but the money payable upon them.

Cologne Mark Weight. 3608 grains Troy.

Commassee. An Arabian copper coin, but contains a little silver: 60 to a dollar at Mocha.

Commission. Latin, *committĕre,* to entrust, consign, commit; from *con* and *mitto.*

(*a.*) Primarily, *commission* signifies the act of committing to any one the discharge of some duty for which he is supposed to be specially fitted.

(*b.*) Secondarily, the term is applied to the payment made for the service rendered, and in financial circles this secondary meaning has almost entirely overridden the primary. Hence, by *commission* is most commonly understood a sum paid for the performance of a given service, and especially that of buying and selling on behalf of a principal.

Commodatum. Latin, *commodo, commodare,* to lend, to accommodate for a length of time; used by the best writers for things which are themselves returned, as books, clothes, a sword; and is thus distinguished from *Mutuum* (*which see*).

Commodatum in mercantile law signifies a loan of such things as are expected to be returned, and not to be repaid or replaced by an equivalent. In loans of Bonds, Share Certificates, and the like, bearing numbers which the lender wishes to retain, it should always be stipulated that the same identical papers are to be returned; if this precaution be not taken, there may be a difficulty in reclaiming them in a court of law.

Commodities. Objects of any kind which can be bought or sold. It is commonly, but rather inconsistently said, that *money* is a commodity as much as cotton, iron, or sugar. Nothing but a rash desire for generalization could lead to such an assertion; for all our leading economists have made a clear distinction between them. Money furnishes us with a unit in terms of which the value of commodities may be expressed, but no commodity is ever used (except for the sake of some passing illustration) to serve as a unit by which to estimate the value of money.

Compensation. From the Latin, *penso,* to weigh, and *con,* together: *penso* is the frequentative form of *pendo,* to hang, to hang down, like the scales of a balance: *compensatio* is a balancing, whether of services, advantages, or values: exchange; barter.

Compensation is a word used in ordinary speech, bearing the general meaning of requital, satisfaction: or in the sense of an equivalent for loss, damage, or suffering.

It is used also in a technical sense, with the meaning of *Set-off* (*which see*).

Composite Coin. Coins consisting of two or more substances, metallic or otherwise, each substance retaining its distinctive character, and not as in ordinary coins fused into one homogeneous mass. Louis, King of France, had one- and two-dime pieces made of silver wire fixed on pieces of leather. The silver wire gave the value, the leather bulk. Various attempts have been made to diminish the bulk of copper coins, by inserting a disk of silver in the centre. These experiments have not succeeded, but numerous specimens are to be found in the cabinets of the curious.

Condor. A gold coin used in some South American States.

(*a*.) The *Gold Condor of Chili* weighs 15·253 grammes ·900 fine, and is worth 47·28 francs=£1·8743 or £1 17*s*. 5¾*d*. sterling. The coinage of Chili is regulated by the Monetary Laws of January, 1851, and October 1870. The Condor is also called the 10-peso piece.

(*b*.) The *Gold Condor of the United States of Columbia*, or 10-peso piece, according to the Monetary Law of June, 1871, weighs 16·129 grammes ·900 fine, and is worth 50 francs=£1·9821 or £1 19*s*. 7¾*d*. A double Condor of 20 pesos is also struck.

(*c*.) The *Gold Condor of La Plata* is the same as that of Chili and is valued at 9 patacons 20 cents. (*See Patacon*.)

(*d*.) The *Gold Condor of New Granada* is worth £2 0*s*. 3¾*d*.

Condorin. A Japanese copper coin, worth about ¾*d*. English.

Confederate Notes. Promissory Notes issued by the Confederate States of North America, as a means of raising money to carry on the war with the Federal States, during the struggle of the latter in defence of the Union. They are now almost valueless.

Consideration. In mercantile transactions the term "Consideration" may signify—1st. A *benefit received*, as a payment of money, or a delivery of goods.

2nd. A *promise made* to pay money at some given date, or an *engagement* to deliver commodities under specified conditions.

3rd. A *loss suffered* in consideration of which some form of compensation is to be made.

Consign. Consignment. The remitting of goods from one place to another for the purpose of sale. It is usually accompanied by an agreement containing clearly defined conditions as to commission, and return, if unsold.

Consol Certificates. Documents issued by the Bank of England certifying that the Holder is entitled to £50, or some multiple of £50 in the Consolidated Three per cent. Annuities. Until within the last few years, Consol Holders had their claim recorded or "inscribed" in the books of the Bank, and Stock to any amount not including fractions of one penny might thus be inscribed. The Certificates were issued in order to afford certain advantages to those who were willing to forego the additional security which inscription secured. Two of those advantages were—1. Increased facility of Transfer. Merchants and Bankers, holding these Certificates, might transfer them from one to another without the trouble attending the usual method of transfer, and the expense of transfer fees.

2. Consol holders living in the country might cut off the coupons attached to each certificate, and pay them into their bankers or to

their local tradesmen, and so avoid the necessity of coming up to London to receive their half-yearly dividends, an expense which pressed heavily on small holders, and caused a serious deduction from their annual income.

The following is the form of the certificate printed on the face of each bond:—

"*This is to certify*, That the Bearer of this Certificate is entitled to ONE HUNDRED POUNDS Consolidated Three Per Centum Annuities, subject to the Provisions of the Act 26 Victoria, Cap. 28, and to the regulations affecting the same.

JNO. FRANCIS,
Chief Cashier,
Bank of England."

A kind of fly-leaf is appended to each certificate, consisting of ten half-yearly coupons.

COPY OF A CONSOL COUPON.

257 *Div.*	CONSOLS.	*Div.* 257
08142	£100	08142

Coupon for One *Pound* Ten *Shillings.*

(LESS INCOME TAX.)

Being the half-yearly Dividend on Stock Certificate

for One Hundred Pounds.

Consolidated 3 *per cent Annuities.*

Due January 5, 1881.

£1 10*s.* 0*d.* S. O. GRAY,
Chief Accountant Bank of England.

Consols. A contraction of the term "Consolidated Funds." In the beginning of the eighteenth century several Government funds were in existence; the customs, the excise, stamps, and other sources of revenue were each the basis of a distinct and separate fund, and were made the security for sums advanced on each, and for those advances only. These different funds were by degrees classed together, till in 1787 they were *consolidated* into one, when the debt amounted to £245,466,855, and the annual charge to £9,666,541.

Since then several additions have been made to the Consolidated Fund, so that in the year succeeding the close of the Bonaparte struggle, 1816, the total of the public debt of the United Kingdom, consisting largely of Consols of different denominations, was upwards of £860,000,000. It has subsequently been reduced, and at the present moment is less than £780,000,000, but varies from time to time as greater or less demands are made upon it, through the exigencies of war or other national responsibilities. Of the above Debt, about £400,000,000 consist of Consols properly so called.

Consumption. Latin, *consumere*, to take to one's self, to use, to spend, to employ.

Consumption is the correlative to Production (*see Production*), and signifies the buying of a thing for one's use and enjoyment, and not for the purpose of sale. The French equivalent is *Consommation*, but both the English and French words are often used in popular speech in the sense of *destruction*, and this sense of the word has somewhat disguised its original meaning. Economists have consequently preferred the use of the terms Supply and Demand in lieu of Production and Consumption, as they answer to the idea intended to be conveyed quite as well, and are not so liable to misconstruction. (*See Supply and Demand.*)

Consumption is a term applied to two radically different things. There is one kind of consumption which affords an immediate gratification, and leaves nothing behind. It uses up wealth, without leaving anything to fill its place. This is called "Unproductive Consumption." There is another kind which enriches: it uses up wealth, but in such a way as to leave a greater wealth in its place. This is called "Productive Consumption."

Contango. This appears to be one of those cant terms so common amongst business men, and especially among the habituès of the Stock Exchange. It seems to be connected with some of the following words in the Italian and Spanish languages, but the derivation is irregular and uncertain:—

Spanish, *contar*, to count, to reckon; *contante*, ready money; *conta*, reason, satisfaction; Italian, *conta*, delay (an obsolete word, but coming very near to *contango* in meaning); *danaro contante*, ready money; *a contanti*, in cash; *contare*, to count, to reckon; *conto*, account, reckoning.

Contango is a word used on the Stock Exchange as a name for the charge made by brokers for *carrying over* a bargain from one fortnightly account to another instead of closing it. (*See Carrying Over.*) It often happens that when a purchase has been made by a client, no opportunity occurs in the course of a fortnightly account of closing the bargain with a profit, and perhaps not without a considerable loss; and at the same time there may be a probability that if the bargain be kept open a little longer, a good profit might result. In such a case, a fictitious sale is effected, at the current market price of the stock bought, the *difference* between the buying price and the fictitious selling (the carrying over) price is paid by the client, and the bargain is kept open; for this privilege the client pays a certain rate of interest for the money employed in the fictitious purchase, which will be more or less according to the demand for this kind of accommodation in the market at the time. It is the rate of interest thus charged which is called the "*Contango*," and is usually reckoned at a certain rate per cent. on the money value of the stock bought,

Contango Day. The second day before settling-day on the Stock Exchange. It is sometimes called "continuation day," because bargains, instead of being closed, are *continued*, by the fixing of the *Contango* (*which see*).

Conto. A Conto of Reis (Portugal) is one thousand of milreis (1:000$000).

Contract. An agreement between two parties, the observance of which is enforced by a legal obligation, or right of action. It may be—

(*a.*) A *Unilateral Contract*, binding one party, the debtor, and not the other. An insurance policy is a contract of this kind, which is only signed by the insurer, the insured having discharged his obligation by the payment of the premium.

(*b.*) A *Bilateral Contract*, binding both parties in such a way that each becomes both *debtor* and *creditor*. A broker's contract is of this kind, for although it is only signed by one party, the broker, the simple acceptance of the contract without demur by the client binds him in law to discharge his part of the obligation when the settling-day arrives. Nevertheless, as a general rule, bilateral contracts are signed by both parties.

Contract Note. A slip of paper containing the terms of a bargain entered into on behalf of a client. They are used in various departments of business, and notably in Stock Exchange transactions. The following is a copy of note handed by a broker to his client:—

CUSHION COURT, OLD BROAD STREET,
LONDON, *Oct.* 18, 1879.

Bought for HENRY WALDEGRAVE, Esq.,
(subject to the Rules and Regulations of the London Stock Exchange)
of W. PHIPSON,

£500 Egyptian State-Domain Bonds @ 78			
	£390	0	0
Brokerage .		12	6
	£390	12	6

F. THOMSON,
Sworn Broker.

For account, 30 Oct. 1879.

Convention Money. (*Conventions Münze.*) The old Austrian currency, based on the 20 *Florin Standard* (20 *Gulden-fuss*), in virtue of which 20 Gulden were coined from a Cologne mark weight of *fine* silver. (*See Cologne Mark.*) This standard was in use down to 1857, when it was superseded by the Forty-five Florin Standard (*which see*).

Convertibility. From the Latin, *con*, with, or together, and *vertere*, to turn: *convertere*, to change one thing into another, or to give one thing for another. The necessity of using the word "another" indicates the force of the prefix *con.* It implies that in an act of *conversion* two things are brought "together," and one is made to take the place of the other—*i.e.*, they change places "with" each other.

By convertibility is meant, in commerce, the capability of exchanging one thing for another. Scrip is said to be converted into Bonds or Shares: old Bonds into new Bonds: Bullion into Coin: Gold into Bank Notes, or Bank Notes into Gold, when either of these is exchanged for either of the other.

The term *Convertibility* has a special and technical meaning when applied to Bank notes and other forms of "paper money." It then signifies the capability of exchanging such paper into gold at any moment when the holder wishes to do so. The Convertibility of a note is considered perfect, when the Bank issuing the note holds in its vaults a quantity of gold (bars or coin) equal in value with the nominal value of all the notes issued. No bank in existence actually does this; but the Bank of England offers security for the value of its notes almost equivalent; inasmuch as the whole of its notes are represented by bullion in its vaults together with Government securities of the first class. The Government securities amount to £15,750,000; the bullion varies in amount from time to time, but with every decrease in the amount of bullion, a corresponding amount of notes is withdrawn from circulation. Very few Banks, and very few States can offer security equal to this, hence it is that "paper money" in other States is so often at a discount, or what is the same thing expressed in different words, gold is so often at a premium.

It may be asked, What is the use of paper money at all, if gold and other valuable securities must always be kept in reserve in order to render it convertible? Several advantages arise from the use of paper money, especially when thus secured by a reserve of bullion. (*a.*) It is more convenient to send from place to place than coin or bars would be, and the expense of conveyance is also less. (*b.*) The wear and tear of coins is avoided by the use of paper. (*c.*) As every note is numbered, it is more easily recovered if lost or stolen. (*d.*) The labour of counting, and the mistakes that might arise in counting are avoided. (*e.*) When gold is deposited in the form of bars, the cost of coinage is saved.

Co-operation. Latin, *con*, with, or together; *operor*, I work; *opus*, work or labour.

To co-operate is simply to work with some one in order to secure some desirable result. In this sense the word has been long in use, and unrestricted in its application. Latterly the term has acquired a technical meaning in commerce, where it is used to express the distinctive principle on which certain associations are formed, and which are therefore called Co-operative Societies.

The leading objects aimed at by these societies are:—

(1.) To reconcile the interests of *Capital* and *Labour* by enabling the labourer to become to a certain extent his own capitalist.

(2.) To minimize the cost of distribution of commodities among customers.

(3.) To dispense in some measure with the services of middlemen.

(4.) To avoid the losses incident to "credit" trade among retail dealers.

(5.) To secure unadulterated goods by giving no one an interest in adulterating them.

The success which attended some of the early attempts at trade co-operation, induced men of an enterprising and speculative turn to extend their sphere, and a large number of so-called co-operative societies have been started within the last few years which were nothing more than joint-stock trading companies, based on the principle of doing all business for ready money only. But most of these companies have failed, and the causes of failure in some instances were very palpable. Looking over the reports of several extinct associations the following causes of failure are conspicuous.

(*a.*) Shareholders took up shares merely with a view to profit by the dividends they expected to accrue, but did not lay out a single penny at the stores.

(*b.*) Instead of insisting on each purchaser paying ready money and *taking away his goods with him*, an attempt was made to send all parcels above a certain value to any part of the metropolis at the expense of the Society. In one Society, enough was paid in one year for carriage of goods to pay a fair dividend to the shareholders, but the shareholders had no dividend, nor have they ever had a penny of their capital returned. The true principle of action would seem to be to sell all articles at such a price as would offer an inducement to members to undertake either the trouble or expense of conveying their purchases to their own homes. When this is not practicable the co-operative principle is to this extent inapplicable.

(*c.*) By entering into arrangements with manufacturers for the supply of goods at a large discount off the trade price. It was found in practice that such manufacturers mostly put an extra price on their goods knowing that a discount would be demanded, and when this was done, the necessity of making all purchases through the Society, and passing all articles bought through the Society's books, enormous clerical labour was entailed, and a large staff of book-keepers required.

(*d.*) When co-operation has been applied to manufacturing concerns difficulty has always been found in securing the needful skill in the management. The body of the shareholders are generally incapable of appreciating managerial skill, they pay for it grudgingly, and mostly drive away the one man of all others it would have been their interest to retain.

(*e.*) Shareholders in many instances cherished unreasonable expectations. They seemed to think that the 20 or 25 per cent put upon the wholesale price of goods would fall into their hands. They forgot that the so-called "profits" of the retail tradesman were the wages he received as compensation for his acquired skill, and his daily labour, as well as the interest on his capital.

Notwithstanding all these drawbacks, it is the opinion of all unbiassed observers that there is still some really useful work to be done by co-operative societies, but shareholders and members will have to remember that "*co-operation*" is the essential condition of success, and that mere joint-stock trading is not at all likely to compete successfully with the compact energy, the personal interest and the acquired experience of regular retail traders.

Copeck. A Russian copper coin, the 100th part of a *ruble*, value $\frac{19}{50}$ of an English penny.

The 20 copeck silver piece of 1870 when new is worth $7\frac{1}{2}d.$

Copfstuck. An Austrian silver coin now disused, value about 9*d.*

Cornado. A copper coin formerly circulating in Spain; of small value, whence the proverb "no vale un Cornado" is the equivalent of our "not worth a farthing."

Corner. A term introduced into the London Stock Exchange from America, where it is used to denote a market devoted to some particular stock or commodity, more especially when the dealings in that market are characterized by great activity and perhaps by secresy. Hence arise the distinctions of "gold corner," "railway corner," &c.

Corner, To. Like the last word this phrase also comes from America, and is now in frequent use here. The notion conveyed is that of being driven into a corner, by being out-matched in a speculation; that is, buyers or "bulls" have been inveigled into purchases, and find themselves loaded with stocks which they cannot sell; or, on the other hand, sellers or "bears" have effected sales of stocks which they cannot deliver, nor yet buy back, except at a ruinous sacrifice.

Corõa or Crown. *Corõa* is the Portuguese contraction for the Latin, *corona*, a crown.

A Portuguese gold coin of 10,000 reis; weighs 17 grammes 735 mgrms. (17·735 grammes) ·916$\frac{2}{3}$ fine, and is worth £2 4*s.* $4\frac{3}{4}d.$

There are other gold coins of proportional weight; Meia Corõa (half-crown), Quintos de Corõa ($\frac{1}{5}$ of a crown), Decimos de Corõa ($\frac{1}{10}$ of a crown).

Cost. Two words here appear to be blended into one. The Latin, *constare*, to stand together, to be fixed, to be determined; whence to *cost* would imply a resolution and decision after haggling and huckstering in the market. From *constare*, by dropping the *n* (just as we get Covent Garden from *convent* garden), we have the Italian, *costare*, the old French, *causter*, and the modern French, *couter*, all meaning the same as our word "cost."

Others think that the Saxon, *cyste*; Scotch, *kist*, a chest or box, in which money was kept, is the origin of the word. It seems more probable that it is connected with the Scotch *cose* or *coss*, which Dr. Jamieson says means to exchange or barter, from the Saxon, *ceosan*, to choose. The past participle, *ceosed*, *cossed*, or *cost*, would thus signify when applied to price that which was *chosen* or *taken*. In Sussex (more especially in the secluded districts) the verb to *scoss*, to *scose*, or to *scourse*, was till lately in common use to denote barter or exchange, as distinguished from a sale. The connection of *scoss* with *coss*, and *scose* with *cose*, is precisely analogous with that between *smelt* and *melt*, *smash* and *mash*, *slash* and *lash*, and has an intensitive effect. The Dutch, *kost;* German, *kosten;* Swedish, *kosta*, are the equivalents in other Teutonic dialects.

"And made hym obligacyon and *costage*
hym gan sende."—*Robert of Gloucester*.

"Let not the lufe of this lyfe temporall
Quhilk ye mon lose, but le quhen ye leist were
Stay you to *cois* with lyfe celestial
Quhen ever that the chois comes thame betweene."
DAVIDSON'S *Commendation of Vprightness*.

The *Cost* of a commodity is the sum total of the services required to make that commodity, and to place it in the hands of the consumer.

Cost of Production. A phrase much used in Economics, to signify the sum total of all the services requisite to make an article and bring it to market or place it in the hands of the consumer. These services fall under three heads:—Labour, Endurance, and Abstinence. By *labour* is understood all the efforts, physical or mental expended in the work: by *endurance* the suffering of any disagreeable or painful feelings associated with certain kinds of work: and by *abstinence* the foregoing of any enjoyment that might be derived from the spending of wealth in order that it may be employed as capital.

Neither of these elements of *cost* is susceptible of being measured or priced. In practice, therefore, the manufacturer bases his calculations not on the cost, but on the *expenses of production*—that is to say, he reckons what he shall have *to pay* for the labour and endurance needed in the production of a given article, and what his capital would yield him if put out at the current rate of interest instead of being employed in the production of that article. The *cost* and the *expenses* are quite different things, though closely allied; but it is the latter with which the manufacturer and merchant are chiefly concerned, while the former is of more interest to the speculative economist.

Council Drafts. Drafts issued by our Government against the Government of India. Payments to the amount of £17,000,000 sterling are made by India to the Home Government every year. But since payments have to be made by English merchants to merchants and others in India the transfer of bullion is avoided by the use of these "Council Drafts," which are so called because our Government *draws* upon the "Governor-General of India in Council" for such sums as shall be readily negotiable in the English market, or such as will satisfy any special claims upon the Indian

Government for interest, dividends, &c. The following is a copy of a Council Draft given at the Bank of England in payment of interest on Enfaced Paper representing a capital of 243,000 Company's Rupees :—

No. 462 (First/Second) Crest. Stamp.

London, 21 Aug. 1879. c. Rs. 4860.

On demand, pay to Messrs. P. M. Mondor & Co., or order (Second/First of this tenor and date not being paid) the sum of Company's Rupees Four Thousand Eight Hundred and Sixty—being the amount of Interest for ½ year from 1st Feb. 1879 to 1st Aug. 1879, due on Promissory Notes amounting to Company's Rupees 243,000—of the 4 per cent. Loan of 1842-43 as by advice from us.

To His Excellency
The Right Honourable
the Governor General of India
in Council.

For the Secretary of State for
India in Council.
(Signed)

Any one in England receiving this Draft can sell it on 'Change, and thus obtain cash for it at once, or he may send it to his correspondent in Calcutta who will give him value for it at the exchange of the day.

Counterfoil. Latin, *contra*, against or opposite to; and *folium*, a leaf.

A leaf opposite to, or over against, another leaf. In commercial practice, a counterfoil is more correctly a part of a leaf,—that part which is left in a book when one part has been torn out. Receipts, drafts, cheques, orders, &c., are usually written in books with counterfoils, and the purport of the writing on the leaf torn out, is repeated in a condensed form on the counterfoil, so as to furnish a record of every transaction authorized by the leaves themselves.

Counting Board. A board used in banks and other places where much coin has to be counted. It consists of a flat board with depressions on its surface exactly fitted to the size of the coin to be counted. By shaking a number of coins upon the surface of the board most of the depressions are quickly filled—the remaining ones are filled by the hand. When the board is full, the number is at once known. This rather primitive method is giving way to the weights and scales now to be seen on the counter of every cashier.

Coupon. French, *couper*, to cut.

A piece cut off. It is applied in commerce to the small slips of paper detached from a sheet or bond, entitling the holder to the interest on bonds or the dividends on shares.

Coupons have been greatly multiplied during the last quarter of a century, and the work arising from the sorting, listing, and cancelling of them employs a large number of hands. Hence the importance of constructing coupons in such a form as shall economize labour, promote accuracy, and prevent fraud. There are certain points of considerable importance in designing a coupon, but unhappily the duty of designing them has too often fallen into hands that have had no experience in their manipulation. The following particulars are worthy of especial attention:—

I. Every coupon should have on its face such words as indicate the nature of the Bond, Certificate, or Debenture from which it is detached. Otherwise, when the Bond, &c., is not accessible, it is often impossible to tell to what it belongs.

II. The "house" or bank at which it is payable should be stated thereon.

III. The value of the coupon should be stated in plain figures, or indicated by its colour. In *share* coupons, the value of which varies, this would of course not be practicable.

IV. The date at which the coupon falls due.

V. The Bond or Share *number*, which is best placed midway between the two ends. It is then visible when the coupons are held in bundles at one end, while being turned over by the thumb and finger at the other end.

Coupure. French, *couper*, to cut.

Etymologically, the same in meaning as *coupon*, but is used in practice somewhat differently. The word often appears in correspondence relating to International Stocks, and is usually translated in English as "piece." Thus where we should speak of a number of foreign bonds of different value, as "pieces of different denominations," the French term would probably be "*coupures* of, &c.

Course of Exchange. The variable price (estimated in the currency of one country) which is given for a fixed sum in the currency of another. The same name is also applied to the slips issued by brokers and merchants containing a list of the rates of exchange ruling between the great commercial centres of the world.

Credit. Latin, *credo*, I believe, trust, put confidence in. Whence *creditum*, a loan, a debt.

Credit signifies, primarily, trust reposed in a person with whom one deals. To sell a person goods for which he is not required to pay till after the lapse of some time, is to give *credit*, and implies a *belief* that the person can and will pay the money or an equivalent when it falls due.

(*a.*) When a bargain has been agreed to between two parties, and one of these parties hands over certain goods to the buyer, the other loses all property in them, and if, by the terms of the bargain, the buyer is not to pay for them, say for three months, the seller stands in the position of *creditor* (that is, he has given *credit*) to the buyer, and he can neither claim the goods nor demand any specific money for them. But he has at law a Right of Action against the buyer, which he can put in force, if at the end of three months the money is not paid. Hence *Credit* has been defined as "A Right of Action against a person for a sum of money."

(*b.*) In book-keeping, "to put to one's *Credit*," is to enter a transaction in such a way as to show that the person referred to has a "right to demand" something, not necessarily money, even though the value of that "something" be expressed in money. For example, suppose a Bill of Exchange for £100 be received by a London merchant from his correspondent in Antwerp. The Bill would be placed "to the Credit" of the correspondent in his account, If, however, the Bill was not met for want of funds when it became due, the London merchant would place it "to the debit" of his correspondent at Antwerp, and return it to him; and this is all that the latter has a right, in such a case, to demand.

(*c*.) *A Credit* in banking is an entry in the books of a banker implying that a customer has deposited money or notes with the banker. In such a case, the customer loses all property in the cash and notes, and in return has this entry made in the books, which is called a "credit," and it gives him a right to claim at any time—not *his money or notes*—but money or notes of equal value.

The amount of wealth in the form of "Bank credits" held by individuals in large commercial centres, is enormous, and unsubstantial as it appears, it is one of the safest forms which wealth can assume.

(*d*.) In the mathematical treatment of economic doctrines, Credit is defined as "Negative Capital:" for further elucidation of which term, see MacLeod's "Theory of Banking" and "Economics for Beginners."

Creditor. *Credo*, I believe.

Literally, one who credits, believes or trusts. In Economics, it is used to signify something more, and implies the *acting* on the strength of one's belief. Hence a Creditor is always understood to be one who not only believes in the honesty and ability of another to pay a debt, but one who actually entrusts property to another with the expectation that he will repay it either in kind or by an equivalent.

Crisis. Greek, κρυσις, *krusis*, from κρινω, to judge, decide, separate; whence *krisis* is a decision, determination, the end of a period of dispute or uncertainty. The Latinised form, *crisis*, passes unchanged into the English language. The French, *crise*, is formed regularly from the same word. In Germany the forms *Krisis* and *Krise* are both used.

A Crisis, in commerce, signifies a turning-point in any of those uncontrollable movements which occur in trade from time to time, such as expansion of credit, over-production, reckless speculation, &c., processes which go on for a time till the evils which follow in their train accumulate to such a degree as renders any further progress in the same direction impossible. When matters have arrived at this point, attention is forcibly directed to the causes which have been silently in operation, a general scare ensues, the energies of mercantile men are relaxed, and after a while are turned into different channels, when business resumes its normal course.

Crore of Rupees. *A Crore of Rupees* signifies 10,000,000 of rupees, and is generally taken as equivalent to £1,000,000 sterling. Its metallic value, however, is only £979,166 13*s.* 4*d.*, reckoning the Rupee at 1*s.* 11½*d.*, and as the price of silver has fallen very much during the last few years, even this reckoning is too high.

The arithmetical notation for rupees is peculiar, and requires explanation. For anything less than 100,000 rupees, the ordinary decimal notation is used. But for any sum above that, say 125,000 rupees, a different mode of statement is adopted. Thus, 125,000 rupees is written 1,25,000, and is read 1 lac, 25,000 rupees. This suffices for any number of rupees less than 10 millions, for which another comma is inserted. Thus, 7,13,12,500..6..5, is read 7 crores, 13 lacs, 12,500 rupees, 6 annas, and 5 pice. (*See Rupee*).

Crossed Cheque. A Crossed Cheque is so called because it has two transverse lines drawn across it. If between the lines the letters "& Co." be written, it is said to be crossed *generally*, and the holder can make use of it only by paying it in to *some banker.* If the name of any bank or banker be inserted between the lines, it is said to be crossed *specially*, and can then be paid in only at that particular bank or bankers. The object of crossing a cheque is to enable the drawer to trace through what hands it has passed, in the event of its going astray through error or fraud. The abbreviation "& Co." is not essential, however, and may be omitted.

Cheque Crossed Generally.

& Co.

London, 16 *Dec.* 1878.

To the London Joint Stock Bank, Princes Street.

Pay to James Brown, or Bearer,
Two Hundred and Fifty Pounds.

£250 0 0 Allen, Watson & Co.

By simply writing the name of a Bank or Banker before the letters "& Co.," the cheque is said to be crossed "specially."

Crown. (*a.*) An English coin of circulation, value one-fourth of a sovereign. It weighs 18 dwts. $4\frac{4}{11}$ grains Troy; and is made of silver, of the "ancient right standard." The half-crown is exactly half the above weight and value.

(*b.*) A gold coin used in Austria, called also the Union Crown, worth 13·8 florins. Weight, 11·111 grammes. Fineness, ·900. Since 1 gramme of gold ·900 fine is worth 29·4986*d.*, we find the value of the Austrian Gold Crown in sterling, £1 7*s.* 3¾*d.*; but as the gold coin of Austria, is a mere commodity, notwithstanding the care bestowed on its mintage, it is found, after allowing for mint remedies and fair abrasion, that it is rarely worth 27*s.* and often not more than 26*s.*

(*c.*) A gold coin used in North Germany, valued at 9·3 thalers.

Its weight and fineness are the same as that of the Austrian Crown above described, and its value in sterling therefore identical.

(*d.*) A gold coin used in South Germany worth 16·3 florins. Identical in weight, fineness, and English value with the two crowns above described, and for that reason is called the Union Crown (*Vereins Krone*).

(*e.*) A gold coin of Portugal. (*See Corôa.*)

Crusado. A Portuguese gold coin of 400 reis. The silver Crusado Novo or Pinto is equal to 840 reis. (*See Rei.*)

Cum Dividendo. Latin, *dividendum*, something to be divided; from *divido*, to divide, and *cum*, with.

With the dividend; often contracted to *cum dividend, cum div.* or *cum d.* This phrase is attached to prices and quotations about the time that a dividend is to be paid, and it indicates that the price quoted gives the purchaser a right, not only to the stock he is buying, but also to the dividend or interest just falling due.

Cum Drawing. Latin, *cum*, with. (*See Ex-Drawing.*)

If bonds are bought or sold just about the time when a drawing takes place, it is necessary to specify whether the Bonds transferred carry with them any benefits that may result from the Drawing or not. If the benefit goes with the Bond, it is said to be sold "Cum Drawing" (with the benefits, if any, of the drawing about to take place).

Currency. From Latin, *curro*, I run.

The property or quality of being current, or of circulating freely. Owing to the fact that this property is found in the things we call money, such as coins, banknotes, &c., the term *currency* (by a process very common in most languages) has been transferred from the property or quality itself to the things possessing it. Hence, money, notes, bills of exchange and the like are commonly called "the Currency" but might with much more correctness be called the *Circulating Medium*" (*which see*).

The term *currency* is by some writers restricted to the money *current* as a legal tender in any given country. When the precious metals are the legal tender, and bank notes are always *convertible* into coins equal in amount to the value printed on their face, it is called *Metallic Currency*. When paper notes are made by law a legal tender, and are *inconvertible*—in other words, when the holder of bank notes or Government notes is not entitled to claim gold or silver for them—it is called *Paper Currency*. In almost every instance of an inconvertible paper currency, it is depreciated in value, or, what is the same thing, gold and silver are at a premium. (*See Premium*)

Under the name of currency are sometimes included unrecorded debts, as well as book debts, and deposits with bankers. Hence the dictum "*the amount of Currency in any country is the sum of all the debts due to every individual in it.*—That is, all the money and credit in it." (MacLeod, page 27.) This, however, is a wide extension of the meaning of *Currency*, the prominent idea of which is that of *running* or circulating freely among traders, which book debts and unrecorded debts can hardly be said to do.

Currency is classified by MacLeod as follows:—

1. Coined money—gold, silver, copper.
2. Paper currency—*i.e.*, promissory notes, and bills of exchange with all their varieties.
3. Simple debts of all sorts, such as credits in banker's books, called deposits; book debts of traders; and private debts between individuals.

The mediums of exchange comprised in the name *Currency* are classified by Seyd thus:—

Gold coins Silver ,, Copper ,,	Metallic Currency.
Bank Notes State ,,	Paper Currency.

In England, where gold forms the basis of valuation, the currency may be divided into:—

Gold Coins	Free Currency.
Silver Coins Copper ,, Bank Notes State ,,	Conditional Currency.

Currency by Tale. That form of currency which admits of being passed from hand to hand by simple counting, without the use of scales, or touchstone, or other test of weight or purity. Coins of some shape or other are always used when currency by tale is established, and it is probable that among the earliest of such coins the Greek *obolus* would be found. Oboli were stamped spikes or bars, and six of them made up a *drachma* or handful and thus gave origin to the Greek unit of value.

Currency by Weight. The primitive form of most metallic currencies. In the earliest times, and before the invention of coining, wedges, bars, or fragments of metal were used as the medium of exchange, and payments were made by weight only. The inconvenience of always having to carry about a balance and weights when accounts were to be settled was so great as to render any contrivance welcome which would enable merchants to dispense with so cumbrous an apparatus; the contrivance hit upon and ever since practised was the division of a given metal into pieces of equal weight, and impressing a seal or stamp upon them under the authority of the Government, to assure those who received them that the pieces of metal were of the lawful purity and weight. After that it was only necessary to count the pieces instead of weighing them. (*See preceding article.*)

Currency Principle. This phrase is used to signify the principle on which certain banks have conducted their business, and which some financiers still maintain should be followed. Essentially it consists in exchanging credit for specie, so as always to maintain an exact equality between the two. As this would prevent a banker from making any profit by the business, while the advantage to customers would be very great, it is necessary to charge a commission in such banks on all business done, in order to meet the expenses of the establishment. The Banks of Amsterdam, Hamburg and Venice were formerly conducted on this principle, and they rendered good service in their day, but modern banks make their profit chiefly by employing the specie of their customers in discounting bills of exchange, or by lending money against securities, retaining sufficient in the form of ready cash for all probable demands as they occur from day to day.

Currency Value. In Hamburg, the value of the silver coinage as compared with bank money. (*See Bank Value.*)

Customs. French, *coutume*, from *couter*, to cost. Law Latin, *custuma*, which appears to be a mere adaptation of the French term to the requirements of the Latin language.

Customs are the *costs*, duties, tolls, or tribute paid by importers and exporters on goods brought into, or sent out of, the country. By a statute of Edward I., the king promised to take no customs from merchants, saving those on "wools, skins and leather," which were called the hereditary customs of the Crown. The list of dutiable articles has varied from time to time since then, and is liable to alteration by Act of Parliament whenever the exigencies of the Exchequer demand it.

D.

D, occurs in the following:

Dbk., Drawback.
d/d, Days' date.
Dft., Draft.
Div., Dividend.
Dis., Discount.
Dr., Debtor.
d/s, Days' sight.

Dandy Note. For goods removed from the warehouse of H. M. Customs, a form of dandy note and pricking note combined is used.

A dandy note is a document used for the shipment of goods. This paper is filled in by the exporter, and is then passed at the office of the Controller of Accounts. In the case of the delivery for exportation of casks of wine or spirits, the gauger who examines them, notes, on the back of the dandy, the bung and wet dimensions, and the contents and ullage of each cask. On the dandy note the Export Examining Officer also records his examination of the goods, and on the shipment of these it is forwarded to the Principal Searcher's office.

The following is the form of dandy and pricking notes combined, used when the goods are removed by cart:—

To the Out-door Officer at

Deliver the under-mentioned Packages for the Examining Officers at

Shipping Marks, Numbers, and Description of Packages, and Species of Goods, in words at length.	Merchant's Name, Ship, Captain and Destination.
	Ship Master Destination Exporter Carman Warehousing Department 187

To the Out-door Officers on Board the Ship

Master, for

Receive the following Goods for Shipment

Shipping Marks and Numbers.	Exporter's Name and Date of Bond.	Quantity and Description of Packages of Species of Goods in words at length.
	Exporter. Date of Bond.	

Examined 187 Examining Officer	Received the above-mentioned Packages on Board this Ship, 187 Master, Mate, or Out-door Officer.

Date. French, *date;* Italian, *data;* Spanish, *data;* Latin, *datum;* from *do, dare,* to give, meaning generally a given *time* and a given *place.*

Any *given* time; any fixed or settled time. The common derivation of date from *day* is of course a vulgar error, as the word applies as much to place as to time.

Dating Forward. A practice adopted by wholesale dealers in textile fabrics of *dating* an invoice or a bill some months later than the time when the goods are actually delivered. The object aimed at by the large wholesale houses is to attract buyers by the offer of long credit; but the evils attending the practice when carried to excess are so great, that an attempt has lately been made to confine it within narrower limits. An experienced buyer thus describes the process in a letter to the *Daily News*:—

"I have this day received a circular from a house in the City offering cambric handkerchiefs (a large trade), delivered in November, dated as February, 1881, with 2½ per cent. discount in April or four months' bill. These long dating forward terms are of very little use to sound cash buyers, but the reverse, as they know that certain calculations of interest and deductions for bad debts are charged on the goods which they and the public have indirectly to pay. This system of long dating enables a large amount of questionable trade by re-sales, &c., to be carried on by persons who get their goods on long credit with scarcely any capital of their own. The old system of retailers visiting the various markets every month, and making their purchases with the fair discount of 2½ in six weeks was a sounder system of business, both for buyers and sellers, as I know that many a young beginner has been ruined through overstocking himself through the facilities thrust upon him for dating the goods forward."

Days of Grace. From Latin, *gratia*, favour, kindness.

Bills of Exchange, when drawn upon, that is, payable in England, otherwise than *on demand*, have three "days of grace" allowed over and above the time specified on the face of the bill, so that the bill really becomes due upon the third day of grace, and not earlier, unless it fall upon a Sunday, Christmas Day, Good Friday, or a day of public fast or thanksgiving, in which cases the bill becomes due the day *before*. If on a Bank Holiday, the day *after*. (*See Holidays.*) No other country in Europe except Austria (3 days) and Russia (10 days) allows days of grace.

Dead Account. An account standing in the name of a person deceased. "When the probate of a will is lodged at the Bank, the stock specified only is placed at the command of the executors. But should there be any other funds in the name of the deceased party, the word 'deceased' is placed against the name; and this prevents unauthorised persons from receiving the interest. By the rules of the Bank also, no more stock can be added to that which is technically termed a 'dead account.'"—FRANCIS's *History of the Bank of England.*

Debasement. Etymology uncertain. It is said by some to be derived from the Latin *de*, down; and *basis*, the bottom or base. By others it is derived from the French *bas*, low, mean, vile; but the French have no compound word like *debaser*, *debaisser*, and it seems more probable that the English word has been formed like many modern scientific words directly from the Latin elements above named.

Debasement is a fraudulent process practised on the coinage, to which dishonest governments have on many occasions had recourse in order to supply themselves with funds which they could not extort from the people. To a limited extent it has also been practised by forgers and swindlers, but this is usually called "making counterfeit coins," and debasing the coinage as a national act is understood to be the work of those whose business it was to maintain its purity. The consequences of a debasement of the coinage are so disastrous to a nation that all civilized governments now take the greatest precautions against it. The ceremony called the "Trial of the Pix," (*which see*) is performed with the express object of maintaining the purity of the currency as established by law.

Debenture Bond. Latin, *debeo*, a contraction of *dehibeo* (from *de* and *habeo*) to have something from someone; hence, to owe. The present participle *debens*, owing, is also applied to a debtor, or one who owes. A Debenture is therefore a simple acknowledgment of a debt.

Debentures or *Debenture Bonds* are bonds issued by the State or by Commercial Companies, acknowledging a debt or obligation, and containing *an engagement to pay* a specified sum at a specified date, with interest on that sum at a specified rate, until the date of repayment of the Bond itself. The Victoria Government Debentures, and most Railway Debentures, are examples. (*See Debenture Stock.*)

Debenture Stock. It sometimes happens that when Debenture Bonds have matured, the parties who have incurred the obligation of paying them off find it inconvenient to do so. In other instances, holders of Debentures have not wished to be paid off, but rather to receive the interest thereon. In these cases the convenience of both parties is met by converting the Debentures or Debenture Bonds into Stock, that is, by exchanging them for a new document, on which is inscribed an engagement to pay a certain *annuity, by way of interest*, for the money lent, but not to repay the principal itself. When Government Bonds and Exchequer Bills are thus converted into Stock, the process is called *Funding*, (*which see*).

Debt. Latin *debeo, debere*, to owe. *Debitum*, a debt, a sum of money owing.

A duty or obligation to pay something. By a process very common in language, the name of debt is often applied to the sum of money, or other commodity, owing; but in law and in commerce it is correctly used only in reference to the duty to pay. Since, wherever there is imposed on any person a duty to pay, there is also vested in some other person a right to demand, it is clear that two different and apparently contradictory names may be applied to the same thing, that is, the name Credit or Debt, right or duty may be used in reference to one and the same transaction. In using one term rather than the other there is a reference, expressed or implied, to the person. When no such reference is made, the terms Debt and Credit are synonymous both in law and trade. The opposite significations attached to the two words, as used in popular language are nevertheless quite correct, when used in reference to the *person owing* or the *person claiming* the same due, as every one who examines his banker's pass-book may see, the Credits being placed all on one side, and the debits or debts on the other, the entries on the Creditor side cancelling an equal amount on the Debtor side.

This opposition between the two terms is also seen in the fact, that while anyone would be willing to buy a Credit (a right to demand) no one would be so foolish as to buy a Debit (that is, a duty to pay).

Decime. A French copper coin, the tenth of a Franc.

Decimo. (*a.*) The tenth part of the Chilian *peso*. It weighs 2·500 grammes of silver, ·900 fine, and is worth half a franc, or rather more than $4\frac{3}{4}d.$ English.

(*b.*) The tenth part of the Venezolano. It consists of 2·500 grammes of silver, ·835 fine, and is worth 46 centimes, or $4\frac{1}{2}d.$ English.

(*c.*) The tenth part of the peso of the United States of Columbia. It weighs 2·500 grammes of silver, ·835 fine. Hence, although its weight is exactly proportional to that of the peso, it is a mere token coin owing to its inferior fineness. (*See Peso.*)

Decussis. A Roman silver coin, marked X. Ten asses, same as denarius.

Defacing of Coins. Coins may be *defaced* by punching, cutting, clipping, sweating, or abrasion. The last process is always going on while a coin is in circulation, (*see Abrasion of Coin*) and so long as a coin is not reduced beyond a prescribed limit, it is a legal tender. But if a sovereign be punched, or cut, or clipped, it ceases to be a legal tender, and will only pass for its value as bullion. In the Bank of England, light coins are only partly cut through, and this is sufficient to ensure their passage to the melting-pot.

Deferred Annuities. Annuities the enjoyment of which is deferred, sometimes for several years, at others, but a few months. When once the annuity has commenced to run, it may be *perpetual*, or may terminate on the occurrence of some event, as for example, the death of the annuitant. The present value of a Deferred Annuity depends partly on the length of time that must elapse before payment commences, and partly on the contingency of its ever having to be paid at all; as happens when the proposed annuitant dies before the first payment becomes due.

Deferred Bonds and Shares. Deferred Bonds are bonds issued by a Government or by a company, entitling the holder to a gradually increasing rate of interest, till the interest amount to a certain specified rate, when they are classed as, or are converted into *Active* Bonds.

Deferred Shares, are shares issued by a Trading Company, but not entitling the holder to a full share of the profits of the company, and sometimes to none at all, until the expiration of a specified time, or the occurrence of some event. Founders' Shares in joint stock companies are often of this kind, and do not bear interest or receive profits till the ordinary shares are in the enjoyment of a given annual return.

Delegation. Latin, *dēlēgo, dēlēgare,* to send to a place, to assign over a debt to be paid; whence *delegatio,* an assignment of a debt.

A letter or other instrument employed by bankers for the transfer of a debt or credit, with a view to economize the use of Bills of Exchange, Cheques, and other instruments which require a stamp. Letters of Credit are mostly simple Delegations, and thousands of claims are daily discharged, by a written order, requesting the required sum to be placed to the credit of the claimant, or that a certain account may be debited with the sum. The examples given at foot are familiar to all engaged in London business, and are fair illustrations of the different kinds of documents which have been known as Delegations from the time of the Romans. As the stamp duty is evaded by the use of these forms, they are much employed by merchants and bankers well-known to each other, and very frequently they pass from one department of the same house to another. But they are wanting in validity as negotiable instruments, partly from the absence of the stamp, and partly because of their vagueness. At the same time, this vagueness and non-negotiability, add to their value for that particular purpose on which they are employed; as they are useful only to that particular person or firm for whose service they are intended.

Delegation in Form of Letter of Credit.

To Messrs. Berg & Co., Berlin.

Please hold at the disposal of Mr. Brown the sum of Ten Thousand Marks, and debit the same as per advice.

John Whitaker.

London, Sept. 28, 1879.

Delegation in Form of Debit Note.

No. 2487.

The Continental Bank, Lombard Street,

Debit Foreign Coupon a/c the sum of Eighty-Three Pounds for sundry coupons left by B. B. and Co.

For the Company,

£83.

Robert Prince.

This form is very vague, and would be of no use to any one but the party who left the coupons. The signature is that of a junior clerk.

Delegation in Form of Credit Note.

To the Cashiers of the Bank of England.

Credit Messrs. Martin and Co.
on a/c of Messrs. Holz and Stein
£17 6*s*. 8*d*.

Dividend Pay Office, 30 Aug. 1878.

This form of Delegation is issued by a department of the Bank of England, and is addressed to the officers of another department of the same Bank.

Delegation in Form of a Remittance to a Foreign Country.

Londres, 17 Oct., 1870. In 1,000.

A vue payer par le present cheque a l'order de M., P., Q. & Co. ——— la somme do MILLE FRANCS a valoir sur les fonds portes au credit de notre compte avec ou sans avis de B. C. and Co.

To Messrs. N. M & Co., Bordeaux.

The term Delegation is also used in French in the sense of a Share Certificate. The following form is found on certain Suez Canal Shares assigned to the Egyptian Government.

Delegations de Coupons d'Actions de la Compagnie Univ. du Canal de Suez.

Ces Coupons au nombre de 8,883,100 *proviennent* de 176,602 Actions appartenant au Gouvernement Egyptien.

Delegation in French is used also in the sense of "proxy."

Delivery, For. When the price of Consols or other Stocks is quoted "for delivery" it usually means that such stock is to be paid for and delivered on the day when the bargain is struck, and that the settlement is not to be deferred to the fortnightly account. (*See For Account.*) The same expression is also used to distinguish a *bona fide* sale of stock, from a mere speculative sale, in which latter case, there is no intention to "deliver" the stock, but to take the profit or pay the loss when the settling day arrives.

Delivery Order. A written or printed document, entitling any person therein named, or the legal holder thereof, to the delivery of any goods, wares, or merchandize of the value of forty shillings, or upwards, lying in any dock, port, wharf, or warehouse; this document must be signed by the owner of the goods, or by some one on his behalf, upon the sale or transfer of the property named therein. The duty on a "delivery order" is paid by means of a penny stamp, which must be cancelled by the person who executes or issues it. Delivery orders, like dock warrants, are often deposited with bankers as security for money advanced thereon.

Demand. Latin, *mando, mandare,* to enjoin, to entrust. French, *demander,* to ask, to have need of.

The origin or cause of value. Human needs give rise to a *desire* for some commodity; if the person desiring that commodity has anything of equal value to give in exchange for it, and wishes to make the exchange, a "demand" for the commodity arises: if he have nothing to give in exchange for it, the mere desire does not amount to a "demand." Hence the meaning of "demand" is a desire in the mind of some one who has something he is anxious to give in exchange for the thing desired.

Demonetization. From the Latin *moneta,* coin, or money, and *de* with a privative force. French *demonetiser.*

By *Demonetization* is meant the removal of certain coins from the rank of legal tender to that of mere token money. Germany, Holland, and the United States have treated their silver coinage in this way within the last few years, and the action on the part of those States, is commonly thought to be one of the efficient causes of the much-talked of depreciation of silver; which has varied in price from 62*d.* to 49*d.* per ounce.

Demurrage. French, *demeurer,* to dwell, remain, stop; *demeure* (in law) signifies *delay; mettre en demeure,* to demand in due form of law.

The idea which lies at the base of all cases of *demurrage* is that of delay, stopping, or staying, but in the application of the term to business affairs, it has acquired rather divergent meanings.

Thus, *Demurrage* is the allowance of 1½*d.* per oz. made to the Bank of England in exchanging coins or notes for bullion. The metallic value of standard gold is £3 17*s.* 10½*d.* per oz. At the Bank of England £3 17*s.* 9*d.* is given for it without any delay. If it were taken to the mint there would be a delay of some days before it could be converted into coin. The difference of 1½*d.* per oz., by which this delay is avoided, is called *demurrage.*

Demurrage is also a payment made by anyone who charters a vessel, and afterwards causes it to be delayed in port after the proper time for leaving.

Denarius. From Latin, *deni,* ten; *denarius,* consisting of ten; hence, a coin consisting of ten units. (*See As.*)

A Roman silver coin, marked X. [10 assi or asses], value 8*d.*; it was lowered both in weight and value from time to time, and became at length in law Latin what we now call a penny, thus giving the origin of the *d* in our familiar £ s. d.

Denaro. Italian money of account, value of $\frac{1}{24}$ a penny. Also in Tuscany, 12 Denari=1 Soldo=⅝*d.*

Denier. A French copper coin, the twelfth part of a sou. The name was once well known in several European countries, but is now rapidly disappearing from all.

Deposits. Latin, *de,* and *pono,* I put or place; *depositum,* something put into one's charge.

A deposit in the widest acceptation of the term is anything placed in the custody of an individual or of a company either for the sake of safety, or as a security, or with the desire of obtaining interest on it. The term is more restricted in its use in commerce, and bears two or three technical interpretations.

(*a*) Deposits of money are sometimes received by commercial companies with a view to employ it in their business. Interest of varying amounts will be given on deposits of this kind, according as the deposit is subject to withdrawal at a week's, or month's, or six months' notice.

(*b*) Deposits of Bonds, Share Certificates, and other negotiable instruments, are often deposited, for the sake of safety, with a merchant, or banker, in exchange for which a "deposit receipt" is given. When deposits of this kind are made the depositor usually pays a commission, or some other form of remuneration for the trouble and expense of their custody.

(*c*) Similar documents are frequently placed in the hands of merchants and bankers as a security for loans made to the depositors. In these cases, the deposit is made at the time the loan is advanced, and withdrawn when the loan is repaid.

(*d*) But the most important of "Deposits" are those which technically bear this name among bankers; and they merit the more consideration from the fact, that the want of knowledge on this point often leads to egregiously fallacious deductions. When on one side of a banker's periodical balance sheet there appears the item—

Deposits £20,560,000.

the inference made by the uninitiated is that so much actual money has been deposited in the bank by its customers, and that the bank has this amount of money to lend. It will often happen that when deposits stand at the figure above quoted, the actual available cash would not amount to one-tenth that sum, and yet be amply sufficient to meet every probable demand; and the reason is this:—The business of a bank consists largely in the purchase of commercial bills with a view to profit. These bills, when bought, are paid for, not with money, but by an entry in the banker's books to the credit of the customer who sells the bills. It is this "entry to the credit of the customer," or more shortly this "CREDIT" that is technically called a *Deposit*, and from the nature of the case it is at once seen, that the number of deposits shows very fairly the *amount of business* done by the bank, but is no indication whatever of the money actually in hand. Of course, some of the Credits in a banker's books are given in exchange for Cash as well as for Bills. Nevertheless, it is to these Credits the term "Deposits" is applied, and not to the cash itself.

(*e*) There is an important distinction to be made between what a customer places in his bank to his Current Account, and what he places there on Deposit, although it is common for people to call, in a vague unmeaning way, everything a "deposit" which is carried to a bank. What a customer takes to a bank and places to the credit of his Current Account is to all intents and purposes sold to the banker in exchange for credit, and the customer loses all claim to it, all control over it. If the bank stopped payment, and went into liquidation, the customer could only recover a *pro rata* distribution of the assets, like an ordinary creditor in any other case of bankruptcy. But if he has placed bonds, or bills, or bullion at the bank on deposit, simply for safe keeping or as security for a loan, these deposits would be placed in a totally different category from those which went to his current account, and would form no part of the assets of the bank, nor could they be applied to its liquidation. The one is a *Venditum* or Sale, the other a *Depositum*, or Deposit.

Depositum. Latin, *depositum*, something committed or entrusted to the care of any one. French, *depôt*.

A term used in Roman law signifying that the commodity deposited was is due course to be returned *in specie; i.e.*, the thing itself was to be returned. Goods deposited in wharfs, docks, and warehouses are of this nature, and are thus distinguished from *money, notes, and bills*, which are of the nature of the thing called by the Romans *Mutuum*, which became the absolute property of the person holding them, and for which he paid, or gave in return property of equal value. (*See Mutuum.*)

Deposit Warrant. An acknowledgement, receipt, or certificate showing that certain commodities have been deposited in a certain place for safe keeping, as security for a loan, or some other defined purpose. They are of two kinds:—

(1) *Special Deposit Warrant*, such as bills of lading, pawn tickets, dock warrants, certificates of deposits, which entitle the holder to claim certain specific goods, and not merely others of equal value in exchange for them. Documents of this kind unless fraudulently issued, are among the best of securities, as they are always based on articles of value, and cannot be issued in excess of the goods actually deposited.

(2) *General Deposit Warrant*. A warrant of this kind does not require that certain specific goods shall be delivered up in exchange for it. Still less when the deposit consists of money is it expected that any specific coins shall be delivered. Hence contracts, promissory notes, bills, &c., may be paid by any coins which constitute a legal tender; and warrants for the delivery of coal, corn, pig iron, are legally met by the delivery of these commodities of the required quality and value, and may be the same as those actually deposited or not. If, however, there be any clause in a contract or warrant which states that certain articles named therein shall be delivered and none other, the warrant becomes Special, and is no longer General, even though the deposit consist of coins, as may very well happen in the case of a collection of coins, illustrating the monetary systems of the world, or the coinage of some particular portion of English history. From this it will be seen that the distinction between a General and a Special Warrant is very important, and

the non-observance of that distinction may possibly lead to unpleasant consequences.

Depreciation. Latin, *de*, down; *pretium*, value, or price; *depretio, depretiare*, to value at a low rate, to despise.

This term is often confounded with *Debasement*, especially when used with reference to the coinage. But *debasement* is the wilful act of a dishonest Government, or of dishonest persons; while *depreciation* whether of coin, bullion, or commodities is usually altogether beyond human control. As the price, or value, of a thing is the ratio in which that thing exchanges for some other thing, it is obvious that if any one commodity becomes unusually abundant in the market, the ratio in which it exchanges with all other commodities is altered, and the same may be said if the supply be abnormally scant. When, in the course of these fluctuations, the quantity of any commodity given in exchange is greater than usual, the value of that commodity is said to be depreciated.

Depreciation in commerce is mostly understood to have reference to the diminished value of coins, of bullion, or of a paper currency. The most notable case of *depreciation* in modern times is that of silver coin and bullion. Silver, which a few years ago was worth, when measured in gold, about sixty pence per ounce, is now only worth fifty pence; this diminution in value has arisen from the large quantity thrown on the market through the disuse of it as a legal tender in Germany and one or two other States, while large supplies came over from America, for which there was no corresponding demand.

Paper Money is liable to still greater fluctuations in value, owing to the facility with which it can be manufactured, and made by law a legal tender.

The different forms of Bank Notes and State Notes illustrate very clearly the nature of *Depreciation*, varying as they do from perfect security to almost utter worthlessness.

I. Bank Notes would be considered *perfectly safe* from depreciation if issued only against an equivalent amount of Bullion held in reserve by the issuer. No banks issue notes of this kind.

II. Bank Notes are considered *practically safe* when issued partly against bullion held by the issuer, and partly against Government or other undoubted securities. Bank of England Notes are chiefly of this kind, and they pass from hand to hand as readily as hard cash, that is, they are not *depreciated*.

III. Bank Notes or State Notes are *depreciated* in value when issued against a small reserve of bullion, but resting on the credit of the country issuing them, and the good faith of the Government. Austrian paper florins, and Russian paper roubles are of this kind, and in a more marked degree the Turkish caimès lately issued in such enormous quantities, to meet the expenses of the Russo-Turkish war.

IV. State Notes issued against little or no bullion reserve, and under the guarantee of an unstable Government, French *Assignats* of a former day, and the *Confederate Notes* of more recent times are examples of depreciation amounting almost to worthlessness.

Dime. A silver coin current in the United States, value 10 cents, or $\frac{1}{10}$ of a dollar; weighs 38·4 grains; fineness ·900; value, nearly $4\frac{3}{4}d.$ (4·7353*d.*).

Dinar. The unit of value and of account in Servia. It consists of 5 grammes of gold $\frac{9}{10}$ fine, and is therefore identical in value with the French franc. It is divided into 100 paras.

Dinero. The tenth part of the Peruvian sol, represented by a silver coin worth 4.7578*d.* ($4\frac{3}{4}d.$ English). It consists of $2\frac{1}{2}$ grammes of silver ·900 fine.

Discount. A deduction made in the payment of a bill or settlement of an account. In the discounting of bills (the method in which bankers' advances are usually made), the profits are obviously greater than when interest at the same rate is charged; inasmuch as interest is paid at the expiration of the time for which money is advanced, whereas the discount is subtracted at the beginning of the term. Thus, if £100 be lent out at 5 per cent. interest the lender will receive at the end of the year £105—that is, £5 for the use of £100. But if the borrower accept a bill for £100, and the banker *discounts* it at 5 per cent, the banker will give £95 only, and will acquire a two-fold advantage, (1) he will get £5 for the use of £95 instead of £100 as in the former case, and (2) he will have the £5 to trade with for a whole year; this at 5 per cent. is equivalent to adding another 5 shillings to the interest.

In discounting foreign Bills of Exchange the course adopted is somewhat different from that in use for Inland Bills. Instead of making a deduction from the amount given for a discounted bill, it is the usual practice to give a different rate of exchange. To take a simple case, suppose it is desired to discount a three months bill in Paris at the rate of 4 per cent. per annum. Let the current rate of exchange for three months bills be F.25·45, the purchaser of the bill will then receive F.25·45 centimes for every pound at the end of 3 months. If he wishes to discount the bill, at the rate of 4 per cent per annum, and to obtain cash for it immediately, he will sell it at the rate of F.25·20 centimes to the pound, that is, he will give up 25 centimes in each 25 francs (roughly), which is 1 per cent. for the three months or 4 per cent. per annum, and this represents the discount at which he sells the bill.

To *discount* news or intelligence, a cant phrase much used in City circles, is to anticipate or expect such intelligence, and then act as though it had already arrived. The common result of discounting news is, to find that when it actually arrives, the markets take a turn the very opposite of what might be expected to follow as a consequence of such news.

Discount, To To discount a bill or note is to buy from the holder of it the right to receive the money due upon it.

Dishonour. *See Notice of Dishonour.*

Dividend. Latin, *dividendum,* something to be divided.

The sum periodically payable as *interest* on loans, debentures, &c. or that periodically distributed as *profit* on the capital of a railway or other company. The sum to be divided is broken up into as many portions as there are bondholders or shareholders to claim them, and the fractional part falling to each holder, bears the same proportion to the whole dividend as the amount of stock or shares he holds, bears to the whole capital from which the dividend is derived. These fractional parts therefore are more properly called "quotients," but the term is never used in this connection. Bondholders are never said to receive their quotients of the dividend or profit due to them in respect of their holdings, though this would be the correct term to use, but they are always said, though incorrectly, to receive their "*dividends*," and the process of paying them is called, in banks and other offices, the "payment of dividends." This inaccurate mode of expression has obtained such wide currency, that no mistakes are likely to arise from its use, so that it is not likely, even were it desirable, that the practice should be interfered with.

Dobbeltdaler.—The silver double daler of Denmark, value 192 skilling, or 4*s.* 4½*d.* sterling.

Doblon or Doubloon. Literally a "double one" referring to the monetary unit of value, and more particularly in Spain to the *double-pistole*. The name is now used in several of the Spanish and Portuguese colonies without reference to its meaning, and is applied to coins of very different values, of which the following are the most important for the purpose of comparison in working the exchanges.

(*a.*) The *Isabella doubloon* (Doblon d'Isabel) still circulating in Spain (value 100 reals or 5 dollars) weighs 8·3865 grammes of gold, ·900 fine, worth £1 0*s.* 7½*d.* sterling (247·839*d.*) Several doubloons have been used in Spain at different times, varying greatly in value, but the one above described has taken their place in the currency, and the old ones pass at a valuation.

(*b.*) The *Gold Doblon of Chili* weighing 7·626 grammes, ·900 fine, value 5 Chilian dollars, or 18*s.* 8·95*d.*

(*c.*) The *Doblon of Mexico* (the Gold Onza) value 16 dollars, weighs 27·067 grammes or 417·7 Troy grains, ·875 fine, worth £3 4*s.* 8*d.* sterling.

(*a.*) The *Doubloon of Bolivia* is the same in weight and fineness as that of Chili, as fixed by the monetary laws of January, 1851, and October, 1870.

Dobrao or Dobra. A Portuguese gold coin valued at 12,800 reis, or £2 16*s.* 10*d.* sterling. It is no longer current, but passes at a valuation.

Dock Warrant. A Dock Warrant is a kind of receipt given by the owner of a Dock in return for goods deposited with him. It passes freely from hand to hand like a Bill of Exchange, but differs from it precisely in the same particulars as does a Bill of Lading. (*See*

Bill of Lading.) They are often deposited with bankers as security for money advanced by way of loan.

Doit. (*a.*) A Hindostan copper coin, 120 to a rupee.

(*b.*) A Dutch coin (called also *Duit*), value 160th part of a guilder, about ½ of a farthing, English. Hence the provincial expression of contempt "Not worth a *doit*."

Dollar. The word *dollar* is a corruption of the German *thaler*, low German, *dahler;* Danish, *daler;* and the Italian, *tallero.* All these forms were derived from *Joachim's-thal,* a town in Bohemia where the Count of Schlick, in 1518, coined some excellent pieces in silver, one ounce in weight. From the name of the town came the regular adjective *Joachim's-thaler,* which was applied to the above-named coins, as well as that of Schlicken-thaler. Hence *Joachim's-thaler pieces* first was contracted into *Joachim's-thalers,* and this again into *thalers.* The subsequent modifications were easy and obvious.

The dollar is a favourite coin, and under different names is found in almost every part of the globe. In many cases where the name is different (as in *piastre, peso, sol*), the value is nearly the same, while in others where the name is the same, the value is widely different (as the dollar of the United States, 4*s.* 2¼*d.*, and the dollar of Buenos Ayres, 2*s.* 1*d.* The following is a list of the principal dollars in circulation, with the data requisite for a comparison of values.

(*a.*) The new *Gold dollar of the United States,* first struck in 1870, weighs 25·8 grains, ·900 fine, and is worth 4*s.* 1·316*d.* sterling. It is divided into dimes, cents., and mils. The gold pieces of 3 dollars and 2½ dollars (the Quarter Eagle) are of the same fineness, and are proportional in weight.

The *Silver dollar of the United States* (1870) weighs 412·5 grains, or 26.7295 grammes, ·900 fine. Taking the value of fine gold to that of fine silver as 15½ to 1, the value of the silver dollar is rather greater than that of gold, namely 50·868*d.* At 16 to 1 it is almost exactly equal to the gold dollar.

By the Coinage Act of the United States Congress of 1873, gold was made the standard of monetary value, and the gold dollar the legal unit—all silver coins being thus reduced to the condition of token money. (*See Trade Dollar.*)

(*b.*) The Silver dollar is the unit of value in Mexico. It consists of silver ·900 fine, and is well known in all those parts of the world which trade with Europe and America. It weighs 27·067 grammes, or 417·7 grains troy, and is worth 4*s.* 3½*d.* sterling. The coinage of Mexico is somewhat rough and irregular: some silver dollars contain gold in sufficient quantities to pay for extraction: others are rather superior in fineness to the legal standard, but generally they bear a good name, and pass almost everywhere at their full nominal value.

(*c.*) The unit of value in Gibraltar, worth 4*s.* 2*d.* sterling, and is sometimes divided into 12 reals, and sometimes into 100 cents. The revenues of the garrison are kept in sterling.

(*d.*) The old unit of value in the Ionian Islands before the introduction of the French system into Greece in 1872. It was divided into 100 oboli, and was worth in English 4*s*. 2*d*.

(*e*.) The unit of value in Canada, represented by paper only, Canada having no coinage of its own, and fixed at a par value of 4*s*. 2*d*. English.

(*f*.) The Spanish dollar, now called also the piastre, is one-fifth of the Gold doblon d'Isabel, giving for the value of the Spanish dollar in gold, 49·478*d*. sterling.

The Silver dollar, or Duro, weighs 25·960 grammes, ·900 fine, and is worth 49·403*d*. sterling.

The dollar or piastre is used in the quotation of the foreign exchanges, but accounts are kept in pesetas, each peseta being equal to the franc.

1 dollar = 2 escudos = 5 pesetas.

(*g*.) The dollar of Central America (Guatemala, San Salvado, Honduras, Nicaragua, and Costa Rica), is represented by the French five-franc piece, and is therefore worth 47·580*d*.

(*h*.) The dollar or thaler of Hamburg is a silver coin valued at $2\frac{1}{2}$ marks courant or 35·32*d*. sterling. (*See Thaler of Hamburg*.)

(*i*.) The Specie dollar of Norway or Species daler, consists of 28·893 grammes of silver, ·875 fine, and is worth nearly 4*s*. $5\frac{1}{2}$*d*. sterling (53·46*d*.).

(*k*.) The Rix dollar of Sweden, or Rigsdaler weighs 8·502 grammes of silver, ·750 fine, worth 13·483*d*. sterling.

(*l*.) The Rix dollar of Denmark, or Rigdaler weighs 14·447 grms. of silver, ·875 fine, and is worth 26·730*d*. sterling.

(*m*.) The dollar of Peru is now called the sol. (*See Sol*.)

(*n*.) The dollar of Chili is now called the peso. (*See Peso*.)

(*o*.) The new dollar of Uruguay is now called the patacon. (*See Patacon*.)

(*p*.) The dollar of Bolivia when of the full legal weight and fineness, is worth 4*s*. 2*d*. English. But the coinage of Bolivia has been so debased, that taking metal for metal, it is scarcely worth 3*s*. 1*d*.

(*q*.) The dollar of New Granada is identical in weight and fineness with the French five-franc piece, and is called the peso. (*See Peso*.)

(*r*.) The dollar of the Argentine Republic is now called the patacon, and is represented by *paper only*; and therefore furnishes no data available for estimating the rate of exchange.

(*s*.) The dollar of Arabia, the Mocha dollar, or piastre, is valued at 3*s*. 5*d*. Since 100 Spanish piastres exchange for $121\frac{1}{3}$ Arabian piastres, the exact value in exchange is 1 piastre = 40.82*d*. It is divided into 80 caveers or cavears.

There are several other countries in Asia, Africa, and America besides those above named, where the principal unit of account is the dollar, but it is not represented by any coinage of their own. The best coins of other States circulate at a valuation, and the Mexican dollar especially is very extensively used.

The sign $ now so generally used to signify a dollar is commonly supposed to date from the time of the celebrated Pillar dollar of

Spain. This dollar was known as the Piece of Eight (meaning eight reals), and the curved portion of the sign is a rude representation of the figure 8. Tho two vertical strokes are thought to be emblematical of the Pillars of Hercules which were stamped on the coin itself. (*See Pillar Dollar.*)

The dollar being decimally divided, the ordinary decimal notation is sufficient theoretically for all requirements. In practice, however, it is found convenient in the United States to use the following modifications of it:

$\$75.22\frac{1}{2}$ cents.

$\$75.\frac{22\frac{1}{2}}{100}$

$\$75.\underline{22\frac{1}{2}}$

$75.22.5

all of which mean precisely the same amount.

Domiciled. From *domus*, a house.

Made payable at some specified house. Thus all the Brazilian Loans are said to be domiciled at Messrs. N. M. Rothschild & Sons; the Russian 1850 Loan at Messrs. Baring Bros.; partly because they were issued respectively by those houses, and partly because the half-yearly interest coupon is also payable there. The phrase is also used in reference to bills payable in a given country, as "bills domiciled in France," "bills domiciled in Germany, &c. &c.

Doppia. A Papal gold coin, value 13*s.*; called also the pistole. Now superseded.

Dore. From the French *d'or*, of gold; whence the verb, *dorer*, to gild, and the participle, *doré*, gilt or golden; all from the Latin *de-aurare*, which, according to Littré, signifies to spread over with gold.

Doré silver is silver mixed with gold in sufficient quantity to make it worth *parting* or refining. One part of gold in a thousand of the mixed metal is sufficient to pay the expense of the process, and to leave a profit.

Double Standard. In Economics, the phrase "Double Standard" is used to signify a "Double Standard of Monetary Value." It implies the existence of what is known as the "Gold Standard" on the one hand, and the "Silver Standard" on the other. Wherever the Double Standard *in its integrity* is in use, a creditor is bound to accept payment of any sum, in coins of either of the metals, gold or silver, which the debtor may choose to tender. If gold is scarce and dear, while silver is plentiful and cheap, the debtor will pay in silver, and for the time being *Silver* becomes the Standard of Value; if silver is scarce and gold plentiful, Gold will be made the medium of payment, and, for the time being, the Standard of Value. This by Gresham's Law of the Coinage (*which see*) is inevitable. Hence it is at once evident that the term "Double Standard" is a misnomer. It may be called an "Alternative Standard," but at any given time, there is but one Standard of value, and the metal adopted at the moment as the Standard, will always be the cheapest, while the other is bought and sold like any other commodity or will be used to make payments abroad, thus draining the country of that particular metal.

The phrase above used, "in its integrity" has been inserted advisedly. For, at the present time, there is scarcely a single country in which the Double Standard *in its integrity* is retained. In France, Italy, and other countries included in the Monetary Convention, and which profess to have adopted the "Double Standard," a check has been given to payments in Silver by the refusal on the part of the respective Governments to coin more than a given quantity of silver Five-franc pieces (the only coins which were of full metallic value before the recent depreciation of silver, and which are now considerably less in value than the gold Five-franc piece), as it was found that gold was rapidly leaving those countries for payments abroad, and silver was accumulating to an inconvenient degree. By this restriction of the silver coinage, the Double Standard is virtually suspended, since the choice of the legal tender is no longer practicable. Payments may, it is true, be still made in silver bars, but they will only be valued at the price of silver current for the day, and not at the fixed rate of 15½ parts of *fine* silver for one part of *fine* gold.

Drachma. The Latinised form of the Greek δραχμη, *drachmé*, a coin divided into six obols. Originally it was written δραγμα, *dragma*, which signified a handful, and appears to have referred to the six obols (spikes, bars, or wedges of metal) which made a "handful."

The Drachma is the unit of value and the unit of account in Greece. In virtue of the Latin Monetary Convention of November, 1878, and the Greek Monetary Law of April 1867, the coinage of Greece was assimilated to that of France, the drachma having the same weight and fineness as those of the franc. It is divided into 100 *lepta*, the lepton consequently being the equivalent of the centime. The multiples of the drachma, whether in gold or silver, are all now struck in conformity with the requirements of the Latin Monetary Convention, so that the coinage of Greece is described by substituting *drachma* for *franc*, and *lepton* for centime in that of France and Belgium. (*See Franc.*)

Draft.—A written order for the payment of a sum of money addressed to some person who holds money in trust, or who acts in the capacity of agent or servant of the drawer. Documents of this kind often pass between one department of a bank or mercantile house, to some other department, and are distinguished from Bills of Exchange and Cheques, in not being drawn upon a debtor.

"It is essential to the character of a *bill*, that it should be addressed to a person who owes the money as a *debtor*. If the order be addressed to a person who merely *holds* the money as a *Depositum*, as a *Baillee*, or *Trustee*, or *Agent*, or *Servant* of the writer, it is not a Bill, but a *Draft*; and there are most important economic distinctions between the two instruments."—*McLeod.*

Drain of Bullion.—By a *Drain of Bullion* is meant the flowing away of gold and silver in coins or in bars, to such an extent, as to leave insufficient in the country to meet the requirements of trade. This is a matter of the utmost importance to a commercial people, and the right understanding of the cause or causes of a "drain" is essential on the part of those whose business it is to remedy the evils arising from a deficiency of the precious metals.

The circumstances which lead to the transfer of bullion from one country to another are numerous; but there are three which exert a paramount influence, and which, perhaps, may be so stated as to include all others; these are:—

I. *The Relative Indebtedness of the Country to others with which it Trades.*—When imports greatly exceed exports, the importing country becomes indebted to other countries; the difference must be partly paid in coin or bullion, and if this goes on for any length of time, the drain of bullion will be so great as to cause a serious deficiency of bullion in the country. This evil tends to cure itself in course of time (though, perhaps, not till after serious disturbances to trade have resulted), because the difficulty of selling the imported goods would induce merchants to cease buying. But this cause of "a drain" is frequently mixed up with some other cause or causes, and the phenomenon is often so complicated that a merchant finds it hard to say to what the monetary disturbance is due.

II. *A Depreciated Paper Currency.*—This evil has not been felt in England for many years. But in 1810, when a large number of inconvertible bank notes were in circulation, they became so depreciated that £4 10*s.* had to be paid for an ounce of standard gold, whose metallic value was £3 17*s.* 10½*d.* Again, in 1813, the price of gold bullion, when paid in paper, was £5 10*s.* per ounce. Since 1823, bank notes have always been convertible into gold on presentation at the Bank of England, and, therefore, from that time, have never been depreciated. When paper money is thus depreciated, it is a legal tender only in that country where it is issued. All payments abroad must be made in gold or silver. Hence the inevitable "drain."

In Turkey during the last few years, a drain of bullion has been experienced in its most exaggerated form. For 100 Turkish silver piastres, as much as 620 paper piastres have been demanded. The paper currency of Turkey has been therefore almost worthless, and the drain of the precious metals has been so absolute that a coin is scarcely to be found in circulation among the mass of the lower and middle classes—with what result to Turkey herself, is only too well known. Russia, Austria, Italy, the United States, and many other countries, have suffered in the same way, though in a minor degree, but all severely enough to make them long for a return to specie payments, and a more healthy condition of the national finance.

III. *A Lower Rate of Interest for Money than prevails in Neighbouring Countries.*—Whenever the rate of interest paid for the loan of money, or the rate at which bills are discounted in two different countries differs considerably, it becomes profitable to send bullion to that country where the interest (or discount) is highest. The ordinary competition between the dealers then causes it to flow from that country where the rate is low, towards that where it is high. This process went on in London after the panic of 1866, to such an extent, that the Bank rate of discount was pushed up till it reached 10 per cent., and even then the drain was not checked. But the paper currency of England was not *depreciated;* owing to the simultaneous withdrawal of notes with the drain of bullion, paper money was rather *appreciated*, and the suspension of the Act of 1844 enabled the bank to issue a large supply of paper money, and then the demand for gold abated.

The actual difference between the Rate of Interest (or Discount) in two countries, which suffices to set bullion flowing from one to the other, depends partly on the distance and partly on the means of transmitting metals from one country to the other. By a detailed calculation, Mr. Goschen, in his "Theory of Foreign Exchanges" shows that a difference of 2 per cent. must exist before it becomes profitable to send gold from Paris to London, or *vice versâ.* Between London and Berlin rather more. Hence we might expect to find that the bank rate prevailing in these great monetary centres would rarely differ by much more than 2 per cent., and generally by considerably less. And this we find actually to be the case. In a carefully constructed table exhibited at the *London Statistical Society*, April 1, 1879, in the course of a Paper read by Mr. Stephen Bourne, it is shown that the rates prevailing in France and Germany gave a yearly average during thirty years as follows:—

Table Showing the Yearly average Bank Rates of Dividend in England, France, and Germany, from 1849-78.

Year.	England.	France.	Germany.
	Bank Rate.	Bank Rate.	Bank Rate.
	Per cent.	Per cent.	Per cent.
1849 . . .	2·93	4·00	4·05
'50 . . .	2·50	4·00	4·00
'51 . . .	3·00	4·00	4·00
'52 . . .	2·15	3·17	4·00
'53 . . .	3·69	3·23	4·25
'54 . . .	5·11	4·33	4·35
'55 . . .	4·89	4·44	4·10
'56 . . .	6·06	5·54	4·95
'57 . . .	6·67	6·16	5·75
'58 . . .	3·23	3·69	4·50
'59 . . .	2·73	3·46	4·20
'60 . . .	4·18	3·64	4·00
'61 . . .	5·27	5·53	4·00
'62 . . .	2·53	3·77	4·00
'63 . . .	4·41	4·63	4·10
'64 . . .	7·40	6·50	5·30

Rates of Dividend in England, France and Germany—continued.

Year.	England.	France.	Germany.
	Bank Rate.	Bank Rate.	Bank Rate.
	Per cent.	Per cent.	Per cent.
1865 . . .	4·77	3·72	4·95
'66 . . .	6·95	3·67	6·20
'67 . . .	2·54	2·71	4·00
'68 . . .	2·10	2·50	4·00
'69 . . .	3·20	2·50	4·10
'70 . . .	3·10	3·99	4·85
'71 . . .	2·89	5·71	4·15
'72 . . .	4·10	5·16	4·30
'73 . . .	4·79	5·15	5·05
'74 . . .	3·69	4·29	4·35
'75 . . .	3·23	4·00	4·70
'76 . . .	2·60	3·40	4·15
'77 . . .	2·90	2·25	4·40
'78 . . .	3·75	2·25	—

This table is very instructive. A glance down the three columns will show that with the exception of the years 1864 and 1866, the average difference of the Rates rarely amounted to 2 per cent.; which proves, not that the difference *never* amounted to so much, for scarcely a year passes but several transits of bullion take place, but that when the "Specie Point" was exceeded, these transits of bullion immediately brought down the higher rate, and thus restored the equilibrium.

The above principles being established, the inferences are obvious. (1) If the Board of Trade Returns, glutted markets, or depressed prices indicate that importations have been carried to excess, and the indebtedness of the country unduly increased, merchants must cease to buy. (2) If a Paper Currency has been so largely introduced into a country as to raise gold and silver to a high premium, the only thing to be done is to withdraw it quickly as the exigencies of the occasion will admit, just as France and the United States have done, and as Italy is rapidly doing. (3) If the Bank Rate is too low, and the general interest for money is unremunerative, the Rate must be raised. This is now so well recognized that in London and Paris, at least, gold and silver are always speedily brought back into those centres by a prompt rise in the minimum rate of discount.

Drawee. The party on whom a bill, draft, or cheque is *drawn*. In the ordinary course, he subsequently becomes the acceptor, or payer, or both.

Drawing. French, *tirage*, from *tirer*, to draw; German, *Ziehung*, *ziehen*, to draw.

A process made use of to determine what bonds or shares shall be paid off or amortized from time to time, by the application of the Sinking Fund attached to public loans. A *drawing* is in every respect a lottery, but, taking all things into account, it is generally felt to be the fairest and most satisfactory way of making a distribution of the moneys arising from the operation of a Sinking Fund, notwithstanding the objection entertained against lotteries by the English people. If Governments could always be trusted, it would be far better to apply a Sinking Fund by the purchase of bonds and Shares on the market, and then cancelling them in the presence of duly authorised officers. But Governments are not always honest, and some have been known to take measures to bring their bonds into disrepute, in order that they might buy them on the market at a cheap rate.

With a view to secure perfect integrity in the conduct of these drawings, they are usually made in the presence of the most highly responsible parties, such as the contractors for the loan, the resident minister of the borrowing Government, and a notary public.

Ducat. From the Latin, *ducatus*, a leader, commander. This coin derives its name from the circumstance that it was first issued in a *dukedom*, under the authority of a *duke*. To what duke the honour is due is not very clear. By some it is ascribed to Longinus, Duke of Ravenna, who lived in the sixth century, but on evidence by no means conclusive. A more probable origin is found in the excellent coin struck by St. Roger II. of Apulia in 1140, which bore for its device the figure of Christ, and for its legend, "SIT TIBI CHRISTE DATUS, QUEM TU REGIS, ISTE DUCATUS," (Be it given to thee, O Christ, whom thou rulest, the same to be LEADER.)

The ducat is no longer the monetary unit in any country. It was formerly a favourite coin with the Dutch, and owing to the excellence of the pieces struck, they were sought for and imitated by several other countries, and especially Russia. The exportation of these coins from Holland to Russia was at one time an important trade. Ducats now everywhere circulate at a valuation, where they circulate at all, or are bought and sold simply as bullion. The following are some of the best known:—

(*a*.) The gold ducat of Holland, weighing 3·494 grammes, ·983 fine, value 9*s*. 4½*d*.; more accurately 112·55534*d*.

(*b*.) The gold ducat of Russia is precisely the same in weight, fineness, and value with the Dutch ducat.

(*c*.) The gold ducat of Austria-Hungary, weighing 3·4904 grammes, ·986 fine, value 9*s*. 4¾*d*. The old Austrian Four-ducat piece is now little known.

(*d*.) The gold ducat of Sweden, weighing 3.486 grammes, ·976⅔ fine, value 9*s*. 3½*d*. sterling.

(*e*.) The gold ducat of Hamburg (a few of which remain in circulation) is valued at 5 marks banco. Taking the mark banco at 1·4846 shillings, the ducat would be worth 7*s*. 5*d*. sterling.

(*f.*) The silver ducat of Sicily was formerly the unit of value. It is now superseded by the Italian system. Its weight, when new, was 22.943 grammes, ·833 fine, and was worth 3*s.* 4½*d.* sterling.

Ducatone. A Flemish silver coin—the crown—value 5*s.* 3*d.* Also in Parma, called the scudo, value 4*s.* 3*d.*

Ducatoon. An old silver coin, worth about 5*s.* 3¾*d.* sterling, sometimes found still circulating in the Netherlands.

E.

E occurs in the following abbreviations :—

E.E. Errors excepted.
E. & O.E. Errors and omissions excepted.
Ex. d. or x/d. Exdividend.
Ex. cp. or xcp. Excoupon.

Eagle. A United States gold coin of 10 dollars; weight, 16·718 grammes or 258 grains; fineness, ·900; sterling value, £2 1*s.* 1*d.* In 1870, coins of the same fineness, and of proportional weight, were struck, called the *double eagle*, the *half eagle*, and the *quarter eagle.*

Economics. From the Greek, οικος, *oikos*, a house; νομος, *nomos*, a law. οικος also signified household property, goods, and was used in Attic law to denote property of every kind. This term is derived in a very indirect manner. Originally the word οικονομια, *oikonomia*, or œconomy, signified the management of a household. Thus:

"The Household Book of Henry Algernon, Earl of Northumberland (1497 to 1527) contains a complete system of antient *œconomies.*"—*Manners and Expenses of Antient Times.* 1770.

Afterwards it came to mean *administration*, or management generally: then again, after passing through the Latin form, it was applied to the management of the internal affairs of any corporation, or State. The modern notion conveyed by the word in the sense of frugality appears to have been derived from the custom of regarding wastefulness and extravagance as resulting from the want of *oikonomia ;* and conversely the practice of utilising everything so as to prevent waste was attributed to the prevalence of *oikonomia*, or good administration.

Hence the word was so habitually associated with saving and frugal habits that it was at length regarded as synonymous with frugality and prudence. The modification of this term as the name of a science is simply in conformity with established practice, so as to adapt it to scientific nomenclature, and harmonize with such terms as mechanics, mathematics, acoustics, statistics, &c.

The Science of Economics lies at the foundation of every sound system of Banking, and is, therefore, one of the most important objects of study to every community engaged in commercial pursuits. It may be defined as the Science which treats of exchangeable things, and of the laws which regulate their exchange. It is a branch of the wider subject known as Political Economy.

Political Economy treats of the laws which control the production, distribution, and consumption of wealth. There are many causes which assist in each of these processes. By the operation of these causes, production may be stimulated or retarded; distribution may be facilitated or embarrassed. Consumption may be increased or diminished; but of all the causes which contribute to these results, by far the most important is the quality of *Exchangeability*, which the various forms of wealth possess, and the facility with which *Exchanges* can be made. So important is this property of *Exchangeability*, that most writers of note, both ancient and modern, have regarded it as the one thing on which wealth depends. It is, therefore, not surprising that the doctrine and practice of *Exchanges* should have been elevated to the rank of a distinct science, and that the laws which regulate the *Exchange* of commodities should have been made the object of special study; for whatever tends to make the exchange of commodities easy, rapid, and safe, tends also to facilitate and encourage the production, distribution, and consumption of wealth.

The science of Pure Economics is, nevertheless, a comparatively modern study. It was, till quite recently, the custom to devote a chapter or two to the Exchanges in every work on Political Economy. But the enormous development of our Banking System, which is wholly concerned with the Exchanges, has rendered necessary a more profound and extensive study of the subject than was in former times ever dreamt of; so that, at the present moment, we have excellent works devoted exclusively to the Theory and Practise of Banking, or Economics, as well as to the more general study of Political Economy in its widest aspects. As examples of a work in each of these subjects, Mr. H. D. McLeod's "Elements of Banking," and Mr. J. S. Mill's "Elements of Political Economy," may be advantageously compared.

The "Elements of Banking" is a work on Economics, properly so called, and is so regarded by the Author himself. It will be seen that it is characterized by the sharpness of its definitions, by numerical exactness, and by making every part contribute to the main idea of the book, which is to determine the laws which control the Exchange of commodities, and to describe the machinery by which this Exchange is effected. In J. S. Mill's "Political Economy" the Exchanges are treated of also, as a most important cause, among *other causes*, which contribute to stimulate the production, distribution, and consumption of wealth. But these *other causes* occupy a larger proportion of the book than would be allowable in a work of pure Economics, and it contains, moreover, some collateral investigations; such as the Theory of Rent; the nature of Capital and Profit; the part played by natural agents, such as minerals, watercourses, climate, &c.; the degree of civilization enjoyed by a community, and other cognate matters. Broadly speaking, the Science of Economics stands in much the same relation to Political Economy, as does a treatise on Pure Mechanics to a work on Physical Science; the former is precise in definition, and exact in demonstration; the latter is more discursive and explanatory, and would introduce much collateral information by way of illustration. At the same time, it is always to be remembered that writers have often spoken of Economics and Political Economy as though they were the one and the same in object and scope, and until the process of differentiation has been carried further by experts in the science, this indefiniteness and confusion are unavoidable.

Mr. McLeod, in his "Economics for Beginners," page 19, makes the following pertinent remarks:—

"Seeing, then, that the term Political Economy was expressly designed by its originators to include the political relations of men, which are now excluded from the science, and that the term Economics clearly indicates that the science is restricted to Property, we shall henceforth use it exclusively in this work; and Economics may be defined to be the science which treats of the laws which governs the relations of Exchangeable Quantities."

Economic Quantities. A technical term for the different orders or kinds of wealth, as Money, Labour, Credit, and the various objects which fall under either of those heads or types. Thus—

Money is taken as a type of all the material things which constitute wealth; as money, properly so called, land, houses, animals, corn, fruit, timber, metals, &c.

Labour is the type of services of every kind, as those of the artisan, ploughman, lawyer, physician, actuary, preacher, schoolmaster, policeman, &c.

Credit, which is of itself merely a Right of Action (*see Right of Action*), is the type of rights of all sorts, as the right to annuities, dividends, rents, copyrights, patent rights, reversions, advowsons, &c.

All these things are wealth, because they are exchangeable quantities; in other words, because they can be bought and sold.

Embezzle, To. This word is supposed by some to be derived from the obsolete verb to *bezzle*, originally meaning to guzzle, to drink hard; then to waste in drinking and riot, or to make off with anything in a dishonest manner.

"It is your fault if you have *bezzled* it away."—BURROUGHS *on Hosea.*

This meaning of the word does not, however, lead to the meaning conveyed by the legal term *embezzle*, and there is more reason to suppose it was derived, though in a very circuitous manner, from the Latin, *imbecillus* or *imbecillis*, an adjective signifying "weak," from which was formed in later times the verb to *imbecile*, to weaken, to waste away, to subtract from. Passing from monkish Latin into French, *im* was changed into *em*, as in many other cases—*e.g.*, *imperium* in *empire*, and under sundry modifications of this nature, we find the word used to express a weakening, a wasting away, misappropriation, and the like.

The history of this word has puzzled etymologists. Johnson derived it from *imbecillus*, and Mr. Walter W. Skeat produces a number of quotations in support of this view. He says:—

"I take the account of the word to be simply this: (1) that *imbecile* was formerly used both as a substantive and a verb; (2) that it was often pronounced with the accent on the *e;* (3) that in course of time the accent on the *e* became permanent when the word was used as a verb, according to the common usage whereby we distinguish the substantive *tórment* from the verb *to tormént;* and (4) that the unlucky substitution of *em* for *im* at an early period, so utterly darkened the etymology that there was nothing whereon to rest the sense of the word, thus leaving it to float about as best it could."—*Notes and Queries.*

In a fifteenth-century poem often printed with Chaucer's works, occurs the following:—

"These wicked wretches, these hounds of hell,
As I have told playn here in this sentence,
Were not content my dere love thus to quell
But yet they must *embesile* his presence."
Lament of Mary Magdalen.

Here Mary laments that the soldiers have *embezzled* or taken away the body of her Lord.

In Palsgrave's "French Dictionary," *temp.* Henry VIII., we read:—"I concede, I *embesyll,* a thynge, I kepe a thing secret. I *embesell,* I hide or consoyle. Je *cele.* I *embesyll* a thynge, or put it out of the way. Je *substrays.* He that *embesylleth* a thing intendeth to steal it if he can convoye it clenly."

Bishop Taylor used the word in its most primitive form:—"Princes must . . . . be guardians of pupils and widows, not suffering their persons to be oppressed or their estates *imbécilled.*"—*Holy Living,* c. iii. s. 2.

"It is a sad calamity that the fear of death shall so *imbecill* man's courage and understanding."—*Holy Dying,* c. iii. s. 7.

In Sharp's "Sermons" the modern form appears. "Religion will not allow us to *embezzle* our money in drinking or gaming." Vol. I. Sermon I.

Dropping the first syllable from *embezzle,* we have *bezzle,* just as we have *sport* from *disport, spend* from *expend.* If this explanation be the correct one, the common derivation of the word from *bezzle* would seem to be a complete inversion of the truth.

Embezzlement is a crime distinguished from *larceny,* properly so called, as being committed in respect of property which is not, at the time, in the actual or legal possession of the owner. As to this it is enacted, that if any clerk or servant, or any person employed for the purpose or in the capacity of a clerk or servant, shall, by virtue of such employment, receive or take into his possession any chattel, money, or valuable security for or in the name or on the account of his master, and shall fraudulently embezzle the same, or any part thereof,—every such offender shall be deemed to have *feloniously stolen* the same; and shall suffer the same punishment as last above particularized; and that if any money, or security for the payment of money, shall be entrusted to any *banker, merchant, broker, attorney,* or *other agent,* with any direction in writing to apply such money, or any part thereof, or the proceeds, or any part of the proceeds, of such security, for any purpose specified in such direction—and he shall, in violation of good faith, and contrary to the purpose so specified, in any wise convert to his own use or benefit, such money, security or proceeds, or any part thereof—every such offender shall be guilty of a *misdemeanour;* and he may be sentenced to penal servitude for a term not exceeding *fourteen* years, or less than *three* years, or to such other punishment, by fine or imprisonment, or both, as the court shall award. Again, if any chattel or valuable security, or any power of attorney for the sale or transfer of any share or interest in any public stock or fund of this country or any foreign State, or in any fund of any body corporate, company or society,—shall be entrusted to any *banker, merchant, broker, attorney*, or *other agent*, for safe custody, or for any special purpose, without any authority to sell, negotiate, transfer, pledge, or in any manner convert to his own use or benefit, such chattel or security, or the proceeds of the same, or any part thereof, or the share or interest in the stock or fund to which such power of attorney shall relate, or any part thereof;—every such offender shall incur the *same penalties* as are imposed in the case last before mentioned.

Endorsee. The party who acquires the right conveyed by any negotiable instrument in consequence of its being made over to him by *endorsement*. Where several endorsees appear on the back of a bill, the last is the one entitled to receive the money or right conveyed.

Endorsement. Latin, *in*, on; *dorsum*, the back; French, *endosser*, from *dos*, the back.

To *endorse* a bill, cheque, note, or other document, is to write one's name on the back of it. Hence endorsing a cheque, &c., is sometimes called "backing" it. The name may be accompanied by other words, or may stand alone, thus giving rise to two kinds of endorsement, viz:—

1. *Special.* An endorsement is called "Special," when it is made payable to the order of the person to whom it is transferred (the Transferee): thus—

Pay to the order of Glyn, Mills & Co.

Thos. Humphrys.

Sometimes the endorsement is rendered still more special by stating the date at which it is to be paid, and the house or firm who may be applied to for payment,—precautions taken to prevent fraud.

2. *General.* An endorsement is called "General," when the holder who wishes to transfer it simply writes his name or that of his firm, thus—

Glyn, Mills & Co.

When thus endorsed, a bill may be transferred from hand to hand without further endorsement, and is freely negotiable. (*See Bill.*)

As to the forms *Indorse* and *Endorse*, practice appears to be entirely controlled by the taste of the writer. In point of correctness, there is scarcely a choice to be made between them. The form "*Indorse*" is derived directly from the Latin. "*Endorse*," comes to us through the dialects of Southern Europe. It is merely a question of derivation.

Endorsements of bills, notes, and similar instruments, are sometimes otherwise classified, thus:—

1. *Full endorsement*, as--

Pay Messrs. Cheston & Co., or Order for value received.

THOMAS WILTON.

2. *Incomplete endorsement*, as—

Pay Messrs. Cheston & Co., or Order.

THOMAS WILTON.

3. *Blank endorsement*, as— THOMAS WILTON.

The practical effect of the first two kinds of endorsement is to limit the transfer of the instrument to the person or firm named thereon; the phrase "for value received" being regarded in law as a matter of no importance. But in the case of a blank endorsement, the instrument is made transferable by simple delivery to any person without further endorsement. If the Payees, Messrs. Cheston & Co., wish to transfer either of the above bills made payable to them or "their order" they must endorse it.

It is to be observed, however, that neither of the above endorsements take effect, or would be valid in law, unless they were followed by "delivery." The delivery may be effected by giving it into the hands of the endorsee, when it is called "Actual Delivery," or the endorsee may be notified that the endorser has endorsed the bill, while the endorser retains it in his own possession; this is called "Constructive Delivery."

Although the literal meaning of the word "endorsement" is writing on the back, it is not *essential* that the writing should be on the back.

By the endorsement of a bill, the endorser incurs the responsibility of a new drawer, and hence, if the drawee does not pay the bill when it matures, the endorser on receiving notice of dishonour must pay the sum due to the holder, together with the notarial charges incurred.

Endorsements are sometimes demanded in a careless and irregular manner, and grave responsibilities are thereby incurred. The object sought in demanding an endorsement, is to secure that an instrument shall be delivered by some person or firm who has a right to deliver it, and that the consideration given in exchange for such delivery, shall be given to the right party. Hence, an endorsement ought to be signed by a person or firm well known to the endorsee, and whose signature is distinctly recognized. But it is not an uncommon thing to find utterly unknown individuals asked to endorse "letters of allotment," "coupon tickets," and the like. Now if a dishonest person gets possession of such papers, and obtains for them scrip or cash by merely endorsing them with an unknown name, and with an unrecognized signature, no useful purpose is served, and the banker or merchant who hands over cash, or any other valuable consideration to a dishonest holder, may very properly be asked, whether he knows the signature, or the person who made it; or, whether he took any pains to ascertain that he was the rightful owner of the "letter" or "ticket;" and if he neither knew the person, nor recognized the signature, nor took any pains to satisfy himself that the claim made was *bonâ fide*, the settlement of the matter might involve some intricate points of law. It seems better in all cases where a name and address are demanded from strangers merely for the sake of information, as they do at the Bank of England when a note is presented for encashment, to say,—"Write your name upon it," and so avoid the use of the legal term, "endorse." Nevertheless, in the case of a cheque "to order," a banker is not bound to inquire into the genuineness of an endorsement.

Endorser. One who endorses a Bill or other negotiable instrument, and so makes over, or transfers, his claim, by writing his name at the back of such instrument.

Enfaced Paper. This name is given to the Bonds or Certificates of certain India Loans. They are so called because they are marked or "enfaced" on the top, bottom, and left margins, by a broad band impressed upon them from an enchased copper-plate, the general appearance of which band, resembles the familiar black and red stamp so well known to everyone who has had to unpack a bottle of medicine or box of pills protected by Her Majesty's Letters Patent.

All the loans quoted in the price lists under the name of "Enfaced Papers," though held and dealt in largely in this country, are, properly speaking *Internal* Indian loans. The terms in which they are described on the bonds, and the interest payable on them are all expressed in "Company's Rupees." The half-yearly interest is payable by council drafts on Calcutta. There are bonds in the market bearing interest at 4, $4\frac{1}{2}$, 5, and $5\frac{1}{2}$ per cent respectively. The following is copy of the contract on a piece of Enfaced Paper;—

"The Governor General of India in Council does hereby acknowledge to have received from *A. B. Lombardi & Co.* the sum of Company's Rupees TEN THOUSAND as a loan to the East India Company, and does hereby promise, for and on behalf of the said Company, to repay the said loan, by paying the said sum of Company's Rupees, TEN THOUSAND, to the said A. B. Lombardi & Co., their executors, or administrators, or their order, on demand, at the General Treasury of Fort William, after the expiration of three months' Notice of Payment, to be given by the Governor General of India in Council, in the Calcutta Gazette, and to pay the Interest accruing on the said sum of Company's Rupees TEN THOUSAND from the 1st February 1878 (seventy-eight) at the rate of four per cent per annum, by Half-Yearly Payments, at the General Treasury of Fort William, to the said A. B. Lombardi and Co., or administrators or their order, until the expiration of three months after such Notice of Payment as aforesaid, when the amount of interest due will be payable with the principal, and (such Notice being considered as equivalent to a tender of payment at the period appointed for the discharge of this Note) all further interest will cease."

When the name of the holder is inserted, as above, it must be *endorsed* by him, before he can transfer it.

Engross, To. French *gros*, large. Italian and Portuguese *grosso*. French *grossir*, to become great, to grow stout; also *grossoyer*, to write in a large hand, to *engross*; as distinguished from the *minute* or small hand in which the notes of a meeting were taken down, and thence called the *minutes* of a meeting.

"Le notaire garde la *minute* et en delivre la *grosse*." (The notary keeps the minutes, and delivers the engrossed copy.) P. MARIN.

All the above modern forms are supposed to be derived from the Latin, *crassus*, coarse, thick, large, dense.

The verb to engross has three different but allied meanings in commerce.

(1.) *To engross* signifies to write out in a large clear hand, copies of deeds, contracts, agreements, indentures, &c. The word is sometimes applied more particularly to certain initial words and phrases which are written in Old English text, or some other conspicuous form of letter.

(2.) *To engross* in ancient mercantile law was to buy up the whole of any specific kind of commodity on its way to market, with the object of creating a monopoly, and so enhancing its price. (*See Engrossers.*)

(3.) The word in the sense last described is often used metaphorically, thus—"This branch of our business *engrosses* (takes up, monopolizes), too large a portion of our time and capital to render it profitable." It is also introduced into colloquial speech to indicate that any one or any thing occupies an undue share of attention; as when we say of an obtrusive guest, that he *engrosses* all the attentions of the host; or of some favourite pursuit, that it engrosses too much of the time and energies of its devotee.

Engrossers or **Monopolists.** A term much used in ancient mercantile law. It was applied to those persons who foreseeing a probable rise in prices would buy up commodities, and hold them in hand with a view to augmented profits. Legislators in their blindness strove hard by means of penalties to suppress this class of persons, and it was not till more light was thrown on economical questions by Adam Smith and his successors, that the futility of these measures was seen. Still less was it seen that the service rendered by Engrossers was a very real and important one. (*See Forestall.*)

Envelope. From the Latin *involvere*, to wrap round, to enclose.

"I rede that our hoste shal beginne
For he is most *envoluped* in sin."
CHAUCER, *The Pardoner's Tale.*

This familiar word, which first became common on the introduction of the Penny Postage in 1840, was formerly pronounced in an affected and Frenchified way, but is now treated in commercial circles as a pure English word, and pronounced accordingly.

Equation of Payments. An arithmetical operation, the object of which is to determine the date at which a single payment should be made in lieu of several different payments due at various dates. The rule usually followed is: Multiply each payment by the time at which it falls due; divide the sum of the products by the sum of the payments, and the quotient is the time required. For example, suppose £75 due at the end of six months; £90 at the end of seven months; £120 at the end of ten months. At what time must the whole be paid in one sum, so that no loss may result to either party?

$$\begin{array}{rcl} 75 \times 6 &=& 450 \\ 90 \times 7 &=& 630 \\ 120 \times 10 &=& 1{,}200 \\ \hline 285 &&)\ 2{,}280\ (\ 8 \text{ months.} \\ && \quad 2{,}280 \end{array}$$

This rule is founded on the assumption that the interest on the sums due before the equated time, is equal to the interest on those falling due after the equated time, which is not strictly correct; since it is the *discount* and not the *interest* which ought to be reckoned on the latter sums. The calculation of these discounts, however, involves the use of algebraical formulæ and is too prolix for counting-house practice. Moreover, the difference in the results is so trifling, that the simple arithmetical process above described is almost invariably adopted. The following examples are further illustrations of the rule.

£27 10*s*. is due at the end of 1 day; £540 at the end of 35 days; £68 5*s*. at the end of 90 days; £75 5*s*. at the end of 111 days. After how many days should all the sums be paid together without loss to either debtor or creditor?

$$\begin{array}{rrcl} \pounds & s. && \\ 27 & 10 \times 1 &=& 27{\cdot}50 \\ 540 & 0 \times 35 &=& 18900 \\ 68 & 5 \times 90 &=& 6142{\cdot}50 \\ 75 & 5 \times 111 &=& 8352{\cdot}75 \\ \hline 711 & 0 &&)\ 33422{\cdot}75\ (\ 47{\cdot}008 \text{ days.} \end{array}$$

This is so near to 47 days, that if the £711 were paid 47 days after the due date of the first payment, neither party would suffer any appreciable loss.

In the next example, the data are expressed somewhat differently. Suppose £28 5*s*. to be due 4th Feb. 1880; £174 10*s*. on 6th March; £37 5*s*. on the 14th April; £344 on 6th May; £203 on 13th July. Find the date at which the whole may be equitably paid in one sum.

(NOTE.—The year 1880 is leap year.)

	£	s.		£	s.
Feb. 4 .	28	5		28	5
Mar. 6 .	174	10 ×	31 =	5,409	10
Apr. 14 .	37	5 ×	70 =	2,607	10
May 6 .	344	0 ×	92 =	31,648	0
July 13 .	203	0 ×	160 =	32,480	0
	787	0	)	72,173	5 (91·7 days

This may be taken as 92 days. Now 92 days from Feb. 4 (reckoning 29 days in Feb.) brings us to 6th of May, the date required.

Escudo. (*a.*) Formerly the Spanish unit of monetary value, worth about 2*s.* 1*d.* English. The old denominations of Spanish currency are connected with the new by the following formula :—

5 pesetas = 2 escudos = 1 piastre or dollar (= 3*s.* 11½*d.*). Hence the value of the escudo at present is only 1*s.* 11¾*d.* English.

(*b.*) The *Escudo* of Central America weighs 50·16 grains of gold ·853½ fine, worth 7*s.* 6*d.* sterling.

(*c.*) The fifth part of the Chilian condor, is also called an *escudo*, value 89·97*d.* sterling.

Escudillo de Oro. The gold escudillo: a coin used in the Philippine Islands, a dependency of Spain. It is called also the *peso*. It weighs 1·691 grammes ·875 fine, and is worth 4*s.* 0½*d.* English.

Escudo de Oro. A gold coin circulating in the Philippine Islands, equal to 2 *pesos*. It weighs 3·383 grammes, and is ·875 fine. Its value is 8*s.* 1*d.* English.

Esquire. Italian, *scudiero;* French, *ecuyer,* a shield-bearer; Latin, *scutum,* a shield.

An *esquire* or *squire* was one who attended on a knight, and bore his lance and shield. The use of the title in commerce is complimentary, but not legal.

Estate. Latin, *status,* a condition, standing, or circumstance, from *sto, stare,* to stand. From *status* we have the French *état,* formed, like many other words, from the Latin by dropping the initial *s*, and replacing it by an *e*, as *schola, ecole, school; stella, etoile, star;* by a similar law of language, the English retains the original *s* of the Latin as well as the *e* of the French, whence we have *estate,* a law which is exemplified in a great number of words coming to us from the Latin through the French.

The popular meaning of the word *estate,* in English, nearly always appears to involve the idea of *landed property,* so that when a gentleman's estate is mentioned, a picture is involuntarily formed of a tract of land, with the buildings, timber, minerals, and probably the cattle thereon. This is correct so far as it goes; but in *commerce* it is common to speak of the estate of a merchant in a sense which may or may not imply the possession of a single foot of land. In commercial law, the estate of a tradesman is simply his *status,* "his condition," the "circumstances," pecuniary or otherwise, in which he *stands;* and when he is insolvent, the "winding up of his estate" is the appropriation of all his property, and the distribution of it among his creditors.

Esterling. An English silver coin, the Anglo-Norman penny. The 240th part of Tower Pound of Silver, of the "Ancient Right Standard." It is the origin of the word "pennyweight," which was divided into 24 grains. This penny was, therefore, a little heavier than our present three-penny bit, which weighs only 21·81818 grains troy. The esterling weighs 22½ grains troy. (*See Tower Pound Sterling.*)

Exchange. Change. French, *changer;* Italian, *cangiare,* formed according to Menage from *cambiare,* and this from the Latin, *cambire.;* to barter, to exchange. Chaucer uses "exchange" in the sense of "change."

> "These women all of rightcousnesse
> Of choice and free election
> Most love *eschaunge* and doublenesse."

Gower brings both forms into juxtaposition:—

> "For thilke time (I understande)
> The lumbarde made non *eschange*
> The bishoprickes for to *change.*"

The transition from *change* to *exchange* is not easily traced. Although *exchange* is the modern form of the word, "'change" is still often used as a contraction.

Exchange in its widest sense is the giving or receiving one thing for another. In commerce, all exchangeable things are classed under three heads, which we have called the three orders of *Economic Quantities* (*see Economic Quantities*), and although any one thing may be exchanged for any other, yet it will be found on examination that all exchanges fall under one of the following six heads:

Let M stand for all *Material* forms of Wealth.
L for all forms of *Labour* and service.
and R for all kinds of *Rights.*

Then we shall have as many species of Exchange as there are combinations of these letters taken two and two together. Thus:

M	may	be	exchanged	for	M
M	,,	,,	,,	,,	L
M	,,	,,	,,	,,	R
L	,,	,,	,,	,,	L
L	,,	,,	,,	,,	R
R	,,	,,	,,	,,	R

It is, however, important to observe that the *combination* of letters here used is not by any means such as falls under the algebraical laws of Combination and Permutation. In Algebra, the combinations, MM, LL, and RR would be inadmissible; and *three* only would be possible between three quantities taken two and two together, according to the formula—

$$\frac{1.\ 2.\ 3}{1.\ 2} = 3$$

As illustrations of each of the above species of exchange, we may take—

(1.) M for M. The payment of money for a joint of meat.

(2.) M for L. The giving of commodities on the truck system as a reward for labour.

(3.) M for R. The purchase of a house, settled by the passing of a cheque.

(4.) L for L. The services of a medical man, balanced by the labour of a gardener.

(5.) L for R. The payment of a clerk's salary by means of a cheque.

(6.) R for R. A sale of bills, in exchange for a credit in the books of a bank.

Thus far the term "Exchange" applies equally to Inland and Foreign transactions, but in financial operations, the expression is employed almost exclusively to signify "foreign exchanges" which may mean the giving or receiving of the money of one country in return for an equivalent sum in that of another; or it may mean the settlement of debts by means of paper documents, bills of exchange, &c. (*See Bills of Exchange.*)

Down to the time of Henry VII., the business of exchange was a royal monopoly, and carried on at the same office as the mint or "boullion," as it was anciently called; and the *royal exchanger* alone was entitled to give native coin for foreign coin or for bullion. This monopoly was infringed by the Goldsmiths in later days, until it was seen that their profits were so great, as to yield them large fortunes. In the reign of Charles I. therefore, a proclamation was issued forbidding all but the royal favourite, Henry Richard, Earl of Holland, on whom was conferred the office of "*changer, exchanger,* and *outchanger,*" to participate in this business. But the privilege was not of long duration. With the fall of Charles, the monopoly ceased, and the commercial needs of the times gave rise to new institutions. (*See Real Exchange, Nominal Exchange.*)

Exchequer. For the origin of this word the learned carry us back to the ancient Persian language, in which *Schach* (modern Shah) signified King. In very ancient times a game was in vogue, which was played on a board with squares marked upon it. Upon this board figures of wood or ivory were moved about, and one of the principal pieces was called Schach (or King), which name, in course of time, was applied both to the board and to the game itself. In Germany, the name in an unaltered form is applied to the game of *chess.* From the peculiar marking of the board, any surface which was divided in squares was said to be *chequered.* Hence, the old Norman French *exchequeir* and modern French *echiquier* applied to the court where the King's revenue officers met, because they sat round a table covered with chequered (or checkered) cloth resembling a chess board. On the squares of this cloth sums were marked, or scored with counters, in the rude and primitive manner prevalent in that age. The Latin root *scac*—which was in use (though not in classical times) at a very early period—is derived from the same Oriental source, and enters into several different words closely allied to each other, as *scaccum,* a chess board; *ludies scaccorum,* the game of chess; *scaccarium,* the Court of Exchequer, and also a chequered cloth. Old Madox, in his "History of the Exchequer," says, in his quaint and amiable way—

"From the Latin *Scaccarium* cometh the French *Eschequier* or *Exchequier*, and the English name from the French. Or if any one thinks it more likely, that the French word was the ancienter, and the Latin one formed from it, I do not oppose him, nay, I incline to believe it was so." And again: "At the coronation of Richard I., Six Earls and Barons carried *unum Scaccarium* (a chequered cloth) on which were placed the Royal Insignia."

The Court of Exchequer is one of the three great courts of the realm. In Anglo-Saxon times there was only one great court—the *Wittenagemote*, but William the Conqueror separated it into two—the *Aula-regis*, or King's Court, and the Ecclesiastical Court. Subsequently a further separation took place and the Court of Exchequer was detached from the Aula-regis.

The Court of Exchequer is now a Court of Revenue, and a Court of Common Law only. In its former capacity, that with which we are here exclusively concerned, "it ascertains and enforces by proceedings appropriate to the case the proprietary rights of the Crown against the subjects of the realm." (*Blackstone.*) And thus deals with all matters relating to the revenue of the Kingdom. The Exchequer and the Treasury are connected offices, and jointly control the national revenues in the interest of the Executive. Its operations are supervised by the Audit Office in the interest of Parliament, and (through them) the taxpayers of the nation. (*See Audit Office.*)

Exchequer Bill. An instrument of credit created by the Commissioners of Her Majesty's Treasury for the purpose of raising money for temporary purposes to meet the necessities of the Exchequer. Exchequer Bills form a large portion of the Unfunded or Floating Debt of the country. The following are some of the most characteristic features of an Exchequer Bill:—

(1.) They are issued for sums of £100 each, or some multiple of £100, and bear interest at a rate fixed at the date of issue, and at the beginning of each subsequent year.

(2.) They bear a sheet of ten half-yearly coupons, and will therefore last for five years, without renewal. On the next page is a copy of the coupon on a £500 Bill.

It will be observed that the amount due on each coupon is not named, because they run for five years, and the interest fixed only from year to year.

(3.) At the end of twelve months, the holder of an Exchequer Bill may claim payment of the principal sum named on the face of it, but if payment shall not be so claimed, then the Bill shall have legal currency for the next following twelve months, and the holder will have no title to claim payment until the close of that period, but will continue to receive interest on the principal sum by presenting the half-yearly coupon in the usual way at the Bank of England. The same rule applies to each succeeding year.

(4.) Even when the coupons are exhausted, the holder of the Bill may, if he so prefer, have it renewed instead of being paid off.

(5.) At any time during the last six months of *every* year from the date of the Bill, such Bill will be received by the collectors of Customs, Excise, or other duties payable to the Government for the sum or principal money contained therein, that is, the sum printed on its face.

(6.) If an Exchequer Bill be defaced by accident, so as to make it difficult of negotiation, a new one may be obtained in exchange for it.

(7.) The interest on an Exchequer Bill can never exceed 5½ per cent. per annum, and it has sometimes fallen as low as 2½.

EXCHEQUER BILL INTEREST CERTIFICATE.

£500.

Per Act 29 *Vict. Cap.* 25.

This Coupon entitles the Bearer to Interest on the above sum for the half-year to the 11th March, 1881.

WM. DUNBAR, Comptroller and Auditor-General.

The reason why Exchequer Bills are so much sought after by monied men is, that they are nearly always quoted in the market at a premium, and are always saleable. They therefore furnish a near approach to that great desideratum among the mercantile community, money that shall yield interest and yet be in the condition of "ready money," two qualities that vary in inverse proportion the one to the other.

The word *bill* in the phrase "Exchequer Bill" is somewhat different from that in "Bill of Exchange" as regards its origin. An Exchequer Bill was originally an Exchequer *Billet* or piece of wood —Norman French, *bille*—which was the primitive form in which Exchequer Bills were at first issued. In practice, the *billet, bille,* or *bill* was a single piece of wood, having notches cut transversely across it. It was thus distinguished from the later *tally*, which was a similar piece of wood, slit longitudinally through all the notches. (*See Tally, Stock.*)

Exchequer Bonds. Exchequer Bonds are issued under the authority of the same Act as Exchequer Bills, and by the same Commissioners. Bonds, however, differ from Bills, as will be seen by a perusal of the following details :—

(1.) Exchequer Bonds are issued to *run for a definite period of time*, in no case to exceed six years. In most cases they run for much shorter periods, and they must be presented for payment at maturity, as interest thereon ceases at that date.

(2.) The interest payable on Exchequer Bonds is fixed at the time of issue, and the amount payable is printed on each coupon. It cannot exceed $5\frac{1}{2}$ per cent., and there are some Bonds in circulation bearing only $2\frac{1}{2}$ per cent. per annum interest.

(3.) They may be registered or inscribed in the books of the bank, and certificates of such registration would be given in lieu of bonds. These certificates would bear no *coupons*, and the half-yearly interest would have to be applied for in a way similar to that followed in the case of consols.

Excise. Latin, *excisum*, from *ex*, out, *cædo*, I cut, or hew; whence, to *excise* is to cut out, and the substantive, *excise*, something cut out.

Excise is an inland tax or impost levied on goods sold by retail, or, as is sometimes the case, on goods before they leave the manufactories. It is thus distinguished from duties and customs which are levied on goods imported from foreign countries.

Ex Dividendo. Without the dividend, often contracted to *ex dividend, ex div, ex d,* or *x d.* When attached to quotations of prices it signifies that the purchaser of the stock is not entitled to the dividend just about falling due, and is thus contrasted with *cum div*, or *cum dividendo* (*which see*).

Ex Drawing. Since the prices of stocks and shares quoted in the official list carry with them the right to claim all accruing advantages in respect of those stocks or shares; and since the "drawings" for the Sinking Fund or amortization are among those advantages, it is usual to state, about the time when drawings take place, whether the prices carry with them the right to the drawing, or whether that right has ceased. This is done by inserting, after the price, the phrase "ex drawing," or "cum drawing,"—words which convey their own meaning.

Ex New. A phrase often appended to the prices of stocks and shares in the official list. In England, the quoted prices always include all accruing rights, as well as dividends, and among such rights, is that of a claim to new shares or new issues of stock in virtue of present holdings. Hence, so long as prices are quoted "cum new," that is "with new," it signifies that the purchaser has the right to claim the advantages of the new issue; when quoted "ex new," that the right has ceased.

Extension of Protest. Under the article "*Protest*," it is stated that simply *Noting a Bill* and returning it, is regarded in law as a sufficient Protest, and this method is often adopted when bills are returned to parties in the same city or town. But when the Protest has to be sent from one town to another, and especially when sent abroad, the Notary may be required to issue the recognized formal document, a copy of which is given under the article "*Protest*," and this proceeding is technically called *Extension of Protest*.

F.

F. occurs in the following abbreviations:—

F.A.A., Free of all Average.
F.O.B., Free on Board.
F.P.A., Free of Particular Average.
F.G.A., Foreign General Average.

Face Value. The value printed on the face of a Bond, Debenture, Share Certificate or other negotiable instrument. This clearly is very different from its *market value*, which may be greater or less, according to the estimation in which a given stock is held by the public. The Face Value is also sometimes called *Nominal Value*, which see.

Farthing. Ferling. Anglo-Saxon, *feorthling*, originally the fourth part of a coin, not confined to that of a penny.

"This yere the Kynge made a neue guyne as the nobylle, half-nobylle, and feodyng-nobylle."—*Grey Friars' Chron.* Camden Soc.

In the Old English we also find *feorthing* and *fourthing* used in the same sense.

An English bronze coin, composed of 95 parts of copper, 4 of tin, and 1 of zinc; value one-fourth of a penny. In English accounts farthings are usually written as fractions of a penny. If a separate column is employed for them, and they are written as integers, the letter *q* is placed at the head of the column, and signifies *quadrantes*, fourth parts, from *quadrans* a quarter.

Favourable, or **In Favour of.** A term constantly used in reference to the rate of exchange between two countries. It is evident that a rate of exchange which is favourable to one country, is unfavourable to the other; and also that a rate which is favourable for drawing in one country, is unfavourable for remitting to it. The term is therefore, ambiguous, when tried by either of these tests. To obviate this ambiguity, it is found convenient in practice to assume that a merchant always means his own country, when he says that the exchange on some other country is favourable or unfavourable; and then he simply means that by the alteration in the rate of exchange *more* or *less* of the coinage of that other country is given for a stated amount in the coinage of his own. Thus, if the rate of exchange between Berlin and London moved from 20·25 marks to 20·30 marks per pound sterling. A London merchant would say the exchange was favourable, and a Berliner would say it was unfavourable, or "against" him; for the obvious reason that the Berliner would have to give, and the Londoner to receive a greater number of marks for a specified number of sovereigns.

Mr. Goschen states the case in different terms, thus; "When it is said that the exchanges are *favourable* to any particular country, the intention is simply to state the fact, that bills of that country upon foreign cities are *difficult of sale*, whilst bills drawn *from abroad are at a premium*. So when it is said that the exchange is *unfavourable*, a situation is described in which *foreign bills are in great demand*, and when consequently their value seems likely to be so enhanced as to render the export of bullion an unavoidable alternative."—*Theory of Foreign Exchanges*, p. 88. (*See Specie Point.*)

There is, however, yet another test which may be applied to the exchanges, and in regard to which we may say they are "favourable" or "unfavourable." Let it be borne in mind, that it is a bad thing for any country to have less gold than is needed for the requirements of trade, and equally bad to have a glut of it, that is, *more* than can be profitably employed. When there is too much, the rate of interest or discount will sometimes fall, as it did a few years since, and again in 1879, as low as one per cent. When there is too little, the rate may rise as it did in 1866 to 10 per cent., or, as in 1878, to 7 per cent. Both of these extreme rates are disastrous to bankers and merchants; and commerce becomes completely disorganized as long as they continue. There is a pretty general consensus of opinion that business never proceeds so smoothly and profitably as when the rate of interest or discount moves about somewhere between 4 and 5 per cent. Hence, whenever the reserve of gold in the vaults of bankers runs so low as to render the safety of the banks at all precarious, that would be considered a "favourable" turn in the exchanges which caused gold to flow into the country. But should the inflow proceed to such an extent as to overstock the market with gold, then any alteration in the rate of exchange which checked the inflow would be considered favourable; from this it is seen that a "favourable" or "unfavourable" rate of exchange is not determined so much by the direction in which the exchanges move, as by the results brought about by their movement. A movement in the rate that is "favourable" up to a given point, is "unfavourable" when pushed beyond that point. The converse, however, is not true; an "unfavourable" rate of exchange never becomes "favourable," but grows worse and worse the further it is pushed.

Fee. Fief. Feudal. This word, in its earlier forms, having been part of the current speech of all classes of society—learned and unlearned, rich and poor—has been subject to the vicissitudes common to words of this kind, and has undergone great changes.

It is traceable to the Greek, πεκω, *pekō*, to shear, to clip; whence is derived πεκος, *pekos*, wool, a fleece; the name being subsequently transferred to the animal of which the fleece was the most valuable part. Hence the Latin, *pecus*, a sheep, afterwards made to include goats, kine, and other domesticated animals. From *pecus* was formed *pecunia*, wealth, riches, property, because the wealth of primitive societies consisted mainly of sheep and cattle.

By Grimm's "Law of *Lautvershiebung*, or Transposition of Sounds," we are led to expect that any word beginning in Greek with π, or in the Latin with *p*, would, if found in the Gothic or Teutonic tongues, begin with *f* or *v*. And this is what actually occurs. We are not, however, to infer that these forms are derived either from the Greek or Latin. It is more probable that the Greek and Latin, on the one hand, and the Gothic and Teutonic forms on the other, were all derived from some common origin anterior to either. Hence we have the Gothic, *faihu*, possessions, riches; Old High German, *fihu*, *fehu*, and the modern German, *vieh*, all signifying cattle; the old Norman, *fe*, cattle, money, wealth; Anglo-Saxon, *feoh*, cattle, riches, money. With the incursions of the barbarians from the North, this word was introduced into Southern Europe, and took the forms of the Italian, *fio*; Provençal, *feu*, *fieu*, and French, *fief*. Adapted to the Law Latin of the Middle Ages, and strengthened by the insertion of a *d*, we have *feudum*, used to denote property in land, from which we have *feudal*, and the English *fee*, in the sense of an estate in land, and *feoffment*, to denote the process of conveying a fief or fee to a new owner. But *feo* or *feoh* was also used in the popular Anglo-Saxon tongue, with the meaning of *money payment* or *reward*, and this meaning held its ground till it was embodied in our modern colloquial speech.

A *Fee* therefore is a sum given for a service rendered, or a payment made for some right or privilege. In this sense we speak of "barristers' fees," "school-fees," "waiters' fees," &c., and they differ generally from wages or salaries, in being given for single acts or detached services, rather than for time service, or service by the week and year.

As used by lawyers, a "fee" also signified an estate held on certain conditions, as a "knight's fee," which was an estate held on certain condition of rendering a knight's service to the King.

Fiduciary. Latin, *fides*, faith, trust in one's honesty: *fido*, *fidĕre*, to trust, confide, place confidence in; *fidus*, that may be relied on; *fiducius*, that is given in trust to any one, not as his own property, but on condition of its being restored at a given time.

The word *Fiduciary* is used in banking and commerce to signify "without securities," or, as it is more commonly expressed, "*uncovered*." Hence, a "fiduciary loan" is a loan made on the honour and good faith of the borrower without deposit of securities, or without "cover."

Finance. Financier. Latin, *finis*, the end, or limit; *finio*, *finire*, to bring to an end. In classical times the word *finis* was used also to signify a measure, or an amount, as being the end at which one arrives by adding several sums, or the limit which includes them all. In post-classical times, *finis* and its derivatives was used in this sense more freely, and in law was made to signify the end of a suit or the payment of a disputed debt. *Finalis dies* was the day of trial; *finale judicium*, the judge's decision; *finalis concordia*, the agreement by which the suit was ended. As suits were more frequently terminated by the payment of money when litigants increased in riches, the *finis* came at length to be thought of as a sum of money almost exclusively. Passages abound in the old law books which indicate how completely the idea of *money payment* had supplanted the original idea of *end* or *termination*. Thus, in Matthew Prior's "History of Henry III.," we read:—

"Clauculo captus fuit, et tacito facto *fine* . . . . caute dimissus. (He was captured secretly, and having quietly submitted to the payment of a *fine* . . . . he was cautiously sent away.)

"Nullum ulterius ab eo *finem* habebimus." (We shall get no further *terms* from him.)—*Duc.*

The antiquary of Sir Robert Cotton relates how, when the king summoned the clergy and even females to London in order to pass over to France on military duty, the archbishop and others "possent *facere finem* per eodem si vellent" (were allowed, if they wished, to put an end to the obligation—*i.e.*, to pay a fine or compound for it). It was a natural step for the old lawyers to pass from this now recognized meaning of *finis*, to the formation of a new Latin verb *finare* which was always used in the sense of paying a fine, exaction, or composition; and from this was formed the participle *finans*, the paying of money, and then in a perfectly regular manner the English and French *finance*, first used in the sense of extortion, and afterwards in that of payment in general.

The word Finance and its derivatives were, till within a late period, applied to the management of the State revenues; and a "great financier" was always understood to be some one conversant with the art of raising and administering the income of the nation. More recently, however, and especially since the rapid expansion of trade during the last forty years, the business of money lending, as a distinct profession, has risen greatly in importance. Wealthy firms, and large joint stock associations, have devoted themselves mainly to this business: and although "Finance" and "Financier" appeared at first rather big words to apply to trade, the popular ear soon became accustomed to them. *Finance* in commerce usually means the raising of capital by subscriptions, and the employment of it in loans for carrying out commercial undertakings.

Fine. Latin, *finis*, the end; *finio, finire*, to put an end to.

In the ancient laws of England, a *fine* was so called because it was the means of putting *an end* to a suit, and to "all other suits and controversies concerning the same matter."—STEPHEN'S *Blackstone*. This idea pervades the modern use of the term at least in law: and although the origin of the word is in popular speech lost sight of, it does not inaptly describe the effect of a fine in such cases as a "fine for trespass," a "fine for default of payment," a "fine for breach of rules," &c. In all these cases the payment of the fine brings to an *end* the grievance or dispute in respect of which it was levied.

Fiorino. A gold coin formerly used in Tuscany, so named from the Fleur-de-Lis, the arms of Florence. (*See Florin.*) Value about 1*s.* 1¼*d.*

First Class Paper. Bills, drafts, and promissory notes, bearing names of the highest class, as acceptors or endorsers. Exchequer bonds and Treasury bills, having the guarantee of the Government, of course rank with quite the best paper.

First / Second / Third of Exchange. Bills of Exchange are commonly drawn in sets of *three*, called respectively the First, Second, and Third of Exchange. On the first is inserted the phrase "this First of Exchange (Second and Third of the same tenor and date unpaid);" on the Second, the phrase, "this Second of Exchange (First and Third of the same tenor and date unpaid);" on the Third, the phrase, "this Third of Exchange (First and Second of the same tenor and date unpaid)." In all other respects the three forms are identical. The object of making out Foreign Bills in sets of two or three, is to facilitate their negotiation, and also to prevent loss or delay in consequence of miscarriage or other untoward event. (*See Sola* and *Via.*)

Fixed Capital. Capital employed in the purchase of land, in executing works, or in erecting machinery with the hope of making a series of profits by their use during a greater or lesser period of time. As everything made by human hands is liable to wear and tear, no capital can be considered absolutely *fixed*. It is fixed only for a time. What the capitalist expects is, that when his buildings, machinery, &c., are worn out, the returns made by their employment shall have been sufficient to replace the same with new, and yield a certain something besides which he calls his "profit."

Floating Debt. When Debts are contracted by a Government, or other public body, with an engagement to repay the same at a specified date, with interest thereon up to that date, the interest being sometimes paid in the form of discount, they constitute a *Floating Debt*. It is synonymous with *Unfunded Debt* (*which see*), Exchequer Bills, Exchequer Bonds, Treasury Bills, Promissory Notes, Drafts, and Bank Credits, all form part of the Floating debt of the nation.

Floating Capital. Floating Capital is that portion of the wealth of a banker or trader, which he employs in such a way that, by parting with it, he replaces it with a profit in a single operation. As there is very little capital that can be said to be absolutely fixed, so there is little, if any, that can be called purely *floating*. The term, however, is a convenient one, and serves to distinguish, in a vague way, that portion of capital which is not appropriated to any fixed or permanent investment. Capital invested in mines, railways, land, &c., often remains fixed there for years. The capital employed by bankers is rarely, perhaps ought never to be, so fixed. It should be lent for short terms, as to brokers from settling day to settling day, or in discounting three months' bills for merchants and traders. It is then never out of their hands for a long time together, and in case of need may be rapidly accumulated, so as to meet any demand that may unexpectedly arise. Capital thus employed is called *Floating Capital*.

Florence. A gold coin formerly used in England, but long since extinct. Like the florin it took its name from the city of Florence, where they were first coined. By the Statute of 18 Edward III. every pound weight of old standard gold was to be coined into 50 florences, to be current at six shillings each, all which made in tale 15 pounds, or into a proportionate number of half-florences, or quarter-florences.

Florin. The name of a coin formerly issued in Florence, from which city it takes its name, the city itself taking its name from the Fleur-de-Lis, the arms of Tuscany, of which Florence was the capital. Florins, owing to the excellent workmanship bestowed upon them, were much esteemed in England and other parts of Europe. The value of the florin, whether in gold or silver, was found a convenient unit of value, and as such became a favourite coin in many parts of the world. The following are the principal coins known under that name.

(*a.*) An English silver coin equal to one-tenth of a sovereign. It weighs 174·54545 troy grains (or 11·31036 grammes). ·925 fine, which gives $\frac{37}{40}$ of fine silver to $\frac{3}{40}$ alloy. The mint remedy or allowance is 4 parts in 1000. In fixing the "Tariff Value" of the coinage this allowance is taken into account, because in foreign countries, coins when exchanged in any important quantity pass simply as bullion. Hence, when compared with French money, for example, the mint par of exchange is 1 florin = 2·32 francs, but the tariff value is 2·30 francs, the difference arising from (1) the *allowance* for weight, (2) the *allowance* for fineness, and (3) for a fair degree of abrasion. (*See Token Coins* and *Legal Tender.*)

(*b.*) The unit of value in Austria, divided into 100 new kreutzers or cents. Its value in sterling is determined by the mint law, which ordains that one metric pound of *fine* silver (500 grammes) shall be coined into 45 florins (or gulden). The florin therefore contains 11·1111 grammes of *fine* silver, or 12·3457 grammes of *standard* silver 900 fine. By arbitrating at the rate of 15½ parts of fine silver for 1 part of fine gold, we find the value of the silver florin = 23·495*d.* sterling. For some time the paper florin has been much more extensively used in Austria than either gold or silver coinage; these latter are therefore simply commodities, and are bought or sold at a premium which varies according to the price of these metals in the market, and the degree of credit enjoyed by the State. In Paris, the mint par value of the florin is 2·47 francs, and the tariff value 2·45 francs.

(*c.*) The unit of value in Holland. In 1850 the gold coinage of Holland was suppressed, and silver was made the standard of value. But quite recently the gold standard has been re-introduced, and the monetary laws of Nov. 1847, and Sept. 1849, re-established. In virtue of these laws the florin is made the unit of value, and the unit of account. Gold is now the standard of value, and the 10 florin gold piece, or William, furnishes the data for calculating the par of exchange, while the silver florin still remains a legal tender. They may both therefore be advantageously described.

The *Gold Florin.* The gold 10 florin piece, by the law of 6th June, 1875, weighs 6·720 grammes, ·900 fine. It is worth 20·83 francs, or 198·23*d.* The value of the gold florin is therefore 2·083 francs, or 19·82*d.*

The *Silver Florin.* The silver florin weighs 10 grammes, ·945 fine, and taking 15½ parts of *fine* silver as equal to 1 of *fine* gold, we have for the value of the silver florin 19·983*d.* As silver is now much depreciated in value, a considerable deduction must be made from this calculated value, in all countries where the gold standard prevails.

The Dutch florin is often called the guilder. It is divided into 100 cents.

(*d.*) The *Silver Florin* of the *South German States* is now superseded by the new German coinage. It is, however, still legal tender. Its full weight was 10·582 grammes, ·900 fine, and was formerly valued at 20·182*d.*, but is now, like other silver coins, when compared with a gold standard, much depreciated. It was divided into 60 kreutzers of 4 hellers each.

(*e.*) The *Polish Florin* of Russia is valued at 15 copecks. It weighs 3·059 grammes, 500 fine, and is worth 3¼*d.* sterling.

Flotsam, Jetsam, and Lagan. "Barbarous and uncouth appellations," says Blackstone, "used to distinguish certain goods cast upon the sea, from certain others which constitute a *legal wreck.*" The barbarism and uncouthness of these words arise from their formation, which follows no recognized law of language. They are nevertheless derived from well known roots.

Flotsam, variously written *flotsen, flotzam,* and *flotson,* is derived from the Saxon *fleotan* or *flotan,* to swim; *flota,* a thing which swims on the surface.

"Flotsen be any goods that by shipwracke be lost, and lie *floting* or swimming upon the water."—Minshew.

Jetsam, or *jetson,* or *jettison,* is from the Latin, *jacio, jacĕre,* to go, to cause to go, to throw, to cast. French, *jeter.*

"Quæ enim res in tempestate levandæ navis causa *ejiciuntur,* hæ dominorum permanent. Quia palam est eas non eo animo *ejici* quod quis eas habere nolit." (For those things which during a storm are thrown overboard for the sake of lightening the ship remain the property of the owners. Because it is evident that they were not thrown overboard with the intention of abandoning them.)—Coke's *Institutes.*

Lagan, or *ligan,* is from the Saxon, *ligan, licgan,* or *léegan,* to lie, to be in an inclined or horizontal position.

To constitute a legal *wreck*, goods must come to land, when they become the property of the king, of the sheriff, or the lord of the manor. They must, however, be kept for a year and a day (in France for a year, in Holland for a year and a half), so that if any man can prove a property in them, they shall be restored to him without delay. But in the case of goods found floating on the surface of the sea—*flotsam*—they remain the property of the owner, since it is assumed that he has not renounced his right to them: but if no owner appears they become the property of the Crown. Goods thrown overboard, and which sink to the bottom of the sea, are dealt with in the same manner, and are treated as *jetsam. Lagan* or *Ligan* is goods sunk in the sea and attached to a cork or buoy in order to be found again. Here it is clear that the owners did not intend to renounce their property in them, as they had done all in their power to assert their right to the goods. Hence *flotsam, jetsam,* and *lagan,* are not the lawful spoils of the finders, but must be delivered up to those who can prove their right to them, the owners paying a reasonable reward to those who saved and preserved them, which is called *salvage.* (*See Salvage.*)

Forestall, To. Saxon, *stoel, stal, stael, steal,* all of which forms were used to denote a standing place, or fixed spot in a market or fair: Danish, *stal;* German, *Stall;* French, *stalle.*

To *forestall* is to buy goods on their way to market, before they are brought to the *stall*, where they are exposed to the competition of buyers.

Forestallers. A name applied to a class of dealers who in former times intercepted goods on their way to market or fair, and bought them up with a view to enhance their price. When roads were bad, travelling laborious, and the population scattered, "forestallers" did a thriving trade. The practice of forestalling was regarded as an unfair advantage taken from the frequenters of the market, and penalties were imposed on those who sought to profit by it, but they were of no avail. It is now practised in all the markets and exchanges of Europe, although not called by that name. (*See Engrossers* and *Regraters.*)

Forfeit. About the latter syllable of this word little doubt can be entertained. The Latin, *facere,* to make or do, the French, *faire,* and cognate words sufficiently indicate its origin. But with regard to the particle *for,* two explanations have been given. It is thought by some to be equivalent to *fore,* in front of, or previous in point of time, but the force of the prefix in such words as *forswear, forbid,* does not support this view. It seems far more probable that the Latin, *foris,* out, without, foreign to; the German, *ver;* Gothic, *fair;* French, *for;* and English, *for* or *fore,* are all variations of some primitive form which, as Mr. Macpherson says, imply "negation, excess, priority, or *vitiation of the natural sense of the word* to which it is prefixed," as *forego,* to go without; *forejudge,* to judge wrongfully; *foreclose,* to close against; *forbid,* to bid away; *forswear,* to swear falsely. On this supposition *forfeit* or *forfait* would signify a misdeed, something wrongly done, a crime, and in this sense it was formerly used.

> "My heart nor I have doen you no *forfeit*
> By which you should complain in any kind."—CHAUCER.

"Oro omnes quibus aliquid *forefeci* ut mihi per suam gratiam indulgeant." (I pray all to whom I have done anything wrong that they grant me their pardon.)—*Pontanus in Duc.*

By a common process in language the name for the misdeed or crime was transferred to the consequences or penalty attached to it. *Forisfactus servus,* in the laws of Athelstan, was one who had made himself a slave by his misdeeds: and the French, *forfaire corps et avoir,* implied the loss of liberty and property by crime. *Bona forisfacta* in English law are lands or goods, the property in which is gone away or departed from the owner.

The general idea conveyed by the word *forfeit,* as distinguished from a fine or penalty, is that of the lapsing of a claim, or a loss arising from misconduct. A fine is *imposed,* a penalty *inflicted,* a forfeit is *incurred;* as exemplified in the case of detected smuggling, when the goods are *forfeited,* and in addition a fine is *exacted.* So when a loan contractor issues the prospectus of a loan, there is usually a clause to the effect that "If the subscriber fails to pay any of the later instalments when due, all previous instalments that have been paid shall be *forfeited,*" that is, he shall not be allowed to claim the repayment of the instalment made; but he may sell his scrip for what it will fetch, and if any loss occurs he must bear it himself: but the loss results from his own default, and is not inflicted by any legal authority.

Forge, To. Most authorities agree in deriving this word from the Latin, *faber*, a smith (which is supposed to be a contraction of *faciber*, from *facere*, to make). *Faber*, in the sense of a maker, was applied to workers in wood and stone, as well as to workers in metal; and as it was much on the tongues of the labouring and unlettered classes, it underwent the usual changes to which such words are exposed. First there was the change from *b* to *v*, preserved to us in the modern names of *Favre*, *Lefevre*, *orfevre* (goldsmith): then the change from *v* to *u*, giving us the old French, *faur*; Wallachian, *fauru*, a smith, and *faurie*, a smithy, or smith's shop. *Faurire*, in Eastern Europe, was used to denote the making or fabricating of anything, but especially the working of metals; and when by the introduction of the tailed *i*, that is the *j*, into the alphabet, *faurire* was converted into *faurjre*, the way was clear for the Spanish, *forjár*, and the modern French, *forge*.

Forgery is a very grave offence in the eye of the law. It is defined to be "the fraudulent making or alteration of a writing or seal, to the prejudice of another man's right, or of a stamp to the prejudice of the revenue." It is necessary in order to convict a man of forgery to show that the instrument forged so far resembles the true instrument as to be capable of deceiving persons who use ordinary observation. Hence, if a cashier or clerk in a bank passed a cheque with a signature that was to ordinary observation a false one, it would most likely lead to a conviction of gross carelessness, on the part of the clerk, rather than to one of forgery against the offender. On the other hand, any material alteration of a document, however slight, is as much a forgery as an entire fabrication; and the fraudulent application of a false signature to a true instrument, or a true signature to a false one, are equally forgeries.

Forgery is one of those offences which increase with the advance of science and education; and hence it has been found necessary to inflict heavier penalties on this offence than our forefathers ever dreamt of. "The punishment of this offence at *common law*, and as a mere misdemeanour, was fine, imprisonment, and pillory;" but when by the Act 11 Geo. IV., it was made "*treason*" to forge the Great Seal, the Privy Seal or any Privy Signet, &c., and when by the same Act it was made "*felony*" to forge stamps, exchequer bills, Bank of England notes, bills of exchange, promissory notes, deeds, receipts, &c., heavier penalties were inflicted and in many cases the extreme penalty of death. Capital punishment for forgery is now abolished, but the penalties are still very severe, as they ought to be, for it is not an offence, in its grosser forms, which is committed under the impulse of a momentary temptation, but is usually the result of long premeditation, and much misdirected ingenuity at the instigation of mere avarice.

Forty-five Florin Standard. The standard on which the Silver currency of Austria is based. The metric Pfund of 500 grammes of fine silver is coined into 45 Austrian florins, 30 Prussian thalers, or 52½ South German florins.

Fractions of Penny. It is a rule in the Custom House, when the precise duty upon any article may produce a fraction of a penny less than a halfpenny to reject the fraction; and where it amounts to a halfpenny or more, the next highest number of pence is to be stated on the entry and brought to account. In making payments all fractions of a penny are to be rejected.

Folio. From the Latin, *folium*, a leaf; which again is from the Greek, φυλλον, *phullon*, the leaf of a tree, herb, or flower.

In Bookbinding, a *folio* is a sheet so folded as to make two leaves without further folding; it is said to be *in quarto* when folded so as to form four leaves; *in octavo*, when folded again so as to form eight leaves.

In Book-keeping, a *folio* consists of the two pages presented to the view when laid wide open, and which are usually indicated by one and the same number.

In Law-writing, a *folio* sometimes means a single page; at others, as in conveyancing, it signifies 72 words; in Chancery proceedings to 90; and in Exchequer proceedings to 80.

Foreign Bill. From the Latin, *forinsecus;* whence the French, *forain*, out, outside, from without; outside the house, home, or country.

A Bill of Exchange may be called "Foreign" from *three* different sets of circumstances, thus giving rise to three distinct classes of Foreign Bills.

1st. It may be drawn in the United Kingdom, and made payable in a foreign country.

2nd. It may be drawn in a foreign country, and made payable in the United Kingdom.

3rd. It may be drawn abroad, and made payable abroad, but be negotiable in the United Kingdom.

Each of these classes may be again subdivided into Short Bills, Sight Bills, and Long Bills, the last including One month, Two months, Three months, Six months, and generally any bills payable more than *ten days* after they are made. They may also be the *First*, *Second*, or *Third* copies. As these minor distinctions are explained under their various headings, and as the peculiarities of Endorsement are the same as for Inland Bills, it will be sufficient in this place to give a single specimen of each of the above-named *three* classes, with such explanations as may be applicable to them.

In the following examples the portions printed in Roman type are the same for all bills of the same firm, and are usually prepared from engraved plates. The numbers and the words printed in italics as well as those in capitals are inserted with the pen to suit each particular case.

First Class.

No. 728. £300. Manchester, 10 *Dec.* 1879.

Ninety days after date pay this first of Exchange (second and third not paid) to the Order of Messrs. BERGMANN & Co. the sum of *Three Hundred Pounds* sterling, value received, *which place to account.*

HENRY BLACKBURN.

To Messrs. MARCHANT FRÈRES, Paris.

Second Class.

No. 7416. £250 10*s.* 0*d.* Frankfort o/M, 3 *Jan.* 1880.

Three months after date pay this First of Exchange (Second and Third of the same tenor and date unpaid) to the Order of Messrs. FRANKLIN & GREEN the sum of *Two Hundred and Fifty Pounds, Ten Shillings*, value received, *and charge the same to account.*

F. SCHWARZWALD.

To Messrs. HARDEN & Co., Birmingham.

Third Class.

No. 406. Fl. 17,000. Madrid, 8 *Dec.* 1879.

Sixty days after date please pay this First of Exchange (Second and Third of the same tenor and date unpaid) to the Order of Mr. JNO. HOWSON the sum of *Seventeen Thousand Florins in Austrian Silver Currency*, value received, and *charge the same as advised.*

WEISS & BLANCO.

To the STAATSBANK, Vienna.

The above are fair specimens of Bills of Exchange as used in the present day. They do not differ very much in point of form from those in use during the last 500 years. One of the earliest Bills of Exchange known is reprinted in McLeod's *Theory and Practice of Banking*, and although written in Italian, yet it is of such antiquated style, and so mixed up with Spanish terms, as to render it very difficult to decipher. The first of the two following bears date 1381, the second 1404. The translations have been furnished by an eminent teacher of the Italian and Spanish languages.

Al nome di Dio. Amen. A primo di Februario MCCCLXXXI pagate per questa prima lettera ad usanza da voi medesimo libre 43 de' grossi, sono per cambio de' ducati 440, che questi chi hone ricevuto da Sejo el Compagni attramente le pagate.

(In the name of God. Amen. On the first of February, 1381, pay this first letter of exchange for the use of yourself 43 pounds of *grossi*, they are for exchange of the 440 ducats which these here have received from Sejo and Company, or pay them otherwise.)

Al nome di Dio. Amen. A di Aprile xxviii, 1404, pagate per questa prima di camb, a usanza a Pietro Gilberte e Pietro Olivo, scuti mille a sold. X Barcelonesi per scuto, e quali scuti mille sono per cambio che con Giovanni Colombo a Gressi xxii de gresso per scuto et Pon. a nostro conto; et Christo vi guardi.

Antonio quart. Sab de Brugis.

(In the name of God, Amen. On the 28 April, 1404, pay by this first bill of exchange to Pietro Gilberte and Pietro Olivo, one thousand scuti at the rate of 10 Barcelonese soldi per scuto, which thousand scuti are for exchange with Giovanni Colombo at the rate of 22 grossi per scuto, and place to our account; and Christ protect you.)

Franc. Although the history of the modern *franc* dates no farther back than the decree of Napoleon Bonaparte, as first Consul of the French Republic in the year XI., there have been coins in existence for centuries called *franks, francks, franckes*, or by the elision of the *n*, *frãkes*. Under one or the other of these names they are often alluded to by our English writers.

"Dan Jon, I say lene me this hundred *frankes*."

CHAUCER, *The Shipman's Tale.*

"But in London, and in the diocese was gathered a tûne of gold, and in the whole realme of England was gathered xxv. c.m. *frankes*, which makes in English money cclxxvii. m. vii. c. lxxvii. p."—BARNES, *Workes*, p. 193.

The name is derived from the coins used by the Franks, a confederacy of German tribes who *freed* themselves from the domination of the surrounding Latinised nations, shortly after the decline of the Roman Empire, and established themselves in the northern part of the country now called France, but which at that period was called Gallia or Gaul.

The modern *Franc*, the only important coin of that name now existing, is the unit of value, and the unit of account in France, and all those countries which have joined with France in the Monetary Convention. (*See Monetary Convention.*)

The following details respecting the French coinage have been furnished by M. Sudre, *Chef des Bureaux de l'Administration des Monnaies*, for the Annuaire par le Bureau des Longitudes for 1879.

The *Gold Franc*. The value of the gold franc is deduced from the 10-franc piece or half-napoleon. Its weight is 3·226 grammes, ·900 fine, giving for the weight of the single franc, ·3226 grammes.

The weight of the 20-franc piece is of course double the half-napoleon; more accurately the napoleon weighs 6·45161 grammes.

The determination of the Mint Par of Exchange between England and France serves as a model on which all similar operations may be conducted, and indicates further the data which should be demanded as the basis of all similar computations.

Suppose, for example, that we wish to compare the value of the sovereign with the 20-franc piece of France. We know that the legal weight of the sovereign is 7·98805 grammes, and its fineness ·916$\frac{2}{3}$. It therefore contains 7·3223259 of *fine* gold. On the other hand, the French 20-franc piece weighs 6·45161 grammes ·900 fine; it therefore contains 5·806449 grammes of *fine* gold. Hence we have the following proportion:—

grammes		francs		grammes		
5·806449	:	20	::	7·3223259	:	x

which gives as the value of the sovereign 25·2213 francs.

Dividing 240 pence by 25·2213 we have for the value of the French franc in gold 9.51576 pence sterling.

The *Silver Franc*. The silver franc is the unit about which the whole monetary system of France turns.

By the law of the Republic dated 1795, it was decreed that the monetary unit should be the *Franc;* that the fineness of the silver should be nine parts of pure silver to one part of alloy; and that the 1-franc piece should weigh five grammes.

Eight years later (March, 1803) it was decreed that the silver franc should have the same weight and fineness as before; and also that new *gold-pieces* should be struck of twenty francs each, 155 to the kilogramme of gold ·900 fine.

Hence the weight of the 20-franc gold piece is $\frac{1000}{155}$ grammes or 6·45161 grammes as stated above; from which we find that 1000 grammes of *gold* ·900 *fine* is worth 155×20 francs, and 1,000 grammes of *silver* ·900 *fine* is worth 200 francs. This gives us the value of gold as compared with silver, in accordance with which the Double Standard was established in France, and which still is nominally maintained, although, in consequence of the recent depreciation of silver, it is practically abandoned.

Since 1,000 grammes of standard gold = 3,100 francs, and
1,000 ,, ,, silver = 200 francs,

we find that gold is reckoned in France to be worth $15\frac{1}{2}$ times the same weight of silver, whether the metals be *pure*, or of the *same degree of fineness.*

These data furnish the means of calculating the Mint Par of Exchange. But, in practice, the Exchange is regulated by the "Tariff-Value" of the coins, which, when sent to foreign countries, are treated simply as ingots of bullion. (*See Tariff Value, Retenue.*)

It is also important to observe that the *franc* above described is represented by 5-franc pieces only; and when we speak of silver as a legal tender in France, it must be understood that it is only when 5-franc pieces are tendered that the tender is legal. All the silver coins of lower denomination have an inferior degree of fineness, so that the metallic value of the 1-franc piece is never equal to $\frac{1}{5}$ that of the 5-franc piece.

The 1-franc piece is ·835 fine and weighs 5 grammes, and its *metallic* value instead of being 1 franc is only ·93 franc. Its value in sterling is therefore

$$\frac{93}{100} \times 9{\cdot}51576 \text{ or } 8.8196568 \text{ pence.}$$

In keeping accounts in francs the arithmetical notation is very simple and almost identical with the decimal notation; thus fr. 9·645 is perfectly clear to any one acquainted with decimal fractions; but it is more common in France to write fr. $9{\cdot}64\frac{1}{2}$ which would be read 9 francs, $64\frac{1}{2}$ centimes; nevertheless when any fraction of a centime other than *one-half* is to be written, the decimal notation is mostly adhered to.

The following table of the French coinage, which is the same as that of all countries included in the Latin Monetary Convention, will be useful for reference; as it has been thoroughly revised by M. Sudre, and gives the latest authorized statement of the weight, fineness, and tariff value of all the coins now circulating as legal tender in France:—

Denomination of Coin.	Legal Weight	Fine-ness.	Par Value.		Tariff Value.	
			Of One Kilo.	Of Each Piece.	Of One Kilo.	Of Each Piece.
	Grammes.		Fr. c.	Fr. c.	Fr. c.	Fr. c.
Gold—						
100 francs.	32·258	·900	3100	100·00	3093·30	99·78
50 francs.	16·129	,,	,,	50·00	,,	49·89
20 francs.	6·452	,,	,,	20·00	,,	19·95
10 francs.	3·226	,,	,,	10·00	,,	9·97
5 francs.	1·613	,,	,,	5·00	,,	4·99
Silver—						
5 francs.	25·000	·900	200	5·00	198·50	4·96
2 francs.	10·000	·835	185·56	1·86	184·16	1·84
1 franc.	5·000	,,	,,	0·93	,,	0·92
50 centimes.	2·500	,,	,,	0·46	,,	0·46
20 centimes.	1·000	,,	,,	0·19	,,	0·18

Frederic d'Or. The gold Frederic is a coin used in the North German Zollverein States, value five thalers, now a mere commercial coin.

It also circulates in Denmark, where it is valued at 7 dalers 36 skilling, but it is here also merely a commercial coin, and averages 16*s.* 2*d.* English.

Freight. German, *Fracht;* French, *fret,* from *fréter,* to take in for transport or conveyance. It is probably connected with the Latin, *fero,* I carry.

Freight is a word used in three distinct senses.

(*a*) *The carriage of goods by water,* as when we say the cost of freight is so heavy as to render the importation or exportation of certain goods unprofitable.

(*b*) *The cargo of a ship,* which includes all those goods which are carried from one port to another with a view to profit, but not those intended for consumption during the voyage, nor the tackle or machinery belonging to the ship.

(*c*) *The charge made for the carriage of goods* whether by land or water.

Fuang. The one-eighth part of the Siamese *tical* worth about 3¾*d.* English.

Fund. From the Latin, *funda,* a purse, or net; and this again from *fundĕre,* to pour.

A *Fund* in commercial language is an accumulation resulting from the *outpouring* of money, or other forms of wealth, into a common stock, and is thus equivalent in meaning to *banck* or *mons,* a mount or heap. This rudimentary notion of a fund being formed, it underwent sundry modifications till it was used to express the idea of a collective amount of anything whatever, as a "fund of information," a "fund of amusement." In economics, the term is used to denote the putting together of sundry sources of revenue, or various contributions to some prescribed purpose. Hence, it still retains much of its primary signification—namely, the *pouring* into some one common stock of a number of things appropriate to the object contemplated.

Funded Debt. The Funded Debt, *par excellence*, in England is that vast total of Annuities paid by the Government to its creditors under the name of Consols—Reduced Three Per Cents, New Three Per Cents, Savings Bank Annuities, &c., amounting to nearly £800,000,000 sterling.

Although the broad distinction between the Funded Debt and the Unfunded or Floating Debt, as they actually exist, is that the latter is, according to contract, to be paid off at a specified date, while the former need never be paid at all, but only the interest thereon; yet there is nothing either in the name or nature of "Funding" to prevent the term being applied, to *Redeemable* debts as well as *Irredeemable* ones. The recent issue of Three per cent. Redeemable Rentes (*Rentes Amortizables*) in France is a case in point. The French "Rentes," like the English "Annuities," merely signifies an annual payment; they each constitute the National Debt of their respective countries, and have, till lately, been regarded as perpetual. They constitute, in fact, precisely what we called a Funded Debt. The Funded Loans of the United States are still more to the point. (*See* Arts. *Funding*, and *Unfunded Debt.*)

Funding. The process by which a Floating Debt is converted into Stock. Governments, railway and other companies often find when the time comes for paying of bills, debentures, or bonds of short date, that they have not money in hand to meet their obligations, although they have abundant means for the payment of the interest on them. Lenders under these circumstances are sometimes not only willing but rather desirous of having their claims commuted by a perpetual annuity in lieu of the lump sum to which they are entitled. In this way our English Consols, the French Rentes, and most Railway Stocks originated. Hence by "Funding the Public Debts" is meant the conversion of debts payable at short specified dates, into an annuity to last for ever, or into one that is to last for a considerable, though definite, time; an arrangement often acceptable to both borrower and lender. In some Funding operations provision is made for the repayment of the debt at the option of the borrowing Government, but not at the option of the lender, as in the case of the United States "Five per Cent. Funded Loan," the object of which was to convert the enormous number of "Six per Cent. Five-Twenty Bonds," then in circulation, into a new Five per Cent. Debt. These "Five-Twenties," as their name is intended to imply, were redeemable at the option of the government after five years from their date of issue, and at the option of the holder after twenty years: six per cent. being paid on them until they were redeemed. The result of the conversion of these "Five-Twenties" was the three great "United States Funded Loans" thus officially described:—

> "The Funded Loan of 1881 is redeemable at the pleasure of the United States after the first day of May, A.D. 1881, and bears interest at the rate of five per cent. per annum, payable quarterly."
>
> "The Funded Loan of 1886 is redeemable at the pleasure of the United States after the first day of May, A.D. 1886, and bears interest at the rate of four and a-half per cent. per annum, payable quarterly."
>
> "The Funded Loan of 1901 is redeemable at the pleasure of the United States after the first day of May, A.D. 1901, and bears interest at the rate of four per cent. per annum, payable quarterly."

The general notion attached to the term "Funding," whatever it may have been in former days, would now appear from a consideration of the foregoing examples, to be simply the blending together of several debts of different denominations into one great debt clearly defined in amount, on which interest is to be paid at a fixed rate until the debt itself is redeemed; or if the debt is not redeemed, the interest to be paid in perpetuity.

G.

Gage. French, *gager*, to wager; *gage*, a pledge or bond. Italian, *gaggio*, all of which Skinner derives from the Latin, *vas, vadis*, a pledge, security, bail. Tooke derives it from the Anglo-Saxon *Cægg-ian*, to shut up, to bind.

This word is little used in English, except in composition, as in mortgage, weathergage, leegage; in these latter it is often written *guage.* In commerce it means that by which a man is bound to certain engagements; a pledge, a stake, a bail.

Gall. A silver coin used in Cochin China, value 4*d.* English.

Gantang. Twenty-five kansang, a coin used in the Philippine Islands. (*See Kansang.*)

Garbling. Spanish, *garbillo*, a coarse sieve; *garbillar*, to sift, to separate the bad from the good. Venetian, *garbelo*, a sieve. Old Ital., *garbellare*, to sift. All these modern forms are supposed to be connected with the Latin, *carminare*, to card, comb, or cleanse wool or flax, but the connection is by no means clearly traced.

Garbling is the practice adopted by many money-dealers of picking out new full-weighted coins from those which pass through their hands, for the purpose of exporting them, or melting them down, retaining the light ones for circulation and for their trade payments at home. (*See Gresham's Theorem*). The word was formerly used to signify the process of separating the dust or dross from spices and drugs, and was gradually extended, first, to denote generally the separation of the good from the bad of anything, and then by analogy to the selection of evidence suitable to a given purpose, and the suppression of the rest.

Gari. A Hindu coin, about 4,000 rupees.

Gazette. In the Gazette. In the Bank Bill of 1879 it is stated that the "Gazette" for the purpose of that Bill shall mean:—

"As respects companies whose head office is in England, the *London Gazette*":—

"As respects companies whose head office is in Scotland, the *Edinburgh Gazette*":—

"As respects companies whose head office is in Ireland, the *Dublin Gazette*."

Gazzetta. A Venetian copper coin, value ¾*d*. This coin has an historical interest in consequence of its being the origin of the now familiar name "Gazette," as applied to a newspaper. In the days of the old "newsletter," before newspapers came into existence, it was customary in Venice to collect a manuscript sheet of news, and to read it aloud in some public place, a charge of *one gazzetta* being made to all who wished to hear it.

General Law of Value. "To discover a single General Law," says Mr. McLeod, "which governs the exchangeable relations of all economic quantities, whatever their nature may be, at all times, and under all circumstances:—

Let A and B be any two economic quantities of any form whatever; then suppose that A remains constant, while B varies; then B, or the value of A, will vary from four causes.

It will increase,—

1. From diminution in quantity.
2. From an increase of demand.

It will decrease,—

1. From an increase of quantity.
2. From a diminution of demand."

Genovino. A Genoese silver coin, value 4*s*. 4*d*.; also a gold coin, value £3 2*s*. 8*d*.

Genuss-Actie. *See Action de Jouissance.*

Genuss-Schein. The same with *Certificate de Jouissance* (*which see*).

George d'Or. A Hanoverian gold coin now disused. Sterling value about 16*s*. 3*d*.

Georgino. A silver coin formerly circulating in Modena, value about 2½*d*., now superseded by the Italian coinage of the Monetary Convention.

Goldsmiths' Notes. Notes issued by the goldsmiths of Lombard Street before the era of London banking. Before the time of Charles I. merchants used to deposit their unemployed cash in the Tower for safe keeping, but that King being in need of ready money, seized £200,000 deposited there, and the merchants finding that their money was not safer in his keeping than in their own houses, adopted the practice of depositing it with the goldsmiths, who had vaults and guards for the protection of their treasures. These goldsmiths gave receipts for the sums thus deposited with them, which are said to resemble our modern dock warrants, and by delivering of these receipts and warrants, gold and silver, in the form of coin, were transferred. Although these "Goldsmiths' notes" were often spoken of and referred to in Acts of Parliament, no specimen has been preserved, and we have as vague a notion of their form as we have of the equally talked of Roman and Greek "Bills of Exchange." The oldest forms extant are those found in the archives of Childs' Bank, which were kept in a room over Temple Bar. During the recent demolition of that structure, several commercial curiosities were brought to light; among them were certain "orders to pay" drawn upon Mr. Francis Child, goldsmith, from which it appears that the old respectable name of "goldsmith" was more thought of than the newly-introduced title of "banker."

These old forms, however, were more commonly called "Cash Notes;" but it is probable that some of them were also called "Goldsmith's Notes," especially when in the form of "promises to pay." The following are copies of the two oldest; the first a "Cash Note" *drawn upon* a goldsmith; the second, a "Promissory Note" *issued by* a goldsmith.

I. Copy of Cash Note.

Bolton, March 4, 1684.

At sight hereof pray pay unto Charles Duncombe, Esq., or order, the sum of four hundred pounds, and place it to the accompt of

Your assured friend,

WINCHESTER.

To Captain Francis Child,
near Temple Barre.

II. Copy of Promissory Note.

Nov. 28, 1684.

I promise to pay unto the Rt. honble. ye Lord North and Grey, or bearer, ninety pounds at demand.

For Mr. Francis Child and myself,

JNO: ROGERS.

This is thought to be at least one form of Goldsmith Note, but not the oldest. Of those said to resemble our Dock warrants, not a single example is known to exist.

Gold Standard. *See Standard of Value.*

Good Delivery. An expression used in the Stock Exchange, and is applied to the delivery of Bonds, Share Certificates, Debentures, or Stocks, if when examined by the broker they are found in sound condition. It is primarily the duty of the seller to see that the securities he tenders are sound and perfect. It is also the duty of the broker to examine all the securities passing through his hands. This is indeed one of the most important functions of the broker, for his clients are often too little acquainted with documents of this kind to be capable of judging for themselves. Moreover, the requirements of some foreign States are so capricious, that none but those professionally occupied in handling papers of this description, can be expected to have a perfect acquaintance with them. For example, a Spanish 3 per cent. Bond must be preserved entire with all its rough and irregular margins, whether on the Bond itself, or on the Coupons; if any of these are removed, the Spanish Financial Commission are ordered to refuse payment for them when presented. Again, on Italian coupons, as well as on those of the United States loans, an official stamp is impressed; if this is removed or mutilated, payment is at least delayed, if not positively refused. In the transfer of Share Certificates of Commercial Companies, there are so many details to be attended to, that no one but a broker or other professional man could be expected to know them. Since, however, a broker's responsibility ceases after three days from the date of delivery, it is important that every person who keeps securities should examine them for himself, so that if any mistake or oversight on the part of the broker is detected, he may be at once informed of it; and the following points at least may be verified by the most inexperienced :—

I. Every Bond, Share Certificate, or other Security should bear the English Government Stamp, indicating that the *duty* imposed on it by the Inland Revenue Office has been paid; otherwise the Bond is not negotiable.

II. The *number* of the Bond, Certificate, &c., should be perfect and neither mutilated nor defaced, and the same number should appear on *every coupon.*

III. The *nominal value* of the Bond, Debenture, &c., as well as that of each of the coupons, should be printed in figures or letters, or both, and should be found uninjured. Share Certificates cannot have these details on the coupons, because the rate of payment is uncertain.

IV. The *date* at which coupons are payable should be marked on each coupon, and free from defacement.

These details are within the comprehension of every one who can read, and carelessness on the part of a customer in the examination of them, might entail loss, or at least trouble, should any defect be subsequently discovered.

Goods and Chattels. A corrupted translation of the old law phrase, *bona et catalla. Bona* is classical Latin, and signifies good things, or as we say, Goods. *Catalla* is mediæval Latin, and is a contraction of *capitalia,* referring to kine, horses, sheep, &c., which were reckoned by the head or *caput;* so that *bona et catalla* meant all the implements and movable things about an estate, together with the live stock in the possession of the owner. The distinction between *bona* and *catalla* afterwards disappeared, but the phrase itself survived, and was translated "goods and chattels" without any difference of meaning between the two words.

In English law, "goods and chattels" signifies all kinds of personal or movable property as distinguished from real property, as land, houses, shops, farm buildings, &c. Blackstone defines *chattels* as comprising "all sorts of things movable which may attend a person wherever he goes." Hence, the artifice of building a conservatory or a shoemaker's shop "on wheels." Such a structure may be built and taken away by a tenant; but if the same structure were built on timbers fixed in the ground, it could not be removed without the landlord's consent. Under the phrase "goods and chattels" are included rights of action, bills, debts, banknotes, copyrights, share certificates, foreign bonds, and, in short, all material or immaterial things which are not attached to the soil.

Goodwill (of a business). The advantages connected with an established business of good repute. A well-established business presents an expectation of profits to any one entering upon it, and is worth paying for. Any one having such a business and who is willing to relinquish the expectation of the profits by transferring it for a consideration to someone else, can do so by what is technically called "selling the goodwill" of that business. These transactions are fully recognized by English law, and an encouragement to industry and integrity is thus held out to those who have the tact and energy to accumulate this form of wealth.

Gourde. The *gourde* or *dollar* or *piastre* of Hayti or St. Domingo, is represented by paper currency, and is nominally worth $3\frac{1}{8}$*d.* but often is not worth more than $2\frac{1}{2}$*d.*

Grain. The unit on which are founded the Avoirdupois and Troy systems of weight used in England. In the Statute 31 Edward I., it is enacted:—

"I. An English penny, now the largest coin in England, which is called a sterling, round and without clipping, shall weigh *thirty-two grains of wheat,* well dried, and gathered out of the middle of the ear,

"II. And twenty of these pence, or twenty pennyweights, shall make an ounce.

"III. And twelve of those ounces make a pound"—Anderson, vol. i. p. 351.

The weights thus determined were preserved by the king's moneyers, but the pennyweight was subsequently divided into 24 grains. Hence, the *grain* now in use is derived from an artificial standard, but the standard itself was derived from the grains provided by Nature. The coin above mentioned was, of course, silver.

Gramme or **Gram.** The unit of weight in the French metric system, now largely employed either compulsorily or optionally in most of the civilized nations of the world. It is the weight of a cubic centimetre of distilled water at the temperature of 39°·2 Fahr., or 4° Centigrade. Professor W. H. Miller when fixing the national standards in 1856, estimated the gramme at 15·432349 grains troy.

From the above data we find the troy grain equal to ·0648 gramme.

The following table will be found useful in converting grammes into grains, or grains into grammes:—

I.		II.	
Grammes converted into Grains.		Grains converted into Grammes.	
Grammes.	Grains.	Grains.	Grammes.
1 =	15·432349	1 =	·0648
2 =	30·864698	2 =	·1296
3 =	46·297047	3 =	·1944
4 =	61·729396	4 =	·2592
5 =	77·161745	5 =	·3240
6 =	92·594094	6 =	·3888
7 =	108·026443	7 =	·4536
8 =	123·458792	8 =	·5184
9 =	138·891141	9 =	·5832
10 =	154·323490	10 =	·6480

Grano. A Maltese copper coin, $\frac{1}{100}$ part of the old Sicilian ducat, and worth about $\frac{2}{5}$ of an English penny.

Gratis. Contraction of *gratiis*, for thanks; thus Cicero, "gratiis reipublicæ servire," to serve the State without fee or reward.

In commerce, as *thanks* have no exchangeable value, any service done for thanks is considered to have been done *for nothing*, and hence the common acceptation of the word.

Gresham's Theorem or Law. Owing to the ease with which coins when much worn circulate among the trading community, a practice has arisen among a limited class of money changers and bullion dealers of picking out new, bright, and full-weighted coins, either for making payments abroad, or melting down into bullion. The extent to which this practice had been carried, not being known to the Government, all efforts made by the Mint authorities to improve the condition of the coinage from time to time were found ineffectual. But it was observed by Sir Thos. Gresham that—

When two sorts of coins are current in the same nation, of like value by denomination, but not intrinsically, that which has the least value will be current, and the other, as much as possible hoarded or exported.

Hence good coins disappeared, and bad ones continued to circulate. The reason was, that so long as a law existed to make all coins a legal tender, or so long as the public showed an indifference about their weight, traders paid for their goods at the least possible cost—that is, by giving light coins for them in preference to heavy ones; and as the heavy coins were the only ones that would be accepted abroad at their denominational value, they were remitted to foreigners in payment for goods received from abroad. Owing to the practice now authorized by Government of defacing all light gold coin that finds it way to the Bank of England, the *garbling* of the coinage (as the process was called) has almost ceased.

Griscio. An Egyptian silver coin, value 1*s.* 6*d.*: 30 medini.

Grivenik. A Russian silver coin, called also the 10-kopeck piece. It weighs 2·039 grammes, and is ·500 fine, worth about 2*d.* English.

Groot. A small silver coin used in Bremen, value 11-20ths of an English penny.

Grosch. A copper coin formerly in use in Russia. Value 2 copecks.

Groschen. A small silver coin used in the North German Zollverein States, value 1-30th of a *thaler*, about $1\frac{1}{6}$*d.*

Gros Ecu. A silver coin used in Geneva, value 4*s.* 8*d.*

Gross. German, *gross*, great, large.

The whole, as distinguished from a part. *Gross weight*, the weight of entire package without any deductions. *Gross amount*, the total as distinguished from the *nett* amount.

Grosso. A Luccese billon coin, value 3*d.* Mezzo grosso, value $1\frac{1}{2}$*d.*

Grote. A bronze coin formerly used in Bremen, worth about one halfpenny English, 96 of which go to a specie rix dollar. (*See Dollar.*)

Guarantee. *Guaranty* or *Warranty*. French, *garantir*, to warrant, to pledge, to make sure. Gaelic, *barantas*. Welsh, *gwarantee, gwarant*, surety, pledge.

These three words although identical in their origin, differ somewhat in their application. *Warranty* is a law term much used in former times, but now little heard of.

A *guarantee* is a contract in writing by one man on behalf of another. If the contract or engagement be by word of mouth only, it will be of no force in a court of law. Whatever difference there may be etymologically between *guarantee* and *guaranty*, that difference has now disappeared. The two words are now used with precisely the same meaning, and there is no obvious reason for preferring one to the other.

The most important distinction to be observed in regard to a *guaranty* in commercial practice, is that which arises when a third party is introduced as a guaranty or surety for one or two others.

The guarantees or securities offered by the customer of a bank are often of the loosest description, and yet are valid in law. A customer wishing to borrow a thousand pounds for three months, might offer on his own behalf a guarantee or security in the form of Government Bonds to the value (say) of fifteen hundred pounds market value; but he would simply deposit them with his banker; he would have no receipt deposit handed to him, no acknowledgment or contract would be placed in his possession, although he would be called upon to sign a form of agreement to be held by the bank. But if a third party comes forward as guarantee for the borrower, more care is requisite in drawing up the contract, as it would certainly be more strictly interpreted than one given by the customer himself; and as the law in relation to this subject is somewhat complicated, although in the present day pretty well established, it is so much the more necessary that third parties when acting as guarantees should carefully scrutinize the Contracts to which they append their names.

Guild. Supposed to be derived from the Saxon, *guildan*, to pay; from which was formed the law Latin, *gildare*, meaning the same. Something more than mere paying towards the support of the company was implied in the term. An essential feature in the ancient *guilds* was the duty of dining or feasting together once a year, which in those days was considered almost a religious obligation, much in the same way as drinking together became in a later age. To pay the expenses of this annual feast, contributions were regularly made, and to these contributions the word *gildare* was applied. The Saxon term for the company was variously written *geld*, *gield*, *gild*, *guild*, and *gyld*.

> " The roome was large and wide
> As it some *gyeld* or solemn temple were."
>
> SPENSER, *Faerie Queene*, b. ii. c. 7.

> " Paying to them that haue saued and kept the same couenable for there trauaille, that is to say, by the discretion of the sherifes and bailifes or other our ministers in the places *guildable*."—RASTALL, *Collection of Statutes*, p. 279.

A guild in the modern acceptation of the word is a company or society formed to carry out some benevolent or other specific object. It still retains something of the old distinction between that and a trading company, inasmuch as all guilds make a point of having an annual or more frequent dinner provided for its members. No such obligation is imposed upon a commercial company, in many cases indeed, such an appropriation of the company's funds would not be tolerated.

Guilder. (*a.*) The Dutch Florin. (*See Florin.*)

(*b.*) The unit of value in the Dutch East Indies divided into 100 cents, and is now identical with the florin of Holland.

(*c.*) The unit of value in Java, also identical with that of Holland.

Guillaume, or William. A gold coin circulating in Holland, belonging to the old system of coinage, which was superseded by the Dutch monetary law of June, 1875. The guillaume weighs 6·729 grains, ·900 fine. Mint Par value 20·86 francs, or 16*s.* 6¼*d.* sterling.

A double guillaume of proportional weight and equal fineness is also in circulation.

Guimuh. A Turkish silver coin, value 20 piastres; called also the *Real Medjidie.* (*See Medjidie.*)

Guinea. (*a.*) A gold coin formerly used in England, and so called because made of gold imported from Guinea. By a proclamation issued Dec. 22nd, 1717, the guinea was made current at 21*s.* Its true value as derived from the market values of gold and silver at that time was 20*s.* 8*d.* At present there is no English coin called a guinea, but the fashion still prevails of quoting prices of some things in guineas, and for the sake of appearances, subscriptions to charities are often recorded in the same denomination.

(*b.*) A gold piece coined in Egypt, value 100 piastres. (*See Piastre.*)

Gulden. The Austrian florin. (*See Florin.*)

Gunda. A nominal coin used in Bengal, worth four cowries, and not convertible into sterling.

H.

H occurs in the following abbreviations:—

H.M.C. Her Majesty's Customs.
H.M.S. Her Majesty's Service.

Hachi-monseng. A Japanese circular coin of iron, and called the eight monseng piece. (*See Monseng* and *Zeni.*)

Halbbatzen. A billon coin formerly used in Switzerland, sometimes called a five-centime piece.

Half Notes. It is a common custom amongst men of business to cut a bank note, bond, and some other negotiable documents in two before sending them by post. This is done with a view to safety; for it is a maxim in law, as stated by McLeod, that "the property in an instrument remains in the owner until he has *entirely* parted with it; if he cuts it in two and sends one part by post, he does not lose the property in it till he has sent the other part, and he may reclaim the first part sent."

Hard Cash. A term used to distinguish *metallic* money, from the different forms of paper money. Nevertheless, the same phrase is often popularly used to denote bank notes, cheques, and other documents of undoubted value, in contradistinction to mere book debts, or commercial rights.

Hard Dollars. The English rendering of the Spanish *pesos duros,* (*duros fortes* or *fuertes*), a term conventionally used in some South

American States to signify "metallic currency," as distinguished from "paper currency," with which they are flooded.

Heller. (*a*) The $\frac{1}{120}$ part of the old silver *florin* of the South German States. English value $\frac{2}{3}$ of a farthing.

(*b*) The $\frac{1}{24}$ part of the Aix-la-Chapelle *mark:* about $\frac{2}{3}$ of a penny.

(*c*) A small coin of account formerly used in Frankfort, worth about $\frac{1}{3}$ of a farthing.

Holder. The holder of a bill, or any other negotiable instrument, is the person who has lawful possession of it for the time being; by having possession of it, is not meant simply having in one's own possession, or in one's own strong box, but having the right to claim it wherever it may be placed for the sake of safety, or for any other purpose whatever. For example, a bill may be deposited with a banker for safety, or as a security against a loan. In neither of these cases does the holder lose his hold upon it; but if he gets his banker to discount it, he loses all claim upon it, for he has virtually sold it, and the banker has paid him for it by a credit in his books.

Holidays. When a bill matures on a Sunday, Christmas Day, Good Friday, a Fast or Thanksgiving Day, appointed by Royal proclamation, the bill must be presented for payment on the *day preceding*. If it falls on a Bank Holiday under Sir John Lubbock's Act, the bill is payable on the *day following*.

Honour. Payment for. Acceptance for. The phrases "To Pay for Honour, or to Accept for Honour," signify in full, to pay with a view to save the honour, or to accept with a view to save the honour, of some one, and it usually implies that the person who performs this act does so on behalf of some friend or of some correspondent, whose bill would be dishonoured unless such a service were rendered. It is always detrimental to the reputation of a merchant or trader to have his bills and drafts dishonoured, and yet it will sometimes happen that when a bill is presented for payment, the drawee may be unable to pay it, and may be unwilling to accept it, because he knows that when it falls due he will not have funds to meet it. Sometimes, too, a bill contains irregularities with respect to dates or amounts, and from any of these causes it might be dishonoured unless some friend or correspondent could be at once applied to on the spot, who would undertake the responsibility of paying or accepting the bill in case of need. (*See In Case of Need.*) The laws relating to the payment or acceptance of bills for honour, contain some rather nice distinctions, and the works of McLeod ("Theory and Practice of Banking"), Byles ("Bills of Exchange"), and Wilson's "Handy-book on Bills, Notes, and I O U's" should be consulted by all who wish to obtain a competent knowledge of the subject. The following is a copy of an "Act of Honour," as given in Brookes' "Office and Practice of a Notary."

Act of Honour.

Act of Honour on acceptance *supra protest* by a third person, for the Honour of Drawer (or Indorser).

On the —— day of —— one thousand eight hundred and eighty-one, I, M—— N——, Notary Public, duly admitted and sworn, dwelling in ——— in the county of ——— and United Kingdom of Great Britain and Ireland, do hereby certify, that the original Bill of Exchange for Five hundred pounds, of which a copy is on the other side written (now protested for non-acceptance) was exhibited by me to E—— F——, one of the firm of E—— F—— & Co., who declared that the said firm would accept the said bill *supra protest*, for the honour of the drawer, holding the drawer and all other proper persons responsible to the said firm for the said sum, and for all interest, damages, and expenses incident thereto. I have therefore granted this Notarial Act of Honour accordingly. Which I attest, &c.

Hypothecation. From the Greek, ὑποτιθεμαι, *hypotithemai*, or ὑποτιθημι, *hypotithēmi*, to deposit as a pledge, to pawn, to mortgage; ὑποθηκη, *hypothēkē*, a pledge, pawn, or mortgage; whence the Latin, *hypothēca*, which signified generally a pledge, security, or deposit of things movable or fixed. It was also used in contradistinction to *pignus*, a pawn; *pignus* being applied to movable things, goods, chattels, &c., and *hypotheca* to immovable things, or real property. This distinction is maintained in the modern use of the word.

Hypothecation is the giving over of a thing by way of pledge or mortgage. When property of any kind is *hypothecated* as a security for a debt, the property remains in the hands of the debtor or borrower, and is thus distinguished from a *pawn*, where the property is given into the hands of the creditor or lender. Hence, when a foreign State pledges certain revenues, as customs, tobacco duties, sheep taxes, or State domains, as security for a public loan, they are said to be *hypothecated*—that is, the right to them is made over to the public creditor, but they are not, for they cannot be, handed over to him, because the lands are immovable, and the revenues are not yet collected. But the case is different when movable things are placed in the hands of a lender or creditor as security for a debt. Bills, deeds, bonds, plate and jewelry are often thus deposited with bankers or with pawnbrokers, and these articles are said to be placed *in pawn*, and are thus distinguished from property or rights which are simply *hypothecated*.

I.

I occurs in the following abbreviations:—

Int. Interest.
Inv. Invoice.

Ikilik. A Turkish silver coin, equal to two piastres. (*See Piastre.*)

Immaterial Capital. A name made use of in Political Economy to denote that form of Capital which consists of mental abilities, physical strength, business capacity, or manual dexterity, which can be employed as a source of income. To a clerk, accountant, or manager, qualities of this kind constitute capital of a very solid nature.

Immaterial Property. A name given by Economists to the right a man has to the use of his own mental and physical powers, and the profits derivable from the use of them.

Imperial. (*a*) A Russian gold coin, nominally equal to 10 roubles. It weighs 13·088 grammes, and is ·916⅔ fine, which gives a value of £1 12*s*. 9*d*. sterling for the Imperial when perfect.

But the largest gold coin now struck by the Russian mint is the half imperial, and this is almost the only Russian gold coin known in commerce. It weighs 6·544 grammes, ·916⅔ fine, and is worth 16*s*. 4½*d*. sterling. The Mint allows a remedy of 2 per mille for weight, but none for fineness. Although it is impossible to work to so great a degree of accuracy, the gold coins of Russia have a high reputation, and a large business is done in them by bullion dealers and refiners.

(*b*) There was formerly a gold coin circulating in Belgium, also called the Imperial. Its sterling value was about 11*s*. 3*d*.

Inconvertible. From the Latin, *verto*, I turn, and *in*, not.

Paper money is said to be inconvertible when it cannot be exchanged at the option of the holder for gold or silver to its full nominal value. By making paper money inconvertible, it usually falls in value immediately, and this fall is expressed by saying that *gold and silver are at a premium*, whereas, it would be more correct to say that "*paper money is at a discount*." Where paper money is always convertible into gold, there never can be any great difference in value between the two. A five-pound Bank of England note, for example, is worth five sovereigns anywhere in England, simply because the holder of it can get five sovereigns for it whenever he chooses. But a hundred-florin note in Vienna will not exchange for 100 gold florins, nor will a hundred-lire note in Italy exchange for 100 gold lire, because no one is bound to give the holders of the notes gold to the nominal amount on their demanding it. Most of these Government notes, however, carry on their face a "*promise to pay on demand*;" only it seems to be understood that no one shall be allowed by law to make the "demand" till it suits the convenience of the issuers to respond to it. Paper money of this latter kind is what is properly and technically called "inconvertible."

Incorporeal Property. From the Latin *corpus*, a body.

In Economics, a term applied to credit, debts, and kindred forms of wealth, as distinguished from money and commodities, which are called corporeal property. In general terms, incorporeal property is that kind of property which is not fixed in any *corpus*, body, or material substance, and which may even not be in existence at the present time. Of this nature are the rights to the produce of lands, trees, cattle, policies of insurance, which may be bought or sold like any other property, although years may elapse before the purchaser can use them. Nevertheless, the *right* to them may exist at the present moment, and it is this right which constitutes one form of incorporeal property.

Indemnity. Latin, *emo*, I take, and *de*, from, contracted into *demo*, to take away, take off; whence *damnum*, a taking from the value of a thing; loss, hurt, injury, harm. From this primary meaning it came to signify loss of property, debt, and then again a fine or penalty.

From *damnum* is derived the verb *damnifico*, to cause a loss, to damnify, and by addition of the negative prefix *in*, we have *indemnis*, unhurt, free from loss or injury, and *indemnitas*, security from loss or injury, or, as we say, "indemnity."

A letter, bill, or contract of indemnity is a document written or signed by one person with a view to secure a second party from loss. A mere oral engagement or promise is of no avail in a court of law, however binding it may be on moral grounds. Hence, it is customary in commerce, whenever one party pays money, or does anything in favor of a second party, to which the latter cannot show a legal claim, although there may be *primâ facia* evidence that such claim is good, to demand of the favoured party a *letter of indemnity*—that is, a writing holding the other harmless in the event of any one afterwards coming forward and presenting the same claim, and fortifying that claim by handing in the legal documents. To take a simple case. Suppose a person, holding a Consol certificate for £100, with a fly-leaf consisting of coupons £1 10*s*. each, but that the document has been damaged by fire in such a way as to destroy one of the coupons, and leave no trace of its existence. This certificate might be presented at the Bank by the holder, and as the holder has an undoubted right to the value of the coupon, the directors, after due inquiry and delay, might authorize the payment of the coupon, although it was destroyed or supposed to be destroyed. At the same time, it is evident that a fraud may have been attempted, that the coupon has not been destroyed, but wilfully cut off, and the marks of fire added, in order to give countenance to the fraud. Hence, as a matter of precaution, the Bank, if it paid the coupon at all, would most likely demand a letter of indemnity, holding them harmless in the event of the coupon, supposed to be destroyed, being afterwards presented for payment, for in such a case it would certainly have to be paid, even though it had been paid before on the good faith of the holder of the certificate. Now the letter of indemnity is brought into requisition. The holder of the certificate is applied to, and as he has engaged to hold the Bank harmless in the event of the coupon being presented, he must refund the money, or to be liable to an action at law, and also to heavy penalties. It is not, however, against fraud that protection is usually sought by an "indemnity," but against those strange "*oversights, inadvertencies*, and *lapses of memory*," which all those officials know something of, who have much to do with the "uncommercial" classes, and whose ways, though honest enough, are often of the laxest description.

Indemnity also is employed in commerce to denote the compensation made to any person for losses or injuries caused by the carelessness or oversight of another.

Indents. Orders, contracts, sent from distant countries (especially

India and China) under certain conditions as to price, &c. These orders were formerly written on forms torn in a zigzag, *indented* line from a counterfoil, so as to afford the means of detecting forgery or fraud. Hence the name, which is derived from the same origin as the more familiar term "*Indentures.*" Owing to the spread of telegraphic communication, and the rapid diffusion of "Price Currents," indents now differ but little from ordinary orders for goods.

Indentures. From the Latin, *instar dentium*, literally, after the manner of teeth, or like teeth.

An indenture is a legal deed written on paper or parchment, in which deed two or more parties are equally interested, so as to render it necessary for each to retain a copy. Hence the term is mostly used in the plural. They derive their name from the fact that they were originally written on a single sheet, the copies being afterwards separated or cut in a zigzag line (*instar dentium*, that is, like the teeth of a saw), so that when brought together, the genuineness of each document might be tested by comparing the indentations of one with those from which it was detached. This practice, formerly much in vogue among merchants who gave receipts or vouchers detached from a margin or counterfoil, is now, to a great extent, discontinued; other methods giving greater security having been devised. (*See Stocks, Tally.*)

Indermille. A Hindu silver coin, value 10*d.*

Inflation. Latin, *inflo, inflare*, to blow into, to blow out, as in the distension of the cheeks; and metaphorically, to augment, to increase. *Inflatus*, distended, puffed out.

The term "Inflation" is used in Economics as a curtailed form for "Inflation of Credit." While credit, when kept within proper limits, is of the utmost importance to the easy working of our mercantile system, there is a limit beyond which it cannot be increased, without danger to all parties concerned in it. It is difficult at all times to say when this precise limit has been reached. As a general rule it may be said that so long as the average prices of most kinds of commodities do not rise to any important extent, and so long as the various instruments of credit are readily convertible or realizable, no great danger is to be feared; but when the prices of commodities rise unduly, when high wages are demanded and freely paid, when bankers find it expedient to contract their issues, it is then time for merchants to look well after their balances, and to examine their bill-books, for these are undoubted signs of a coming storm, due to Inflation of Credit.

Ingot. From the German, *ein*, in, and *giessen*, to pour; *eingiessen*, to pour in; *Eingiess*, something poured in. Dutch, *ingieten*, to pour in, to cast in. French, *l'ingot*, now shortened into *lingot*. The original meaning of *ingot* in English was a vessel or mould into which molten metal was poured, and it was not till a later age the term was applied to the metal itself.

"He put this once (ounce) of copper in the crosslet (crucible)
And on the fire aswithe he hath it set
And afterward in the *ingot* he it cast."

Yeoman's Tale.

Ingot was the name formerly applied to the mould or matrix into which molten metal was poured for the sake of forming it into bars. It is now applied exclusively to the bars of metal themselves which have been cast in a mould. Conventionally the term is applied only to bars of the precious metals, as gold and silver. Copper, tin, lead, &c., in the same form are simply called bars.

Ink. From the Greek, *εγκαυστον*, *enkauston*. Latin, *encaustum*, something burnt in, from the ancient practice of making letters or figures on tablets of wax by means of a heated rod or *stylus*. *Encaustum* was the name given by the Romans to a kind of red ink or vermilion used in the signature of the Emperor. From this we have the Italian, *inchiostro*, *incostro*: the French, *encre* and *enque*; the Dutch, *inkt*; and the English, *ink*. The German, *Tinte*, and Spanish, *tinto*, with other kindred forms, are derived from a different origin.

The name of this familiar substance finds a place here simply on account of any interest that may attach to its etymology.

In Need. (*See Case of Need.*)

Inscribed Stocks. (*See Registered Stocks.*)

Instalment. Saxon, *in*, in, *steal*, a place.

Instalment signifies etymologically the same as *Installation*—that is, the putting into, or promotion to some place, dignity, or office. But a difference is made in the use of these terms, the latter only being employed in the sense here given; the former being now almost exclusively devoted to the service of finance. *Instalment* in this application would mean literally the putting one into the position of a bondholder or shareholder, and as this is commonly done by making successive payments, and as these stand much more prominently in the mind of the candidate for bondholdership than the dignity itself, a custom has grown up of calling these successive payments *instalments*, thus diverting the meaning of the word from its true object to another that is merely subsidiary thereto. When the term had thus become familiar as indicating a sum of money, it was found so convenient that it came to be applied to all fractional parts of a sum of money when paid in succession, so that to "pay by instalments" is a phrase in such common use in this sense as to be always understood.

Instrument. Mr. MacLeod makes the following important distinction between the two meanings of the word Instrument in the phrases "Instruments of Credit" and "Instruments of Exchange." In "Instruments of Exchange" it signifies the means by which circulation or exchange is effected. In "Instruments of Credit" it means a *Record* or *Document* of the Debt.

Interest. Money paid for the use of money. Unless otherwise expressed, any rate per cent. is understood to be that rate *per cent per annum*. It is important to observe, however, that interest though specified as a given rate per annum is often paid half-yearly or quarterly in which case the profit to the lender is somewhat increased. Thus, if £100 be lent at five per cent. payable quarterly, £1 5*s.* may be put out at interest for nine months, the second £1 5*s.* for six months, and the third for three months, and the interest thus coming in must be added to the five per cent. in order to determine the true return to the lender.

Bills, balances in accounts-current, and many other sums have the interest on them calculated to the day, and for this purpose tables have been compiled, and are to be found in most counting-houses. Where such tables are not at hand the following rule will be found of great service :—

Multiply the principal by the number of days, and this product by double the rate per cent. per annum. Of this result take $1\frac{1}{3} + \frac{1}{30} + \frac{1}{300}$, and cut off five figures for decimals of a pound. For example :—

Find the simple interest on £154 for nine days at the rate of $3\frac{1}{2}$ per cent. per annum —

Principal	154
Multiply by No. of days	9
	1386
Multiply by double the rate	7
Take the product once	9702
,, ,, $\frac{1}{3}$	3234
,, ,, $\frac{1}{30}$	323
,, ,, $\frac{1}{300}$	32
Cut off 5 right hand figures and call them decimals of a	£·13291

pound, giving 2*s.* $7\frac{3}{4}$*d.* as simple interest on £154 for 9 days at $3\frac{1}{2}$ per cent. per annum.

Again, as another example, find the interest on £9 for 30 days at $4\frac{1}{2}$ per cent. per annum :—

Principal	9
Multiply by No. of days	30
	270
Multiply by double the rate	9
Take the product once	2430
Add $\frac{1}{3}$ the product	810
,, $\frac{1}{30}$,,	81
,, $\frac{1}{300}$,,	8
	£·03329 = 8*d.*

Note.—In all cases similar to the last, when the number of digits is less than five, ciphers must be added to the left in order to make up that number.

Interest, is either *Simple* or *Compound*. Simple Interest is so called because the interest is simply added on from year to year and no additional interest is reckoned on the amounts thus accruing. Thus £100 put out at 4 per cent. *simple interest* for 5 years would amount to £120, the £20 being the simple interest added on in 5 successive instalments.

Compound Interest is so called because the interest is paid not only on the original capital, but also on the successive additions as they annually accrue. So that £100 put out at compound interest at 4 per cent. would amount in 5 years to £121 13*s*. 3½*d*.

International Coinage. Most experts in monetary science have had to face the problem of international coinage, and not a few have tried their hands at devising a system which should not only be practicable, but acceptable to the great trading nations of the world. The enormous loss of time and labour entailed by the complexity and incommensurability of different monetary systems, has attracted the attention of all who have studied the subject. There is a great loss of time in converting statements of accounts, lists of prices, and tables of statistics when expressed in the moneys and weights of foreign countries. There is a further loss of labour incurred by the statistician and merchant who receive their information from various sources, sometimes expressed in pounds sterling and hundredweights, at another in francs and kilogrammes, at another in marks and metres, at another in thalers and centners. Worse than all, there are many countries in which the Mint regulations are so imperfect or are so loosely observed that special knowledge or personal research is required on the part of those who do business with them. So numerous and weighty are these difficulties that many people make a business of them, and the money laid out in the remuneration of these men is so much sheer waste.

The only attempts at an International coinage that have yet been made, are those of the two European monetary conventions. (*See Monetary Convention.*) But the laws which the members of these bodies have laid down for their guidance are too rigid to admit of their becoming widely *international*.

Nevertheless, they are being adopted wholly or partially by several trading communities, and the success they have achieved will have to be taken into account, in any future scheme that may be devised. One hopeful feature has been developed in the course of the inquiries and investigations arising from the discussion of this question, and that is, the almost perfect unanimity with which the Gold Standard has been accepted as the true basis of the currency. There is also a pretty general agreement, that the size or denomination of coin suitable for one country, would not be the most suitable for another; and hence the practical inference that it is more desirable that the coinage of one country should be exactly *commensurable* with that of every other country included in the scheme—in other words, that the coins should be exact multiples or submultiples of all the other coins, rather than that one unit should be adopted by each and all. To take a favourite example: it is said that a coin equal to 1 sovereign = 25 francs = 10 Austrian florins = 20 marks = 5 dollars, would be a good coin to serve as a Standard of Value, and for international payments, and that all these values might be impressed on its face. It so happens, however, that although a coin of this size and value would *very nearly coincide* with the coinage of those countries respectively concerned, there are no two of them which *exactly coincide;* and in order to assimilate them, four out of the five, if not all of them, would have to make a slight alteration in the value of their unit. This is the great difficulty. No country is willing to make the requisite change. There is one reason why England should not make the change, which cannot be urged by either of the others; the English sovereign has been in circulation without any change in weight or fineness longer than any other. On the other hand, there is one very good reason why other States might be asked to make some change in their unit of value. The Gold and Silver coinage of France, Germany, and the United States has within a few years from the present time been replaced by a forced paper currency, while in Austria, Italy, and some other States of the Convention, a paper currency still prevails. The consequence is that the sovereign is a coin better known than any other coin in all parts of the commercial world, and which circulates freely and without question wherever it is found. Too much importance, however, ought not to be attached to the fact, for it is well-known that the smaller values of the franc, and of the dollar, render either of those units more acceptable to some countries than the large and, to certain poor countries, almost incomprehensible pound sterling. After all, the main difficulty is assimilation of value, for, as above stated, the international gold coin, if once agreed upon, might be called by a name that should be expressed in terms of the monetary unit of either country, and if such value were stamped on the face, no mistake could possibly arise, or inconvenience be felt.

International Stock. (*a*) Bonds or Shares whose dividends are payable in two, three, or more commercial centres, as London, Paris, Berlin, &c. Russian, Egyptian and some Turkish stocks are of this character.

(*b*) Bonds or shares which can be freely bought or sold in several commercial centres, and which afford facilities for arbitrage operations, or which can be employed as remittances so to avoid the cost of sending out bullion. The bonds of the United States 5 per cent. Funded Debt, as well as the more recent issues of that country, are said to be largely employed in this way; as are also the 4 per cent. bonds of our Indian Empire.

Intrinsic Value. Latin, *intrinsecus* (*intra* and *sĕcus*), within, in itself.

The phrase "Intrinsic Value" has been much objected to by economists, with a good show of reason, but the arguments used have not always indicated that the objectors quite appreciated their opponents' position. A promissory note for a sovereign, and a gold coin called a sovereign, have the same value—that is, each can be exchanged for the same quantity of any commodity—but everyone is conscious that the note depends for its value on the signature appended to it, and that if the person who signed it became bankrupt, or proved to be a rogue, its value might be entirely destroyed. On the other hand, a sovereign, even though the legend were effaced, and the device pressed out, would still have the same, or nearly the same value—provided it were of full weight, since it derives none of its value from the words impressed upon it, or from the character of the persons who impressed them. Stating the question somewhat differently, a coin and a good promissory note have the same value—that is, they will exchange for the same commodity. Deface the coin by the rolling press, and the writing of the note by means of chemicals, the exchangeable value of the coin is scarcely at all impaired, while the paper is worthless. This is the distinction which most men have in their minds, when they speak of the *intrinsic value* of a gold coin. The gold has a value independent of the words impressed on it, or the character of the person who impressed them, the paper has no value apart from the words on its face, and the character of the person who wrote them. At the same time, it is well known that the phrase does often lead to confusion, and economists have therefore done wisely in refusing to use it, the substitution of "Metallic" for "Intrinsic" answering every purpose.

It is, however, important to observe that many recent writers of repute, both in England and France, still adhere to the term "intrinsic," so that dogmatism on this point is out of place. Professor Bonamy Price, one of the latest writers on Political Economy, for example, has this sentence—

"It is the *intrinsic* value of the metal, its cost as a commodity which does all the work of a coin."—*Practical Political Economy* p. 368.

Mr. Seyd also uses the term freely, and in the *Annuaire par la Bureau des Longitudes* for 1881, the same word is used without the slightest reserve.

Investment. By *investment* is meant the outlay of money in the purchase of land, houses, stocks or shares with a view to receive the interest, rent, or dividends accruing thereon. The term, however, so like many others used in commerce, is employed somewhat vaguely; and it is not unusual, nor can it be said to be improper, to employ it when money is put into a business, wholesale or retail. Nevertheless, even here, there is a distinction made between the putting of money into a business with a view to receive a fixed rate of interest, and the employment of it in the same business with the intention of receiving a share of the profits, or bearing a loss as the case may be. In the former case, it would be called *investment* more properly, and in the latter, it would be called *trading* with it.

Invoice. The etymology of this word is very doubtful. It is often derived with great confidence from the French, *envoyer*, to send, *envoi*, a sending or message. *Envoi* was the term formerly used to signify the concluding address, the message from the Author when the Volume was ushered into the world. It seems more probable that the real origin of the word is the Italian, *avvise*, a notice, an advice. *Lettera d'avviso*, a letter of advice. The insertion of the *n* in words which come to us through the French is very common.

An invoice is a statement on paper concerning goods sent to a customer either for sale or on approval. It usually contains the price of the goods sent, the quantity, and the charges upon them made to the consignee. Any other details respecting which it is important for the consignee to be informed are added, and in these respects it differs from a trade bill or definite account.

I O U. A recognized contraction of the sentence, "I owe you." It is a simple acknowledgment of indebtedness to some particular person. As it is neither a promissory note nor a receipt, it requires no stamp. It is not a negotiable instrument, but as it is an acknowledgment of a debt, that debt can be sued for at any time, and is so far equal to a promissory note payable on demand. The following simple form of I O U should be adhered to since any addition to or deviation from it by inexperienced hands might render it invalid :—

Form of I O U.

Manchester, Sept. 11, 1878.

To Mr. John Cassel.

I O U One Hundred and Twenty Pounds.

£120 0 0

HERBERT BENSON.

If any words were added which might be construed into a promise, it would then become a "promissory note," and would be invalid without a stamp. Hence the necessity of care when interest is to be paid; for if it promises to pay *interest* only, no stamp is required, but if it were so worded as to imply a promise to repay the *principal* at a given date, it would require a stamp like any ordinary promissory note.

Isabel de Oro. A gold coin still circulating in Spain, valued at 100 reals, or 10 escudos or 5 piastres (dollars).

Ishu. A Japanese silver coin equal to the quarter of the itziboo or boo; worth about $4\frac{1}{4}$*d.* sterling. Gradually giving place to the new decimal system.

Issue. From the Latin, *exire*, to go out, to go forth; whence the French, *issir*, with the same meaning, and the participle, *issu*, meaning, gone out, descended, &c.

To issue signifies to give out, to distribute; hence, to issue notes, as by a bank, is to give out promissory notes in exchange for gold or silver, whether in the form of coin or bullion. *To issue* shares, as is done by commercial companies, is to give out certificates in exchange for money or other consideration, which certificates entitle the holder to certain advantages and profits which may accrue from the undertaking. *To issue* bonds or debentures, as is often done by railway and other companies, is to give out in exchange for a money payment certain instruments which entitle the holders to a fixed rate of interest. *To issue* a bill, note, or draft, is to deliver it to some one who thereby acquires a right of action on it.

Issue Department of the Bank of England. The Bank of England is divided into two great departments, called the Issue Department and the Banking Department (*see Bank Return*), which, although occupying the same building are, nevertheless, quite distinct.

The business of the Issue Department, although conducted by the officers of the Bank of England, is under the control of the Government, which control is exercised through the operation of the Bank Act of 1844, the directors of the Bank having no voice whatever in the matter. In Mr. Thomas Hankey's lectures on "The Principles of Banking," a very clear account is given of the issue department and its functions. He says:—

"In order to understand the action of the Bank of England correctly, it must always be borne in mind that, since the Act of 1844, the directors have had no control of that part of the currency which consists of bank notes; that is, they have had nothing whatever to do with the amount at any time in circulation in the country. The only function of the bank in this respect is to give notes for sovereigns when these last exceed five in number, or for bar gold, and to give or return sovereigns for every bank note presented for payment.

"Gold uncoined, that is, in the shape of bars, is received by the bank, and notes given in exchange at the rate of £3 17*s.* 9*d.* per ounce of 22 parts out of 24 of pure gold. In consequence of this operation, which it is, by law, compelled to make, the bank is commonly said to *buy* gold at £3 17*s.* 9*d.* per ounce. But, in truth, there is little in the transaction which resembles an ordinary *purchase*. The bank note given in exchange for such gold is more in the character of a receipt than a payment for a purchase. The bank, as I have already stated, is obliged by law to give bank notes for *all* the gold brought to them for that purpose, and to give gold coin, *i.e.*, sovereigns, for bank notes whenever presented for payment. The transaction is carried on in this way:—

"An importer or holder of, say, 1,000 ounces of gold desires to convert it into coin. He can do so by sending it to the Mint, where the operation will be effected free of charge, the Mint delivering him sovereigns at the rate of £3 17*s.* 10½*d.* for every ounce of gold when it has been properly assayed, and this coined money is given him at that rate for every ounce of standard (*i.e.*, of 22 carats fineness); but, the operation is a troublesome one to an importer, and must cost something in sending to and from the Mint, and is attended with some loss of interest during the period of coinage. The usual, and, I may say, invariable course is for the importer to send his gold to the Bank of England, which is compelled by law to buy it at £3 17*s.* 9*d.* per ounce, and this difference in price of 1½*d.* per ounce is readily paid, and is a great accommodation to the importer, who gets his gold coin without delay and without further expense.

"Every note presented at the Bank of England for payment must be immediately paid in gold coin; but as it was known that the wants of the community in this country were such as to require, for the ordinary trade, from seventeen to twenty million pounds of Bank of England notes to be always in circulation, the bank was permitted to make use of, at first fourteen and afterwards of fifteen million pounds of their own notes by investing them in securities, so as to make interest; which interest the Bank was to retain for its own use, and this enabled the Bank to pay, and the nation had a claim to exact, a payment for such privilege, which payment now amounts to nearly £200,000 a year —the profit which the nation derives from the issue of Bank of England notes. Beyond this sum of fifteen million pounds, the Bank is prohibited from issuing a single bank note without having an equivalent sum of gold in its vaults, and it is compelled to publish weekly an account of all the gold so held.

"I have already stated that the Bank is bound at all times to pay all its notes, when presented, in gold. It has frequently been asked how this could be effected when fifteen million pounds of such notes are not represented by gold in hand, but have been invested in securities. The mode is very simple. Supposing that all the notes outstanding beyond fifteen millions, were presented for payment, the gold in the bank reserved for that purpose would have effected this operation; but before the amount was reduced to fifteen millions, indeed long before, the bank would commence to realize its fifteen millions of securities. £4,000,000 consist of securities perfectly saleable at all times; the remainder—viz., eleven millions—has been lent to the Government. If there was any need of that money, the Chancellor of the Exchequer would not have the smallest difficulty in turning the Bank debt into three per cent. stock, which would be put into the names of the Governor and Company of the Bank of England, who would sell it as required, receiving for all such sales *their own notes, which, not being required to be re-issued for the purposes of circulation, would be completely cancelled*, and so, when all the securities were realized, and all the outstanding notes paid off, this part of the function of the Bank of England would be terminated; and thus, be it observed, all its bank-note liabilities would have been discharged without any disturbance of its other business, or without having touched a shilling of the capital."

At the present moment all Bank of England notes in circulation are secured as follows:—

£11,015,100 by Government Debt,
£4,734,900 by Securities,

and a variable amount against gold and silver.

The security thus offered for the convertibility of the bank note is so complete, that it circulates everywhere at its full value, and for many purposes is far preferable, and is actually preferred to gold. (*See Bank Return.*)

Issue of Loans and Shares. By the issue of a loan is meant the issue of documents called bonds, declaring that the holder has contributed a certain nominal sum towards a specified loan, and giving him a claim to interest on that sum at a fixed rate per cent.

By the issue of shares is meant the issue of certificates in return for a payment (called a subscription) declaring that the holder is entitled to a share in the profits of any given commercial undertaking, proportioned to the amount he has subscribed.

The method of procedure in each case is nearly identical, and consists of the following steps:—

(*a*) The publication of the Prospectus. (*See Prospectus.*)

(*b*) The taking in of Letters of Application. (*See Letter of Application.*)

(*c*) The sending out of Letters of Allotment. (*See Letter of Allotment.*)

(*d*) The issue of Scrip (*see Scrip*), in exchange for the Letters of Allotment.

(*e*) The exchange of Scrip for definitive bonds (*see Bond*) or Share Certificates. (*See Shares.*)

Itziboo, Itzebu, Itzib, or Itchebo. A Japanese coin which, through the introduction of the decimal coinage into the country, is falling into disuse. There were two coins called the itziboo, one of silver, and the other distinguished as the itzibookin, a compound of silver and gold. Their fineness is not to be relied on, so that these coins vary in metallic value from 1*s.* 4*d.* to 1*s.* 5½*d.* sterling. They are thin oblong plates, with square corners, thus differing from the kobang, which has rounded corners. The old coinage of Japan is gradually being superseded by the decimal system recently introduced. (*See Yen.*)

J.

J occurs in the following abbreviation:—

J/a. Joint account.

Jacobus. An old English gold coin of the time of James I., value about 25*s.*

Jettison or **Jetson.** Goods thrown overboard to lighten a vessel when in distress. It includes also the cutting away masts or cables, or any other part of the ship with a view to ensure the ship's safety. *See Flotsam.*

Joanese. A disused Portuguese gold coin, metallic value about £3 11*s.* 2*d.*, familiarly called the Joe.

Jobber. The origin of this word is best determined from its obsolete diminutives, *jobbel, jobbet,* which signified a small lump or load of anything. Hence, *job* would mean a lump or piece, and in a secondary sense is applied to a piece of work, or a task. From the noun, *job* is derived the verb, to *job,* and from this again the name of one who jobs, a *jobber.*

A dealer, one who does chance work; in Stock Exchange parlance, one who deals in Stocks, Shares, and the Public Funds. Although there is a slight taint of opprobrium attaching to the name of a stock-jobber, on account of the disreputable characters that too frequently take up the business, the profession is one which demands great tact and knowledge, and the duties pertaining to it are of a very onerous nature. Many of the jobbers on the Stock Exchange are men of considerable substance, and often hold as their private property large quantities of the Stocks in which they deal. It is the business of the stock-jobber to ascertain the market prices of the stocks asked for by the brokers; the prices being determined by the proportion subsisting from time to time between the buyers and sellers. If sellers preponderate, prices fall; if buyers predominate, prices rise. An experienced and skilful jobber discovers this relation by inquiry and observation among his fellow-jobbers, and by intercourse with the brokers. Acting on the knowledge thus acquired, he is prepared when a broker appears in the "house" to "make a price" for any of the special stocks in which he deals. By "making a price" is meant the quotation of two prices for the same stock, at one of which he is prepared to buy, at the other to sell, not knowing at the moment whether the broker wishes to buy or sell. But having quoted the two prices, he is bound by the Rules of the House either to buy or sell as the broker may decide. For example, suppose a broker to go to a jobber, and ask the price of Russian 1873 Bonds; the latter might say 86¼ to ½, meaning that he was prepared to buy them at 86¼, or sell them at 86½. The broker might say I will buy them at 86½, and then the jobber must conclude the bargain, and he would do so in the hope of being able to buy them of some one else at 86¼. The difference between the two prices quoted is called the "jobber's turn" or the "turn of the market," and it constitutes the profit made by the jobber on the transaction. By this simple arrangement all the stocks and shares commonly dealt in pass from hand to hand with the greatest facility, and it is only "out of the way" securities that require more detailed and leisurely treatment. The advantages enjoyed by the holders of bonds and shares, in thus having provided for them a ready market, is immense, as every one has felt, if he has experienced the difference between selling these securities and the selling of a house or a plot of land. Bring a house or a plot of land into the market, and it is known at once whether you wish to buy or sell. If you wish to sell, no one is anxious to buy, and the price is run down; if you wish to buy, no one is anxious to sell, and the price is put up. Apart from this exaggerated difference between the buying and selling price, there are heavy costs for transfer, conveyance, and registration, and it is on comparing these costs with those attending the transfer of Stock Exchange securities under the admirable régime of the "House," that the advantages of the latter become so conspicuous.

Joint Stock Banks. Banks constituted on the principle of Joint Stock Companies. They were at first founded on the principle of *Unlimited* Liability, and the oldest of them—namely, the London and Westminster, established 1834; the London Joint Stock, 1836; the Union Bank, 1839; the London and County, 1839, till lately remained on that footing. More recent establishments have been started on the *Limited* liability principle, and at the present time a lively discussion is going on as to the expediency of adopting the principle of *Reserve* liability. These three classes, however, all fall under the laws of Joint Stock Companies, which laws are supplemented by special clauses adapting them to the business of banking, and defining the powers of the directors. For a detailed account of the rise and progress of Joint Stock Banking; see McLeod's *Theory and Practice of Banking*, vol. ii. p. 379. See also next article.

Joint Stock Company. A Joint Stock Company is defined by Act of Parliament to be, "A Company consisting of seven or more members having a permanent paid up or nominal capital of fixed amount, divided into shares, also of fixed amount, and formed on the principle of having for its members the holders of shares of such capital, and no other persons." This definition excludes those companies consisting of six or fewer members, whose affairs fall under the Law of partnership.

Journal. From *dies*, a day. Latin, *diurnum*, the book in which the proceedings of each day were entered in the Roman Senate; whence the adjective, *diurnalis*, daily, in mediæval Latin, and the French, *journale;* Italian, *giornale;* Spanish, *jornal;* and English, *journal.*

In book-keeping, a *journal* is a book in which the transactions of each day are entered in the order in which they occur. The separate items are afterwards copied into other books, as the ledger, balance-book, &c. The journal is considered one of the *principal* books, in contradistinction to those which are auxiliary or accessory.

Journey. Fifteen pounds weight (701 sovereigns) of coined gold, or 60 pounds weight of coined silver. It is to be observed that 701 sovereigns do not weigh precisely 15 pounds troy, nevertheless, if they were found to be exactly of that weight, they would be so well within the Mint *remedies* as to satisfy all the requirements of the law.

K.

Kabean. A Hindoostanee copper coin, valued at $\frac{1}{40}$ of a rupee.

Kansang. A silver coin used in Mindanao, Philippine Islands, $2\frac{1}{2}$ of which go to the Spanish dollar, thus giving 1*s.* $7\frac{1}{2}$*d.* for its English value.

Karub. A Tunisian coin worth $\frac{35}{96}$ of a penny. There are two coins bearing this name, one of billon, and the other of copper.

Katib. A copper coin of Mysore $\frac{1}{8}$ of the *pie*, or $\frac{1}{64}$ of the English penny.

Kazneh or **Khuzneh.** A sum of money (not a coin), sometimes called a "Treasury." It is equal to 1,000 Egyptian Purses (*see Purse*), or £5,127 1*s.* 8*d.* sterling.

Kees. The Arab name for the Egyptian *Purse*, a sum of money equal to £5 2*s.* $6\frac{1}{2}$*d.* sterling.

Keran. A Persian silver coin—20 shahis, about $11\frac{1}{4}d.$ English. (*See Zabkran.*)

Kheyreeyeh. An Egyptian gold coin equal to 9 piastres or 1*s.* 10*d.* English.

Khodabandi. A Persian silver coin worth about 7*d.* sterling.

Kibear. An Abyssinian denomination of money, equal to 3 glass beads called *borjooks,* and estimated to be worth about $\frac{5}{32}$ of a penny.

Kilogramme. The unit of weight in the French metric system, for heavy goods. As its name implies, it consists of 1,000 metric grammes.

Kites. A slang term for Accommodation Bills; and, generally, for paper credit, not based on commercial transactions. In Scotland they are called also *Wind Bills.*

Kitze. In Turkey a "bag" of gold worth 30,000 piastres.

Kivan or **Quan.** The unit of value in Cochin China. The Kivan is a piece of silver (it can hardly be called a coin) very variable in value, but reckoned as a basis of exchange at about $\frac{2}{3}$ of a dollar. This gives 2*s.* $9\frac{1}{3}d.$ as the value of the Kivan. It is divided into 10 mas.

Kronen Thaler. The old Brabant crown or dollar, now superseded by the new German coinage. It was worth about 4*s.* 4*d.*

Kobang. A Japanese gold coin, in the form of a thin oblong disc, about 2 inches long, and $1\frac{1}{4}$ inches broad, rounded at the ends, and weighing about 200 grs. troy. It is an evidence of the rude condition of the Japanese coinage, before the recent introduction of the decimal system (*see Yen*) that the Kobang was so irregular in fineness as to be valued at 4 itziboos only, whereas its real metallic value was found on assay to be from 15 to 16 itziboos. Foreign traders soon discovered this, and by paying for merchandise in silver, and then exchanging the silver for gold, their gains were enormously increased, and gold was drawn from Japan at a rate which aroused the attention of the Government. Severe measures were adopted to prevent the circulation of the gold kobang, till at length it was reduced to about $\frac{1}{4}$ its original weight. The new kobang weighed about 51 grs. troy, with an average fineness of ·650, thus giving a sterling value of about 5*s.* 10*d.*

Kopek or **Kopaika.** A Russian copper coin, worth about $\frac{3}{8}$ of a penny. (*See Copeck.*)

Kopfstuck. An Austrian silver coin, worth 20 kreutzers, or 4·694*d.* sterling.

Kran or **Karann.** An Arabian denomination for a sum of money equal to 10,000 piastres.

Kreutzer. From the German, *Kreuz*, a cross.

(*a.*) An Austro-Hungarian copper coin nominally valued at $\frac{1}{100}$ of the Austrian florin—that is, ·2375*d.*, or about $\frac{7}{30}$ of the English penny. It is also represented by two silver coins, which have different degrees of fineness. Thus, the *silver florin* of 100 kreutzers weighs 12·345 grammes ·900 fine, and is worth francs 2·47 centimes = £·0978; or about 1*s.* 11½*d.* sterling. The value of the *kreutzer* as derived from this coin is therefore ·2349*d.* sterling.

The silver 10 *kreutzer piece* is only ·400 fine, weighs 1·666 gramme, and is worth 1¼*d.*, from which we find the kreutzer worth only half a farthing, English.

(*b.*) A silver coin formerly used in the South Zollverein States, the 60th part of a *florin*, and worth about ⅓ of an English penny.

Krona / **Krone** / **Kroner** or **Crown.** The unit both of value and account in Norway, Sweden, and Denmark, in conformity with the requirements of the Scandinavian Monetary Convention of May 23rd, 1873. It is represented by both gold and silver coins.

The Gold Krone. The 10 kronen piece weighs 4·480 grammes, ·900 fine. Its par value is francs 13·89 = £·5505, or 11 shillings sterling, and the krone as thus estimated is worth 1*s.* 1¼*d.*

The Silver Krone. The silver krone weighs 7·500 grammes, ·800 fine. Mint par value franc 1·33 cents. = £·0522, or 1*s.* 0½*d.* sterling. The krone is divided into 100 öre.

L.

L. Occurs in the following abbreviations :—

L/6/2. Our Letter of 6th Feb. &c.
L/C. Letter of Credit.
L.T. Lira Turca, the Turkish pound.

Labour. From *laborare*, to work or labour, and is connected with *lapsus*, a slipping, a falling, or gliding away in a gradual and unobserved manner.

Labour is the putting forth of effort in the production, preservation, or distribution of wealth. The term *Labour* is used in economic science as the type of services of all sorts, just as "money" is made the type of instruments of credit, and "land" the type of all material objects possessing exchangeable value.

Physical and *mental* effort may be expended under three different sets of circumstances giving rise to results bearing different names, thus :—

Labour is effort put forth in the production, preservation, or distribution of wealth as above said. It implies a wasting, or slipping away of energy, physical or mental, and sometimes both, and is rarely undertaken except from necessity, or to supply some urgent need.

Work also is effort put forth with the same object, but not so much from necessity, as with a view to procure gratification. That gratification may consist in the increase of the means of comfort and luxury; or it may be in the mere pleasure of activity, as is the case with many men of public spirit who devote immense effort to political and social enterprises with no other object than that of the public weal. Effort of this nature, however, is put forth rather from choice than necessity, and so far from being painful or wearisome, is mostly a source of keen enjoyment. Still it is work, and often work of the most useful kind. The work done by a steam engine, a galvanic battery, or a discharge of dynamite implies still less the idea of anxiety or suffering; hence we never speak of the "labour" of a steam-engine, of a galvanic battery, or of dynamite. When, however, human work is so excessive as to become painful and exhausting, we commonly hear it said that such work has "become a labour" to one, and this form of speech marks the conventional distinction between the two words.

Recreation, although often involving immense physical or mental effort is still farther removed from the idea of labour. Indeed, as the term implies, it is expected to replenish and renew the energies rather than exhaust them.

In Economics, the term Labour is made to cover what is above described, both as labour and work when resulting from human effort—as Mr. McLeod says "Labour in Economics means an exertion of the mind, however manifested, either by the hand, the tongue, or in any other way. However simple work may be, it must be directed by thought. All Labour is in reality Thought, accompanied by muscular exertion; and the sedentary scientific student—the lawyer, the clergyman, the professor, the painter, the Cabinet Minister, the banker, the merchant are as truly labourers and working men as any carpenters, masons, or ploughmen.

Lac, or Lakh of Rupees. A *Lac* of Rupees signifies 100,000 Company's Rupees, which, taken at 2*s.* per rupee, would be £10,000 sterling. At 1*s.* 11½*d.*, which is nearer its metallic value, £9,791 13*s.* 4*d.*

The caution often repeated in this work respecting the depreciated value of silver is especially applicable to this article, owing to the immense interests involved.

For the arithmetical notation of the lac *see Crore of Rupees.*

Laches. From the Latin, *laxus*, wide, roomy, loose, slack; *arcus laxus*, an unbent bow; *funis laxus*, a slack cord.

"Male *laxus* in pede calceus hæret." (A shoe which sets loosely on the foot—that is, which does not fit.)—HORACE, *Satires.*

From *laxus* is derived the French, *lache*, loose, weak, negligent; and from this again is formed the English noun, *lache;* plural, *laches;* the pronunciation of which is Anglicised into *lahsh* or *lahsh-ez. Laches* is sometimes used as a singular noun; it is then derived from the Norman French, *lachesse*, weakness, negligence.

Laches in commercial law are those acts of negligence and carelessness which entail inconvenience and sometimes loss to those who commit them. As examples may be mentioned—(1.) The taking of a bill or note in satisfaction of a debt, and failing to present it in due course. (2.) If a person receives a cheque in payment of a claim and neglects to present it at the bank on which it is drawn, while there are funds to meet it, and afterwards presents it when the funds are insufficient, the loss and inconvenience will fall on the holder of the cheque. (3.) If a banker pays a cheque which a little care would show to have been forged, he has committed a lache, and must bear the loss. (4.) If a bill is dishonoured by the refusal of acceptance or payment, the holder must give notice of the fact to the antecedent parties, or he will have no claim against them.

On the other hand, when mistakes are made which no ordinary care would have prevented, they are not called laches, but are set down as frauds on the part of those who cause them, and as it is often difficult to draw the line between *laches* and *frauds*, it not unfrequently happens in courts of law that some of the most troublesome points which a jury is called upon to decide is whether a fraud has been intended, or a mere lache committed.

Law Merchant. A branch of the Common or Unwritten Law of England, embodying the customs and usages of merchants, and is thus distinguished from Statute Law, or Written Law, which is founded on definite Acts of Parliament passed from time to time. The Law Merchant dates from a very early period, and is referred to in a Statute of Edward III., and from that time till now, many usages have acquired the force of law, although never fortified by an Act of Parliament, while other usages have been found so useful and important, that special Acts have been passed with a view to place their authority beyond dispute. The rules relating to the negotiation of bills of exchange, to partnership, apprenticeship, and some other things, are now incorporated in our Statute Law. But many customs still remain which have no other force than that of long usage and the consent of merchants. As a familiar example may be mentioned the practice of depositing coupons with the agents authorized to pay them when they are due. It is the universal practice to require those who present coupons for payment to make a list of them, containing the number of each one, and then to leave them three or more clear days for examination. Now there is nothing on the bond to authorize this delay, or to justify the imposition of this labour. And yet if any cantankerous bondholder insisted on immediate payment on presentation, and that payment were refused, he would assuredly discover, perhaps to his cost, that the law merchant justified the delay, for the custom is general, and is enforced by merchants and bankers in the interest of bondholders generally, and not for their own sakes, as by these means they ensure the payment of the coupon to the rightful claimant, and prevent irregularities and losses which might result from a more hasty course of procedure.

So again with regard to "stopped payments," "stopped notes," "stopped cheques," or "stopped bonds;" there is nothing to justify the stopping of these instruments, but the desire to secure the payment or transfer of them to the rightful owner. Nevertheless, the stopping of them is so common, and is of such manifest importance, that the law merchant will always support those who put on a "stop," provided it be shown that no negligence or unnecessary delay has been practised. (*See Stopped Payment.*)

Leang. The Chinese name for the *Tael* (*which see*).

Lease. Anglo-Saxon, *lesan*, to demise, to leave; French, *laisser*, to loose (as it were from our own possession), to let away, or apart, to bequeath.

A *Lease* is the letting or giving up the care of lands, tenements, machinery, &c., for a consideration, and for a stipulated time; after which time the use and enjoyment of the property leased reverts to its original owner. The term is also applied to the deed or document containing the terms on which such property is let.

Ledger. This word, as applied to one of the principal books used in book-keeping, has a pure Saxon origin. The corresponding book on the Continent derives its appellation from a totally different source, in French, *le grand livre;* in German, *das Haupt Buch.* The Dutch, *legger*, is probably from the same source as the English—namely, the Anglo-Saxon, *lecgan*, to lie, stay, or remain; whence a *leger-book* is a book that lies ready for entries of all kinds, and that remains, or is kept for reference.

Hakluyt used the word in a now obsolete form:—

"All which particulars doe most evidently appeare out of certaine auncient *ligier* books of the R. W. Sir William Locke, mercer of London."

Davies, in "The Immortality of the Soul," writes the word in its modern form:—

"This *ledger book* lies in the train behind
Like Janus' eye which to his poll was set.

Fuller, in his "Worthies," uses another modern form:—

"It happened that a stage player borrowed a rusty musket which had lien long *leger* in his shop."

Dr. Warton, a later writer, reverts to another disused form:—

"Many *leiger* books of the monasteries are still remaining wherein they registered all their leases.

The *Ledger* is one of the principal books used in every merchant's office. It is commonly said that a well-kept ledger would show the actual condition of a bank or merchant's office, even though all the subsidiary books should be destroyed by fire or other accident. If for "ledger" we substitute "ledgers," this would probably be true. For there are different kinds of ledgers used in all large offices. Indeed, it may be said that most books into which entries are posted from the auxiliary and subsidiary books are called ledgers, if they are intended to be kept for reference, and as a permanent record of business done.

Legal Tender. Latin, *tendo*, I stretch; *tendĕre*, to hold out, to offer.

Since *To tender* signifies to offer, or present for acceptance, we have the derivative noun *tender*, used in Economics in two technical senses. First it refers to an act, and this means an *offer* or *proposal*. Secondly it means a sum of money, or instrument of credit, as when we say "Gold is the only *legal tender* for sums above two pounds sterling." "Bank notes are a *legal tender* for sums above five pounds," in the United Kingdom. No tender of payment is valid unless made in the current coin of the realm or in Bank of England Notes. The meaning of which is, that when a debtor wishes to discharge an obligation, he is bound to do it by the payment of bank notes or by the current coin of the realm, if his creditor demand it. On the other hand, if the creditor refuses to accept the same, his claim on the debtor lapses, provided the tender has been made subject to the following conditions—namely, (1) that no bank note tendered was of less value than five pounds; (2) that the silver did not exceed in value forty shillings; and (3) that the copper or bronze coins did not exceed the value of *twelve pence.*

"By *legal tender* is denoted such money as a creditor is obliged to receive in requital of a *debt* expressed in terms of money of the realm."—JEVONS' *Money*, p. 76.

"If a debtor tender to his creditor the amount of a debt due in legal tender money, and it be refused, the creditor may indeed sue for it afterwards, but the costs of the action will be thrown upon him."—*Ibid.*

Legal Tender "does not mean, as many absurdly suppose, that a shopkeeper is obliged to sell for a legal tender note; but the legal tender law compels him to take the note on presentation for a debt recorded in his books."—BONAMY PRICE, *Practical Political Economy.*

Hence a trader may make any contract he likes for *gold*, *silver*, or *notes.*

Modifications of Legal Tender—

(*a.*) *Single Legal Tender System.* A Government while emitting various coins in various metals, may ordain that all contracts expressed in money of the realm, shall, in the absence of any express provision to the contrary, be taken to mean money in *one kind of metal* specially named, while other coin shall be left to circulate at varying market-rates, compared with the principal kind of coinage.

(*b.*) The Government may emit coins of two or more kinds of metal, and enact that contracts may be discharged in one or the other kind, at certain rates fixed by law. This is the *Multiple Legal Tender System.*

(*c.*) While maintaining one kind of coin as the principal legal tender, in which all large money contracts must be fulfilled, coins of other kinds of metal may be ordered to be received in limited quantities as equivalent to the principal coin. This may be called the *Composite Legal Tender System.*

Legend. Latin, *legendum*, something to be read from *legĕre*, to read.

The *words* inscribed on the face or rim of a coin; the busts or other figures constituting the *device.*

Leopold. A gold coin formerly circulating in Belgium. When first issued it was valued at 25 francs, but is only worth $24\frac{1}{4}$ francs of the present coinage, or 19*s.* $4\frac{1}{2}$*d.* sterling.

Lepton, plural **Lepta.** The one-hundredth part of the Greek Drachma, and equal to the French centime, in conformity with the requirements of the Latin Monetary Convention.

Letters of Administration. (*See Administration.*)

Letter of Allotment. A letter issued in answer to a letter of application for a portion of a public loan, or for shares in a commercial undertaking. The various points of importance in documents of this nature are best illustrated by a specimen. Appended is a copy of the "Letter of Allotment" issued to applicants for a portion of the late Egyptian State Domain Loan.

C *No.* 854. ***

EGYPTIAN STATE-DOMAIN MORTGAGE BONDS.

LONDON, 14*th November*, 1878.

In answer to your application, we have allotted to you £ 500 say *Five Hundred* Pounds nominal Capital at £73 for each £100 payable as follows:—

£5	on	application.
£15	,,	allotment.
£20	,,	16th January, 1879.
£20	,,	17th April.
£13	,,	19th May.
£73		

The first instalment on this allotment being £ 100 , the exact amount of your deposit, we have merely to inform you that Scrip Receipts will be prepared as early as possible, and when ready be delivered against this Letter in due course.

A Coupon for the dividend due on the 1st June next, will be attached to the Scrip.

We remain,

Your obedient Servants,

** In all communications respecting this Letter, please quote this Number.

Letter of Application. A form issued to persons who wish to subscribe towards the capital of a company, or to take part in a Government loan, &c. The following are forms well known in City circles, and give a fair idea of the nature of all similar forms:—

FORM OF APPLICATION FOR ALLOTMENT.

Payment to be made in Cash only.

ROYAL HUNGARIAN 6 PER CENT. RENTES.

Issue of £8,000,000 (Eight Million Pounds Sterling)

Nominal Capital 6 per Cent. Rentes.

To Messrs. N. M. —— & Co.

Gentlemen,

________ request that you will allot to ________ £ ________ say ________ Pounds nominal Capital of the above Stock, on which ________ enclose the deposit of five per Cent., or £ ________, and ________ agree to accept that amount, or any less sum that may be allotted to ________ and to pay IN CASH the balance of such allotment according to the conditions of your Prospectus of the 8th October, 1877.

Gentlemen, Your obedient Servant,

Name at length ________

London, *Address* ________

____

1877.

RHODES REEF GOLD MINING COMPANY
LIMITED.

No.

FORM OF APPLICATION.
(To be retained by the Bankers.)

This Form should be sent intact to the Bankers.

To the Directors of

THE RHODES REEF GOLD MINING COMPANY, LIMITED.

GENTLEMEN,

Having paid to your Bankers* the sum of £——— being a deposit of 2*s.* 6*d.* per Share, I request that you will allot me———Shares of £1 each in your Company, and I hereby agree to accept the said Shares, or any smaller number which you may allot to me, and I agree to make the payments thereon, and I request you to place my name on the Register of Shareholders in respect of the Shares which may be allotted to me.

I am, GENTLEMEN,

Your obedient Servant,

Signature———

Name (in full)———

Address (in full)———

Profession or Business———

These particulars must be written legibly.

Date ———, 1880.

The £1 per Share is payable—2*s.* 6*d.* on application, 7*s.* 6*d.* on allotment, 5*s.* on 15th day of January, 1881, and 5*s.* on the 15th day of March, 1881.

* In the event of no allotment being made to the public, the amount paid on this application is to be returned in full.

Letter of Credit. A letter of credit is a letter sent to a distant town, or foreign city, requesting that a certain sum may be placed to the credit, or held at the disposal, of some person named therein. It is not a negotiable instrument, owing to its vagueness. Indeed it has been called the most primitive form of bill. Considering how obscure the origin of trade bills is, it is not improbable that they originated in mere business letters, and were afterwards reduced to the regular form, as found in use among the Lombards and Venetians. How easy the transition is may be seen by a comparison of the following note sent from London to Glasgow:—

To Mr. Macfarlane, Glasgow.

Dear Sir,

Have the goodness to hand the Secretary of the Glasgow Infirmary the sum of Five Pounds, and debit my account with the same.

Yours truly,

ROBERT STEPHENS.

Such a note might be written by any man on friendly terms with another, without a thought or knowledge of such things as bills, negotiable instruments, &c., and yet how near it comes to the form of an inland bill of exchange is obvious to everyone. Doubtless, thousands of such notes have been and are still written by persons who have no knowledge of business in its more complicated aspects. A still more curious foreshadowing of the Letter of Credit is to be found in the Bible. It is the oldest form of letter or bill extant, and is found in 2 Chron. ii. 11, where it is expressly stated that "Huram, the king of Tyre, answered in writing, which he sent to Solomon." In this letter is a clause to this effect. "Now therefore the wheat, and the barley, the oil, and the wine, which my lord hath spoken of, let him send unto his servants: and we will cut wood out of Lebanon, as much as thou shalt need: and we will bring it to thee in flotes by sea to Joppa; and thou shalt carry it up to Jerusalem."

Here we have a clear case of exchange: on the one side wheat, barley, oil, and wine; on the other, cedar wood, and service. The contract was reduced to writing, and appears to have been honourably fulfilled. Of course the whole document is verbose and vague, but it shows that when antiquarians are looking about for the origin of instruments of exchange, they must be prepared to go a long way back, and traverse very obscure paths. It is commonly said that the Romans made use of writings similar to our modern bills of exchange, or promissory notes, but no specimen has, as yet, been discovered in any extant Latin author, which is a little surprising when we reflect on the completeness of mercantile law in Rome, as illustrated by the Pandects of Justinian and some earlier works on the same topic. (*See Circular Letter of Credit.*)

Form of Letter of Credit.

Messrs. Bruce & Co.,

New York.

This letter will be presented to you by *Mr. Holland* in whose favour we beg to establish a credit for *Two Hundred* pounds sterling. You will please hold this sum, or any part thereof, at his disposal, less your usual charges, and take in exchange his drafts upon this

Bank, which will be duly honoured. It is understood that this credit is to be available for one year from this date, at which period if *Mr. Holland* has not made use of it, you will consider it cancelled. We shall forward you, in our next letter the signature of *Mr. Holland*, to which we refer.

I am, &c.

Letter of Regret. A form of letter issued the same time with "Letters of Allotment" informing certain applicants that owing to the number of applications, the contractors "regret" they cannot comply with their request.

Letters of Probate. (*See Probate.*)

Levant, To. Spanish, *levantar*, to raise; *levantar el campo*, as in French, *lever le piquet*, to decamp.

A slang term applied to the conduct of fraudulent debtors, who run away rather than face their creditors.

Levy, To. French, *lever*, to raise.

To *levy* a rate, tax, or contribution is simply to raise one.

Ley. The unit of value and of account in Roumania. By the Roumanian Monetary Law of April, 1879, the coinage of Roumania was assimilated to that of the Latin Monetary Convention, although Roumania has not formally subscribed to it.

The *Gold Ley*. Coins of 20, 10, and 5 leys in gold are struck by the Roumanian Mint. The 10 ley gold piece weighs 3·226 grammes, ·900 fine. This gives for the single ley ·3226 grammes, which, like the French franc is worth about 9½*d.* English.

The Silver Ley weighs 5 grammes, ·835 fine, and is worth 93 centimes, or 8·94965*d.* English.

The Ley is divided into 100 banis; whence the bani is equal to the French centime.

Liability, Liable. French, *lier*, to bind: from the Latin, *ligo*, with the same meaning. The word *liable*, used somewhat vaguely in common speech, in the sense of "obnoxious," "exposed," "subject," is employed in commerce with a meaning more in accordance with its etymology. *To be liable*, is to be "bindable," "able to be bound," and a man may render himself thus *liable*, by placing himself under the action of the laws of the realm, or by entering into a private contract, or by inadvertently exposing himself to the devices of fraudulent individuals. Thus the law of the land cannot *bind* a man to pay a penalty, or to go to prison, if he has not committed the offence to which such punishment is attached; but if he does commit such offence, the law is empowered to bind him; in other words, he is "liable" or "able to be bound." Again, I am not bound, nor can any one bind me to pay the debts of my next-door neighbour; but if I have entered into a contract or agreement, or have become surety for him, then, in the event of his failing to pay his debts, his creditors are able to bind me, or the contract binds me, to make good the deficiency—that is, I have incurred a *liability*, or am *liable* for his debts. As to the possibility of rendering oneself "liable" through inadvertence, the history of the recent Glasgow Bank failure affords melancholy illustrations. Many honest persons became shareholders in that concern, with an unwavering belief that their capital was placed in the hands of managers whose integrity and ability were unquestionable; but their confidence was misplaced, and they have been made to feel that they are capable of "being bound" to make good the defalcations of those whom they trusted.

Limited Liability. Liability is said to be *limited* when the person liable is bound under clearly defined conditions. The phrase is chiefly used in connection with Joint Stock Companies, and here it means that the members or shareholders shall not be called on under any circumstances to contribute more than the amount of the shares for which they have subscribed. If the debts of such a company when wound up, amount to more than the resources of the company, can meet, the creditors must bear the loss.

Unlimited Liability. As implied by the name, companies formed with *unlimited liability* place their members in a much more precarious position than those with limited liability. In the event of a failure in any such company, the creditors may call upon all the shareholders, or any one of them, to contribute, if necessary, his last penny towards meeting their claims. The fear of such a catastrophe, probably, acts as a stimulus to care and exertion; for some of the banks, constituted under the system of the unlimited liability, are amongst the soundest and most prosperous in the kingdom. Many banks, however, which were originally founded on the principle of unlimited liability, are being reconstituted under the Reserve Liability Act.

Reserve Liability is "liability held in reserve," and is not called into operation so long as the share capital and revenues of a Joint Stock Company are sufficient to meet all the demands made upon them. Under such favourable circumstances a Joint Stock Company may be even wound up, and its accounts closed, without recourse to this reserve liability. But should the assets of a company be found insufficient to meet the demands made upon them, the law authorising a reserve liability acts as a twofold protection: (1.) In favour of the shareholders themselves, all of whom may be called upon to contribute, *pro ratâ*, to make up the deficiency, but who cannot be required to contribute more than the amount specified in the Articles of Association. Except in some unusally unfortunate cases, this might mean distress, it by no means implies ruin. (2.) In favour of the creditors, who can demand, in liquidation of their claims, a sum from the shareholders, at least equal to the original share capital of the company for that purpose, and in some double that amount. In the Act of 1879, entitled a "Bill to Amend the Law with respect to the Liability of Members of Banking and other Joint Stock Companies," the characteristics of a Reserve Liability Company are thus described:—

(1.) The words "reserve liability," or "limited by reserve," shall form part of the name of every Reserved Liability Company.

(2.) In the event of a Reserve Liability Company being wound up, there shall be payable in respect of each share in the company (in addition to such portion, if any, of the nominal amount of such share as is not paid up) the amount of the reserve liability attaching to such share; and the amount of such reserve liability shall be payable by the same persons, and in the same manner, as if such amount were part of the nominal amount of each share.

(3.) The amount of the Reserve Liability attaching to each share shall be regulated by the amount of such share, and shall be *a sum equal to, or some multiple of, the nominal amount of the share* in respect of which it is payable.

(4.) The amount of the Reserve Liability attaching to each shall, in the case of a reserve liability company formed in pursuance of this Act, be stated in the Memorandum of Association, and in the case of an unlimited company registering as a reserve liability company in pursuance of this Act, be stated in the resolution passed by the members when assenting to registration.

(5.) The limit of liability required by an unlimited company registering as a reserve liability company shall not apply to any debts or liabilities of the company contracted prior to such registration; and such debts and liabilities may be enforced in the same manner in which the debts and liabilities of a company registered as an unlimited company are enforceable.

Liabilities by Indorsement. Liabilities incurred by banking and commercial firms in consequence of having indorsed Bills of Exchange or other negotiable instruments, whereby they become responsible for the payment of such bills, &c., in the event of all the other parties failing to do so. Liabilities of this kind form a distinct item in the balance sheet of Joint Stock Banking Companies under the Act of 1879.

Lien. From the Latin, *ligare*, to bind, to tie; whence *ligamen*, a band, tie, or bandage. Old Norman, *lian*, a band, bond, or pledge; Provençal, *liain;* Catalonian, *lligam;* Portuguese, *ligame;* Italian, *legame*, all bearing a similar meaning.

A *lien* is the right of retaining anything given as a pledge or security until the claim upon it be satisfied. It also includes the more general right of any one who has been employed to bestow his labour upon any article to retain that article until his labour is paid for. An innkeeper who bestows his care on the property of his guest—a carrier who has conveyed goods from one place to another—a joiner who has repaired a desk—each has a *lien* on the articles on which he has bestowed his labour, which *lien* he can lawfully enforce if he be so minded until his work is paid for. Hence the distinction between a *particular* and a *general* lien.

Particular Lien is the right of retaining any particular article or chattel, until some legal claim upon it be satisfied. A bookbinder has a particular lien on a book that he has bound, a joiner to a desk he has repaired, a banker to any securities pledged for the payment of a specified debt, which lien he may enforce by retaining the articles named until the debt is paid; but he may not seize or retain any other securities or chattels for that *one* debt.

General Lien. An hotel keeper has a general lien upon the baggage and other property of a guest which he may retain till his bill is paid. A banker has a general lien upon all banking securities as bills, notes, stock, coupons, bonds placed in his hands by a customer, and which he may retain as security for any sums due to the bank; and that lien extends not only to debts already accrued, but to any that may accrue while the said securities are in possession of the bank. There are, however, many nice points of law in relation to *liens*, whether general or particular, and it is a kind of business about which it is always expedient to have the advice of a solicitor.

Light Coin. A sovereign is a light coin whenever it weighs less than 123·27447 grains (7·98805 grammes.) But it does not cease to be a legal tender till it is reduced in weight to 122·50 grains (7·93787 grammes). The last person who uses and tenders such coin bears the loss.

Silver coins are allowed to fall much lower from their mint weight before they are withdrawn from circulation, and sixpences may sometimes be met with in trade which scarcely exceed one half their legal weight. Even then they are often accepted as readily as though they were of full mint value, every one hoping to be able to pass them on to some one else, and so avoid the loss which is sure at last to fall on some unlucky holder.

Professor Jevons maintains that the only thorough "remedy for this state of things is for the Government to bear the loss occasioned by the wear of the gold, as it already bears that of the silver currency. . . . . No one would then have any reason for keeping the light gold away from the bank; the currency would soon be purged of the illegally light coins, and would thenceforth be kept up strictly to the standard weight; all loss of time and trouble would be saved to individuals, a consideration which we should not lose sight of, and lastly, no injustice would be done, as at present, to the last holder of a light sovereign."

"In opposition to such a proposal, it is usually urged that encouragement would be given to the criminal practice of sweating or otherwise diminishing the weight of the currency. I answer that on the contrary, it is the present state of things which gives the best opportunity for illegal practices, because it renders the population perfectly accustomed to handling old and worn coins. No one now actually refuses any gold money in retail business, so that the sweater, if he exist at all, has all the opportunities he can desire. I have met with sovereigns deficient to the extent of four or five grains, or 8*d.* to 10*d.*, but they nevertheless circulate. . . . . Under the proposed new system, such practices would be rendered almost impossible."

Limitations, Statute of. Whenever an injury has been done, or a debt incurred, a *right of action* has been set up. That action must, however, be brought within a reasonable time, and what shall be considered a reasonable time is fixed by the *Statute of Limitations.* After that period, the remedy is "barred" by mere lapse of time.

The use of these Statutes of Limitation is to preserve the peace of the kingdom; and to prevent those innumerable perjuries which might ensue, if a man were allowed to bring an action for an injury committed, at any distance of time. Upon both these accounts the law, therefore, holds that *interest reipublicæ, ut sit finis litium* ("it is of importance to the commonwealth, that there should be a limit to litigation"), and upon the same principle, the Athenian laws in general prohibited all actions, where the injury was committed five years before the complaint was made. Nor are these the only reasons on which the bar by lapse of time is founded; for if the plaintiff were permitted to bring a claim forward at any period, however remote, there would be danger of its being delayed until the defendant had, by some casualty, been deprived of the documentary or other evidence by which it might once have been successfully encountered; and the delay might even be practised with the fraudulent design of exposing him to this disadvantage; besides which, it is to be considered, that great hardship always attaches to the case of a party, who, after a long possession—not originating in any fraud or other misconduct of his own — finds himself unexpectedly liable to eviction, while on the other hand a supine claimant is entitled to no favour or protection from the law; the maxim being that *vigilantibus non dormientibus, jura subveniunt.* (Laws come to the help of the watchful, not to the sleeping.)

The Statute of Limitations covers a great number of cases, but those most frequent in commercial and banking practice are the following:—

1. All debts on simple contract, arrears of rent, and actions for trespass, are limited to six years after the cause of action has accrued. Exception is made in favour of persons labouring under *disability*, such as being *under age*, or of *unsound mind*, in which cases it is provided that such person shall be at liberty to sue after the removal of the disability within the same period as is allowed to persons having no such impediment.

2. A bill or a note may be negotiated for the space of six years after it has become payable. After that period no action can be taken. The exceptions are, when a fresh promise *in writing* is signed by the party to be charged, or his agent, and when part payment has been made, or interest paid, when the remedy will be revived and continued in force from the date of the last payment.

3. If a customer leaves a deposit or balance at his banker's and neither adds to it nor draws upon it for six years, the banker is not liable. But if the balance has been above the recognized minimum, and interest on that balance has been added from time to time in the banker's books, the banker is liable for six years after the date when the last addition was made.

4. In regard to real property considerable alterations have been

made in the law from time to time. Till very recently, if a person or persons had enjoyed a right of way, or the use of side lights looking upon an adjoining property, and had been in peaceable possession of that privilege for twenty years, he could not after that be dispossessed. But by an Act passed in 1874 the term was shortened from twenty years to twelve years. Hence the necessity of closing such rights of way, or blocking up windows, the use of which is enjoyed only by sufferance, every few years, in order to prevent any piece of property from being encumbered by claims to which strangers or neighbours have no legal right, but to which they can establish a right, if these simple precautions are neglected.

Limited Liability. *See Liability.*

Limit of Credit. There is scarcely any doctrine in Economics of greater importance than that which relates to the Limit of Credit. Most commercial catastrophes have been caused by the overstepping of those limits, and that again has in many instances been done in consequence of the want of a clear understanding of the signs which indicate an undue Extension of Credit. Not that any one sign would of itself indicate that the Limit of Credit had been reached. It is the concurrent appearance of several signs that enables the prudent trader to guard against the coming storm; and some of these signs may with advantage be here noted. First, there is a large extension of manufacturing industry and commercial enterprise, and as there is little or no corresponding increase of metallic money in the world at these times, this great increase of business is carried on chiefly by means of credit, and instruments of credit, in the form of commercial bills. Such an increase is commonly known as the "Inflation of Credit" and is one of the first signs that the limit of credit is being approached. Secondly, since it is the business and in the interest of Bankers to watch these signs, those who interpret them most correctly, and act upon them most promptly, find it expedient to charge a higher rate of discount for their advances, in other words, when applied to by merchants to buy debts, by discounting bills of exchange, they give less for them than they have been in the habit of doing. Bills then are less freely offered, or if freely offered, bankers continue to increase the rate of discount, and thus discourage the creation of further credit. This is called in banking parlance a "Contraction of Issues." When bankers generally show an inclination to contract their issues, we have a second indication that credit is approaching its limit. Thirdly, as a consequence of Contracted Issues by the bankers, the prices of certain commodities are seen to fall. At one time it will be railway property, another mining shares, another textile fabrics, at another the shares of commercial companies. At this point, the public become aware for the first time of the storm that has been brewing, and as manufacturers and merchants cannot any longer get credit at the Banks they are obliged to sell their commodities at the low prices prevailing in order to meet bills falling due day by day. This depresses prices still more, and it soon becomes obvious to the whole community, that commodities of some kinds, and perhaps of several kinds, have been produced more rapidly than they were wanted by the people. Hence this phenomenon has received the name of "Over-production," which is a third sign that the limit of credit has been very closely approached. Finally, as a co-operation of the foregoing causes, a fourth phenomenon reveals itself in the complete "Disorganization of Commerce." High rates of interest are offered for loans, while capitalists refuse to lend on any terms. Merchandise and commodities are piled up in warehouses, docks, and wharves, while thousands under the shadow of their walls, are perishing for lack of food and other necessaries of life. Everyone is offering his services in his own particular line of business, and no one can be induced to accept them. Trust and confidence which lay at the very foundation of all healthy trade, are supplanted by doubt and suspicion. These are the leading characteristics of most commercial crises which result from the abuse of credit—that is, by not restraining it within safe limits,

Liquid Assets. A term used by bankers to denote coin, bank notes, and securities which can be instantly converted into cash. It excludes all bills which have several days or weeks to run, bonds and shares whose market value is depressed, so that they cannot be sold without a loss, and generally all such securities whose value cannot from any cause whatever be at once realized in an emergency.

Liquid Reserve. That portion of a Bank's Reserve which can at any moment be converted into cash, or otherwise realized.

Liquid Securities. Securities that can be easily and promptly converted into cash.

Lira. From Latin, *libra*, the Roman pound; French, *livre;* Italian, *lira.*

The unit of value and of account in Italy according to the terms of the monetary laws of April, 1862, and July, 1866, and of the Latin Monetary Convention of 1878.

Both the gold and silver *lira* are identical in weight and fineness with the French Franc. It is divided into 100 *centesimi.* (*See Franc.*)

The old Lira of Tuscany was worth 7¾*d.* sterling, and was divided into 20 Soldi; it is now superseded by the Italian coinage.

The Lira of Turkey and Egypt is of the same fineness as the English sovereign ·91666, and is worth 18*s.* sterling. (*See Medjidié.*)

Livre. Old French computation, value 10*d.*; 20 sous.

Lloyd's. A name given to the place of general insurance business, from that of the proprietor of a coffee-house, formerly used for a similar purpose in Lombard Street. The concern was afterwards removed to Pope's Head Alley, where it was called New Lloyd's; and subsequently, in 1773, to some rooms in the upper part of the Royal Exchange and the interest of it having long been purchased of the then proprietor, it has from that time been placed under the management of a committee of the members. This institution, now known simply as "Lloyd's," is devoted entirely to Marine Insurance, and to such business as is subsidiary thereto; as the classification and registration of vessels, &c.

Lloyd's Policy. The form of policy authorized by the Committee of Lloyd's.

Appended is a form of "Lloyd's Policy," the body of which is printed in Roman type, with blank spaces for the portions here filled in with Italics, as well as for the amount stated on the margin at the left. The letters S. G. are the initials of the Latin words "*Salutis Gratiâ*" (for the sake of safety.) Taken with the figures immediately below, they mean "insured—or made safe—to the extent of 1,000 pounds.

S. G.

£1,000.

Be it known that *G. Cowen & Co. & or as Agents* as well in *their* own name, as for and in the name and names of all and every other person or persons to whom the same doth, may, or shall appertain, in part or in all, doth make assurance and cause *themselves*, and them and every of them, to be insured lost or not lost, at and from—

Genoa to London. With leave to call at any ports or places for all purposes. Additional conditions as attached.

upon any kind of goods and merchandises, and also upon the Body, Tackle, Apparel, Ordnance, Munition, Artillery, Boat, and other furniture, of and in the good Ship or Vessel called the *Waterford* whereof is Master, under God for this present Voyage, ALFRED WATSON or whosoever else shall go for Master in the said ship, or by whatsoever other name or names the same ship, or the Master thereof, is or shall be named or called, beginning the adventure upon the said Goods and Merchandises from the loading thereof aboard the said ship *as above* upon the said ship, &c., and shall so continue and endure, during her abode there, upon the said ship, &c., and Goods and Merchandises whatsoever, shall be arrived at *as above* upon the said ship, &c., until she hath moored at anchor Twenty-four Hours in good safety, and upon the Goods and Merchandises until the same be there discharged and safely landed; and it shall be lawful for the said ship, &c., in this Voyage to proceed and sail to and touch and stay at any Ports or Places whatsoever *and wheresoever, &c.*, without prejudice to this insurance. The said Ship, &c., Goods and Merchandises, &c., for so much as concerns the Assured, by agreement between the Assured and the

Assurers in this Policy, are and shall be valued at *as under*.

Touching the Adventures and Perils which we the Assurers are contented to bear and do take upon us in this Voyage, they are of the Seas, Men of War, Fire, Enemies, Pirates, Rovers, Thieves, Jettisons, Letters of Mart and Countermart, Surprisals, Takings at Sea, Arrests, Restraints and Detainments, of all Kings, Princes, and People, of what Nation, Condition, or Quality soever, Barretry of the Master and Mariners, and of all other Perils, Losses, and Misfortunes that have or shall come to the Hurt, Detriment, or Damage of the said Goods and Merchandises and ship, &c., or any Part thereof; and in case of any Loss or Misfortune, it shall be lawful to the Assured, their Factor, Servants and Assigns to sue, labour, and travel for, in, and about the Defence, Safeguard, and Recovery of the said Goods and Merchandises and ship, &c., or any Part thereof, without Prejudice to this Insurance; to the Charges whereof we, the Assurers, will contribute each one according to the Rate and Quantity of his sum herein assured. And it is agreed by us, the Insurers, that this Writing or Policy of Assurance shall be of as much Force and Effect as the surest Writing or Policy of Assurance heretofore made in Lombard Street or in the Royal Exchange, or elsewhere in London. And so we the Assurers are contented, and do hereby promise and bind ourselves, each one for his own Part, our Heirs, Executors, and Goods to the Assured their Executors, Administrators, and Assigns, for the true Performance of the Premises, confessing ourselves paid the consideration due unto us for this Assurance by the Assured, at and after the Rate of *Seven Shillings and Sixpence per cent.*

IN WITNESS whereof, we the Assured have subscribed our names and sums assured in *London*, 18*th December*, 1879.

N.B.—Corn, Fish, Salt, Flour, and Seed, are warranted free from Average, unless general, or the ship be stranded; Sugar, Tobacco, Hemp, Flax, Hides, and Skins are warranted free from Average under Five Pounds per cent.; and all other Goods, also the Ship and Freight, are warranted free from Average under Three Pounds per cent., unless general, or the Ship be stranded.

On Merchandises, &c., valued as above.

Lloyd's Bond. A Lloyd's Bond is a form of agreement authorized by the Committee of Lloyd's. It differs from a policy, inasmuch as a policy is issued before a ship sails, and contains a *promise* contingent on certain eventualities. But a Lloyd's Bond supposes a ship to have returned, and to have already suffered damage; and the object of the Bond is to protect shipowners from losses as specified in the Bond. The following is a copy of a Lloyd's Bond as amended and authorized by the committee in 1878:—

An Agreement made this day of 188 BETWEEN Master of the Ship or vessel called the and the several Persons whose Names or Firms are set and subscribed hereto, being respectively Consignees of Cargo on Board the said Ship of the other part.

WHEREAS the said Ship lately arrived in the Port of on a Voyage from and it is alleged that during such voyage she met with bad weather, and sustained damage and loss, and that sacrifices were made and expenditure incurred which may form a Charge on the Cargo, or some part thereof, or be the subject of a general average contribution, but the same cannot be immediately ascertained; and in the meantime it is desirable that the cargo should be delivered.

NOW THEREFORE THESE PRESENTS WITNESS and the said Master on his own behalf, and on behalf of his owners, in consideration of the agreement of the parties hereto of the second part hereinafter contained, hereby agrees with the respective parties hereto of the second part, that he will deliver to them respectively their respective consignments, on payment of the freight payable on delivery, if any, and the said parties hereto of the second part in consideration of the said Agreement of the said Master for themselves severally, and respectively, and not the one for the others of them, hereby agree with the said Master that they will pay to the said Master or the Owners of the said Ship, the proper and respective proportion of any general average, or particular or other charges which may be chargeable upon their respective consignments, or to which the Shippers or Owners of such consignments may be liable in respect thereof to contribute to such damage loss sacrifice or expenditure, and the said parties hereto of the second part, further promise and agree, forthwith to furnish to the Captain or Owner of the said Ship a correct account and particular of the value of the goods delivered to them respectively, in order that any such general average and other charges may be ascertained and adjusted in the usual manner.

This addition to be made to the agreement in those cases which justify the shipowner in asking for a deposit.

AND WHEREAS at the request of the Owner of the said Ship the parties hereto of the second part have respectively deposited or agreed to deposit in the Bank of in the joint names of nominated on behalf of Shipowners and nominated on behalf of such Depositors the sum of £ per cent. on the amount of the estimated value of their respective interests NOW IT IS HEREBY further agreed, that the sums so deposited by the said parties respectively shall be held as security for and upon trust for the payment to the parties entitled thereto, of the general average and particular charges payable by the said parties hereto of the second part respectively, as aforesaid, and subject thereto upon trust for the said depositors respectively.

IN WITNESS

Loan. Saxon, *læn, hlæn,* a lending, a thing lent or borrowed. Dutch, *leening;* German, *Anleihe, Aulehen;* French equivalent, *emprunt.* Old English, *lone.*

"1508. Received of my lord of Dudley . . . . whose soul God pardon, for the *lone* of a vestment. . . . . . £1 0 0."

Manners and Expenses of Antient Times. 1770.

There are two distinct operations denoted by the word *loan,* as well as by the French and German equivalents. If I lend a man a sum of money, or if a friend, whose cellar is exhausted, asks me to lend him a bottle of wine, or if a warehouseman asks a neighbour to lend him a piece of silk, to enable him to execute an urgent order, the lender does not expect, in either of the cases, to have returned to him the same *indentical* money or bottle of wine, or piece of silk, but some other money, some other bottle of wine, or some other piece of silk, of equal quality and value; the loan would be useless to him on any other terms. In the Latin this kind of loan is called a *Mutuum.*

But if one person lends to another a book or a horse, a knife or a pencil for his temporary use, the lender always expects the same articles to be returned as that he lent. This kind of loan is called in Latin a *Commodatum.* In the first kind of loan, the relation of debtor and creditor is set up, in the second there is no such relation.

Lock-out. A combination on the part of employers, as a "strike" is a combination on the part of workmen.

Long Annuities. Annuities issued by Government for a long term of years, and are thus distinguished from "Perpetual" Annuities on the one hand, and "Short Term" Annuities on the other. (*See Annuities.*)

L.S.D. The first letters of the Latin, libra (pound), solidus (shilling), denarius (penny). Plural, libræ, solidi, denarii.

Lot, Lottery. The *Lottery,* or scheme for arriving at decisions by an appeal to the *Lot,* is of great antiquity, and is found among all peoples, even the most primitive. Associated in the earliest ages with religion, it was regarded as an appeal to the supernatural powers for guidance in affairs beyond the control or judgment of the human mind. It rapidly degenerated into a medium for mere gambling, to which purpose it has in modern times been largely applied. It is, therefore, of great importance to draw a clear distinction between a "lottery" properly so called, and "drawing by lot" or "ballot."

A Lottery in the modern sense of the term is a device for the distribution of prizes or privileges by an appeal to chance. They are attended with the following grave objections. (1) They divert the minds of men from the fields of industry, and foster a hope that by a stroke of fortune, wealth may be acquired without labour. There is something unaccountably attractive to some minds in the thought of being one amongst fifty thousand others, any one of which may be entitled on a given day to a sum of £1,000. (2) There is always a dead loss to the subscribers of a lottery; in other words, the sum total of their subscriptions is always much greater than that which the prize winners receive. The balance is pocketed by the promoters of the lottery, or sunk in the costs of management: and (3) the capital thus employed, notwithstanding all the excitement and turbulence attending the operation, is distributed among the prize-winners and promoters, without increase—that is, the capital has been employed, time expended and energy exhausted unproductively. These pastimes may be occasionally indulged in without much harm resulting to any one, but their influence is radically bad, and when a mania for them breaks out, as is too often the case, the consequences to individuals are most disastrous.

Drawing by Lot, as practised in commerce and finance, stands on a totally different footing, and is based on the scientific doctrine of probabilities. It is adopted as the fairest method of assigning certain advantages to individuals when those advantages cannot be distributed among a greater number who have naturally an equal claim. Thus, suppose a Government Loan represented by 200,000 bonds of £100 each, and that by the terms of the contract 500 of these bonds are to be paid off at par and cancelled every year. These 200,000 bonds may all be held by different individuals, and the question must arise, Whose bonds shall be thus paid off? Now the question is practically answered by putting into a bag 200,000 tickets, each bearing a number corresponding to the numbers on the bonds, and in the presence of responsible and authorised parties, drawing out in succession 500 of them. These 500 are paid off and cancelled, and the owners of them are entitled to such benefits as result from the operation. It is the aim of the higher class of merchants—in England at least—to reduce even this small amount of chance work as much as possible, so that although it may be difficult to eliminate it entirely from commercial transactions, its deleterious influences may be reduced to a minimum. (*See Ballot.*)

M.

M occurs as an abbreviation in the following:—
- -/M., a thousand, as e.g., 50/m., fifty thousand.
- Mbco., marks banco.
- M/c., metallic currency, or *moneda corriente* (i.e., the paper money of S. America).
- M/d., months' date.
- M/S., months' sight.

Mace. The one-tenth part of the Chinese *Tael,* and is worth 7*d.* English.

Macute or Macuta. A unit of account among the tribes of West Africa in cowry shells (in one instance 2000), but variable in number according to the tribe. A silver *macute* was coined by the Portuguese for use in the African colonies, and was worth about 2¾*d.* English.

Made Bills. *Made Bills* are distinguished in commerce from *drawn bills*, by having the name of a third party upon them in the character of *indorser* and *negotiator*. A drawn bill is a foreign bill negotiated *direct* from the drawer to a London foreign banker; but a made bill is usually a foreign bill sent up from some provincial town to a correspondent in London, who indorses it with his own name, and then negotiates it. Hence it follows that a foreign bill may be either a drawn bill or a made bill according to the way it is dealt with by the drawer. Take for example the following:—

Birmingham, 8 March, 1880.

£560

Thirty days after sight pay this First Bill of Exchange (Second and Third unpaid) to the order of ourselves Five hundred and Sixty pounds sterling, value received.

CUTLER & Co.

To Mr. Adolph Bergmaun, Hamburg.

Suppose the above bill to be sent by the drawer direct to the London offices of the Bank of Hamburg, it would then be simply a drawn bill.

But if instead of sending it direct to the office of the Bank of Hamburg, it was sent, say to some London correspondent, and by him indorsed and negotiated, it would become in virtue of that act a made bill.

It follows, from the above, that all "bills drawn abroad, and payable abroad, but negotiated in London, are *made* bills," since they always bear the indorsement of some London firm or correspondent. —SEYD, *Bullion and Foreign Exchanges.*

Making up Price. A Stock Exchange term, denoting a price fixed for carrying over every kind of stock not taken up on the settling day. "The *making-up* price is a price fixed for each stock at every settlement. Every member, through whose hands a ticket passes, makes an entry of the amount of the stock on the ticket in his account with the member to whom he passes it, at the price on the ticket in the case of registered stocks, and at the *making-up* price in the case of securities to bearer. An imaginary bargain in fact, is in each case entered against, that is, on the opposite side of, the account, the real bargain and the account is thus closed so far as the amount *of stock* is concerned. But it is evident that there may be, and probably is, a balance on one side or the other in the *money* of the accounts. Those balances go by the name of differences, and are claimed and paid on the settling day. The deliverer of stock receives from the issuer of a ticket payment at the price on the ticket, or at the *making-up* price in the case of securities to bearer; and if the price at which he sold the stock is higher than that on the ticket, he claims the difference of the member to whom he sold the stock; or if it is lower, then he pays the difference."—MADDISON.

Mandats. French, *mandate;* Latin, *mandare,* to enjoin, to command.

Mandats, a kind of paper money issued in France at the time of the revolution after the failure of the *assignats,* but which, like them, derived their value from the confiscated property of the Church pledged for their redemption, though, unlike them, they had *special* portions of that property assigned to them, while the assignats had only a *general* claim. Their fate, however, was similar to that of the assignats, and after short forced circulation they became worthless.

Manifest. A ship's manifest is a formal statement of a cargo for the use of the Custom-house officers, and usually contains a list of all the packages on board, with their distinguishing marks, numbers, and descriptions; all of which details are indicated by a printed form.

Manifolding. A slang term applied to a certain method of feloniously dealing with bank notes, in virtue of which *one* bank note is made to do the purchasing work of *two.* The following is a case which occurred a few years ago. A man, some distance from London, sent an order for boots and shoes to the amount of £20, for which he sent half a bank note, with a request that the goods might be dispatched immediately, and promising the other half of the note on their arrival. He did just the same at another house in London, with the other half. It is needless to say that when he had received the goods he was not long in disposing of them, or in decamping as soon as the transaction was complete.

Marine Insurances are contracts to indemnify the owners of goods, vessels and freight, from any stipulated loss which may arise from the destruction or injury of the ships, cargoes, or other property insured.

Mark. Anglo-Saxon, *mearc*, a mark. Old Norse, *merkia*, signifying a mark of any kind, whether in the form of a stake driven into the ground, or by a furrow made by spade or plough, and this seems to be the origin of the term *mark*, as a measure of land. The same words were also used to denote a *mark* when signifying a numerical unit, whether made by a stroke of the pen, a piece of chalk, a notch on a stick or tally; and hence was very commonly employed to indicate the monetary unit of primitive times, thus giving rise to the name of *mark* as applied to a coin.

Several coins are known by the name of *Mark*. The most important are the following:—

(*a.*) The unit of value and the unit of account in Germany, by the monetary laws of December, 1871, and July, 1873. Its value is determined by the weight of the gold 20-mark piece, or *double-crown*, the 10-mark piece or *crown* and by the *silver mark*.

The *German Gold Mark*. The 20-mark gold piece weighs 7·965 grammes (122·88 grains), and is ·900 fine. From these data we find the weight of the single gold mark to be ·3982 gramme, or 6·144 grains and its sterling value £·0489 or almost exactly $11\frac{3}{4}$*d.* sterling. French value—Fr. 1·$23\frac{1}{2}$ centimes.

The *Silver Mark* weighs 5·555 grammes, and is ·900 fine. Taking fine gold as $15\frac{1}{2}$ times an equal weight of fine silver, the Silver Mark is worth Fr. 1·11 centimes, or $10\frac{1}{2}$*d.* sterling.

The German Mark is divided into 100 Pfennige, and accounts are consequently kept in the Decimal notation.

Three Marks are equal to the German Thaler, which was the monetary unit up to 1871.

(*b.*) The sixth part of the Danish Rigsdaler, value 16 Skillings or nearly $4\frac{1}{2}$*d.* English.

(*c.*) The fifth part of the Norwegian species daler, called also the Ort, value $10\frac{2}{3}$*d.* sterling. These two latter coins are now superseded by the coinage of the Scandinavian Monetary Convention of 1873.

(*d.*) An old silver coin used in Mecklenburg, value 1*s.* 2*d.* sterling, still circulating.

(*e.*) The old unit of value in Hamburg, value about 1*s.* $1\frac{1}{3}$*d.* sterling. To a great extent superseded by the new monetary system of Germany.

(*f.*) A coin used in Lubeck equal to $\frac{1}{3}$ of a Thaler, value about 1*s.* $1\frac{1}{3}$*d.* Also supplanted by the new German system.

(*g.*) The unit of value and of account in the Grand Duchy of Finland. It is represented by both gold and silver coins.

The *Gold Mark of Finland*. The value of the gold mark of Finland is derived from that of the 10-mark piece which weighs 3·226 grammes, ·900 fine. This gives for the single gold mark ·3226 grammes, worth exactly 1 franc or £·03964=$9\frac{1}{2}$*d.* sterling, and thus brings one more nationality into financial relations with the Latin Monetary Convention.

The *Silver Mark of Finland* weighs 5·182 grammes, ·868 fine, and is worth 99 centimes, or $9\frac{1}{2}d.$ sterling.

The Finland Mark is divided into 100 Pennis. A Penni is therefore the equivalent of the French centime. Silver pieces of 50 and 25 Pennis, are struck in silver ·750 fine.

Mark Banco. In Hamburg and the Hanse Towns, the Mark Banco is an imaginary unit of value consisting of a record in the books of the Bank. Silver is paid into the Bank in the form of bars or coin, and credit is given for the amount of *fine* silver they contain, at the rate of $27\frac{3}{4}$ Marks per Cologne Mark weight, or 3608 Troy grains. These credits may be transferred from one bank to another, or to merchants, but no notes are issued. The Mark Banco taking $15\frac{1}{2}$ parts of *fine* silver as equal to one part of *fine* gold, is therefore equal to 1·4846 shillings, or 1*s.* $5\frac{4}{5}d.$ English. As the use of the Mark Banco always represents a definite weight of fine silver, and is not subject to deterioration by abrasion or clipping, there being no coin to clip or wear, the system is much prized by those who are accustomed to it, although it is somewhat embarrassing to foreigners.

Mark Courant. In Hamburg and the Hanse Towns there exists, side by side, two modes of valuation, the *Bank Value* and the *Currency Value.* (*See Mark Banco.*)

The Cologne Mark weight, 3608 grains Troy, of *fine* silver is coined into 35 *Marks Courant.* Before 1856 it was coined into 34 *Marks Courant.* The present Mark Courant reckoning $15\frac{1}{2}$ parts of fine silver as equal to 1 part fine gold is found to be 14·1246*d.* sterling, or 1*s.* $2\frac{1}{7}d.$

Market Price of Bullion. The Market Price of Bullion differs from the Mint Price only when the coinage has been worn or depreciated. When the coins have been worn, the amount of deterioration in each coin is variable, and it is impossible to say, without weighing each one, how many of them should be exchanged for a given number of full weight; in this case they are treated simply as bullion, and exchanged weight for weight. When the coinage has been debased by a dishonest Government, the value of each separate coin is more uniform, and the exchange is effected by giving a greater number of light debased coins for a specified number of standard coins. From the nature of the case, the Market price of bullion is therefore always higher than the Mint price, since when the coins are diminished in weight and fineness, a greater number of them must be given in exchange for an equal weight of standard coins. (*See Mint Price of Bullion.*)

Markings. The prices marked on a board in the Stock Exchange for the information and guidance of its members, and when published in the "Official List," for the information of the public. It is necessary in order that any price may be recorded, that the bargain shall have been done in the Stock Exchange, between members, at the market price, and it will not be recorded on the authority of one member, "if he refuse, when required by a member of the committee, to give up the name of the member with whom he has dealt." It is evidently necessary that the recording of false or artificial prices should be prevented; and the fact that every member who records a price signs his name to it, and that the two members to a bargain must be known in doubtful cases, in a great measure checks anything of the kind. In addition to this, the recording of a price that was altogether beyond the figure of the actual market price would immediately attract the notice of the jobbers in the particular stock quoted, and measures would then be immediately taken to inquire into the case. The prices recorded, are therefore, as a rule, with very few exceptions, the actual prices of business done, and, to some extent, show the course of business during the day."—MADDISON.

Marque, Letters of. Letters of Mart. Most authorities agree in referring the origin of the word *marque* to the old French, *marche*, a boundary or border, and in treating the form *mart* as a corruption. In the old law books the word occurs in several Latinised forms. *Marchationes* signified raids beyond the borders of a tribe for the purpose of pasturage or plunder. *Marcare* was the right of pasturing in a forest adjoining the boundary of a tribe. *Marchagium* was defined to be the *droit de marchage*, or the right of pasturage on neighbouring *marches*. The verb, *marcare*, or *marchiare* in Latin, and the French, *marquer*, acquired at a very early date a secondary meaning, which implied not only the passing over the borders as a necessity or right, but as a means of revenge or reprisal; thus in a document dated 1389, we read:—"Lesquels habitans n'ayant voulutenir et payer le dit accord, le prestre s'en retourna aux Anglais, et fit par iceulx Anglais *marquer* piller et prendre prisonnieres les bonnes gens et habitans de la dite paroisse St. Victor." ("The inhabitants not having observed the said compact, the priest returned to the English, and with their aid *passed over the borders*, to plunder and take prisoners the simple people and inhabitants of the said parish of St. Victor.")

Letters of Marque or Reprisal is a name given to the document issued by the supreme government in time of war to merchants and others, authorizing them to fit out privateers or armed vessels, and granting commissions to the owners of such vessels. The prizes captured are directed to be divided between the owners and the crews. This mode of dividing the spoil is somewhat different from that in use in former times, when the sovereign claimed one-half of the spoil. The modern practice is adopted with a view to encourage men of substance to fit out such vessels, and to assist the Government by embarrassing and enfeebling the enemy.

Mas or **Mathen.** The tenth part of the Kivan (Cochin China), worth about $3\frac{1}{3}d.$, and is divided into 60 sapeks. Mas in Chinese means a heap.

Material or **Corporeal Property.** Property embodied in some material object or *corpus*, and which has come into the possession of the proprietor, such as land, houses, money; they are thus distinguished from debts, credits, rights, &c., which are called Immaterial or Incorporeal property.

Mature, To. A Bond, Bill, or other negotiable instrument is said to *Mature*, or arrive at maturity, at the date when it becomes payable. Hence, a bill payable on demand or sight, matures on being presented for payment. A bill at thirty, sixty, or ninety days *after date*, matures thirty-three, sixty-three, or ninety-three days after date, the three days of grace being added on. When drawn so many days *after sight*, it matures so many days after presentation for acceptance, the days of grace in this case also being added. When drawn, one, two, or three *months* after date or sight, calendar months are understood: and a bill dated 7th March, matures on the 10th April, May, or June, as the case may be. It therefore follows that a sight bill ought always to be presented for acceptance as promptly as possible, whenever it is desired to bring it to maturity at the earliest possible date.

Maundy Money. Small silver coins including twopenny and penny pieces, specially struck for distribution as alms by the Sovereign on Maundy Thursday.

Measure of Value. The common standard adopted by a country, by which the *price* of everything bought or sold is measured, and in terms of which it is expressed. The term has been much objected to by various economists, and Prof. F. A. Walker has proposed to use instead of it, the phrase "common denominator of exchange," but the proposal has not been extensively adopted at present.

In order to measure anything accurately, a unit of measurement is indispensable. To measure the length of a line, a *simple* unit only is required, as an *inch*, a *foot*, or a *mile*. To measure a surface, a *compound* unit is essential; it must have two dimensions, length and breadth, as the *square inch*, the *square foot*, or the *square mile*. To measure a force, the unit employed is compounded of two dissimilar elements, the foot of length and the pound weight, shortly called the *foot-pound*, and it measures the amount of force necessary to raise a pound weight, one foot high.

The *measure of value* is much more complicated and indefinite than either of these,—more complicated because at least three if not more elements, enter into it,—more indefinite because neither element is susceptible of exact numerical or geometrical measurement, while each element is liable to incessant change. They are as follows:—

(1.) *Labour.* The labour expended in producing an object is a very important determinant of its value. All other things remaining the same, an object requiring twice or thrice the amount of labour to produce it, will, *in so far as the labour affects it*, be twice or thrice as valuable. The balance-wheel of a watch depends for its value almost entirely on the amount of skilled labour expended on it, and will vary in cost very closely in proportion to the number of hours consumed in making it.

(2.) *Capital.* The capital employed in producing an object is also an important determinant of its value. All other things remaining the same, an article requiring double the amount of capital to be employed in its manufacture, will, *in so far as the element of capital affects it*, be twice as valuable. A bill of exchange depends for its value on the capital at the disposal of the party who accepts it, and which must be held in readiness to meet it when it falls due. It requires no more labour, skill, or otherwise to draw a bill for £50,000 than for £1,000, but the capital requisite to meet it when due, will be fifty times as great.

(3.) The intensity of human desire as compared with the means of satisfying it. If a strong desire for an object prevails, while the means of satisfying that desire is limited and fixed, its value will be immensely enhanced. A piece of rare china, a picture by a deceased painter, the voice of a fine singer, the services of an eminent barrister or physician, are commodities that cannot be multiplied at pleasure, and some of them are absolutely fixed in quantity. Hence, if the caprices of fashion, or the pressure of human needs, give rise to a great desire for any of these things, their value is enormously enhanced, and is out of all proportion to the capital and labour employed in their production.

Thus it is seen that, from the nature of the case, what is called by economists the "measure of value" does not by any means answer to our popular notions of a standard of measurement, but is of a very unstable and fluctuating character. Nevertheless, the expression is a convenient one, and at any given moment the "measure of value" as above described is a very real and effective one when some substance is chosen as gold or silver which is universally desired, and the trouble of acquiring which has been pretty nearly the same in all ages. It is because gold possesses these qualities in a degree superior to that of silver, that gold is now being adopted in several States (both in Europe and America) which have hitherto been content with silver as a "standard of monetary value."

Medium of Exchange. A substance, or substances in use among traders, which they offer in exchange for any commodities they may desire, and which the possessors of those commodities are always willing to accept in exchange for them. A medium of exchange serves the further purpose of furnishing a standard of value to which all other commodities may be referred, and in terms of which they may be appraised or their value recorded. Any substance may be used for this purpose, and different communities have adopted different *Media*. Lumps of salt of a given size, strips of cloth, cowry shells, cows, beaver skins, discs of leather, cubes of compressed tea, whale's teeth, pieces of amber, have all been used as media of exchange, but none have been found so suitable for commerce on a large scale, as certain metals, and of these, three stand pre-eminent—namely, gold, silver, and copper. These, from their durability, divisibility, and comparatively small bulk, are used almost exclusively by civilised nations, and by the most civilised, gold and silver exclusively. The term "Medium of Exchange" is properly applied to that metal alone which forms the *Standard Coinage* of a nation, since all other coins and all negotiable instruments, are valued in terms of that coinage. Nevertheless, as coinage mostly consists partly of metals other than that adopted as the standard, and have a definite value as a fractional part of the standard "unit of value" it is customary to call all the metallic money in use in a community, the medium of exchange. In course of time, instruments of credit, such as Bills of Exchange, Treasury Bonds, Exchequer Bills, are used as substitutes for the metals, and these then take their place as Media of Exchange, but these, like the inferior metals, have their value recorded in terms of the Standard Unit of Value.

Medjidie. The Medjidié is only another name for the Turkish Lira, derived from that of the late Sultan, Abdul Medjid, in whose reign it was struck. It consists of 7·216 grammes of gold ·916 fine, and is worth almost exactly 18*s.* sterling.

Meia Coroa. The Gold Half-crown of Portugal. (*See Corōa.*)

Memorandum of Association. A short extract provided by Limited Joint Stock Companies, stating the following particulars:—

1. The name of the company.
2. Whether the registered offices of the company are situated in England.
3. The object or objects for which the company is formed.
4. That the liability of the members is limited.
5. The capital of the company.

Mercantile System. The *Mercantile System* is a name given to that mode of conducting the trade of the nation which maintains the *exports* at a money value equal to or greater than the imports. It is inferred—erroneously as modern economists believe—that when the value of the exports exceeds that of the imports, coin must be sent into the country to pay for the excess: and this is thought by some to be a desirable thing. On the contrary, when the imports exceed in value the exports, it is supposed that money must be sent out of the country to pay for the excess. This inference is certainly not warranted, as may be shown by an example.

Suppose goods of the value of £100 to be shipped in London for Paris; assume that duties, carriage, and other charges amount to £5, and that when they arrive in Paris, the goods are sold at the moderate profit of £5. The exporter will then have £110 placed to his credit in the books of his correspondent.

Now let the £110 be laid out in the purchase of some article produced in Paris, say kid gloves, and then forwarded to London. Suppose that by the time they reach London, the cost of commission, freight, duties, and other charges, brings their value up to £115, and at this point their value is recorded. We should then have imported goods to the amount of £115, against goods exported to the amount of £100: and it may be further assumed that these gloves will sell for considerably more than £115, so as to leave the merchant a profit, for without this expectation he would scarcely have entered on the transaction at all.

Here then we have a case in which the balance of trade appears to be against this country, and yet, as we have seen, no money passes either one way or the other; and the parties to the transaction will have so conducted it as to yield a profit to each.

Most modern works on Political Economy devote a chapter to the consideration of the Mercantile System: but one of the most complete and explicit refutations of the fallacy involved in that system, is furnished by Mr. Mac Leod in his "Theory and Practice of Banking" (vol. ii., pp. 333-348), and to this the reader is referred for further details.

Metallic Value. A term used by Prof. Jevons, and some other economists as a substitute for *Intrinsic Value,* an expression which some economists consider to be doubtful of meaning, or without any meaning at all. When thus employed, *Metallic Value*—that is, its value as merchandise—is distinguished from its *nominal* or *legal value,* at which a coin is required to exchange for other coins. Thus, the English bronze penny when offered in quantities not greater than 12 at a time, is valued as the 240th of a sovereign, this is its *legal* or *nominal* value; its metallic value is about ¼th as much. (*See Intrinsic Value.*)

Middlemen. A general term applied to agents, brokers, factors and others whose business it is to bring together producers and consumers, buyers and sellers, &c. The name is now but little used, owing to the taint of opprobrium attaching to it, in consequence of the malpractices of several disreputable members of the profession. The primary and essential duty of a middleman is to *facilitate* intercourse between principals and clients, producers and consumers, buyers and sellers; but it was found in some cases that have since become notorious, that with a view to enhance their own personal gains, a combination amongst middlemen was formed in order to obstruct and embarrass the intercourse between the parties whose interests it was their proper business to serve. These abuses have brought the whole profession of middlemen into undeserved disrepute, for there is an immense variety of commercial operations which none but a skilled hand can safely conduct: and on the other hand, there are many transactions in which no such skill is needed, and if middlemen could be content to offer their services where they are wanted and not to force them on parties who can do very well without them, there is no reason why the opprobrium attaching to their name should not speedily disappear.

Mil or Mill. From Latin, *mille,* a thousand; *millēsimus,* a thousandth part.

Mil is used to signify the thousandth part of the monetary unit in several different countries. Since the *unit* adopted in one country is often very different from that in another, the *mil* necessarily varies in value in the same proportion. Thus the English mil is in practice taken as one farthing, and the United States mil is, therefore, about ⅕ of a farthing.

Milreis. (*a.*) The unit of value in Portugal, gold, weight 1·7735 grammes, fineness ·9166, value in sterling 53·284*d.* Its value is thus deduced. The *corōa* (or crown) consists of 17·735 grammes of gold ·916⅔ fine, and is equivalent to 10 *milreis*. Hence the *milreis* weighs 1·7735 grammes, and this at 30.04488 per gramme gives 53·28458 per *milreis* (*see Price of Gold*). Its value in French money is fr. 5·60 centimes or £·222 sterling. From either computation we have the same English value—namely, 4*s*. 5¼*d*.

(*b*.) The unit of value in Brazil, formerly represented by gold coins, but now replaced by a much depreciated paper currency. The 20 milreis piece weighs 17·927 grammes, ·9166 or $\frac{11}{12}$ fine, and is worth, when of full weight, 538·61455*d*., giving for the gold milreis the value of 26·930727*d*. This must, therefore, be considered the mint par of exchange between Brazil and London.

There is also a silver milreis piece coined in Brazil weighing 12·750 grammes, ·9166 fine, value 24·8465*d*. Both these coins are now comparatively scarce.

The paper milreis is worth only about 15*d*., but varies with the exchange of the day.

Mint. Anglo-Saxon, *mynet*, coin; *mynettian*, to coin; Dutch, *munte*; German, *Münze*; Latin, moneta, which meant not only money, but the stamp with which it was struck, or place where it was done. Dutch, *munten*, to mint, or strike money.

A place where coins are struck. There were formerly several in different parts of England, but their number has been gradually reduced till now there is only one, that on Tower Hill. All transactions between the Mint and the public are now conducted through the Bank of England.

Mint Par of Exchange. The weight of pure gold or silver in a coin of one country, as compared with that in a coin of another. The determination of this proportion lies at the basis of every system of foreign exchange, and is usually calculated from the data furnished by the Governments of the countries concerned. Hence, for example, the Mint par between the English sovereign and German mark is thus found:—

	Grains.
The sovereign weighs	123·274
Deduct $\frac{1}{12}$ alloy	10·272
Leaving fine gold	113·002
The 20-mark piece weighs . . .	122·880
Deduct $\frac{1}{10}$ alloy	12·288
Leaving fine gold	110·592

The value of the sovereign, therefore, is to that of the 20-mark piece as 113·002 : 110·592, or as

d.		*d*.	
240	:	235	nearly.
s.		*s*. *d*.	
20	:	19 7	nearly.

In the *Course of Exchange*, published daily, the "Mint par" would however be expressed thus:—

£1 = mks. 20·43.

It is determined by the proportion

				s.		Marks.
110·592	:	113·002	::	20	:	20·43.

In all cases, where the foreign money is variable, and the English fixed, the Mint par of exchange is found in a precisely similar way.

Mint Price of Bullion. A term applied to bullion, and signifies the number of coins into which a given weight of bullion is divided. Forty pounds weight of *standard* gold are cut into 1869 sovereigns; therefore, 1869 sovereigns is the *Mint price* of 40 pounds of standard gold—that is, standard gold is worth £46 14*s.* 6*d.* per pound troy, or £3 17*s.* 10½*d.* per ounce. (*See Market Price of Bullion.*)

Mixed Currency. By mixed currency is meant a currency consisting partly of the precious metals, and partly of paper, both being made a legal tender by act or decree of the supreme Government. That it may *flow* or *run* freely—that is, become current—it is further necessary that the paper shall at all times be convertible into gold or silver, and that gold and silver shall be convertible into paper. When these conditions do not obtain, it is either not "*mixed*," or it is not "*currency*."

Moeda. A gold coin circulating in Brazil before the introduction of a paper currency. It was worth 4,000 reis—*i.e.*, 4 milreis, or 8*s.* 11¾*d.* It has almost disappeared from circulation, owing to the excessive amount of paper with which the country is flooded.

Mohur. The gold *mohur* of India, or 15 rupee piece, weighs 11·664 grammes (180 grains troy), ·9166 fine. Its value in sterling when of full weight is therefore £1 9*s.* 2¼*d.* The gold mohur is of the same weight and fineness as the silver rupee, and an attempt was made to fix this relation between the value of gold and silver—*i.e.*, 1 to 15—but the experiment failed, and the mohur is now a commercial coin. During the past few years, while silver has been depreciated in value, the gold mohur has been valued at rates varying from 16 to 20 silver rupees.

Gold pieces of ⅔ of a mohur or 10 rupees, and ⅓ of a mohur or 5 rupees, are also in circulation,

Moidore. An old Portuguese coin worth 4,800 reis, about £1 1*s.* 3*d.* English.

Monetary Convention. There are two groups of European nations, between whose members an agreement has been entered into for the regulation of their coinage. They are called, for the sake of distinction, the Latin Monetary Convention, and the Scandinavian Monetary Convention.

Latin Monetary Convention.—An agreement entered into between France, Italy, Belgium, and Switzerland, in December, 1865, in virtue of which the coinages of those countries are of the same weight and fineness. The French franc and the Italian lira have therefore the same metallic value, and constitute the monetary unit in all the countries above named. The "Double Standard," or more correctly the "Alternative Standard," in virtue of the same convention, is also adopted by all these countries.

More recently, Greece has entered into the Union in virtue of the right reserved by Art 12 of the Convention, and the *drachma* is made the unit of value, and of equal weight and fineness with the *franc* and *lira*.

Sundry other countries, especially Roumania, and most of the Republics of South America have adopted the same system without actually entering the Monetary Union. Austria-Hungary has made an approach to the same system by striking off *gold* pieces of 8 florins, each equal in weight and fineness to the 20-franc piece, and Spain has silver pieces on bases corresponding to those fixed by the Union in 1865.

The following is the drift of the Latin International Monetary Convention, stripped of superfluous legal verbiage :—

Latin Monetary Convention.

Art. 1. France, Belgium, Italy, Switzerland and Greece are constituted a Union as regards the weight, fineness, and form of their gold and silver coinage.

The token coinage remains for the present unaffected, and follows the customs and laws of the respective countries.

Art. 2. The high contracting parties engage to fabricate no gold coins but those which correspond with the requirements of the following table, in respect to weight, fineness, remedy, and diameter.

Nature of pieces.		Weight.		Fineness.		Diameter.
		Full wght.	Remedy.	Fineness.	Remedy.	
	fr.	grammes.	millièmes.	millièmes.	millièmes.	mm.
Gold.	100	32·25806	1	900	2	35
	50	16·12903				28
	20	6·45161	2			21
	10	3·22580				19
	5	1·61290	3			17

They receive without distinction, into their public treasuries, all gold pieces made in accordance with the preceding conditions in either of the five States, with the reservation, however, that any pieces shall be rejected whose weight has been reduced by wear and tear one-half of one per cent. below the allowances above indicated, and of which the impression shall have been effaced.

Art. 3. The contracting parties agree to coin no silver pieces of five francs except of the weight, fineness, remedy, and diameter that are named in the following table:—

Weight.		Fineness.		Diameter.
Full weight.	Remedy.	Fineness.	Remedy.	
25grammes	3 millièm.	900 milli.	2 millièm.	37 mm.

All the States of the Union agree to accept without distinction the pieces herein described with the same reservations as in Art. 2, except that *one per cent.* is the allowance permitted for wear and tear, &c., instead of the *half of one per cent.*

Art. 4. The high contracting parties engage henceforward to make no silver pieces of two francs, one franc, fifty centimes, and twenty centimes, except under the conditions indicated in the annexed table:—

Nature of pieces.		Weight.		Fineness.		Diameter.
		Full wght.	Remedy.	Fineness.	Remedy.	
	fr. c.	grammes.	millièmes.	millièmes.	millièmes.	mm.
Silver	2	10·00	5	835	3	27
	1	5·00				23
	·50	2·50	7			18
	·20	1·00	10			16

These pieces are to be recoined by the Governments who have issued them, when they shall have been reduced by wear and tear 5 per cent. below the allowance above indicated, or when their impressions have been effaced.

Art. 5. The silver pieces of two francs, of one franc, of fifty centimes, and of twenty centimes, not conforming to the conditions presented in the last Art, shall be withdrawn from circulation before the first of January, 1869. In the case of Switzerland, this delay is extended to the first of January, 1878, in virtue of the law of January, 1860.

Art. 6. The silver pieces made in conformity with the conditions of Art. 4, shall be legal tender between private individuals in these States where they are coined, to the amount of fifty francs in one payment.

The State which has put them into circulation shall receive them from their own countrymen without limitation as to quantity.

Art. 7. The public treasuries of each of the five States shall accept the silver coins made by one or more of the other contracting

States, conformably to Art. 4, to the amount of 100 francs in each payment made to the said treasuries.

The Governments of Belgium, France, and Italy, shall receive on the same terms till the 1st of January, 1878, the Swiss coins of two francs and of one franc issued in virtue of the law of 1860, and which conform to the conditions of Art. 4.

Art. 8. Each of the Governments engages to accept from private individuals, and from treasuries of other States, the small token coins of silver which they have issued, and to exchange them against *current* coin of equal value (gold pieces or 5-franc silver pieces) on condition that the sum presented for exchange shall not be less than 100 francs. This obligation shall be in force for two years from the expiration of the present treaty.

Art. 9. The high contracting parties shall be allowed to issue pieces of two francs, of one franc, of fifty centimes, and of twenty centimes, only to the extent of six francs per head of the population.

Art. 10. The date of fabrication shall be impressed on all the gold and silver coins struck by the five States.

Art. 11. The States shall report annually the number of their issues, and communicate any facts relative to the circulation which may be of reciprocal interest.

Art. 12. Any other State may enter the Union provided such State accepts the obligations above described in reference to their gold and silver coinage.

Art. 13. The execution of the reciprocal engagements contained in the present Convention, is subordinate as far as need be, to the observance of the formalities and laws of each State, with the understanding that the execution shall be delayed as little as possible.

Art. 14. The present Convention remains in force till the 1st of January, 1880. If before that date no State has communicated its intention of withdrawing from the Union, it shall remain in force for the next fifteen years, and after that from fifteen years to fifteen years in default of formal withdrawal.

The above is a close approximation to the text of the *Latin Monetary Convention*. In one particular it may be said to have broken down. The French Government finding that bar silver, owing to its recent depreciation, was brought into the country in immense quantities and coined into five-franc pieces, according to Art. 4, and finding further that this silver was sent into the treasury for the payment of large sums, while gold was being exported to other countries outside the Convention, it was decreed that no more than a specified number of those pieces should be coined. The effect of this decree was to reduce bar silver to its market value, which was much less than its value in the form of coin, and to make unlimited payments in silver coin impossible, simply because sufficient silver coin was not to be obtained.

The Scandinavian Monetary Convention.

The *Scandinavian Monetary Convention* dates from the year 1873, and includes Norway, Sweden, and Denmark. Up to that time, silver had been the standard of value in those countries, and very little gold was in circulation among them. But by this Convention gold was made the sole standard of value, and gold coins of equal weight and fineness were to be coined by each country, and allowed by law to circulate freely between them. They are fully described in their proper places, and it is not necessary here to do more than name them.

GOLD COINS.

Name.	Fineness.	Grammes.
20-Kroner piece	·900	8·960
10-Kroner piece	·900	4·480

SILVER COINS.

Name.	Fineness.	Grammes.
2 Kroner	·800	15·000
1 Krone		7·500
50 öre	·600	5·000
40 ,,		4·000
25 ,,		2·420
10 ,,	·400	1·450

The silver coins are obviously mere tokens, although the two-kroner and one-krone pieces are much superior to the others. The coins of lower denomination fall almost into the rank of "billon" coins. (*See Billon.*)

Money. Latin, *moneta;* Italian, *moneta;* Spanish, *moneda;* Dutch, *munten;* German, *Muntze;* Anglo-Saxon, *mynet.* Vossius derives *moneta* from *monēre,* to warn, advise, instruct, inform, and says it is so-called because the marks inscribed upon it "inform us of the authority under which it is issued and its value" ("quia nota inscripta *monet* nos autoris et valoris.") The Roman mint was set up in the temple of Juno, which was called, in consequence, the temple of Juno Moneta. The Anglo-Saxon, *mynet,* was also derived from the verb *munan* or *menan,* which, like the Latin, *monēre,* signified to show, inform, or to stand as a sign.

"All mints impress a stamp on their coins; for what purpose? To give information, to make known, on the word of the government that the sovereign, dollar, or franc is made of standard gold or silver, and possesses the requisite weight. In the words of Aristotle, it is impressed on the money to relieve men of the trouble of measuring it, or as Mr. Adams says, 'to save every man the trouble of carrying about with him a bottle of acid and a pair of scales.' A stamped sovereign or dollar tells every one what it is. Nothing can be more obvious than this fact, yet, strange to say, many intelligent men are puzzled to say what the stamp it bears does for the sovereign."—BONAMY PRICE, *Pract. Polit. Econ.*

In its essential nature *Money* is a *ticket* or *order* entitling the holder to receive a quantity of any commodity or some service equal in value to the amount indicated on the face of the order. The Claim or Title may be impressed on metal as in the case of coins, or on paper as in Bills of Exchange, Bank Notes, and other negotiable instruments, thus giving rise to the two great divisions of Money into metallic money and paper money which, however, must not be confounded with *metallic currency* and *paper currency*. (*See Currency*.)

Many attempts have been made to produce a good definition of the term money; the following claim special notice:—

"Money of every kind is an *Order* for goods."—HENRY THORNTON.

"The pounds or shillings which a person receives, weekly or yearly, are not what constitute his income; they are a sort of *Ticket* or *Order* which he can present for payment at any shop he pleases."—JNO STUART MILL.

"A guinea may be considered as a *Bill* for a certain quantity of necessaries or conveniences upon all the tradesmen in the neighbourhood."—ADAM SMITH.

"Money is a Right or Title to demand something from some one else. It is a kind of *Bill of Exchange* or order payable at the will of the bearer."—McLEOD.

"Money is in reality the 'Tool of Exchange,' and it furnishes a measure of value."—BONAMY PRICE.

Professor Jevons, although devoting an entire volume to the discussion of Money in all its forms, hesitates to give a definition of the term. It is not difficult, however, to discriminate among all the things which he enumerates on pp. 248–9 of that work as Money or "as good as money" some which would certainly be called money, and others which though as good as money would not be called by that name. Thus a Consol Bond or Exchequer Bill would if taken at the Market Price of the day be certainly as "good as money" to some people, but it would be quite contrary to usage to call them money. The fundamental notion which underlies all our conceptions of money is, that it is something which everybody desires, or at least something which everybody is willing to accept in exchange for that which he is willing to part with. This willingness may arise from two distinct causes:—First, the thing called "money" may be made of some material which renders it desirable to everybody, and would be sought for by everybody; or secondly, it might be made of some material, as paper, in itself worthless, but yet endowed by force of law with the property of exchangeability—that is to say, a piece of paper having printed thereon a promise to pay Fifty Francs, shall be accepted as fifty francs by anyone who has a claim on the holder of it for that sum. These two distinctions give rise to the two great divisions of Money into Metallic Money and Paper Money, the qualities of which must be looked at somewhat more in detail.

METALLIC MONEY.—English sovereigns and half-sovereigns are true money. In the British Islands, and the Colonies, they are universally desired, and creditors will receive them willingly to any amount. For the same reason, in France, Italy, Belgium, Switzerland, and the other countries included in the Monetary Convention, the gold Napoleon and the silver five-franc piece are true money. In Austria, the silver florin is the coin universally desired; in Russia, the silver ruble; in those countries, therefore, the florin and the ruble are true money; and in other countries wherever a coinage exists which is desired and willingly accepted by the whole population in exchange for commodities or services, that coinage constitutes true money.

Silver shillings and bronze pence are willingly received by everyone in England *within certain limits*. Forty shillings are as good to the owner as two good sovereigns, and twelve pence as good as one silver shilling; but in any larger amounts they are *not willingly* accepted, except in some few cases where they serve a useful purpose for paying wages or distributing small sums. Hence they lose their character of true money, and are frequently spoken of in a depreciatory tone, as "token coins" or "mere counters." Gold or silver bars are still less welcome when offered to one as money. The trouble of assaying, weighing, and dividing it into smaller portions would render it very inconvenient to any but those who had large payments to make in one sum. They cannot, therefore, be called "money."

PAPER MONEY.—A five-pound Bank of England note possesses the characteristics of true money. Partly because it is made by law a legal tender, and partly because of the high credit of the establishment from which it is issued. The bank note is one of those things which everyone in the kingdom is wishing to get as many of as he can, and which therefore he is willing to receive in exchange for what he has to part with. But a five-pound note issued by an obscure provincial bank, though circulating freely in the immediate neighbourhood of that bank, and within that limited circle passing as true money, loses something of its character as it leaves that centre, and in London would very likely be refused by every tradesman to whom it was presented. And yet all notes of this description are convertible into gold on presentation at the bank from which they are issued.

There is another kind of paper money which is "inconvertible," that is, "not convertible" into gold or silver at the wish of the holder, and yet is the only legal tender in the country where it is issued. Some of this paper is worth nearly as much as the gold or silver coin indicated by the amount named on the face of it, like that of France and the United States; in Austria, Italy, and Russia its value is much less, and in Turkey, the State paper, or Caimè, is so depreciated that at the present time (1880) more than 1200 piastres are given for 100 piastres in gold. Nevertheless, in all these cases, and notwithstanding the depreciation, it is the recognized medium of exchange in the country where it is issued, and as such is desired and accepted in payment of debts. It thus fulfils the functions of money, and is properly called by that name.

There is yet one more property by which true money is distinguished—namely, that it bears some mark or marks by means of which *it is easily recognized.* The device and legend of good coins, and the printing on the face of bank notes or State paper are obvious marks. But among more primitive peoples, marks of some kind or other were essential to the idea of money. The iron and leather coins of ancient Greece bore a stamp, and the rude ingots of other countries were also stamped. The blocks of compressed tea in Assam were marked by their size and cubical form, the silver plates of the Chinese by their shoe-like shape, and the copper "cash" of the same people by the square hole in the centre.

From the foregoing considerations we are enabled to form a tolerably correct definition of money.

"Money is the standard by which the value of all other commodities is measured, the medium by which they are exchanged, and it bears certain marks by which it is easily recognized." All other negotiable instruments, though as "good as money," and a great deal better than some of it, are excluded by this definition; but the exclusion is justified by the common usage of all commercial peoples and does not clash with any fully established theory.

Money, For. Bargains "for money" in Stock Exchange parlance as distinguished from bargains "for account" signifies the buying and selling of stocks for *ready money*, and not on *credit*.

Moneys of Account. The denominations and divisions of money in which accounts are kept. They may or may not correspond with the moneys in circulation. Thus, a shilling is a money both of account and circulation at the present time; a sixpenny-piece is not a money of account, but is one of circulation. But in the Anglo-Saxon period, the money in circulation, the money of account, and the unit of value were all different. The *unit of value* was the Saxon pound of twelve ounces of silver; the principal *coin of account* was the shilling or twelfth part of the pound, but no shillings were coined till the time of Henry VII. The coins in circulation were chiefly silver pennies and half-pennies, which, with some token coins, supplied all the needs of the limited trade of those days.

Monied Interest. A phrase which came into use towards the close of the seventeenth century, to distinguish that class of men who had enriched themselves by trade and speculation, and which served to separate them in public estimation from what had been known from time immemorial as the "landed interest." At first it was a term of reproach, and justly so, considering the means by which many of them enriched themselves, and the disreputable characters found amongst them. At the present time the "monied interest" is neither better nor worse than other "interests," but the political and social influence of the class was never greater than during the last twenty or thirty years.

Turgot describes the two similar classes in France under the name of the *intérêt terrier* and the *intérêt rentier*.

Mono-metallism. Greek, μονος, *monos*, alone, single; and μεταλλον, *metallon*, a metal.

That system of currency which is based on a single standard of value, and which makes one metal only a legal tender for any and every amount. (*See Bi-metallism.*)

Monseng. The same with the Japanese *zeni* (*which see*).

Mortgage. From the Latin, *mortuus*, dead; *vas*, a surety, pledge, or bail. Whence in law Latin, *mortuus vadium*, a dead pledge, as distinguished from *vivum vadium*, a living pledge, a term now rarely used. From *mortuus vadium* was formed the old French, *mortgage*, which at an early period found its way into English law books in an unaltered form.

A *mortgage* or dead pledge, says *Blackstone*, "is where a man borrows of another a specific sum (*e.g.*, £200), and grants him an estate on condition that if he, the mortgagor, shall repay the mortgagee the said sum of £200 on a certain day mentioned in the deed, that then the mortgagor may re-enter on the estate so granted in pledge, or (as is now the more usual way) that then the mortgagee shall reconvey the estate to the mortgagor; in this case, the land which is so put in pledge, is by law, in case of non-payment at the time limited, for ever *dead* and gone to the mortgagor; and the mortgagee's estate in the lands is no longer conditional, but absolute; but so long as it continues conditional—that is, between the time of lending the money and the time allotted for payment—the mortgagee is called "*tenant in mortgage.*"

The term *mortgage* is now often used in a lax sense by City men to signify the borrowing of money upon securities deposited with a banker or other lender; this is more correctly called a *pawn* (*see Pawn*). It is also used to denote the anticipating of the payments of debts or dividends, by borrowing a sum of money and giving an agreement to repay the same when such debts or dividends fall due. *Mortgage* when used in these senses, though very common, is incorrect.

There is one other use of the word "mortgage," which, from the way it is employed, and owing to the position of the gentleman who employs it, demands attention. Mr. Thomson Hankey in his "Principles of Banking," says :—

"A relative of mine, C. Poulett Thomson, many years since, used to say to me that nothing was easier to conduct than the business of a banker, *if he would only learn the difference between a Mortgage and a Bill of Exchange.* This saying may appear absurd, but I believe it is full of wisdom. It may be supposed that anybody accustomed to such matters must know the difference between a mortgage and a Bill of Exchange, but the confusion easily arises, and I am convinced that if anyone were critically to examine into the origin of a very large part of what are ordinarily called Bills of Exchange, they would find them to be nothing more than Mortgages; they may be promises to pay; so such a document is indeed provided and given with every mortgage of land, but there is no ordinary provision incident to the document which will secure that on the date of the Bill becoming due, there will be assets forthcoming to meet it. An ordinary Bill of Exchange has such a provision or security; it is based on the transfer of capital in some shape or other in a manner which contemplates that at a fixed date such capital will have passed into the required hands, and that means will be provided to meet it. Even all ordinary Banking Bills are founded on such a supposition. It is a transfer of capital to be met by special provision at a particular day. Now, a Bill of Exchange, which I call for this mere explanation a Mortgage, is based on no such expectation, for example:—

1st January, 1866.

Six months after date pay to the order of ———— £5,000, value received as per contracts.

A. B.

To the ———— Railway Company.

"This Bill, drawn by a railway contractor, will become due on the 1st of July, 1866. The railway company will have no cash in hand to pay the Bill, unless they are able, as they intend, to raise it on their debentures—that is, borrow the money from some capitalist to enable them to meet this engagement.

Sunderland, 1st January, 1866.

Six months after date pay to the order of ———— £3,500, value received in ship ————.

C. D.

To ————, shipowners.

"The acceptors, shipowners, intend to provide means for paying this Bill by mortgaging the ship.

1st January, 1866.

Six months after date pay to the order of ———— £2,000, value received as per contract.

E. F.

To ————, Builders, Pimlico.

"This Bill of £2,000 is intended to be paid by borrowing the money from some insurance company on this and other blocks of houses now under construction.

Liverpool, 1st January, 1866.

Three months after date pay to the order of ———— £10,000, value in cotton, ex *Victoria* and *Jupiter*.

G. H.

To ————, Brokers, Liverpool.

"The cotton here referred to is in course of shipment from America, and when it arrives it will be put into the hands of the acceptors of this Bill of £10,000, who will then be enabled to borrow money for his bankers by pledging the dock warrants.

"These four transactions I consider Mortgages, but the Bills referred to are called Bills of Exchange."

It would appear from the above examples, and the explanations appended to each, that Mr. Hankey considers every so-called Bill of

Exchange a simple mortgage when nothing on the face of it shows that provision is made to *secure* the payment of the Bill when it becomes due; but that in every Bill of Exchange properly so called, there is something on the face of it which shows that such provision is made; and that the certainty of such provision being made is what constitutes its security, and gives it its value.

Mortmain. From Latin, *mortuus*, dead; *manus*, the hand in *mortuâ manu*, in a dead hand. French, *mortmain*.

Property is said to be sold or transferred in *mortmain* when it passes into the hands of a corporation. As these purchases were originally made chiefly by religious houses who held the property in trust, and as these corporations never die, though the individuals composing them do, lands once held by such corporations never again reverted to the king or to the feudal lord; "in consequence whereof," as Blackstone expresses it, "the lands become perpetually inherent in one *dead hand*," and occasioned the general appellation of mortmain to be applied to such alienations, and the religious houses themselves to be principally considered in forming *statutes of mortmain*. The design of the statute was to prevent the accumulation of real property in the hands of ecclesiastical corporations, and other religious bodies, so as to be applied "to superstitious uses." In recent times these laws have been much relaxed, and a man may give lands, notwithstanding the statutes, for the maintenance of a school, or the sustenance of poor people, or any other *charitable* uses. "But," says Blackstone, "as it was apprehended from recent experience that persons on their deathbeds might make large and improvident dispositions even for these good purposes to the disherison of their lawful heirs, it is therefore enacted by the statute of 9 Geo. II. c. 36, that no lands or tenements, or money to be laid out in the purchase thereof, shall be given or conveyed or anyways charged or encumbered, in trust for, or for the benefit of, any *charitable* uses whatever, unless by deed indented, executed in the presence of two witnesses, twelve calendar months before the death of the donor, and enrolled in the Court of Chancery within six calendar months after its execution. It is this last clause which the general public ought to understand, as well as the reason for it. All other matters connected with the law of mortmain are better left to be dealt with by professional lawyers.

Mutuum. From Latin, *mutuor, mutari*, to lend, to borrow, especially said of things not to be returned in kind, but in the form of an equivalent.

Whence *mutuum*, that which is borrowed, a loan; said of things to be returned *in genre* and not *in specie; dare frumentum mutuum*, Cic., to lend corn; *sumere ab aliquo pecunias mutuas*, Cic., to borrow money of any one; *pecunias mutuas exigere*, Cæsar, to request a loan, *cogor mutuari*, Cic., I am compelled to borrow.

It is also used more rarely when the things themselves are to be returned in the same condition as lent, as *mutuari domum*, to lend or let a house.

Mutuum is a term used in mercantile law to signify something lent with or without interest in such a way as to imply an exchange for something equivalent. Money when lent is of this nature, for the object of borrowing money is that it may be spent and therefore cannot be returned. It is repaid by a sum equal in amount, but not with the same coins or notes. Bonds and debentures are lent on the Stock Exchange in enormous quantities on settling days; these also are in the form of a *Mutuum*; but when the lender desires to retain the particular numbers which he possesses he stipulates for the return of the same particular bonds or shares, as was the case with American Five-Twenty Bonds a few years ago, when every holder found an advantage in possessing those bonds bearing the highest numbers. A loan of this kind is called a *Commodatum* (*which see*).

N.

N occurs in the following abbreviations:—

N.S., new style.
No. (*numero*) number.

Napoleon. A gold piece of 20 francs. Owing to the scrupulous care with which the mint regulations of France are carried out, Napoleons are much in favour among merchants and bankers all over Europe, and their price is regularly quoted at most of the Bourses. It weighs 6·45161 grammes ·900 fine. Its metallic value in sterling is £·79286, or 15*s*. 10¼*d*.

Nett or **Net.** French, *net, nette;* Italian, *netto.*

Clear after all deductions are made. For example, an English holder of Italian 5°/₀ Rentes, on presenting his coupons for payment, receives in sterling a certain sum dependent on the current rate of exchange after deduction of 13·20°/₀ Italian income tax; when these deductions have been made, the sum he receives is called the *nett* value of his dividend. So with a hogshead of sugar—the nett weight of the sugar is the difference between the *gross* weight and the weight of the wood and nails of which the hogshead is composed. See *Tare* and *Tret—Gross.* As to the orthography of the word, custom is divided; but as the single consonant is used in the name of the implement used by fishermen and cooks, common sense would suggest the expediency of using the double consonant in the word when employed with the signification here denoted, so as to mark the distinction between them.

New Style. A short and convenient name given to that change in our chronology which resulted from the adoption of the Gregorian in place of the Julian Calendar.

The Roman Calendar, in which our own originated, and which was in use from the time of Numa to that of Julius Cæsar, consisted of 13 months or 355 days. This *lunar* year was about 10¼ days shorter than the *solar* year, so that the end of one year and the beginning of another fell upon all seasons in turn, and would have caused great inconvenience, had it not been for the shifts and expedients enforced by priests and magistrates, in order to bring chronology into accord with the business of life, and especially with the demands of agriculture. In spite of all efforts, however, the confusion had become so great in the time of Julius Cæsar, that in order to make the year 45 B.C. commence on the 1st January, it was necessary to prolong the previous year and make it consist of 445 days. The Julian calendar being thus inaugurated, the adoption of the simple rule, of reckoning 365 days to every common year, and 366 days to every fourth year, or leap-year, served the purposes of chronology for fifteen centuries; at the end of which time certain small errors in the Julian system had accumulated to such a degree as to render a correction necessary. It assumed that the tropical year—that is, the interval between two successive arrivals of the sun at the vernal equinox—consisted of $365\frac{1}{4}$ days. The true value is 365·24224 days.

The intercalation of one day in every fourth year is therefore a little too much. At the end of the 16th century, these trifling errors had amounted to 10 days, when Pope Gregory ordained that the 4th of October, 1582, should be called the 15th October, 1582, and to prevent similar errors in the future, he further ordained as an addendum to the Julian rule, that every year divisible by 100, but not by 400, should consist of 365 days; and every year divisible by 400, again of 366. This change is what is denoted in chronology as the *New Style*. Owing to the religious antagonism between the Greek Church and the Roman, the Christians adhering to the former (Russia, Greece, and the East generally), regarded this ordinance as a usurpation of authority on the part of the Roman pontiff. They therefore refused to adopt it, and continued to use the Julian calendar, or *Old Style*. The difference between the dates in the Old Style and the New, is, of course, always increasing. It now amounts to twelve days.

New Three and a Half per Cents. In 1830, the interest on the New 4°/₀ Annuities which had already been reduced from 5 per cent., was again reduced to $3\frac{1}{2}$, from which operation they derived their name of the "New $3\frac{1}{2}$ per Cents." At the end of 1880, they amounted to a capital sum of £225,746. They terminate in 1894.

New Three per Cent. Annuities. The same as are usually known as New 3 per Cents., and on which interest is payable 5th April and 5th October. They amounted in December, 1880, to a capital sum of £204,153,372.

New Two and a Half per Cents. Annuities bearing $2\frac{1}{2}$ per cent. per annum, payable 5th January and 5th July. They amounted in December, 1880, to a capital sum of £4,168,504, and terminate in 1894.

Niboo. The Ni-Boo or Two Boo piece is a Japanese coin in the form of an oblong plate composed of an alloy of gold and silver. Its value in sterling is double that of the Itzi-Boo (single Boo) and varies according to fineness between 2*s.* 8*d.* and 2*s.* 11*d.*

Nishu or **Nishi.** A Japanese silver coin in the form of a thin oblong plate, equal to half the Boo, and worth about $8\frac{1}{2}d.$ sterling.

Nominal Exchange. The state of the exchanges which depends upon the moneys of the countries, and not on the current demand for them at any given time. It is therefore closely connected with what is more commonly called the "Mint Par of Exchange, but differs from it, inasmuch as it involves a comparison of the fluctuating values of gold and silver: and when a paper currency enters the calculation, the depreciation to which most currencies of that nature are subject.

Nominal Value. The nominal value of a coin is that value which is assigned to it by law, and often differs very materially from its *real* or *metallic* value. A shilling, for example, is nominally worth $\frac{1}{20}$ of a pound sterling or 12*d.* Its metallic value varies from 9*d.* to 11*d.*, according to the price of silver in the market.

Notary. From the Latin, *notarius*, one who took down in writing (*notæ*) the words of a speaker. It was applied more particularly to a quick writer; or one who took down notes in short hand. (*See Engross.*)

The Notary of ancient times was simply one who took down the words of a speaker in a rapid or short hand. Amongst the Romans this kind of work was usually performed by slaves.

The *Notarii* as they increased in ability, and raised themselves above the servile ranks, gradually assumed the duties and functions of the *tabelliones*, a class of writers who, under the Roman law, were employed in drawing up contracts, wills, and commercial documents, and the work which fell to them in this capacity, corresponded very closely to some of the business now undertaken by the modern notary public, the solicitor, attorney, and conveyancer. In modern practice, the business of the notary is more special. He is generally called in to attest signatures in deeds, contracts, affidavits, declarations, and especially such as are to be sent to foreign countries. The noting and protesting of bills of exchange is almost entirely given over to them. They also draw up protests after receiving the affidavits of mariners and masters of ships; and the administering of oaths is a business which they share with magistrates, justices of the peace, and other public functionaries.

From an old document, bearing date 1574, it appears that the Company of Notaries in London at that time numbered *sixteen*, and that they got their living by the "Making of Policies, Intimations Renunciations, and other writings" for the doing of which a monopoly had just been granted to one Richard Candler. This document is curious as showing the number of notaries employed at that time, and also as indicating roughly the kind of duties which fell within the scope of that profession. Since then, not only has the number of notaries increased, but the duties undertaken by them have become more clearly defined, and somewhat more extended in their range.

Note. Latin, *nota*, imperative of *notare*, to mark, observe, to make *nota*. *Nota* is the plur. of *notum* something known, the participle of *nosco* to know. The primary conception of a Note therefore is that of a something known, with which you are asked to make yourself acquainted. It afterwards came to mean something written or recorded, then a letter or epistle, and at length a commercial instrument.

In commercial law, the term *note* is applied to *promises* to pay, and is thus distinguished from a Bill (*see Bill*). It is, therefore, merely a contraction of the familiar term "Promissory Note."

Notice of Dishonour. If when a Bill is presented for acceptance, the person on whom it is drawn refuses to accept it, or if when presented for payment, the acceptor refuses to pay it, or if a promissory note is not paid when it falls due, such default is termed *Dishonour*; and the holder of the Bill or Note is bound to give notice to the parties who drew the Bill or Note, or to those who have negotiated it. This notice is called Notice of Dishonour, and if the holder fails to give notice of the same, the parties who would otherwise have been responsible are discharged from their liability. Notice may be given by word of mouth, or in writing, but as a matter of practice it is usual and generally desirable that the notice should be delivered in writing, no matter how short, so that the meaning is clear. A mere ticket pinned on to the Bill is often used, and the few formal words on the face of the ticket constitute a sufficient notice. The following is an example:—

"I beg to inform you that the undernoted Bill has been duly presented for payment to ——— ———: and as it has been dishonoured, that I shall look to you for payment.

"Date ——— "Yours, &c.,
"Amount ——— "R. S———.
"Drawer ———
"Endorser ———

Noting a Bill. To *note a bill* is to record the non-acceptance or non-payment of a bill when it becomes due. It is done officially by a notary, and the following is the form given by Mr. Justice Byles as a sufficient notice of dishonour from the holder to an endorser.

No. 1, Fleet Street, London.
26 Sept. 187—.

Sir,

I hereby give you notice that the Bill of Exchange dated the 22nd ult., drawn by A.B., of ———, on C.D., of ———, for £100, payable one month after date to A.B. or his order, and endorsed by you, has been duly presented for payment, but was dishonoured and is unpaid. I request you to pay me the amount thereof.

I am, Sir,
Your obedient servant,
G. H.

To Mr. E. F., of ———, merchant.

This form may be, and obviously must be, modified to suit varied circumstances. (*See Protest.*)

Not Negotiable. Words added to a cheque for the protection of bankers and innocent holders against fraud. "This is a new-fashioned cheque altogether," says Mr. Justice Lindley: it dates, indeed, only from the passing of "the Crossed Cheques Act, 1876. The clauses bearing on the phrase "not negotiable" are as follows:—

> "5. Where a cheque is uncrossed, a lawful holder may cross it *generally* or *specially*."
>
> "Where a cheque is crossed *generally*, a lawful holder may cross it *specially*."
>
> "Where a cheque is crossed *generally* or *specially*, a lawful holder may add the words "Not negotiable."
>
> "12. A person taking a cheque crossed generally or specially, bearing in either case the words "not negotiable," shall not have and shall not be capable of giving a better title to the cheque than that which the person from whom he took it had."
>
> "But a banker who has in good faith and without negligence received payment for a customer of a cheque crossed generally or specially to himself shall not, in case the title proves defective, incur any liability to the true owner of the cheque by reason only of having received such payment."

Ever since the passing of the Act, these clauses taken together have been a puzzle to men of business: not one in a hundred seems to have any clear idea of what they mean; and the explanations given by the lawyers themselves do not make the meaning much clearer.

The following practical maxims may, however, be relied on:—

1. Never take a cheque marked "not negotiable" from a stranger, nor even from one who is not a stranger, unless his general reputation for honesty and integrity is known to you.

2. With this proviso, a cheque so marked may be safely taken, and passed through any number of hands: but, as a rule, the sooner it finds its way to the banker, the better.

Novation. Latin, *novatio*, a renewing.

The substitution of a new debt for a former one; a familiar case is when the holder of a bill is not prepared to meet it with cash when due, and gives another bill in place of it. *Novation* also takes place when a debtor, instead of paying a debt, transfers to his creditor a debt due to said debtor; thus, the payment of debts by cheques drawn on a banker are examples of *novation*, because by the passing of the cheque, a debt payable to the bank's customer is thereby transferred to the new creditor, that is, the person who receives the cheque. Among the Romans (to whom we owe the term) the *novatio* was a process of some importance. As debts, before the invention of written instruments of exchange, were not transferable by manual delivery, it was necessary that the three parties to a transfer, namely, the creditor, the debtor, and the transferree, should meet together in person. Then they entered into an agreement before witnesses, and the creditor transferred his claim against the debtor to the transferree. "The contract established between the transferree and the original debtor was termed a *novatio*, and the assignment of the debtor to the transferree as a new creditor was termed *delegatio*." (*See Delegation.*)

"By a novation, a new debtor might be substituted even *without the consent* of the original debtor. If it was done *with the consent* of the original debtor, the new debtor was termed *delegatus*, and the process, *delegatio*." This extract from the Institutes of Justinian shews the technical distinction between a novation and a delegation very clearly.

Nusf. A modern Egyptian coin, silver, equal to ten piastres.

O.

O, occurs in the following abbreviations.

$^{o}/_{a}$, on account.
$^{o}/_{o}$, per cent.
$^{o}/_{oo}$, per mille, per thousand.
O.S., old style.

Obang. A Japanese gold coin, now rarely met with, oblong in shape with rounded ends, and worth 100 Itziboos (*see Itziboo*).

Obligation. Latin, *ob*, over or to; *ligare*, to bind; *obligatio*, a binding or bond.

Obligation has two meanings in the original Latin, and also in its modern applications. (1.) It signifies the relation of a debtor to his creditor, whether it be in regard to a debt of honour, of service, or of money. (2.) It is applied to documents in which an obligation is recorded. Hence the terms "Foreign Bonds," "Railway Bonds," or "Mortgage Bonds." Bonds or obligations are usually distinguished from shares in railway and other companies, by an engagement expressed on their face to pay a fixed amount of interest on the capital invested in the bonds, quite irrespective of the amount payable to ordinary shareholders, which may be more or less than that paid to bondholders. Hence it follows that the payment of the interest on bonds or obligations, must be provided for before any profits are divided amongst ordinary shareholders, and for this reason their price in the market is exposed to less violent fluctuations than that of shares, and are more suitable as media of investments than shares, which are better adapted to speculation.

The fundamental notion borne by the term *obligation* is that of a "tie between two parties of such a nature as to confer on the one a power of compelling by action, the other to give, do, or make good something. The obligation does not give *any interest in a thing*, to get which might be the ultimate object of the proceeding, but only gives a means of acquiring it . . . or its value."

There are two main sources of *Obligations*. *Contracts* in which the debtor is bound by having undertaken to be bound; and *Delicts* in which he has done an injury, and is bound to make good his wrong.

Obolus. (*a.*) In the Ionian Islands, before the introduction of the system of the French Monetary Convention, the *Obolus* was 1-100th part of the Ionian Dollar, worth ½*d.* English.

(*b.*) There was formerly also a Rhenish coin, both in gold and silver, worth about 1*s.* 2*d.*, called by this name.

Ochava, Ochavo, or **Octavo.** A copper coin formerly circulating in Mexico, value ⅛ of a Rial, or 1·64th of the Mexican dollar.

Official List. The list of prices with other details of importance relating to the Stocks and Shares dealt in, on the Stock Exchange. It is published with the sanction and under the authority of the Committee of the Stock Exchange. The prices given in the Money Article of the morning papers, are taken from this list up to three o'clock in the afternoon. After that hour, up to half-past four or five o'clock, they depend for their value on the assiduity and tact of the city editors (and their assistants) of the respective journals. These extra official quotations are often the most important of the day.

Old Style. (*See New Style.*)

On-beshlik or **Onbeshlic.** A Turkish billon coin, valued at 15 paras, or about ¾*d.* English.

Onza or **Onza d'Or,** or **Doubloon.** A Spanish gold coin, value 320 reals = 16 piastres or dollars. It is sometimes called the Isabella Doubloon, and is worth 247·389 pence, or £1 0*s.* 7¼*d.* English. (*See Doblon.*)

Open Cheque. An *uncrossed* Cheque, payable to Bearer or to Order on presentation. (*See Crossed Cheque.*)

Open Credits. Open Credits are defined to be Credits given by Bankers to their Clients without personal guarantees, or deposit of securities. An open credit, therefore, closely resembles a fiduciary loan (*see Fiduciary*), the principal difference being, that in a loan, a sum of money or cheque is handed over to the borrower, while in the case of a credit, an entry is made in the books of the bank to the credit of the client, against which he can draw.

Open Policy. One in which, at the time of effecting the Insurance, it is stated that the Interest is to be hereafter declared.

Options. An *Option* is a bargain in which a dealer has the right to buy, or sell, or both, a certain amount of stock at a given price, during a specified time. The consideration paid for this right is called the "price of the option." Suppose Mercer gives a jobber 1 per cent. for the right of selling £1,000 Russians at a stated price on or before the 15th of the month. Mercer risks £10, but he cannot lose more. If the price falls before the 15th one per cent. he may buy £1,000 Russians, and he will neither gain nor lose by the transaction. If it falls 2 per cent. he may gain £10. If it rises from the first, he simply does nothing and his option expires, and his loss is limited to the £10 he paid for his privilege. *Options* may be dealt in, and often are, in other markets as well as the Stock Exchange, but they are more common in the latter than elsewhere.

When money is paid for the option of buying at a given price, the operation is called "giving for the *call*." When it is paid for the option of selling, it is called "giving for the *put*." Sometimes both operations are combined, and then it is called "giving for the *put* and *call*."

At other times, options are combined with regular purchases and sales. Mercer may, for instance, buy £5,000 Turkish at twelve, with the option of calling for an equal amount before settling day in addition. This is buying £5,000 "*with the call of more*," or he may sell £5,000 at the same price "*with the put of more*"—"more" meaning in each instance an amount equal to that bought or sold.

Or or Ore. The $\frac{1}{100}$ part of the krone of the Scandinavian Monetary Convention (Norway, Sweden, and Denmark), value about half a farthing English. Silver pieces of 50, 25, and 10 ore are struck, the two former ·600 fine, and the last ·400 fine.

Order, to. The phrase "to order" is a curtailed expression covering any of the following—viz., "In obedience to the order," "In obedience to *his* order," "In obedience to *her* order," "In obedience to their order," "According to order." To novices the phrase is mostly unintelligible, and it is probable that many, who are not novices, use it many times in a day without any clear idea of its origin. The manner in which the order is given too, is a little curious, and is another of the many abbreviated forms which pass current in the commercial world. Take for example, a banker's cheque payable "to order." On the face of it we see "Pay to Messrs. Bullion, Bros. & Co. or order" the sum of, &c., &c. And how is the *order* given by Messrs. Bullion, Bros. and Co.? Why by simply writing their name on the back of the cheque. The form, however, is so well understood, that it suffices for all practical purposes, and the abbreviation prevents much useless repetition and waste of time.

By the insertion of the words "to order," a bill or cheque is rendered negotiable according to English law. Without this addition (or the words "to bearer" the transferee could not sue the debtor in his own name.

Or Order. The origin of the phrase "*or order*" is found in the practice of merchants of old time, who were not allowed to pay a debt to any one but the *payee* himself; or, as was afterwards provided, "*to his certeyne atturnai*," or to "*his assignes*," or to "*his certain order*" (that is, to the clearly ascertained order of the payee.) These phrases gradually gave way to the short and now familiar term "*or order*." It means, therefore, that if a debtor does not pay a stated sum to the payee himself, it is to be paid to some one whom he has *ordered* to receive it, and to whom the debtor is *ordered* to pay it. That *order*, in modern commerce, is given by the payee, sometimes by simply writing his name at the back of the instrument, at others by adding the name of the transferee, with other details, thus giving rise to the various forms of endorsement. (*See Endorsement.*)

Origin, Source, or Cause of Value. "There are a great variety of things of different natures which have value. We must search for some single cause which is common to them all; which being present, value is present; which, when it increases, value increases; which, when it decreases, value decreases, and which, being absent, value is absent. The sole *cause of value* is human desire. When there is a demand for things, they have value; when the demand increases (the supply being supposed the same), the value increases; when the demand decreases, the value decreases, and when the demand altogether ceases, the value is altogether gone."—H. D. McLeod.

It is to be observed that this definition applies simply to the term "Origin (source or cause) of value." Human desire is not the *sole determinant of* value. Two things may be equally desired, but if one requires double the labour to produce it that the other does, it will be more valuable than the other. Again if two things be equally desired, and one exists in abundance, while the other is to be obtained only in very limited quantities, this latter will be the more valuable of the two. (*See Value, Measure of Value, Unit of Value.*)

Original Bills. Bills which have been drawn and sold before any endorsements have been added. It is only when original bills have been *drawn* and *accepted* by first-class houses, that a good price can be obtained for them. If the drawer and acceptor of an original bill be comparatively unknown, the buyer of such bill will not pay for it until time has been allowed for inquiries, and to compensate for this trouble, he offers an inferior price for it. When a bill has one or more endorsements, and a well-known name of high repute is amongst them, the obscurity of the original drawer and acceptor is of minor importance. Hence the value attached to bills with numerous endorsements, since every endorser is placed in the position of a guarantor of the soundness of the bill to which his name is attached.

Over Construction. A term recommended by Bonamy Price, to prevent the confusion of certain economic phenomena with *over-production.* He says, "In true *over-production* the fault lies in the supply; eager producers have carried their operations too far. In *over-construction*, the fault rests with the demand which sinks below its previous level. These are phenomena of different kinds; they had better not be indicated by the same word." As examples, the supply of cotton cloth in 1877-8 was greatly in excess of the demand owing to the stimulus given to manufacturers in the five or six previous years, while the demand remained much as usual. The consumption of cotton cloth is spread over a wide area, and after certain limited needs have been satisfied, any further supply is superfluous; the demand for it is therefore not liable to violent fluctuations. Here was a case of *over-production*. But there are other articles (especially such as are intended to gratify the caprices of fashion) the demand for which is very precarious, and may at any moment fall much below the supply, even though the supply has not been augmented in any appreciable degree for years. The straw hat and bonnet trade of Dunstable and its neighbourhood furnishes a case in point. The use of straw-plait had been uninterrupted for a long time; demand and supply had balanced each other; there had been no excessive stimulus to production, and yet a mere freak of fashion was sufficient to throw hundreds out of work. Straw hats and bonnets, a few years ago, were superseded by those of other materials, and the demand for them almost ceased. This was a case of what Prof. Price calls *over-construction*. These two phenomena are, as he says, quite different; but the term "over-construction" is not well chosen. In each phenomenon there is a variable or fluctuating factor, in the first, it is the *supply* that has fluctuated to excess, and the term "over-production" naturally points to that as the cause of the evil. In the second, it is the *demand* that has fallen off, and some word which would describe this falling off would point to the cause of the evil at once, which the word "over-construction" does not.

Over-Production. Over-production is now very generally regarded as one of the chief causes of those convulsions in trade called *panics* or *crises*, and which sometimes reach dimensions which give them the character of a national calamity. Hence the importance of understanding clearly what *over-production* consists in, of tracing its causes, and devising, if possible, suitable remedies. There are three phases of over-production which merit particular notice.

I. Over-production may take place in one or two commodities and no more. This, although a serious matter to those persons specially employed in the production of those commodities, does not affect to any appreciable extent the nation in general. Capital and labour are usually transferred to some other branch of trade, at least for a time, and business then resumes its usual course.

II. A much more disastrous form of over-production is that in which several of the large staple industries or the nation are unduly developed. An example of this occurred in England during the five years which followed the outbreak of the Franco-Prussian war. A great stimulus was imparted to English trade during that period, and railways, ironworks, coal mines, cotton mills and numerous subsidiary industries were forced into unusual activity. But a moment at length arrived when it was found that enormous sums had been expended in the accumulation of fixed capital in the form of railways, iron furnaces, new coal shafts, mills, &c., for which no return could be made till after the lapse of years; at the same time immense stocks of goods were manufactured, first under the stimulus of a brisk demand, and afterwards in the hope of a continued demand. Had all this activity been paid for out of *profits* and *savings*, no evil would have resulted; but the lamentable fact was that the greater part of it was due to an *abuse of credit*. Services were paid for by means of bills; bills were discounted, and with the proceeds additional enterprises were started, and this went on under the sunshine of an apparent prosperity till a cloud began to gather. That cloud was a suspicion on the part of those who *lent* money, or *sold* credit—namely bankers—that it would not be safe to carry their discounting operations much further, a suspicion aroused probably in the first place by learning that here and there some great manufacturer or contractor had a difficulty in taking up his bills when they fell due. A suspicion of this kind soon spreads, and bankers under those circumstances begin to contract their issues. Failures occur, and then everyone is on the *qui vive* to learn who is likely to go next. Then comes the crisis, and happy is the community if the crisis does not break out into unreasoning panic. Whether it does go to this length or not, a severe crisis is sure to be followed by great depression, and it is a long time before confidence is restored. Meanwhile trade languishes, wages fall, and multitudes are thrown out of employment, and it is not till past troubles are to some extent forgotten that the energies of the people revive, and business resumes its normal course. The remedy for this evil lies almost exclusively with the bankers, and those who deal in credit.

III. There is further the supposititious case of universal over-production, that is the over-production of all kinds of commodities. Some economists have rashly said that this is impossible, inasmuch as if all commodities had been produced in superabundance the producers would have nothing to do but live on past produce and cease from producing until the surplus was exhausted. This, however, is neither a correct statement of the case, nor is the inference warranted. Even were it possible, and for the nonce we will assume it possible to produce every kind of commodity in superabundance, yet it is not at all probable that those commodities would be at all proportionately distributed among all the producers. Some would have vast accumulations on their hands, half or perhaps more than half the population would have none whatever; and as these would have nothing but their services to offer in exchange for a share of the surplus, and since, by the supposition, those services for the time being are not required, it follows that they must be reduced to extreme want, if not starvation. The remedy for this evil lies chiefly with the labourers and producers, who must be taught in seasons of prosperity to make provision for the evil day which must inevitably arrive. Instead of living luxuriously and even wastefully in favoured times, they ought to economise and save. They then would have a store on which to fall back in the days of reduced wages, short hours or no work, as the necessities of the occasion may impose. The months or years following a period of over-production are a fine time for persons of fixed and scanty incomes, and for the thrifty class in general. Commodities are then cheap, and consumers luxuriate in the produce showered upon them, while the thriftless and self-indulgent are at their wit's end to procure a meal.

P.

P, occurs in the following abbreviations:

P/N., Promissory Note.
pm, premium
P.O.O., Post Office Order.
P.p., *Per procurationem*, or Please pay
Prox., proximo (in the next.)
P.P.I., Policy Proof of Interest

Pagares. Italian, *pagare;* from Latin, *pacare,* to appease, to quiet, from which also is derived our English word, *pay.* Spanish, *pagaré,* a bond, or writing of obligation to pay a sum of money.—SEOANE'S *Span. Dict.*

Pagares are Bonds or Promissory Notes printed in the Spanish language. They derive their name from the word *pagare* (I will pay) which is printed conspicuously on their face. The only Stocks referred to under this name in the English Market are those of the Sociedad Civil of Madrid, but the name is applied to other Stocks and even to coupons, when the significant word is inserted upon them.

Panic. Said to be derived from the name of the great god *Pan,* who is described by the ancients as so hideous a monster that even his nurse fled away and deserted him. He was the terror of rustics who dwelt in the woods and mountains where he made his home. Stories of this sort easily and naturally give rise to the forms of adjectives and nouns in modern languages, just as Herculean is derived from Hercules, and Mercurial from Mercury. The Spanish and Italian have the word *panico,* and the French, *panique,* all used in the same sense as the English, *panic.*

A *Panic* in commerce is an unreasoning and uncontrollable fear which often seizes a trading community on the occurrence of a financial crisis. The effects are often most deplorable, and multitudes who can ill afford to lose their scanty possessions rush into the market to buy, or to sell, or to withdraw their deposits from the bank just at a moment when common sense or the most ordinary discretion would dictate absolute abstention from any action whatever, and not unfrequently would counsel a course of action the very opposite of that pursued under the influence of a passing fright.

Paper Credit. Orders or Promises to pay a stated sum of money recorded on *paper*. The term as commonly used includes book-debts, I.O.U.'s, and instruments of credit of all kinds.

Paper Currency. The term *Paper Currency* is employed technically with a restricted meaning which it is important to distinguish, since it is a curtailed expression for what is more correctly called a *Forced* Paper Currency, or an *Inconvertible* Paper Currency.

Although in those countries where a gold or silver standard is adopted, *paper money* is in constant use, and forms a part of the *Currency*, there is another sense in which the term *Paper Money* or *Paper Currency* is used, and which separates it from all other forms of paper employed as a medium of exchange. The word *Inconvertible* is adopted to indicate this form of paper money, and the propriety of so describing it is seen by comparing it with other forms of paper money. Thus, a Bank Note, a Bill of Exchange when due, an Exchequer Bond, or Treasury Bill must be paid in cash if demanded. In other words, Instruments of the kind enumerated may be "converted" into cash whenever demanded by the holder of the document. Paper money and currency of this nature is for this reason called "convertible." It sometimes happens, however, that Governments, owing to wars or other adverse circumstances, are much straitened for want of money. They then print bank notes in great quantity, and pay their debts with them; thus distributing them to their immediate creditors. These state creditors also pay their obligations to their debtors with the same paper. On their face, is the usual promise to *pay on demand* the amount stipulated, but it is well known that payment on demand is impossible at the time, and that such payment can only be made at some *future time*. Notwithstanding this drawback, the Government declares these notes a *legal tender*, so that when offered to a creditor they constitute a legal discharge of a debt. As this operates as a sort of compulsion upon a creditor, paper money, when made a legal tender, is called a *Forced Paper Currency*. Further, since no one will give gold or silver which is scarce, when paper, which is plentiful, can be made to do duty for it, it follows that paper becomes "inconvertible." The characteristics of a "Paper Currency" properly so called, are therefore, that it is made a *legal tender*, and that it is thus *forced* into circulation, becoming thereby *inconvertible* into metallic money except at a discount. (*See Paper Money.*)

Paper Money. A general term applied to instruments of credit which pass readily from hand to hand in lieu of metallic money. It applies to Bank Notes *par excellence;* to Commercial Bills, to Promissory Notes of good character, and with somewhat of hesitancy to commercial paper of inferior reputation. The advantages of using paper money in lieu of coin are manifold, but the following are among the most conspicuous;—

(1.) *Portability.* A thousand sovereigns is an inconvenient sum to carry about, and silver of an equal value would form a heavy load, but a bank note or bill for the same amount would lie in one's waistcoat pocket and be scarcely felt.

(2.) *Economy of time* in counting, weighing, &c. To count a thousand pounds in gold occupies considerable time; in silver or copper, or all three combined, much longer. The value of a bank note is seen at a glance.

(3.) *Security.* Coins if stolen or lost are not easily identified, and are difficult to recover. A bank note or bill being numbered and otherwise marked, is not so attractive to a thief, and in case of accidental loss is more easily traced.

(4.) *Saving of Interest.* By employing a comparatively valueless material like paper instead of a valuable metal like gold or silver, there is a saving of interest in so far as the amount of paper money exceeds the amount of metallic currency kept in reserve to meet it. The private and Joint Stock Banks of the United Kingdom in this way enjoy the interest upon fully fifteen millions sterling: and it is probable that the good bills in circulation average an equal sum.

(5.) *Freedom from Wear and Tear.* But there is a clear gain also in the use of paper even when gold and silver are kept in reserve to meet it. The precious metals suffer little from wear and tear when stored up in the vaults of a bank, and it may seem but a trifling amount that is lost by a sovereign though kept in circulation for years. Nevertheless, small as may be the loss on a single coin, that upon coins when counted by millions is very serious, and forms an important set-off against the cost of the paper and printing of the notes.

Par.

From the Latin, *par*, equal (in size, power, or nature), whence *par impar ludere*, to play at "even and odd," a favourite game with Roman children, as with English. It is derived from the Greek, παρα (which was often written παρ), beside, alongside of; and the notion of equality appears to be connected with the practice of putting two or more things beside, or alongside, each other in order to compare them.

This word is used in various senses, some of which it is important to distinguish.

(1.) *Issue Par.* When the Bonds of a New Loan are issued, or the Debentures of a commercial company are placed on the market, the said Bonds or Debentures are distributed to the public at a given price. Thus the Egyptian State Domain Loan was issued in 1878 "at the price of 73," meaning, of course, £73 for every £100 Bond. If the market value of these bonds fell below 73 they were said to be at a discount; if above 73, at a premium; if precisely at 73, "at par." *Par,* when used in this sense and in all analogous cases, is the *Issue Par.*

(2.) *Nominal Par.* Every bond has impressed on its face a *nominal* value, such as £10, £20, £50, £100, £500, or £1,000, or some intermediate amount. The Egyptian State Domain Loan, above mentioned, has rapidly increased in market value, so that now, in June, 1880, it is standing at 95 for each £100 bond, and is spoken of as approaching *par*. Here the meaning of the word *par* has evidently shifted; it now means *nominal par*, or the "face value" of the bond.

(3) *Mint Par*. A contraction of the phrase Mint Par of Exchange, which signifies the value of the coins of one country, expressed by those of another using the same metal. The Mint Par lies at the basis of all international exchanges. (*See Mint Par of Exchange.*)

(4.) *Arbitrated Par*. A contraction of the phrase Arbitrated Par of Exchange, which signifies the amount of currency in one country which is equivalent to a given amount in another, taking into account (1) the balance of indebtedness between the two countries, and the consequent demand for bills on one or the other; (2) the relative value at the time of gold and silver in the case of those countries having a different metallic standard; (3) the amount of interest that would be lost by waiting certain days or months for the payment of a bill, and which is dependent on the rate of discount prevailing at the time; and (4) the amount of risk which is run by receiving a piece of paper representing a promise to pay several days or months hence, in exchange for cash paid down or goods delivered.

Para. The 40th part of the Egyptian piastre, worth about 1-16th of the English Penny. It is sometimes called the Fuddah, which see.

The *Para* of Servia is the 1-100th part of the Dinar, and is the equivalent of the French centime.

Pars of Exchange. There are two modes of denoting the COURSE of EXCHANGE between London and foreign countries; in one, the Sterling is fixed and the foreign money variable; in the other, the Foreign money is fixed and the sterling variable. For convenience of reference when comparing the "Mint Par" with the fluctuating "Course" of Exchange, some of the most important "Pars of Exchange" are here brought together under the two classes. In several cases, both methods of denoting the Par of Exchange are used; notably those of the United States, and some of the South American Republics, and these, therefore, may be placed indifferently with one class or the other.

(*See Table* on the following page.)

First Class.

Sterling Fixed and Foreign Money Variable.

LATIN MONETARY UNION.		
Countries that have joined the Union:—		
France . . . / Belgium . . . / Switzerland . . .	£1=Fr. 25·2213	
Italy . . .	£1=Lirae 25·2213	
Greece . . .	£1=Drachmæ 25·2213	
Countries that have adopted the Latin Monetary System without joining the Union:—		
Spain[1] . . .	£1=Pesetas 25·2213	(1) Although the Peseta is equal to the Franc, the exchange with England is always expressed in terms of the Piastre of 5 Pesetas; thus Piastre= 47½d.
Monaco (Principality)	£1=Fr. 25·2213	
Finland . . .	£1=Mks. 25·2213	
Roumania . . .	£1=Leys 25·2213	
Servia . . .	£1=Dinars 25·2213	
Countries that have assimilated their coinage to that of the Latin Union, without adopting the system in its entirety (2):—		(2) The coinage of these countries is only so far assimilated to that of the Latin Monetary Union as consists in making their *unit of account* exactly equal in weight and fineness to the French Five-Franc piece. It thus facilitates international payments, and opens the way to a further extension of the Latin system.
Colombia . . .	£1=Pesos 5·044	
Chili . . .	£1=Pesos 5·044	
Peru . . .	£1=Sols 5·044	
Venezuela . . .	£1=Venez 5·044	
Uruguay . . .	£1=Piast. 5·044	
SCANDINAVIAN MONETARY UNION.		
Denmark . . . / Norway . . . / Sweden . . .	£1=Kron. 18·16	
Austria-Hungary .	£1=Fl. 10·21½	
German Empire[3] .	£1=Mks. 20·43	(3) The new coinage of Germany is now made compulsory in all the States forming the Empire, although many of the old coins still circulate at a valuation.
Holland . . .	£1=Fl. 12·107	
Turkey . . .	£1=Piast. { 110·70 or 110·28 paras	
Egypt[4] . . .	£1=Piast. 97·50	(4) Coins of various nationalities circulate in Egypt, and all of them have a "Tariff Value" assigned to them by the Government. The mint regulations of Egypt are of the most imperfect character.
United States[5] . .	£1=$1·84	(5) The exact Par of Exchange is £1= $1·86½, but it is taken at $1·84 according to Tariff. This really means that a minute deduction is made for "Mint Remedies" and a moderate amount of wear and tear.

Second Class.

Foreign Money Fixed and Sterling Variable.

Spain[1] . . .	Piastre=47·5785*d*.	(1) Piastre=5 pesetas or francs (Monetary Law of 1868).
Portugal . . .	Milreis=53·284*d*.	
Russia . . .	Ruble=38*d*.	
India . . .	Rupee=22·60*d*.	
Japan . . .	Yen=49·17*d*.	
Mexico . . .	Dollar=51½*d*.	
Brazil . . .	Milres=26·93*d*.	

Particular Average. (*See Average.*)

Partings or **Parting Bullion.** Mixtures of gold and silver. When the Gold is greater in quantity, the mixture is called a Gold Parting, and when the Silver is greater, a Silver Parting. Native gold is always found alloyed with silver, and native silver is sometimes found alloyed with gold. It is only when the alloy is in sufficient abundance to pay for extraction or *parting*, that it is called *Parting Bullion.* As a rule, it may be said, that when a mixture of gold and silver is below the British Standard, that is, lower than 22 carats fine, the amount of silver will pay the cost of parting. Also, when a mixture of gold and silver contains 1 per mill. of gold, the gold will pay the cost of parting.

Passive Bonds and Shares. Bonds or Shares issued by a Government or by a commercial company, on which no interest is paid, but entitling the holder to some future benefit or claim.

Patacon. (*a.*) The unit of value in the Argentine Republic (La Plata). It bears also the alternative names of Peso Duro, and Hard Dollar. Originally it was worth 4*s.* 2*d.* but is now represented by paper currency valued at about half that sum. There is no national coinage in the country, and foreign coins of various denominations circulate at a fluctuating rate of exchange.

(*b.*) A gold coin of Uruguay. The Four Patacon Piece is reckoned equal to 4 Spanish Dollars, or 5 Pesos Corrientes. It weighs 6·730 grammes, ·875 fine, value 16*s.* 1*d.* sterling. The Patacon is, therefore, equal to 4*s.* $0\frac{1}{4}$*d.*

Pataka. The Abyssinian name for the old Spanish or Austrian Dollar, which (as Abyssinia has no coinage of its own) circulates freely in the country. It is valued at about 4*s.*

Patent. Letters Patent. Latin, *literæ pătentes,* open letters.

Patents, a contraction for *letters patent,* are royal grants whether of lands, titles, honours, privileges, or profits from new inventions, or copyrights, and they are called letters patent, because they are contained in *open* letters; that is, letters not closed by a seal, but with the royal seal at the bottom, and addressed by the sovereign to all subjects of the realm. They are thus distinguished from *literæ clausæ,* or closed writs, which not being intended for public perusal are sealed upon the outside.

Rights secured by letters patent fall under the class of property called Incorporeal, and may be bought or sold in the same way as all other property of that description,

Pawn. Latin, *pignus;* Belgian, *pand;* Germ. *Pfand;* Ital. *pegno.*

To put property in *pawn* is to hand it over to a creditor or lender as security for a debt: it is thus distinguished from *hypothecation,* in which case the property remains in the possession of the debtor or borrower. (*See Hypothecation.*)

Payee. The party to whom a sum of money is, or is to be, paid.

Payment. Latin, *pacare*, to appease, to satisfy; whence French, *payer*; Italian, *pagaro*. The original meaning in Latin was not to pay money, but to pacify, or quiet, by any means, whether by force or otherwise. The Latin for payment by means of money was *solvere* or *dissolvere*, to loosen, disengage, release, &c., or *numerare*, to count (referring to the counting of coins); *alicui pecuniam numerare*, to pay down. But in Roman mercantile law the idea of *appeasing* or *satisfying* the claims of a creditor gained such prominence that *pacare* found its way into all the Latin dialects, and acquired those modifications which are now everywhere current in the South of Europe, and throughout America.

In commercial law, *payment* signifies the giving of something in exchange for something else.

Payment may be made in money, and in small transactions generally is, but in modern trade, payment is usually effected by means of bills, cheques, and other instruments of exchange. When goods are offered in exchange for goods, it is popularly distinguished as "payment in kind." Payment in legal tender and payment in kind are the only forms of payment which amount to a "satisfaction." Bills do not afford this satisfaction, till they have matured and are paid. Cheques do not until they have been presented and passed the Clearing House.

Payment Supra Protest. The mongrel phrase "*supra protest*," half Latin, half English, is used in commerce in the sense of "over protest" or "after protest." The circumstances under which payment is made *after protest* are, when the person on whom a bill is drawn, refuses acceptance or payment, or the holder requires better security than that implied by the nature of the bill. (*See Protest, Honour, &c.*) In all cases, when a person accepts a bill for Honour, a *protest* is necessary as a bill can be so accepted only *after* a formal protest for non-acceptance, or for better security.

Peca Antiga. Literally, *Old Piece*. A Portuguese gold coin equal to 8000 reis (8$000), worth £1 15*s*. 6⅓*d*. sterling.

Penni. The hundredth part of the Finland Mark, the equivalent of the French Centime. Silver pieces of 50 and 25 pennis are struck, having a fineness of ·750.

Penny. The root, *pen*, is found in the languages of several European countries, and appears to have been used originally to signify not a coin, but a piece of money of any kind, or money generally. In the Saxon chronicle occurs the phrase "Thritig scylinge penega" (thirty shillings in money), and in the Bohemian, *penizek* is a piece of money. In the Magyar, *pengni* signifies to ring, and in allusion to this quality of the metal the coin is called *penz*. Dutch, *penninck*; German, *Pfennig*; Manx, *peng*.

"The king procured artists as supposed from Florence, and in 1344 the first pieces of gold coin appeared, called Florens, halves, and quarters; but so strong was the impression on people's minds, *of a penny being a whole piece of money*, that these pieces obtained the appellation of *gold pennies, gold halfpennies*, and *gold farthings* or fourthings.—WALTER MERREY.

A bronze coin used in England, and first introduced in 1860. The 12th part of a shilling. Composed of—

95 parts copper.
4 ,, tin.
1 ,, zinc.

100=bronze.

It is a token coin, and worth *in metal* about ¼ its normal amount. Its weight is 145·83333 grains Troy.

In Canada, the Penny is only equal to ⅚ of our English penny; in Nova Scotia, only ⅘.

The old silver penny was the only coin struck in England for many years. It was of the "Ancient Right Standard," like our modern coins, and weighed the 240th part of the Tower Pound; that is 22½ grains Troy. It was, therefore, rather larger than our present three-penny piece, which weighs 21·8181 grains. (*See Tower Pound and Esterling.*)

Perpetual Annuity. An Annuity which goes on for ever, and is thus distinguished from *Terminable* Annuities, which may be *Long* or *Short*, but which terminate at a specified time. Consols—commonly called Bank Annuities—are perpetual; the United States Funded Loans are Terminable, as are also most Bonds issued by Foreign States.

Per Procuration. *Per*, a Latin preposition signifying through, by, by means of, followed by the accusative case. *Procuration* is from *pro*, for, on behalf of, and *cura*, care; whence also *procurare*, to care for, to take care of, to look after anything.

A phrase in common use, half Latin and half English, contracted from the Latin *per procurationem*, meaning "by procuration." *Procuration* means by itself, administration, doing some duty, discharging some office, and the power of procuration is usually conferred by mercantile firms on some trusty servant or clerk for some specific duty. The most common case is the duty of signing cheques, drafts, and other commercial instruments on behalf of a firm or a bank. In some cases, the principals of a London house are empowered jointly and severally to sign on behalf of a foreign firm, or of some foreign correspondent. The duty of signing "by procuration," or on behalf of some one, is assigned sometimes in a very lax way by mere oral instructions, sometimes by a letter duly signed and sealed by the principals; but in cases where great interests are involved, by "power of attorney" (*See Power of Attorney*). The phrase "per procurationem" is commonly contracted into "*p. p.*" so that a clerk or manager (say Charles Benson) signing on behalf of Bergmann & Co., would probably write,

"P.p. Bergman & Co.
Charles Benson."

Personal Capital. That kind of capital which an individual possesses in his own person, in the form of natural energy, acquired skill, proved character, and capacity for business. Capital of this nature is so highly esteemed that those individuals who are so fortunate as to possess it are often able to form partnerships on equal terms with firms who find all the *material* capital required for carrying on the business. It is more common, however, to find *personal* and *material* capital in the possession of one and the same person, for there are few individuals who accumulate wealth, but have done so in virtue of those mental and moral endowments which have been put into exercise in the conduct of their particular business of whatever nature it may be. Viewed in this light, personal or immaterial capital forms a very large proportion of the total capital employed in any highly civilized commercial community. (*See Capital, Wealth, &c.*)

Perte. A French word signifying "loss." It is commonly used in the sense of "loss on exchange." This term is chiefly employed in France and Italy, in reference to the loss resulting from the payment of debts in the paper currency of the latter country instead of in gold or silver, and is commonly stated as a percentage on the sum paid.

Peseta. Diminutive of *peso* (*which see*).

The unit of value in Spain. By a recent Act, Oct. 1868, the coinage of Spain is assimilated to that of France, and the silver Peseta weighs like the *Franc* 5 grammes ·835 fine. Its value in English sterling is therefore very near 9½*d.* Pieces of 5 *pesetas* each are struck, and are called the piastre or dollar, and it is in terms of the dollar that foreign exchanges are quoted in Madrid. Hence, it is necessary, since accounts are kept in *pesetas*, to divide the *pesetas* by five, and call the resulting integers dollars (or piastres), and in the case of England to cast them out at the rate of 47½*d.* per dollar, or whatever other price rules in the market from day to day. The peseta, like the franc, is divided into 100 parts called *centimos*.

Gold coins of 5, 10, 20, 25, 50, and 100 pesetas are also introduced by the new Act. The new gold five-peseta piece weighs 1·6129 grammes, ·900 fine, and is almost indentical in value with the silver piece of the same name.

The Peseta de Columnas is a silver coin formerly used in Spain, and distinguished by two pillars on its face, from which the coin takes its name. It is, nominally, worth 5 reals, or 1*s.* 0½*d.* Its true value, at the present price of silver, is less than one shilling.

The Spanish Monetary Law of June 1864 is still in force, so that two systems of coinage exist side by side in Spain. (*See Doblon, Duro, Escudo, &c.*)

The peseta of Peru is also ⅕ of the silver sol, and equal to the French franc.

Peso. From the Spanish *pesar*, to weigh, to be of a certain weight: whence *pesa*, a piece of determined weight, and *peso*, weight, gravity, heaviness, and, subsequently, a mass by which, as a standard, the weight of other bodies is measured. Formerly a Spanish coin weighing one ounce, afterwards called the *dollar* or *piastre*.

The *Peso of Mexico*. The unit of value and of account in Mexico. By the Mexican Monetary Law of 1867, the peso is represented both by gold and silver coins, silver, however, being retained as the standard of value. It is more commonly known as the Mexican dollar.

The *Mexican gold peso* weighs 1·692 grammes, ·875 fine. It is worth 5·10 francs, or 4*s.* 0½*d.* sterling. Pieces of equal fineness and proportional weight are struck for 20, 10, 5, and 2½ pesos.

The Mexican *silver peso* weighs 27·073 grammes, ·902 $\frac{1}{10}$ fine and is worth 5·43 francs, £·2152, or 4*s.* 3½*d.* sterling. The excellence of the Mexican peso, or dollar, renders it a favourite coin with all countries, and has given it much of the character of an international coin.

The *Peso of Chili*. The *peso* is the unit of value and of account in Chili, and is represented both by gold and silver coins according to the monetary laws of January 1851 and October 1870.

The *gold peso* weighs 1·525 grammes, ·900 fine. It is worth 4·73 francs, £·1874, or 3*s.* 9*d.* sterling.

The silver peso weighs 25 grammes, ·900 fine. It is worth 5 francs, £·1982, or 3*s* 11½*d.* sterling, and is therefore identical with the five-franc piece of the Latin Monetary Convention.

The *Peso of Columbia*. The unit of value and of account in the United States of Columbia. By the Monetary Law of June 1871, the peso was represented by both gold and silver coins of equal nominal value, namely, five francs, thus assimilating their coinage to that of the Latin Monetary Convention.

The *gold peso* of Columbia is represented by the ten peso piece called the condor. (*See Condor.*)

The *silver peso* weighs 25 grammes, ·900 fine, and is worth five francs—3*s.* 11½*d.* sterling.

The *peso of the Philippine Islands* is only another name for the *escudillo* (*which see*), value 4*s.* 0½*d.* sterling. It was formerly divided into 20 reals, but now into 100 centavos.

The *Peso of Uruguay* is more commonly known as the *piastre*. (*See Piastre.*)

Peso Corriente. The "*dollar current*," the unit of value in Uruguay, formerly represented by a silver coin, but now only used as a coin of account. It is valued at ⅘ of the Patacon, and is therefore equal to 38·60*d.* sterling. (*See Patacon.*) The peso is sometimes called the piastre.

Peso Duro. Latin, *durus*, hard.

The *hard peso* or *metallic peso*, to distinguish it from the paper peso, which is in extensive use in several South American States.

Pfennig. (*a.*) A small copper coin used in the North German Zollverein States, value about $\frac{1}{60}$ of an English penny, or $\frac{1}{360}$ of the thaler.

(*b.*) A copper coin used in the South German Zollverein States, worth about $\frac{1}{12}$ of a penny.

There are some other coins bearing the same name, but are now superseded by the *Pfennig* of the German Empire, which is the $\frac{1}{100}$th part of the Reichsmark.

Piastre. From the Greek, εμ-πλασσω, emplasso, to plaster, to spread out like a plaster, whence εμπλαστρον, emplastron, and the Latin, *emplastrum*, a plaster; subsequently anything spread out; a disk; and eventually in the Italianised form, a coin. The change of the *l* into *i* is in strict conformity with the usage of the Italian language through which the word was introduced in the commercial vocabulary of Europe.

(*a.*) *The Piastre of Turkey* is the unit of value and of account in Turkey. It is represented both by gold and silver coins, thus giving rise to two different exchange values.

The Gold Piastre. The value of the gold Piastre is best deduced from the gold 100-piastre piece, or Turkish pound, which weighs 7·216 grammes, ·916$\frac{2}{3}$ fine. Mint par value Fr. 22·78 = £·903. Dividing by 100 the value of the gold piastre is francs ·2278 = £·00903, or 2·16*d.* sterling.

The Silver Piastre weighs 1·203 grammes and is ·830 fine. Its par value is ·22 centimes = 2·11*d.* English.

The Turkish Piastre is divided into 100 Aspres in keeping accounts, and into 40 Paras for currency purposes.

(*b.*) *The Piastre of Tunis.* The unit of value and of account in Tunis. It is represented both by gold and silver coins.

The Tunisian Gold Piastre is best calculated from the 100-piastre piece, which weighs 19·5 grammes, and is ·900 fine. Its value is 60 francs 45 centimes, or £2·3963, giving for the value of the gold piastre, francs 0·6045, or £·024 sterling; say 5$\frac{3}{4}$*d.* nearly.

The Tunisian Silver Piastre weighs 3·097 grammes ·900 fine, and is worth 62 centimes, or a minute fraction more than 5$\frac{3}{4}$*d.* English.

(*c.*) *The Piastre or Ckirsh* is the unit of value in Egypt, of which, according to "tariff," 97$\frac{1}{2}$ go to the English sovereign. Hence the value of the piastre is 2·461*d.* English. It is divided into 40 paras. Gold pieces are coined in Egypt worth 100, 50, 25, 10, and 5 piastres each; and silver pieces worth 20, 10. 5, 2$\frac{1}{2}$, and 1 piastre each. The gold is $\frac{11}{12}$ or ·916 fine.

Another mode of determining the value of the Egyptian Piastre is to take the actual coin and calculate the Mint Par of Exchange; and as both gold and silver coins are struck, it may be deduced from each separately.

The Egyptian Gold Piastre is best determined from the 100-piastre piece, which weighs 8.544 grammes ·875 fine. Its value is 25 francs 73 centimes, or £1·0199 sterling, giving for the single gold piastre 25$\frac{3}{4}$ centimes, or £·0102 sterling or 2·4477*d.*

The Egyptian Silver Piastre weighs 1·250 grammes ·900 fine, and is worth 25 centimes, or 2·378*d.* English.

In either case the Piastre is divided into 40 paras, and not decimally as in most other cases of modern coins.

(*d.*) *The Spanish Piastre* is synonymous with the *dollar or duro*, sterling value 49·478*d.*, which is thus determined. The Five Dollar piece, called also the Isabella Doubloon, weighs 8·3865 grammes, ·900 fine. At 29·4986*d.* per gramme the doubloon is worth 247·389*d.* sterling, and dividing by five we have for the dollar 49·478*d.* Though still circulating, this coin is gradually being displaced by the coinage of the Latin Monetary Convention.

The *Spanish Piastre* for exchange purposes is an imaginary coin of 5 pesetas or francs = 47.578 pence.

(*e.*) *The Piastre or Peso of Uruguay* is identical in weight, fineness, and value with the French five-franc piece. Silver is the standard of value in Uruguay, and no gold is coined. But so far as silver is concerned, it is assimilated to the coinage of the Latin Monetary Convention.

(*f.*) The Piastre or Mocha Dollar is the unit of value in Arabia, and is worth nearly 3*s.* 5*d.*

Piatak or **Pietak.** A Russian silver coin, value 5 copecks. It weighs 1·019 grammes, ·500 fine, and is worth about 1*d.* English.

Pie, Pice. A Hindoo copper coin, 12 of which are equal to 1 anna, 16 annas making 1 rupee. (*See Rupee.*)

The Pie of Singapore is of the same value.

Piece of Eight. The old name for the dollar or piastre valued at 8 reals, from which circumstance it takes its distinctive title. It is commonly supposed to be the origin of the commercial sign for a dollar—$—which in former times resembled an 8, the vertical strokes through it indicating the pillars of Hercules on the pillar dollar. (*See Pillar Dollar.*)

Pillar Dollar. The dollar with the Pillars of Hercules impressed thereon.

Pistole. (*a.*) A gold coin, circulating in Brunswick, Denmark, and Hanover, equal to 5 thalers.

(*b.*) A gold coin used in Hamburg, value 10 marks, 14 schillings. (*Bank value*). (*See Bank Value.*)

(*c.*) A gold coin used in Bremen, value 5 rix-dollars.

(*d.*) A gold coin used in the West Indies, value £1 6*s.* 8*d.*

(*e.*) A Spanish gold coin, worth about 16*s.*

All these coins are now bought and sold, or exchanged at the current value for the day.

Platinum. One of the noble metals, somewhat heavier than gold, and of a greyish-white colour. It is one of the most indestructible of metals, but owing to its hardness, is not suitable for the coinage. Hence, although platinum is a comparatively scarce metal, it is only about one-sixth the value of gold, the demand for it being much less than that for gold.

Platinum Coins. Coins made in Russia of the metal platinum of the value of 12, 6, and 3 rubles respectively. They were soon withdrawn from circulation, as the metal was found unsuitable for coinage.

Policy. Italian, *polizza*, a promise.

The word policy was introduced into England by the Lombards who did a large business in Marine insurance. A policy of insurance is a document containing a *promise* to pay a certain sum of money on the occurrence of some event. In return for this promise a sum of money is paid down called the *premium*. (*See Premium.*) By far the largest part of insurance business is applied to disasters at sea—*Marine Insurance:* to destruction of property by fire—*Fire Insurance :* and to making provision for heirs and successors in case of death—*Life Insurance.*

The practice of Insurance has, however, been much extended of late years, with a view to make provision against loss of crops from bad weather, against destruction of glass from storms, against sickness and accidents of all kinds. In every case a form is filled up containing a promise to pay a certain sum, and this document is always called the *policy*. Although an insurance policy is a *contract* it is only signed by one party, the insurer, who for that reason is called the *underwriter*, and forms, therefore, what is called in law a unilateral contract.

The form of policy now in use is precisely the same as the original printed form adopted by the members of "Lloyd's" on January 12, 1789, except that the old pious expression at the beginning, "IN THE NAME OF GOD, AMEN" has given place to the phrase "*Be it known that.*"

"Policies are of two kinds," says Mr. Park in his "System of the Law of Marine Insurances."

(1.) *Valued Policy*, one in which the goods or property insured are valued at prime cost.

(2.) *Open Policy*, one in which the value of the goods or property is not mentioned.

Hence, "in the case of an open policy the value must be proved; in a valued policy it is agreed, and is just as if the parties had admitted it at the trial." (*See Lloyd's Policy.*)

Political Economy. From Greek, πολις, *polis*, a city; also a country, a state; sometimes it means the citizens who form the state; πολιτης, *polites*, a member of a city or state, a citizen, a freeman; πολιτικος, *politikos*, pertaining to a citizen, befitting a statesman; ὁ πολιτικος, a statesman; τα πολιτικα, *ta politika*, State affairs.

For "Economy," *see Economics.*

The first great work on Political Economy published in England was that of Adam Smith, and was entitled "An Enquiry into the Nature and Causes of the Wealth of Nations," a title which may be made to cover most definitions of the science that have since been made.

Courcelle Seneuil, a French writer, says the main problem of Political Economy is "to satisfy our wants with the least amount of labour;" a definition which has the advantage of using no words but such as are well understood without explanation.

Every writer on Political Economy endeavours, by definition or description, to give some idea of the aim and scope of the science. Without further quotation it may be said that they mostly agree in regarding it as the science which treats of the Production, Protection, and Distribution of Wealth.

So large an amount of literature has been devoted to economy during the last twenty years, as to necessitate a sub-division of its subject matter, which may be advantageously viewed under the following aspects :—

I. Theoretical Political Economy.

II. Practical Political Economy.

Political Economy in its Theoretical or Scientific aspect deals with the facts of industrial life with a view to establish general principles for the guidance of mankind in commercial pursuits; to furnish clear and correct definitions of the terms used; and to dissect the complicated phenomena of political economy so as to be able to examine each element separately, and free from the distorting influences which, in practice, modify the action of every social force. Just as in Theoretical Dynamics, we find it convenient to investigate the laws of motion in a *heavy point*, supposed to be without magnitude, in disregard of *atmospheric resistance* and *friction*, while we know that in practice we could not so much as walk across the street, or fire a gun, without taking these forces into account; so, in the study of the Theory of Political Economy, we endeavour to free ourselves from the consideration of those *moral* and *social* influences which invariably mix themselves up with every transaction in commercial life. The phenomena pertaining exclusively to Economic Science, when thus detached, are few in number. Wealth, utility, value, demand, supply, capital, interest, labour, exchange, rent, and a few others constitute the subject matter of the science, and Bastiat sums them all up under three heads:—*Wants, Efforts* and *Satisfaction.*

Prof. Jevons has carried his theoretical investigations to such a point as to be able to represent the movements of these phenomena by means of curves, to which he has applied the notation of the Differential Calculus.

In common with most scientific economists, he declines to be diverted from his investigations by a consideration of what *ought* to be, and endeavours to determine *what is*, what *goes on*, and *will go on*, as an inevitable result of individuals holding the right to exchange their services for such other services or such other things as they most desire.

But when we take up political economy in its *Practical* aspects, we are no longer able to detach its phenomena from those of our moral and social life. We cannot help being fettered in every contract by the consideration of *what ought to be*, because we are so often dissatisfied, and justly dissatisfied, with *what is*; and the complications which thus arise are thus forcibly put by Prof. Bonamy Price, "Practical Political Economy :"—

"Men are presumed to be keen in the pursuit of riches, and to be sure to act always for their interest, but, unhappily, they are found not to do so, even here, to the end of the chapter. They rush into ruinous wars from passion. They know that the way to be rich is to labour, and they prefer idleness. Whole nations like better to bask in the sun than to take the trouble to accumulate wealth. They are well aware that the tradesmen with whom they deal oppress them with unjust prices; they will not be at the pains to seek out the shops where good commodities are to be had at fair rates, thus making the boasted economical principle of competition to be anything but universal. Saving, they would confess to be the foundation of wealth and security for old age; they spend all they can on drink. Governments and peoples have been taught the reasonableness and profitableness of Free Trade; they persist in Protection. 'The Wealth of Nations' was written to paint the folly of the Mercantile Theory, and few educated men in England would like to confess their belief in it; but it lives on, nevertheless, with indestructible vitality. It reigns supreme in all the Stock Exchanges of the world, and every merchant and shopkeeper loves to hear that exports exceeds imports." To this may be added:— We waste our pity on the poor, who are overburdened with families which they can neither adequately feed nor fairly start in the battle of life, and yet take no pains to warn them at the proper time, or instruct them in the course they ought to pursue. We are for ever preaching to them the duties of self-reliance and foresight, and then encourage them in improvidence by giving them a claim on the hard earnings of others through the agency of an antiquated Poor Law."

Between Professor Jevons's elegant equations, and Prof. Price's stern facts, it is evident that there is plenty of work set out for those who are prepared for yeoman's service in the field of Economic research.

Poltinnick. A Russian silver coin, value 50 copecks. It weighs 10·367 grammes ·868 fine, and is worth fr. 1·99*c.*, or 1*s.* 7*d.* sterling.

Pool. Pooling. To Pool. An Americanism now rendered familiar to the English ear through the reports of the Railway Market in the United States.

The object of a "pool" is to put an end to the "war of rates" which breaks out so frequently between two or more competing lines; and which mostly entails loss to the shareholders as well as injury to the lines themselves. Sometimes the proceeds of the traffic on competing lines are put into a common fund, and afterwards distributed according to conditions previously agreed on. This is called a "Financial Pool." In other cases, arrangements are made for a distribution of the traffic, each line agreeing to accept a specified proportion. This is called a "Physical Pool."

Port of London. In modern speech a "port" is usually understood as a *seaport.* That was not the idea exclusively conveyed by the word as used by the Romans, from whom it was derived, nor by the English when they introduced it into our language. Besides signifying the mouth of a river, or a place into which ships might come, it meant also a warehouse, or magazine, a place for the storage of goods; it signified also a custom-house, or place for the collection of the public revenues.

"In portu operam dabat" (He was a collector of customs).

"Portus est conclusus locus qui importantur merces et inde exportantur. Est et ratio conclusa et munita." (A *port* is an enclosed place to which goods are brought and whence they are sent out. It is also any fortified enclosure.)

In the ancient Laws and Institutes of England, printed by command of William IV., there is one dating from the time of Edward the Elder, son of Alfred (901-924), which is thus officially translated :—"And I will that every man have his warrants, and that no man buy out of *port* (that is, *market*), but have the portreeve's witness, or that of unlying men, whom one may believe. And if any one buy out of *port*, let him incur the King's oferhyrnes"—Quoted by H. D. McLeod, *Theory and Practice of Banking.*

The importance attached to the buying and selling in *port*, or as it was sometimes called, a *market overt*, in the presence of one or more witnesses arose from the educational deficiences of the times when reading and writing were rare accomplishments; so that in order to have legal proof of a contract or bargain, it was necessary that it should be made in presence of some trustworthy officer who might be appealed to in case of dispute. When dealers could put their contracts into writing, these ancient formalities were gradually dispensed with.

Post, To. Latin, *ponere,* to place, to put, or to fix; *positum,* placed, put, fixed.

To Post is a term much used in the counting-house, and signifies to place an entry in some book or ledger where it is to remain permanently. Hence entries made from journals or auxiliary books when placed in the ledger are said to be *posted.* Similarly, the numbers of bank notes, of coupons, bills, &c., when placed in books to be kept for reference are said to be posted.

Post-Date. Latin, *post,* after *datum,* given (meaning a given time).

To attach a date to a cheque or other writing subsequent to that on which it is written. Bank Post Bills are intentionally post dated 7 days; the 7 days' interest being a compensation for the convenience afforded. An ordinary cheque is sometimes post dated, in which case the holder ought not to present it till it has matured, as it is liable to cause error or unnecessary trouble by its return.

"All instruments which are post-dated are void the moment it is shown that the apparent date was not contemporaneous with the date on which they were issued."—Brookes, *On the Office and Practice of a Notary in England.*

When a Cheque is payable *to Order,* a post-date does not invalidate it.

The Post-dating of Invoices is a practice which, from very small beginnings, has acquired dimensions threatening serious inconvenience to those who are its victims. It is not unusual for travellers or canvassers to obtain orders for goods with the understanding that the invoice shall bear a date, three, six, or nine months later than that on which the goods are delivered, at which date payment is made by means of a three months' bill. These long credits added to others which are given by producers of raw material, are among the efficient causes which lead to those terrible commercial crises with which the country is agitated every few years. The practice of post-dating, or as it is sometimes called "dating forward," grows up by such insensible degrees, and over so wide an area, that although no one approves of it, no one is able to suppress it. It is only when the evil has attained such a magnitude as to call forth the united action of a number of the larger trading firms that any effective check can be imposed.

Pound (In weight). From the Latin, *pondus*, a weight. *Pendo*, to cause to hang down like a pair of scales; hence, to weigh. *Libra pondo*, a pound in weight. *Auri quinque pondo*, five pounds of gold. From this way of speaking of *pondo* (in weight), without the noun *libra*, arose the practice in latter times of using *pondus*, as equivalent to the word "libra" in England.

1519. "A monstre of silver and gilt to bear in the Sacrament on Corpus Christi day, the *pondre* (weight) thereof 31 ounces and dimid."—*Churchwarden's Accompts of St. Margaret's, Westminster.*

Pound Avoirdupois. The unit of weight employed in England for weighing heavy goods and merchandize. It is equal to 7000 Troy grains, or 453·59265255 metric grammes. It is also divided into 16 ounces of 437½ grains each.

Pound Troy. The unit of weight used in England for weighing the precious metals. It is equal to 5760 Troy grains, or 373·2419541 metric grammes. It is divided into 12 ounces of 480 grains each.

Hence the grain is the only unit common to the two systems of weight. (*See Grain.*)

Pound (In money). The principal English coin of account, and corresponding to the "coin of circulation" called a sovereign (*see Sovereign*). It is divided into 20 shillings or 240 pence, and weighs 123·27447 Troy grains (7·98805 grammes), as determined by the Mint regulation, in virtue of which 40 lbs. Troy of gold is coined into 1869 sovereigns.

The name is derived from the fact that in the time of the Conqueror, one Tower pound of silver was coined into 240 silver pence; whence the Tower pennyweight was really and truly the weight of a penny. Twelve of these silver pence were called a shilling, or *solidus*, and twenty *solidi* made a pound. The weight of the shilling was reduced from time to time till in the reign of Elizabeth, the pound Troy of silver was coined into 744 pence (*see Shilling*), but 12 of these smaller pence were still called a shilling, and 20 shillings a pound in coin. (*See Troy Weight.*)

The pound is also the unit of value in the Channel Islands, and is divided into shillings and pence as in England. The *pound*, however, is of less value than the English pound sterling, being worth only 230·40 pence, instead of 240 pence; in other words, £1 sterling is equal to £1 1*s.* 8*d.* Channel Islands currency.

There are three monetary units called a *pound* used in Canada, one of which is the English pound sterling, and the other two purely ideal coins founded on the different valuations of the dollar.

(*a*.) The English pound sterling is used almost exclusively in the Goverment accounts, and is represented by the British sovereign coined in England, as above described.

(*b*.) The Halifax pound sterling, which is an imaginary coin, having no metallic representation, is based on an Act of Parliament, which assigns as its metallic value 101·301 grains Troy of gold, ·9166 fine. By the table (*see Price of Gold*) this is found to be 197·2229*d*. say, 16*s*. 5¼*d*.

(*c*.) The Halifax pound currency, also an imaginary unit, founded on the valuation of the Canada dollar, which is the real monetary unit of value in Canada, although represented by nothing but paper issued by the banks. The currency dollar is assumed to be equal to 50 pence English, and four of them are equal to the Halifax currency pound, which is therefore, by the same assumption, equal to 16*s*. 8*d*. English. The Halifax currency dollar is therefore equal to 60 pence Halifax currency, and 50 pence English currency.

These Canadian denominations, having no metallic representations, and the exchange being always quoted in dollars, are of little importance.

The pound in Nova Scotia currency is worth 16*s*. English.

The pound in New Brunswick currency is equal to 16*s*. 8*d*. English.

The pound in Newfoundland currency is equal to 16*s*. 8*d*. English.

Power of Attorney. A *power of attorney* is a written or printed document authorizing some person named therein to act in place of, and with the full powers possessed by, some other person. They are largely used in commerce to enable individuals living in remote districts, or in foreign countries, to obtain payment of moneys, which, without the use of a "power," would require their attendance in person. The following is a form of power of attorney used to obtain payment of an annuity from an Assurance Company :—

Know all men by these presents that I (A.B.), in the county of ———, have made, ordained, constituted, and appointed, and by these presents do make, ordain, constitute, and appoint (C.D. and E.F. jointly and severally) my true and lawful attorneys or attorney, for me in my name and behalf, to ask, demand, sue for, recover, and receive of and from the cashier, treasurer, or whom else it may concern of the Assurance Company (   ), a certain annuity granted for the remainder of my life by policy (   ) of (   ) pounds per annum, payable in half-yearly payments, the first whereof became due the (   ) of (   ) instant. And upon payment or receipt of the said annuity, as the aforesaid half-yearly payment shall respectively become due for me, the said constituent, and in my name to make and give good and sufficient release and discharge for the same. And upon non-payment of the same for me, the said constituent to take and use all such lawful ways and means for the recovery thereof, as the said constituent might or could do were I personally present. And generally in the premises to do, perform, execute, and accomplish all such acts, deeds, matters, and things whatsoever as my said attorneys, or either or any of them shall judge, see, or think fit and necessary to be done in the premises as fully and effectually as I, the said constituent, might or could do were I personally present; and I, the said constituent, do ratify and hereby promise to allow, ratify, confirm, and hold for good, effectual, and valid in law, all and whatsover my said attorneys, or either or any of them shall lawfully do or cause to be done, in and about the premises by virtue of these presents. In witness thereof, I, the said (A.B.), have hereunto set my hand and seal the ( ) day of (A.D. one thousand eight hundred and

A. B.

Signed, sealed, and delivered
in presence of

G. H.

K. L.

P. P. Endorsements. Endorsements by procuration—that is, *per-procuration.* (*See Per-procuration.*) The following is the usual form of a per-pro endorsement.

"Pay to the Order of Blanc & Co.
"Per Pro. Shipley & Sons.

"Thos. Brown."

In this form of endorsement, "Blank & Co." are the endorsees, "Shipley & Sons" the endorsers, and "Thos. Brown" the person authorized to sign on behalf of Shipley & Sons.

Preference Bonds and Shares. It often occurs in the experience of commercial bodies that the capital with which they commence business is found insufficient for the objects they have in view. Under such circumstances it becomes a question how additional capital shall be raised. As a first resource it is usual to adopt one of the two following alternatives. (1.) To issue a series of bonds, which shall receive a fixed dividend, before any part of the company's profits are divided among the ordinary shareholders, thus giving them a preferential claim over the ordinary shares; or, (2.) To issue a series of new shares, which, though not entitled to a fixed interest, shall enjoy a preferential claim to profits up to a specified point, before anything is paid to ordinary shareholders. It is this prior claim which gives to bonds and shares of this nature the right to the title of *preference bonds and shares.* A second or third series of bonds is sometimes issued by companies whose finances are embarrassed, and these are called *second preference* and *third preference* bonds respectively. In these cases, however, the successive series of issues take rank after those that have been previously issued, so as not to impair the security given for those already in circulation.

Pre-preference Bonds and Shares. When a commercial company is in great straits for want of capital, and preference bonds have already been issued by such company, recourse is sometimes had to an expedient which could never be justified, except by a conviction almost amounting to a certainty, that existing preference bondholders would find their position rendered more secure by its adoption. That expedient is the issue of a series of bonds which shall have a prior claim on the income of the company, over those who, till then, had a first claim on that income, namely, the first preference bondholders. Legally, the consent of such preference bondholders must be obtained before any such issue of bonds can be made. When that consent is obtained, and the new series of Bonds is issued, they are distinguished from all the others by the name of pre-preference bonds, and they are so called because the interest on them is paid out of the first revenues of the company, whether there be sufficient to pay the interest on the remainder or not.

Premium. From the Latin, *præmium*, a recompense, or reward; *præmio aliquem afficere*, or *alicui præmium dare*, to reward or recompense anyone.

The meaning of Premium is much the same as that of its Latin original. In general terms it may be said to be a recompense made in return for money paid down for a purpose, or for some service rendered. The word has sundry applications in commerce, the following being some of the more important.

In currency, the premium on gold or silver is the difference of value between gold and silver coins and paper notes of the same nominal amount. Thus when the United States gold dollar was at a premium of 25, it meant that 125 paper dollars were given for a 100 gold dollars. This was the customary mode of recording the difference of value. It would have been more correct in a scientific sense to have said that the paper dollar was at 20 per cent. discount or that 100 of them were worth 80 gold dollars, as determined by the proportion—125 : 100 :: 100 : 80.

Premium when used in this sense is almost identical in meaning with the continental term *agio* (*see Agio*).

In life insurance, the *premium* is the sum periodically paid by the insured in order to secure to his representatives after his death, a stated sum of money from the society to whom the premium is paid. Similarly in Fire Insurance, it is the sum periodically paid in order to obtain compensation for loss of property by fire, and is usually a fixed percentage on the nominal value of the property insured.

In Marine Insurance the *Premium* paid is commonly for a specified voyage, as from one port to another, or to various ports; or from a ship's departure from a given port until her return, as out and home; and sometimes, when upon the ship or freight, it is for a limited time, as a rate per month; but when the time is thus specified, the insurance cannot be in force for a longer period than twelve months, without being renewed in a fresh policy.

In finance, stocks, bonds, or shares are said to stand at a *premium* when their market price is higher than that paid for them when originally issued. For example, if £100 of Russian Stock is issued at the price of £94, then if the quoted price on the Stock Exchange is 95½, it is said to be at 1½ premium; that is, £95 10*s.* would have to be given for £100 of stock. The same applies *mutatis mutandis* to bonds and shares.

One very objectionable use of the word "premium" has lately made its way into the English market from the Continent. A number of Lottery Loans of the worst class have been started in some of the German States, and also in Austria. Owing to the bad odour in which lotteries are held in England, it would be impossible to get subscriptions to them to any great extent in this country if called by their proper name. The name of Premium-Loans (*Præmien Anleihen*) has therefore been substituted; they are persistently advertised and otherwise forced on the attention of persons, who have no means of ascertaining their real character, and the money that has been extracted from the pockets of unfortunate dupes by these means is enormous.

Present, To. Latin, *præsens*, present, immediate, directly, in person; whence the verb *præsentare*, to show, to present, to exhibit.

In ordinary speech, "to present" means simply to place anything before someone, to be seen, or to be accepted. In commercial law, it bears a signification somewhat more technical: thus—

To present a Bill for "Acceptance" is to bring it to the person on whom it is "drawn," and request him to undertake to pay it, which he does by writing the word "Accepted" on its face, and signing his name thereto. Bills should be presented for acceptance as soon as possible; otherwise, the holder may incur loss by the delay.

To present a Bill or Promissory Note for "Payment" is to bring it to the principal debtor and demand payment of it. It should be presented for payment punctually on the day when it falls due; otherwise, all the parties to it except the Drawer and Acceptor are discharged from their liability.

A Bill or Note is considered in law as *duly presented* if left at the residence or business office of the drawer, drawee, or acceptor, that is, it is not essential that it should be delivered to him in person.

Present Value. There are three principal methods of calculating *present values* in use. (1.) The rough method of discounting, as in the negotiation of Bills of Exchange. (2.) The determination of the present value of a deferred payment reckoning compound interest on the sum paid; and (3) The determination of the present value of a series of payments due at regular intervals, as in the case of an annuity. The first of these operations is so simple as to need no formula. For the second and third, a good knowledge of algebra is essential, as they involve rather prolix logarithmic calculations, although in practice the clerical work is much abbreviated by the use of Compound Interest Tables which have lately been brought to great perfection.

For determining the Present Value of a sum due at the end of a given number of intervals; the following formula is used,

$$V = \frac{M}{(1 + r)} n.$$

where V = the present Value.
M = amount due at the end of the time.
n = number of intervals.
r = rate per cent. for each interval.

For the Present Value of a series of payments due at regular intervals, we have—

$$P = \frac{A}{r}\left(1 - \frac{1}{R^n}\right)$$

where P = the Present Value.
A = periodical payment.
n = number of intervals.
R = 1 + r.
r = rate per cent. for each interval.

Priatchek. A Russian silver coin, value 5 copecks, about $1\frac{9}{10}$*d.* (i.e., a little less than *two-pence*) sterling. Often written *Piatachek.*

Price. Latin, *pretium,* worth, value, reward; whence the Italian forms, *pretio, prezzo, pregio.* French, *prix.* Dutch, *prijs.* The English words *praise* and *prize* are also derived from the same root. Thus, to *praise* is to attribute a high value to a thing or deed; *to prize* a thing is to keep it and cherish it, because of the value and worth we assign to it; *a prize* is the reward of industry and excellence in some form or other.

The value of a commodity estimated and expressed in money. Some writers use the phrase "*money or credit*" but this amounts to much the same thing, as the amount of a *credit* is almost invariably expressed in terms of *money.*

Price of Gold and Silver. The Price of Gold is determined by the Mint Regulation which ordains that 40 pounds Troy of Gold $\frac{11}{12}$ or ·916$\frac{2}{3}$ fine, best Standard Gold shall be coined into 1869 sovereigns. By division it is found that 1 ounce Troy of Standard Gold is worth 77*s.* 10$\frac{1}{2}$*d.* Hence, £3 17*s.* 10$\frac{1}{2}$*d.* per ounce is said to be the price of Standard Gold.

Since an ounce Troy is equal to 480 grains we find from the above data that the weight of the sovereign is 123·27447 Troy grains.

Hence the value of the Troy grain of standard gold is found by division to be 1·9469*d.*

Expressed in grammes, the weight of the sovereign is 7·98805 grammes, this gives as the value of the gramme of standard gold 30·04488*d.*

If the gold be $\frac{9}{10}$ or ·900 fine as the French Napoleon, the value of the gramme is 29·4986*d.*

On the same supposition, the value of the grain Troy is found to be 1·9115*d.*

If the gold be *pure* or absolutely *fine,* the gramme is worth 32·7762*d.*

Value of Gold and Silver in Grains Troy.

	Gold $\frac{11}{12}$ fine.	Gold $\frac{9}{10}$ fine.	Fine Gold.	Fine Silver.
1 Grain Troy	1·9469*d.*	1·9115*d.*	2·1239*d.*	.13702*d.*
2 ,, ,,	3·8938	3·8230	4·2478	.27404
3 ,, ,,	5·8407	5·7345	6·3717	·41106
4 ,, ,,	7·7876	7·6460	8·4956	·54808
5 ,, ,,	9·7345	9·5575	10·6195	·68510
6 ,, ,,	11·6814	11·4690	12·7434	·82212
7 ,, ,,	13·6283	13·3805	14·8673	·95914
8 ,, ,,	15·5752	15·2920	16·9912	1·09616
9 ,, ,,	17·5221	17·2035	19·1151	1·23318
10 ,, ,,	19·4690	19·1150	21·2390	1·37020

Value of Gold and Silver in Grammes.

	Gold $\frac{11}{12}$ fine.	Gold $\frac{9}{10}$ fine.	Fine Gold.	Fine Silver.
1 Gramme	30·04488*d.*	29·4986*d.*	32·7762*d.*	2·1146*d.*
2 ,,	60·08976	58·9972	65·5524	4·2292
3 ,,	90·13464	88·4958	98·3286	6·3438
4 ,,	120·17952	117·9944	131·1048	8·4584
5 ,,	150·22440	147·4930	163·8810	10·5730
6 ,,	180·26928	176·9916	196·6572	12·6876
7 ,,	210·31416	206·4902	229·4334	14·8022
8 ,,	240·35904	235·9888	262·2096	16·9168
9 ,,	270·40392	265·4874	294·9858	19·0314
10 ,,	300·44880	294·9860	327·7620	21·1460

On the same supposition, the grain Troy is worth 2·1239*d.*

The price of Silver is determined by the observation that, in France, where the Double Standard (*see Double Standard*) of Valuation prevails, it was found that the value of *fine* gold, as compared with that of *fine* silver, the comparison being extended over several years, was as 15½ to 1. In other words, that 1 part by weight of *fine* gold was equal in value to 15½ parts by weight of *fine* silver. (*See Franc.*) Almost the same proportion was found to prevail in India, where the silver standard is in use. This proportion has been a good deal disturbed of late years owing to the large influx of silver from the mines recently discovered. It was very different also in ancient times. We are told by Herodotus that in the time of Darius, the Son of Hydaspes, that gold was 13 times the value of the same weight of silver. The assay of equivalent amounts of gold and silver coins of that period gives 13⅓ to 1 as the proportion. In Roman times the proportion fell as low as 10 to 1. In later times it rose to 12 to 1. In our first coinage of gold, in the time of Edw. III., about 14 parts of silver was equal to 1 of gold, but this was found to be too low a value for gold. For the last century, or century and a-half, it was about 15½ to 1; and during the late silver panic it was as much as 22 to 1.

Nevertheless, the proportion of 15½ parts of fine silver to 1 of gold is still maintained as a basis of comparison, as it is thought that when business has settled down into its normal course, the old relation between the two metals will be almost unchanged. For this reason, the metallic value of the silver coins described in the present work, have all been calculated on the supposition that 15½ parts of fine silver are equal in value to 1 part of fine gold; and the fourth column in the preceding Tables has been derived from the same data. The series of numbers under the heading "Fine Silver" are obtained from that headed "Fine Gold," by multiplying the latter by 2 and dividing by 31.

When fine gold is taken at 15½ times the price of fine silver, the latter comes out 65*s.* 9d. per oz. troy. But fine silver for the last few years has been nearer 50*d.* per ounce, and has varied considerably at times from that price, so that in calculating the metallic value of silver coins, the market value for the time being must always be taken into account.

Primage. A small contribution, usually about one-tenth the amount of the freight, formerly paid to the captain of a vessel for taking care of the cargo: but which is now regularly charged as an addition to the freight, and applied to the shipowner's benefit.

Prime Entry. Before a Landing Waiter is appointed to the charge of a vessel which has entered the port, and therefore, necessarily before commencing its discharge, it is required that at least two-thirds of the cargo should be entered, and unless the goods are bonded, the duty must be paid up on an estimated amount. This is called making a *Prime Entry*, and when afterwards the goods have been landed, and the net weight or quantity has been ascertained, the consignee is required to make a second or *Post Entry*, and pay the remaining duty.

Principal. (*a.*) The chief, or one of the chiefs of a commercial firm; an employer.

(*b.*) One who employs an *attorney*, to which the term *principal* stands in the same relation as the French *mandant* to that of *procureur*. In this relation, the principal is sometimes called the *constituent*.

(*c.*) A sum of money employed to produce a profit or revenue, and is often used as the equivalent of *capital*. More precisely, however, custom has established a distinction between the two terms, *Capital* being wealth employed to produce profit, and *Principal*, wealth set apart to produce revenue, periodically payable over a length of time under the name of *interest*.

Private Bank. A Private Bank is a bank conducted by a single individual, or by a firm of partners *not exceeding six*. When more than six partners set up a bank it is called a Joint Stock Bank, and falls under the laws established for the control of Joint Stock Companies. No private bank has been established of late years; the large capital requisite for the foundation of a bank, being practically unattainable except by the united contributions of a large number of shareholders.

Probate. Grants of Probate. The official proof of a will or testament. When a solicitor is employed, he will do all that is necessary to obtain such a grant on behalf of his client. But it is not necessary in simple cases to employ a solicitor. The executor of a will should take it to the Court of Probate, Somerset House, Strand, W.C., when the clerks of the department will afford him all the information required.

When application is made to a banker for securities on deposit in the name of a deceased customer, or the balance standing to his credit in the bank books, if over £50, the applicant must produce a Certificate of Probate (or Letters of Administration, if deceased made no Will) to justify the banker in giving up possession of those securities and to prevent their falling into wrong hands.

Mr. Tidd Pratt, late Registrar of Friendly Societies, gives the following useful hints for the guidance of those who wish to prove a Will, without the aid of a solicitor:—

RULES, ETC., *as to Personal Applications for Grants of Probate or Letters of Administration.*

"The department for personal applications is at Somerset House, Strand, W.C. The offices are open to any person who may wish to prove a will or obtain letters of administration without employing a proctor or solicitor.

"The applicant has only to attend (bringing the will, in case there be a will), and state the amount (or thereabouts) of the deceased person's "personal estate and effects." He must also procure (for inspection only) a certificate either of death or burial. This document, however, may be procured and sent subsequently (and it is sometimes dispensed with altogether).

"The applicant will receive all possible assistance from the clerks of the department, with reference to obtaining the grant of probate or administration, and all the papers are prepared, and the parties are sworn in the office.

"As in cases wherein a proctor or solicitor is employed, so in this department, administration bonds, with one or two sureties (according to the amount of property), are required when the application is for letters of administration; not so when an executor applies for probate of a will. The sureties, however, may attend subsequently to the administrator.

"The foregoing outline will suffice for general information in ordinary cases, and parties have only to apply at the department if the case be out of the ordinary course, as any way they will be able to commence the business on their first attendance there.

"All the fees are regulated by a Government table, and are paid in Probate Court stamps, which are obtainable through the messenger. The amount of fees depends on the value of the property of the deceased, and (in case of a will) on the length and nature of that document."

There are about 40 District Registries in different parts of England and Wales: but those who propose to act without the aid of a solicitor will in most cases find it expedient to apply in the first place at the Principal Registry, where all necessary information will be given.

The duties on Probates are now the same as those on Letters of Administration. (*See Administration, Letters of.*)

Procuration. Latin, *pro*, for; *cura*, care; *procurare*, to take care of the affairs of a person in his absence. Hence, to sign a paper by procuration, or proxy, is to get it signed by someone in the place of another.

In commerce it is usual to employ the well-known Latin phrase "per procurationem," to call attention to the fact that a signature is made by proxy. Procurations are used by the employés of small firms in a very lax manner, sometimes to the loss and inconvenience of employers and their customers. In all large and important firms, no one is allowed to sign by procuration except those specially authorized, either by letter, or, as is sometimes the case, by power of attorney.

Production. Latin, *pro-ducĕre*, to lead or bring forward.

In economics, the word production signifies the bringing forward and offering for sale. In this narrow acceptation of the term, it is synonymous with supply (*see Supply*), and differs somewhat from the sense in which the same word is often used in colloquial speech.

Thus, to produce a deed is simply to bring it forward for examination or in evidence. To produce a witness is to bring him forward that he may give his testimony. Again, to produce a poem, a picture, or bale of cloth, is not necessarily to sell it or even offer it for sale, but simply to make it. In all these senses the word is quite correctly used, and it is therefore important to understand clearly in what sense we use it when employed in exact science like economics. By the common assent of economists, it is understood to mean, as defined above, the bringing forward and offering an article for sale.

Productive Labour. Productive labour is effort expended in conferring a service on others.

The services rendered by productive labour may be:—

(I.) *Fruitive*, that is, may minister to human satisfaction and enjoyment immediately, leaving no trace of their existence, being embodied in no material object, and therefore incapable of being stored. They perish in the using, and are, consequently, sometimes called, though incorrectly, "unproductive labour." The services of singers, actors, livery servants, are examples.

(II.) *Protective*, that is, they may serve to protect those who are employed in producing the means of enjoyment, or in protecting the means of enjoyment when they have been produced. Such is the labour of soldiers, policemen, lawyers, judges, statesmen.

(III.) *Accumulative*, that is, services embodied in some material object, and capable of being stored, transferred, or exchanged. The services of artizans, manufacturers, sailors, carriers, are of this kind.

This classification, like all true natural classifications, gives no sharp line of demarcation between the classes. On the contrary, the classes melt insensibly the one into the other. The services of those who minister to immediate human enjoyment are sometimes embodied in the revised energies and improved health of those who participate in them, and thus qualify the participants for the discharge of other services of the protective or accumulative kind. The services of the lawyer or judge, though mainly protective, are sometimes embodied in the title deed, or precedent established by a decision in a court of law. These ambiguous cases do not however invalidate the classification, but rather tend to confirm its soundness and prove that its foundation is laid on the nature of things.

Profit. From the Latin, *pro* and *facio*, whence *proficère*, to gain ground, to advance, to grow or increase. Hence to increase one's wealth or possession. *Profectus*, increase, growth, or profit. French, *profiter*, to gain, to improve; *profit*, gain, advantage, increase.

Profit is the difference between what it costs to produce a thing and what it sells for. Mr. McLeod refines on this definition, and says, "This difference may be in excess of the cost of production, in which case it is positive, and is called gain; or it may be in defect and then it is negative, and is called a loss." This is very true, and in the application of mathematical symbols to economic problems is of great importance. Nevertheless, in popular speech, a *loss* is never called a *profit*, however the word may be qualified.

The cost of production, that is, the expense incurred in producing anything, is made up of four principal items:—

I. Raw material and labour.

II. The interest on capital employed. Many products are not sold and paid for till months after the capital has been expended, and the loss of interest on this capital has to be compensated for.

III. Insurance against risks and accidents. All commercial undertakings are liable to these contingencies, and they are provided against at a certain cost, which must be repaid out of the products.

IV. The reward of management, superintendence, and skill on the part of the capitalist.

Whatever is left after all these charges are met is called *profit*, the end for which all business operations are undertaken.

Pro-Forma. Latin, signifying *for form, according to form, for the sake of form.*

When a document is drawn up or a process gone through after a prescribed model, and with the special object of complying with some legal requirement it is said to be done *pro formâ.* In some large houses of business it is even customary for a firm to draw cheques payable to the same firm and these are called *pro formâ* cheques; the design being to secure attention to the transaction when several different persons are concerned in it, in which case it is not always easy to trace the successive steps of the transaction unless some such means are adopted.

Profit and Loss Account. Part of the account which a merchant keeps for his own information. It is connected with the Stock Account, or Capital Account, and includes among other items, commission, charges, expenses, &c. If the Profit and Loss Account shews a nett gain the balance is placed on the *Cr.* side of Capital Account; if a loss, on the *Dr.* side.

Promissory Note. A written promise to pay a given sum of money to a certain person, at a specified date. The phrase "for value received" is usually inserted, but it has been recently decided in a court of law that it is of no importance and is said to be without meaning. The usual forms of Promissory Notes are given below.

£764 18*s*. 6*d*. London, June 11, 1878.

Three months after date I promise to pay Robert Green or Order, the sum of Seven Hundred and Sixty-four Pounds, Eighteen Shillings, and Sixpence for value received.

ROBERT WATSON.

The above note authorizes Robert Green to claim from Robert Watson, three months after the date written upon it, the sum of £764 18*s*. 6*d*.

£500 London, Nov. 20, 1878.

On demand, I promise to pay Jas. Sinclair Five Hundred Pounds.

HENRY BOUVERIE.

This form of note obliges Henry Bouverie to pay the sum of £500 to Jas. Sinclair whenever the latter chooses to demand it.

N.B. Both these forms require endorsement to make them negotiable.

£350 London, Oct. 6, 1878.

On demand, I promise to pay to bearer the sum of Three Hundred and Fifty Pounds. ROBERT GREEN.

This form of note is not legal, except under special sanction; that sanction, however, is given to certain banks, and notably to the Bank of England, whose notes are essentially in this form. It differs from the other two in not being made payable to any specified person but to anyone who holds it for the time being.

Prompt. From the Latin, *pro-emo*, literally to buy forward, to buy in advance; contracted into *promo, promĕre*, to take, or give forth; to utter, to declare; hence the noun, *promptus* or *promtus*, something set forth, a setting forth, something manifest, visible. In commerce, the setting forth in a written document the record of a bargain or sale, in such a form as to render it negotiable. The French equivalent is *crédit*, or *terme dû paiement*; German, *die Zahlungs-Frist*. The Latin adjective *promptus* is identical in form with the participle of *promere*, and signifies visible, apparent, and when applied to things prepared, ready to hand, quick, expeditious, prompt. In this sense the French equivalent is *prompt*, the Italian and Spanish, *pronto*. The word "prompt," in English, is therefore used in both senses; when we speak of "prompt payment" or a "prompt action," it is used as an adjective, but when we speak of "prompts" as negotiable instruments, the word is employed as a noun.

A prompt is an agreement between a shipper or importer on the one hand, and a merchant on the other; in which the former engages to sell certain specified goods at a given price, and the latter to take them up and pay for them at a specified date. The date may be fixed at three, four, or five months after the sale, and the instrument recording the bargain is called a "three months' prompt," a "four months' prompt," or a "five months' prompt" accordingly. If, however, the buyer wishes the goods to be delivered to him at an earlier date than that assigned, he may have them, if they are in the hands of the importer (as they usually are before such bargains are struck) but payment must then be made on delivery, even though the time recorded on the instrument has not yet lapsed. This is one of the distinctive features of a "prompt." It implies from its nature that the goods shall be "promptly" paid for on delivery, if delivered before the specified date, and at the specified date, whether they are delivered or not. Prompts may be bought or sold through brokers, like other commercial securities, or they may be deposited with bankers as guarantee for a loan.

It is not a little curious that the primary etymological meaning of *pro-emĕre*, which dropped out of the later Latin, is revived in the modern commercial use of the word, where it is always connected with a buying forward, or in advance.

Property. Latin, *proprius*, one's own, *proprietas*, what one enjoys as his own possession.

The word Property is used colloquially to signify money, land, houses, timber, cattle and other material products. Technically, it signifies the *Right* one has in any of these things, and not the things themselves. This, too, is the original meaning of the term as used by old authors, and the colloquial use of it is a perversion of its real meaning, just as the word "drinks" is a perversion when applied to the things we drink.

Property may be conveniently divided into two classes, corporeal, or material property, and incorporeal or immaterial property. Corporeal property is the right one has to the enjoyment of material things as land, ships, buildings, wine, &c. Incorporeal property is the right one has to things not represented by any material objects, as the right to a reversion, or to an annuity, or to things not at the present time in existence, as the produce of a farm or vineyard, or the rental of an estate, &c.; the skill of a manager, the dexterity of a workman, and even the moral character of a servant are also forms of incorporeal property.

Pro-Rata. Latin, *reor*, to reckon, think, judge; hence the participle *ratus*, reckoned, or according to calculation.

According to rate or reckoning in a given ratio. The feminine form of the word is used so as to agree with *pars*, understood, as in Cicero, *pro râta parti*; or more simply in Livi, *pro ratâ*, in each case signifying in proportion, or proportionally.

Prospectus. Latin, *pro* and *specio*, *prospecio*, I look forward; *prospectus*, a prospect, a view.

In commerce, a *prospectus* signifies a document drawn up by loan contractors, directors of public companies, or promoters of joint stock enterprises, when inviting subscriptions towards the capital required for the object in contemplation. A prospectus usually sets forth (1) the amount of capital required (2) the object on which the capital is expended; (3) the security offered; (4) the profits that may be reasonably expected; (5) the contracts that have been entered into, if any; (6) any other details that may assist the public in judging of the feasibility of the undertaking. Appended is a copy of each of two prospectuses, one of a State loan, the second of a trading company.

GOVERNMENT OF PERU.

Issue of £11,920,000 Sterling Nominal Capital Six per Cent. Consolidated Bonds for the Construction of Railroads.

Redeemable at Par by half-yearly Drawings through the operation of an Accumulative Sinking Fund of Two per Cent. per Annum. Commencing in 1880.

PRICE OF ISSUE 82½ PER CENT.

In conformity with the law of the National Congress, dated the 15th January, 1869, which conferred upon the Supreme Government of Peru the right of making contracts for the construction of certain Railroads and of paying for the same by the issue of Consolidated Bonds of the Republic of Peru, the said Government has arranged for the issue of such Bonds as follows:—

For the construction of the Railroad from Callao to La Oroya, to the extent of	27,600,000 soles, or	£5,520,000
And from Arequipa to Puno ...	32,000,000 soles, or	£6,400,000
Total...	59,600,000 soles, or	£11,920,000

Messrs. J. Henry Schröder and Co., being duly authorized, beg to offer the said Bonds for public subscription on the following conditions:—

I. The Bonds will be in amounts of £1000, £500, £200, £100, £50 and £20, bearing interest at the rate of 6 per cent. per annum, payable by Coupons half-yearly on the 1st January and 1st July in each year (the first being payable on the 1st January next).

The coupons will be payable in London in sterling, in Paris at the exchange of 25 francs per pound sterling, and in Amsterdam at the exchange of the day on London.

II. The redemption will be effected by half-yearly drawings at par commencing on the 1st April, 1880, by the operation of a Sinking Fund of 2 per cent. per annum of the entire Capital, plus the interest on the Redeemed Bonds, so that the entire amount will be paid off at the end of 25 years from that date. The funds so drawn will be paid off three months after the date of drawing.

III. The Peruvian Government however reserves the right of putting the Sinking Fund into operation before the date above-named, and of augmenting the amount to be drawn at any of the half-yearly periods.

IV. The Peruvian Government guarantees the exemption of these Bonds from all taxes or imposts of any kind in Peru.

V. The securities specially hypothecated for the due payment of the interest and principal of these Bonds are as follows:

1st, The National Credit of the Republic, solemnly pledged by the Government of Peru in the name of the Republic, with the general hypothecation of all its real property and revenues.

2nd, The Customs dues of the Republic of Peru, amounting annually to 4,000,000 soles, or £800,000.

3rd, The Railways to be constructed from Callao to La Oroya and from Arequipa to Puno, also the existing railroad from Megia to Arequipa, with all their lands, buildings, rolling-stock, workshops and appurtenances. This latter railroad has just been completed at a cost to the Government of £2,400,000.

4th, The surplus proceeds of the guano to be imported into the United Kingdom of Great Britain and Ireland, her Colonies, to the Continent of Europe, and to the United States of America, after providing for the service of the existing 5 per Cent. Government Loan of 1865 (of which £7,199,200 is still in circulation), and of the Guaranteed Pisco-Ica Railway Loan of £290,000. The amount required for the annual service of the Loan of 1865 is £1,000,000, that of the Guaranteed Pisco-Ica Railway Loan £20,800. The sales of guano amount to 550,000 tons per annum, producing a nett revenue of about £4,400,000.

5th, After the 1st July, 1879 (the term fixed for the final redemption of the Loan of 1865), the present bonds become a first charge upon the entire proceeds of guano of the Republic of Peru (subject only to the Guaranteed Pisco-Ica Railway Loan of £290,000), and no other loan can under any circumstances take precedence of these Bonds.

VI. The subscription price is 82½ per cent., payable in the following instalments, viz.:—

£ 5	0	on	application.	
12	10	,,	allotment.	
15	0	,,	the 20th August, 1870.	
15	0	,,	the 20th October, 1870.	
15	0	,,	the 31st December, 1870.	deducting £3 Coupon due 1st January, 1871, less income-tax.
10	0	,,	the 20th February, 1871.	
10	0	,,	the 20th April, 1871.	
£82	10			

Subscribers have the option of paying in full all the instalments, under discount at the rate of 4 per cent. per annum, on any day when an instalment falls due.

Allowing for discount on the instalments, the price is reduced to 81¾ per cent.

The nonpayment of any of the instalments at their due dates subjects all previous payments to forfeiture.

Scrip Certificates to Bearer will be issued against Allotment Letters, to be exchanged for the definite Bonds as early as possible after payment of all the instalments.

The Bonds will be signed on behalf of the Supreme Government of Peru by a Special Commissioner appointed for that purpose, and countersigned by Messrs. J. Henry Schröder and Co. Coupons for the half-yearly interest, due the 1st of January and 1st of July of each year, will be attached.

Applications will be received by Messrs. J. Henry Schröder and Co. on the enclosed form on Tuesday the 7th June, Wednesday the 8th June, and for applications from the country until noon on Thursday the 9th June.

The allotments will be made as early as possible after the close of the subscription. In cases where the amount allotted is less than was applied for, the balance of the deposit will be applied towards payment of the next instalment, and if more than sufficient for that purpose the residue will be returned to the subscriber.

Where no allotment is made the amount of deposit will be returned without delay.

Subscriptions will be opened simultaneously—

In Paris, at the Offices of the Société Générale pour favourer le développement du Commerce et de l'Industrie en France.

In Amsterdam, at Messrs. Lippman, Rosenthall, and Co., and at Messrs. Wertheim and Gompertz's.

In Hamburg, at the Nord Deutsche Bank, and at Messrs. L. Behrens and Sons.

In Brussels, at Messrs. Cassel and Co's.

In New York, at Messrs. Baltzer and Taak's,

but Scrip Certificates, issued in respect of London allotments, can only be paid on and exchanged for Bonds in London.

145, Leadenhall Street, London.
4th June, 1870.

The Clacton-on-Sea and General

Land, Building and Investment Company,

LIMITED.

OFFICES:

CHIEF OFFICE:—33, WALBROOK, LONDON, E.C.

BRANCH OFFICES:

TELEGRAPH OFFICE, CLACTON-ON-SEA, ESSEX; and "KENTISH INDEPENDENT" OFFICE, A 1, WELLINGTON STREET, WOOLWICH.

CAPITAL - - - £500,000,

IN 20,000 SHARES OF £25 EACH.

FIRST ISSUE 4,000 SHARES.

£1 5s. per Share payable on Application, and £1 5s. on Allotment. No Calls will be made at less intervals than Three Months, or of more than £2 10s. per Share.

Discount will be allowed upon Sums paid in advance of Calls.

DIRECTORS.

MR. WILLIAM PARRY JACKSON, Woolwich (*Deputy Chairman of the London Steamboat Company*), Chairman.
MR. THOMAS DANIEL HAYES, Plumstead Road, S.E., Deputy Chairman.
MR. JAMES HARMAN, Clacton-on-Sea, Managing Director.
MR. WILLIAM AGATE, Blackheath, and Clacton-on-Sea.
MR. JAMES ELLIS, 1, Mulgrave Place, Woolwich.
MR. HENRY J. FENWICK GALE, 41, Well Street, Hackney, E.
MR. ABEL PENFOLD, Woolwich, and Clacton-on-Sea.
MR. RICHARD RIXON, Beresford Square, Woolwich.
MR. JAMES SMITH, Allerton House, Finsbury Park, N.
MR. JAMES TOPP, Plough Road, Rotherhithe.

SOLICITORS.

MESSRS. G. F. HUDSON, MATTHEWS, LOPEZ, and COUPLAND, 23, Bucklersbury, London, E.C., and 179, Burrage Road, Plumstead, S.E.

SURVEYORS.

MESSRS. HARMAN and MATTHEWS, 35, Walbrock, E.C.

BANKERS.

MESSRS. GLYN, MILLS, CURRIE and Co., 67, Lombard Street, London.
THE LONDON AND PROVINCIAL BANK, Woolwich.
MESSRS. MILLS, ERRINGTON, BAWTREE & Co., Colchester.

AUDITOR.

MR. JOHN MANN, Maryon Road, Charlton, Kent, S.E.

PROSPECTUS.

Amongst the various Prospectuses issued from time to time offering investments, none can by any means be considered so safe and profitable as the purchase and re-sale of Freehold Land, Ground Rents, and House Property.

It is undoubtedly a difficult matter for the Public in general to decide what is a safe investment; still, when compared with Foreign Bonds and Stocks (the fluctuating nature of which has been lately realized), it does not require much consideration before giving the preference to an association which has for its object the class of business this company contemplates, which is, to enable its Shareholders to obtain a comparatively high rate of interest by judicious investments in,

1st.—Freehold Land in eligible positions, for the purpose of laying out the same, and re-selling it in large or small plots.

2nd.—By the purchase of Ground Rents and House Property, as advantageous opportunities offer, the improvement of the same where possible when advisable, and the re-sale at a profit, unless deemed desirable to hold as a permanent investment.

3rd.—By advancing on Mortgage of Freehold and Leasehold Properties.

The first-named object of the Company cannot be better illustrated than by referring to the only contract entered into—viz., for the purchase, upon very favourable terms, of about Two Hundred Acres of Freehold Land at Clacton-on-Sea, Essex, which it is intended to lay out as a building estate.

Clacton-on-Sea is a comparatively new watering place, with cliffs, fine beach, and sands extending for miles, and a splendid sea, which have already made it a favourite summer resort. The houses built are of a superior class; and there is the nucleus of a fashionable watering place. It is in contemplation to form a railway from Clacton-on-Sea in connection with the Great Eastern line, the terminus of which is shown on the plan of the Company's Estate. The Bill has practically passed the House of Commons, and it is expected the line will be opened about July, 1878.

The Pier is now being lengthened, to enable passengers by the London Steamers to land at all tides, which will increase the number of visitors, and add materially to the value of property in the locality.

That a new watering place near London is required, is an undoubted fact, and when it is remembered that Clacton-on-Sea is nearer London than either Ramsgate, Margate, Hastings, Dover, or Folkestone, it will be seen that there is every prospect of a rapid and great success.

The operations of the Company will not be confined to Clacton-on-Sea.

As the Company is under the Limited Liability Act, no liability beyond the paying up of his Shares can at any time attach to any Shareholder.

The first issue of 4,000 £25 Shares is now offered at par, but the Directors reserve the right of making future issues at such premiums as the success of the Company may justify.

The only contract entered into on behalf of the Company bears date the 28th day of March, 1877, and is made between James Harman, of Clacton-on-Sea, in the county of Essex, Esq., of the first part; James Smith and Henry James Fenwick Gale, of Wilson Street, Finsbury, in the City of London, of the second part; and William

Parry Jackson, of Woolwich, in the county of Kent, Esq. (as Trustee on behalf of the Company), of the third part; being a contract for the purchase of freehold land and hereditaments at Clacton-on-Sea, part of which has been recently purchased by Messrs. Harman, Smith, and Gale, and by Mr. Harman; the remainder having been contracted to be purchased by Mr. Harman, or to be taken on lease with power to purchase. This contract can be seen at the Company's Offices.

For particulars as to the further objects of the Company, see the Articles of Association, which can be had at either of the Company's Offices.

By order of the Board,

W. PARRY JACKSON, Chairman.
JAMES HARMAN, Managing Director.

Protest. Latin, *protestari*, to bear witness, to declare.

In colloquial speech *to protest* is to make a declaration, or to bear witness, and is mostly used in a way implying censure or disapprobation. Hence, to sign a contract or pay a sum of money S. P. (*supra protest*) is to do so under the impression that the signatory is in danger of being wronged.

In *Notarial Practice* to Protest is a usage connected with Bills of Exchange. It is commonly said this use of the word originated with the Venetians, who were exceedingly strict and exacting in all commercial transactions, and who regarded the failure to pay a Bill when it became due as so monstrous a violation of commercial morality, that they were bound to "protest" formally against it. In modern commerce, much less feeling is infused into the process. When a Bill is presented for payment or acceptance, if the Drawee refuse to pay or to accept, the Bill is sent to a Notary, and he in a more formal manner presents it to the Drawee, and if again dishonoured, he issues a Protest in the manner prescribed by law. In England, the process of noting (*see Noting*) is accepted as a sufficient protest for Inland Bills, but Foreign Bills must be protested in a more formal way.

In *Marine Insurance*, a Protest is a declaration made on oath by the captain of a vessel which has met with any disaster at sea, or has been compelled to run into a foreign or intermediate port for safety. The protest should be made as soon as he enters the port, while the circumstances are fresh in his memory, the limit usually assigned being within 24 hours of his arrival. The record is made by a Public Notary in all cases of importance, but this is not essential to the validity of a protest.

Form of Protest on Non-Acceptance.

"On the day of , one thousand eight hundred and , I, R. B., Public Notary, by lawful authority and , dwelling in L——, in the county of L——, and United Kingdom of G. B. and I., at the request of C. D. of L—— (or of the holder or bearer as the case may be), did exhibit the original Bill of Exchange, whereof a true copy is on the other side written, unto a clerk in the counting-house of E. F., the person upon whom the same is drawn, and demanded acceptance thereof, and he answered that it would not be accepted at present.

Wherefore, I, the said Notary, at the request aforesaid, did and do by these presents protest against the drawer of the said bill, and all other parties thereto, and all others concerned, for all costs, exchange, re-exchange, and all costs, damages, and interest present and to come, for want of acceptance of the said bill.

Thus protested in the presence of B. B. and F. F., witnesses.

A. B., Notary Public,
Which I attest.

R. B.,
Notary Public, L——.

It is not indispensable to quote the exact words given in answer to a demand for acceptance—the correct tenor and purport are sufficient.

These forms are varied to suit the various cases that occur.

Proxy. From the Latin, *pro* and *cura*, care: whence a *procurator* was one who took any special business under his care; this word was cut down in Scotch to *prokutor*, in old English to *proketor*, and finally to *proctor*. *Procuratio* in like manner was reduced in the Dutch tongue to *prokuratie*, and to the English forms *prokecy* or *proxy*, from which last, curiously enough, every letter of the root *cura* entirely disappears.

Proxies, or votes by Proxy, play an important part in the meetings of financial companies, insurance societies, and generally of associations whose officers are chosen, or whose rules are made and rescinded by the body of the members. The word is used in three senses. (1.) It signifies the acting in place of another, as in the phrase "voting by proxy;" (2) The person who acts in place of another is called a "proxy;" (3) The written document authorizing one person to act or vote for another is called a "proxy." Proxies, unless fenced round by elaborate precautions, are liable to be, and often are, much abused; but where the members of a society, entitled to vote on a given question, live at remote distances from the seat of an election, it is often the only way of giving them a voice in the management of their own affairs.

Purse. By the Turkish monetary law of 1844, the Purse consists of 500 Turkish piastres. It is of gold and weighs 36·082 grammes, ·916$\frac{2}{3}$ fine; and its mint par value in Francs 113·92 = £4·5153 or £4 10*s*. 3$\frac{1}{2}$*d*. sterling.

An Egyptian Purse (Arab *Kees*) consists of 500 tariff piastres; in English, £5 2*s*. 6$\frac{1}{2}$*d*.

Put and Call. *See Options.*

Pyx or Pix. From the Greek πυξος, the box tree, box-wood; πυξος, a vessel, or chest made of boxwood, and afterwards a vessel made of other kinds of woods, or of metal; whence the Latin *pyxis*, a box or chest, and the Anglicized form of the word for the box or vessel used in Catholic churches to contain the consecrated host, and later on employed to signify the chest in which contributions and offerings for the poor were collected.

1531. For mette for the theffe that stolle the *pyx*.
(For meat for the thief that stole the pyx.)
Churchwarden's Accounts of St. Margaret's, Westminster.

The same name was afterwards applied to the chest in which coins were deposited, previous to the ceremony called the "*Trial of the Pyx.*"

The *Pyx* is a box or chest in which coins are deposited. The name never appears to have been used in the English form except as applied to sacred or ceremonial purposes; first, as the name of the vessel containing the host; subsequently to the box for the collection of pious offerings; and at length to the chest appropriated to the solemn ceremonial called the Trial of the Pyx, originally conducted or presided over by the monarch, some great officer of state, or the Archbishop of Canterbury. (*See Trial of the Pyx.*)

Q.

Quotation. French, *côté*.

The prices quoted for stocks and commodities in the various markets.

Quotient. Latin, *quoties*, or *quotiens*, how often, how many times.

The number resulting from the division of one number by another. In commercial practice the term "dividend" is often used when that of "quotient" would be more correct. Thus, suppose a five per cent. loan of £1,000,000 to be issued; the annual interest, the sum to be divided annually, or *dividendum* would be £50,000. Let a bondholder possess £500 in the stock of this loan; what portion of the interest will fall to his share? It is obvious that "as many times" as his holding is contained in the whole loan "so many times" his share of the interest will be contained in the total interest (the dividenum) to be divided. Now, £500 is the 2,000th part of £1,000,000; therefore, the portion falling due to the holder of £500 of stock must be the 2,000th part of the interest to be divided *i.e.*, £50,000. Divide £50,000 by 2,000, and the result or quotient is £25—the annual interest which a holder of £500 stock would be entitled to. Set out in full, the process appears thus:—

Divisor. Dividend. Quotient.
2,000) 50,000 (25
4,000
———
10,000
10,000
———
. .
═══

The same course of reasoning would apply to "dividends" of all kinds, whether of interest on loans or profits on capital. (*See Dividend.*)

Quadruple. Another name for the gold onza of Spain (*which see*). Value about £3 4*s.*

Quarter Guinea. An English gold coin, value 5*s.* 3*d.* in the times of King George I. and III.

Quartillo and **Cuartillo.** A copper coin of Mexico, $\frac{1}{32}$ of the Mexican dollar, worth about $1\frac{1}{2}$*d.* English, $\frac{1}{4}$ of the Mexican real.

Quartinho. A Portuguese coin of 1,200 reis.

Quattie. A small silver coin used in the West Indies, worth about $1\frac{1}{2}$*d.* English.

R.

Ral. The $\frac{1}{100}$ part of the Bombay rupee, now almost superseded by the division of the Company's rupee in 16 annas of 12 pice each. (*See Pie.*)

Rate of Exchange. The price of the money of one country reckoned in that of another country.

In England, the pound sterling is the monetary unit with which the moneys of other countries are compared.

Between England and those countries using a gold standard, as Germany, the rate is expressed in terms of gold coin with gold coin.

Between England and countries using a silver standard, as India, the rate is expressed in terms of gold coin with silver coin.

Between England and countries using a paper currency, as Austria and Italy, the rate is expressed in terms of gold coin with paper, the nominal value of which, however, is always denoted in the metallic coinage of the country whether gold or silver. (*See Par of Exchange.*)

Rate of Wages. The rate of wages (or salaries) is a subject which has been obscured somewhat in consequence of a mixing up with considerations of pure trade, some others which belong rather to the province of patronage or benevolence. Just as when discussing the subject of "rent," we find it necessary to restrict the term to its application in respect of *agricultural* land, to the exclusion of city lands, and lands devoted to shops, factories, &c., so, when discussing the "rate of wages," we find it necessary to exclude all considerations but those relating to the commercial value of the services for which wages are paid.

A further restriction has to be introduced. Wages are sometimes paid according to the amount of work done; at others, and more commonly, according to length of time over which the service is rendered. The first are called task wages, and partake more of the nature of purchase and sale, as in retail trade. These must be excluded from our discussion on the "rate of wages," and our attention must be limited to wages reckoned according to the length of time occupied by the service rendered, that is, to *time wages*.

With these limitations, it may be stated, as a general rule, that labour, like everything else that is bought and sold, rises and falls in value according to the variations of supply and demand. When there are many labourers in a given field of industry, and a slack demand for them, the competition among the labourers themselves will bring down wages. When there is a brisk demand for labourers, and the supply limited, employers will compete with one another, and wages will rise. Hence, the circumstances which determine the rate of wages will generally be resolved into a modification of the ratio subsisting between the supply of, and demand for, labour; some of the chief of which may be here noted :—

(1.) The time and money expended in learning a handicraft or profession. If much time and money are required, it will tend to keep down the number of those who learn that profession, the supply will be limited, and wages good.

(2.) The repulsiveness and unwholesomeness of the work. Most people endeavour to escape from what is repulsive to them, and unwholesome occupations have a tendency to thin the ranks of those who engage in them by disease or death.

(3.) Trustworthiness, as proved by length of service, or as guaranteed by the recommendation of a friend or patron. This quality is of such supreme importance to many employers, that they can dispense with severity of labour, or even high educational attainments, and yet pay more liberally for the services of workmen of this class than for those whose acquirements are much superior. It was formerly a common experience of railway managers to receive applications for places as guards and station-masters. Those occupations being cleanly and respectable, requiring no manual dexterity, and very moderate education, were sought for by multitudes; but situations of this nature were given as a reward of faithful service for a term of years in some of the lower grades of employment, and thus held out a premium for industry, sobriety, and honesty to men employed in the lower grades.

The wages or salaries of clerks and employés in Government offices, as well as in some merchants' offices, do not fall under the law above stated. The education required of many clerks is of a most elementary nature, but they are required to dress well, to behave courteously, and to comport themselves somewhat as gentlemen; but these are things that many men would do of choice, without being paid for it, and, consequently, the supply of clerks is always much greater than the demand. Nevertheless, the wages of clerks are higher than those of the most skilled artizans, and clerkships are therefore very frequently conferred by way of patronage, or as a reward for services rendered in some other line. If, however, high attainments are required in a clerk, as they sometimes are, the supply of candidates for the office will be curtailed, and the usual law regulating the rate of wages again comes into force.

Ratio of Exchange. A phrase used in Political Economy to denote the proportion in which a quantity of one commodity exchanges for a given quantity of another. The expression can never be used with any degree of accuracy, except in those cases where the commodities are homogeneous in quality, and susceptible of weight or measurement, as in the exchange of gold for silver, copper, iron, &c., or that of wheat, for barley, oats, &c.

Real. The old unit of value in Spain. By the monetary law of June, 1864, the Silver Real was made to weigh 1·298 grammes, ·810 fine, and was worth ·23 centimes in French money, or about $2\frac{1}{4}$*d.* English.

There have been several varieties of Reals circulating in different parts of Spain and her colonies from time to time, differing in value from $2\frac{1}{2}$*d.* to 5*d.* sterling. The confusion arising from so great a number of coins bearing the same name has induced the Spanish Government to adopt the French system, and thus reduce the old coinage to the condition of commercial coin. Ten Reals were equal to one Escudo. (*See Peseta.*)

The *Mexican Real* is $\frac{1}{8}$ the Mexican Silver Dollar in weight, but of inferior fineness. It is worth about $6\frac{1}{4}$*d.* English.

The *Real of the Philippine Islands* is the $\frac{1}{20}$ part of a Dollar, and is worth about $2\frac{1}{2}$*d.* English.

The *Real of Columbia* is $\frac{1}{8}$ part of the Sencilla, and is worth about 5*d.*

The *Real of Uruguay* is a silver coin worth about $4\frac{1}{2}$*d.* English.

Real Corriente. The "Real Current" of Uruguay. There is no coin in Uruguay equal to 1 Real Corriente, but the 5 Reals Corriente piece of Silver furnishes a basis of comparison. It weighs 13 010 grammes, and is ·833·3 fine, value 22·927 pence.

Real Exchange. Real Exchange is also sometimes called Commercial Exchange, and depends on the trade transactions between any two or more countries. It thus differs from the Nominal Exchange, which is based on the relation of the moneys of the different countries. (*See Nominal Exchange.*)

Realization. The process of converting into a reality what was previously contingent or doubtful. Thus, if I buy Consols at $95\frac{1}{4}$, and soon afterwards have an opportunity of selling them at $95\frac{1}{2}$, there is a profit of $\frac{1}{4}$ per cent. upon the operation, but that profit is contingent on my closing the bargain at that moment; for, if I resolve to keep it open, it is quite doubtful whether the price may rise or fall, that is, whether I shall increase my profit or lose it altogether. If I remove the doubt or contingency by closing the bargain the profit is a real one, in other words is *realized*, and the act itself is called *realization.*

Reasonable Hours. It is often notified in commercial documents that bills must be presented, applications made, or certain things done within "reasonable hours," and the question must necessarily arise, "What are reasonable hours?" McLeod cites several cases in point, and notes that the latest hour yet decided to be reasonable is between 8 and 9 p.m. Of course, the decisions here referred to have reference to houses of business open daily; but there are many societies whose offices are open only once a week or once a month, and then only for an hour or two hours in the evening: in these cases the only hours that can be deemed reasonable are those when the office is open and which every member of the society is supposed to know.

Rebate. The same in meaning with *Discount* or *Abatement* (*which see*).

Receipt. From the Latin, *re*, again, and *capio*, I take; whence, *recipio*, I take again, seize, or receive. The imperative form of the word is *rĕcĭpe*, and is found at the beginning of written prescriptions drawn up by medical men, and also in the instructions of old Latin cookery books. When so used it is a direction to "take" certain drugs or ingredients and compound them into medicine or food, and should be pronounced as three separate syllables, *rĕ-cĭ-pe*. To call it, as many people do, a "receipt," is a corruption.

A Receipt is a written document, declaring that certain goods or a sum of money have been received. When made out in full, a receipt should contain, (1) the date when the merchandise or money was received, (2) the name of the person or firm from whom received (3) the name of the person who receives it, (4) for what the money is paid or deposited, and (5) should have a stamp when the money amounts to more than *two pounds*.

Receipt for Money in settlement of an account.

7 Dec., 1880.

Received of Mr. John Watson the sum of Four Hundred and Seventeen Pounds Ten Shillings for goods delivered

£417 10*s*. 0*d*.

RICHARD HENSLOW.

N.B.—The stamp should be cancelled by writing the name or date across it.

Receipt of Bonds deposited as Security for Balance of Account.

20 Jan., 1880.

Received of Joseph Winter, Esq., Five Russian 1870 Bonds of £100 each in deposit as security for Balance of Account.

ALF. ALDERTON.
Broker.

N.B.—This is merely a memorandum and does not require a stamp.

Receipt a Bill or Account, To. To receipt a bill or an account is to write the word "received" at the end of it. The same observations, with regard to date, stamp, and signature apply to a receipt of this kind, as to the more formal one above described. Thus:—

Received 20/1/80.	Henry Warburton.

The other details are furnished by the account itself.

Reciprocity. Latin, *reciproco, reciprocare,* to fetch back, to return by the same way, to turn an argument against one.

A doctrine which has sprung up of late years among certain classes of traders and manufacturers who have suffered from the action of free trade. It does not find much favour with economists, as it is founded on the idea that the whole population of a country ought to be taxed in order to benefit a limited class of producers. Almost every recent work on political economy deals with the question, and to these works the reader is referred for further details.

Reckon. All the Teutonic tongues contain a word or words of which the syllable *rec, rech, rak,* or some combination of vowel sounds with the letters *r* and *k*. These words had a wider signification originally than our present word *reckon,* which is used almost exclusively in the sense of counting or calculation. Thus, the Anglo-Saxon *recan* and *reccean,* to say, tell, number; *Ic marg reccan,* I can relate. Old High German, *rahka,* a narrative or tale. Modern German, *rechnen,* to count or calculate. The equivalent in French is *nombrer* or *compter.*

To "reckon up" is to add up; to "reckon" simply, is to calculate, whether by addition, multiplication, or other arithmetical process. To "pay one's reckoning" is to pay one's bill or account, usually applied to the bill at an hotel or restaurant.

Recoup, To. French, *recouper,* to cut again, as if to correct the fault of a first cutting.

To cut off or keep back a portion of what one is about to pay, in compensation for some damage done by a creditor, or on account of some advantage of which a debtor has been deprived. Errors are sometimes discovered in an account after such an account has been settled and closed. In such a case, the error is often allowed for in the next succeeding account, and the injured party is then said to "recoup himself." This is a distinct departure from the original meaning of the word, but the phrase is in common use, and is best understood without too strict an adherence to its etymology. In like manner, the phrase must be construed, when used in the sense of retaliation for sharp dealing.

Recourse. From the Latin, *recurro*, to run again, to run back, to resort to.

The phrases "with recourse," or "without recourse," are inserted in commercial documents to indicate respectively two opposite conditions on which a bargain is concluded; thus:—

(*a.*) *With recourse* implies that a sale or purchase has been made on condition that the thing sold is of the kind or quality taken for granted at the time of the sale. If on examination it is found to be of an essentially different kind or quality, the buyer is entitled to have "recourse" to the seller, and to claim an annulment of the bargain, or compensation for any loss he may have suffered. A familiar example is that of the purchase of coupons by a money-changer. When a coupon is thus bought, the buyer sometimes finds that the bond, from which it was cut off has been drawn for reimbursement, that all interest upon it has ceased, and that the coupon is not payable. If he has bought it *with recourse*, he returns it to the seller, and claims repayment of the amount given for it.

(*b.*) *Without recourse.* It sometimes happens, however, that buyers are willing to take coupons and other instruments, and at the same time to accept any risk attending the transaction. This occurs when there is much competition among buyers of a particular article, or when a seller is willing to take a lower price for it, in order to be relieved of any risk or trouble attending the transfer of it. The purchase is then said to be made *without recourse.*

In the endorsement of bills or notes, the endorser sometimes finds it necessary to protect himself against any default on the part of other parties to the bill. In such a case he frees himself from liability by adding the words "sans recours," or "without recourse to me," to the words commonly used in an endorsement.

Reduced Annuities. Owing to the defective nomenclature originally adopted in England in reference to annuities, very serious misunderstandings at one time arose between the receivers of annuities on the one hand, and the Government who paid them on the other. An annuity is from its very nature a sum annually paid by one party and received by another. Let the annuity be, say, four pounds; it means that the annuitant, or his heirs, is in the receipt of four pounds a year for ever. For this privilege he has paid a certain sum, say £96. Had this simple language been adhered to, no misunderstanding could have arisen. But a curious fiction was introduced, and this four pounds was *assumed* to be the annual interest on £100 *assumed* to be lent, and the annuitant was said to be the holder of £100 stock, although, as supposed above, he paid only £96 for it. In course of time, this privilege of receiving four pounds a year was so highly esteemed that many persons were found who were willing, and even anxious, to obtain it by paying more than £96 for it, and eventually more than £100, say £105. Now arose a difficulty. The Government saw that the public were willing to pay more than £100 for an annuity of four pounds, which is only another way of saying that the public were satisfied with *less than four per cent.*

for their capital. The Government, therefore, proposed to pay the annuitants their £100 back, and cease to pay the annuity. But to this the annuitants objected. They said—We never lent you £100. We bought an annuity, a perpetual annuity; all this talk about lending and borrowing £100 is a mere fiction. We paid you a sum of £96, in return for which you engaged to pay us four pounds a year. We do not want the £100 you *offer* to pay us, but the four pounds a year you *engaged* to pay us.

The annuitants were right, but the Government had the might, and they used it. They offered to pay back the £100 *assumed* to be borrowed, or pay in future three and a-half pounds a year to each annuitant instead of four pounds. Since that first oversight, a stipulation has always been made by borrowing Governments, in virtue of which they shall always be free to pay off their stock at par, either at any time or after some specified time. Such was the nature of the famous five-twenties of the United States. They derived their name from the fact that, in the terms of the original bond, the Government should be free to pay off the bonds at par after *five* years from the date of issue, and that after *twenty* years the bondholder might legally claim the repayment of them.

Reduced Three per Cents. Certain Government Annuities originally bearing 4 per cent. interest, which was reduced in 1746 to $3\frac{1}{2}$ per cent. and in 1757 to 3 per cent. They amounted, at the end of 1880, to a capital sum of £92,461,985.

Registered Stocks. Registered Stocks are so called because they are entered with the name of the holder in a Register kept for that purpose at the chief office of the Company or State issuing them. Registered Stocks differ from Stocks or Bonds to Bearer in having no sheet of coupons for the half-yearly dividend attached. They are simply certificates declaring that such and such a person is the holder of a given amount of Stock; and that he is entitled to a stated amount of interest thereon. This interest may be called for at the office by the person entitled to it, or it may be paid under Power of Attorney to anyone acting on behalf of the owner. Registered Stocks are considered more secure for those persons who have no strong rooms or safes for the deposit of their bonds, and the trouble attending the collection of dividends is more than compensated by the greater security they enjoy. As examples of Registered securities, may be specially mentioned English Consols, the United States Funded Debt, and French Rentes. Holders of these stocks have the option of receiving Bonds to Bearer with coupons attached, or a simple certificate without coupons, declaring them proprietors of the same; when the dividends are paid in the manner above described.

Rei. An *imaginary* unit of value, on which the monetary systems of Portugal and Brazil are founded. The *real* unit of value in both these countries, is a coin of a thousand *Reis*, called the *Milreis*, but which have a widely different metallic value in the two countries. (*See Milreis.*)

Estimating the value of the Rei from the Gold Milreis, we find:—
Portuguese Rei = $\frac{213}{1000}$ of a farthing.
The *Brazilian Rei* = $\frac{108}{1000}$ of a farthing.

The arithmetical notation of the *Rei* is peculiar, and requires explanation; thus:—

1,000 reis (milreis)	is written	1$000
1,000,000 reis (conto)	„	1:000$000
1,000,000,000 reis (1,000 contos)	„	1.000:000$000
4,800 reis (moidore)	„	4$800
400 reis (crusado)	„	$400
480 reis (crusado nova)	„	$480
100 reis (testoon)	„	$100

Regraters. From the French, *regratter*, to bargain, to huckster.

Dealers who bought and sold in the same market or fair, and on the same day. They were thought to raise the prices of articles which passed through their hands, and were formerly regarded with disfavour. More enlightened views have since prevailed and the practice of "regrating" now proceeds without let or hindrance, although the name of *regrater* has passed out of use. (Compare *Monopoly, Forestalling, Engrossing.*)

Regrets. *See Letter of Regret.*

Reich-mark. The same with the German Mark (*which see*).

Reichs Thaler. (*a*) A Prussian Silver coin, value 2*s.* 11*d.*
(*b*) The same as the Rix Dollar of Bremen (*which see*).

Release or **Acceptilation.** From the Latin, *relaxo, relaxare*, to loosen, to set free, to set at liberty, hence *se relaxare obligatione*, to free oneself from a bond or duty. From the Latin is derived the French *relâcher*, to loosen, to relax, to remit, and also the Italian forms, *rilassare, rilasciare*, and through these the English, *release*.

"Then 'tis thought

* * * * *

And where thou now exact'st the penalty,
Which is a pound of this poor merchant's flesh,
Thou wilt not only *loose* the forfeiture,
But, touched with human gentleness and love,
Forgive a moiety of the principal;"

The Duke *to* Shylock, *Merchant of Venice*, Act. iv.

The Release of a Debt or Obligation is in law equivalent to a Payment or Gift equal in amount to that of the debt. The most familiar examples of Release or Acceptilation which occur in the course of business, are (1) the payment of a sum to a bank in the bank's own promissory notes, and (2) the payment of a sum to a bank by a cheque on that bank by one of the bank's own customers. In either case an obligation or duty rested on the bank to pay a certain sum to its customer whenever he demanded it. By presenting one of the bank's notes, or a cheque drawn on that bank for a stated sum, the customer releases the bank from paying such sum. For, in the case of the promissory note, so soon as it is handed over to the bank for any consideration, the bank may destroy it, and it cannot be afterwards used to set up a claim against the bank, and the bank is thus released from making any payment in respect of it. In the case of the cheque, the customer had claims on the bank equal to the amount of his deposit; but by presenting his cheque on the same bank to the bank in order to discharge some debt (say to pay the interest on a loan), the bank was released from the obligation of returning so much of the customer's deposits as was equal to the value of the cheque.

Remedy. Latin, *remedium*, a cure, a means of cure, a means of protection against anything; *remedium ad magnitudinem frigorum* (*Cicero*), a protection against severe cold. In this figurative sense of "protection," it is used in refinery and coining.—*Mint remedies* being statutory allowances in defect or excess of the legal standard of the coinage, and which serve to protect the mint-master from legal penalties, so long as he works within the limits prescribed. The French equivalent is *tolerance*.

Remedy or Allowance is a technical name for the departures from the standard weight and fineness allowed to the mint-master to cover imperfections of workmanship. There are two ways of denoting this divergence from the standard:—

I. The *Milliemes* system, by which the departure is expressed as so many parts in one thousand. This method is adopted in France, and in most countries where the *Metric System* is in use. The Remedy or *Tolerance* in France, and indeed in all those nations who have joined the Latin Monetary Union, is two parts in a thousand —2 per mille—both for weight and fineness, in respect of the *gold* coinage, and 3 per mille in that of *silver*.

II. The *English* system, which is much more clumsy and complicated. In respect of weight it is denoted by so many grains in the pound troy. In respect of fineness, by so many carats in 22 carats, both of which, however, can be easily reduced to milliemes, when comparison with other coinages is required.

For gold, the remedy in respect to *fineness* is $\frac{1}{16}$ of a carat in 22 carats, which is $\frac{1}{352}$ part of any given weight, or about 3 per mille. In respect to weight, the allowance is 12 grains in the pound troy, which is about $\frac{1}{4}$ of a grain for the sovereign. More accurately, the coinage Act states $\frac{2}{10}$ of a grain as the allowance for weight, and two parts in a thousand for the fineness of a sovereign.

For silver, the remedy in respect to fineness is 4 parts in a thousand, or, as it is sometimes stated, 1 pennyweight in the pound troy, which is 4 parts in 960. In respect to *weight*, the allowance is the same, and is expressed in the same alternative manner.

It is to be observed that the limits above assigned, as *allowance*, *tolerance*, or *remedy*, apply in both directions, that is, the standard must not be departed from either by addition to weight and fineness, or by deduction. In the first case, the mint-master would wrong the Government; in the second, the public who accept the coin. Now, a sovereign, when of full weight and fineness, weighs 123·27447 grains, and the legal remedy $\frac{2}{10}$ of a grain. Hence, a glance at the following Table shows that a sovereign is not a legal issue when it weighs more than 123·47447 grains, or less than 123·07447 grains.

Superior limit	123·47447 grains.
Full legal weight	123·27447 grains.
Inferior limit	123·07447 grains.

Remittance. Latin, *remittere*, to send away, to send forth.

In commerce, a remittance is something sent. It may be a sum of money, a bill or bills, or a quantity of bullion. It is not usual to apply the term to goods or commodities sent out; the words *consignment*, *delivery*, *&c.*, are more commonly employed for this purpose.

Remonetization. By the remonetization of a gold or silver coinage is meant, the re-establishment of such coinage in the position of legal tender after having for a time been degraded to the rank of mere token money. Holland furnishes a case in point. By the monetary laws of 1847 and 1849, the gold florin was made the standard of value, and the unit of account. In 1850, the gold coinage was suppressed and *demonetized*, silver being made the standard of value. Quite recently the laws of 1847 and 1849 have been re-established, in other words, the gold coinage has been *remonetized*, and made again the standard of value.

Rent. From Latin, *re*, and *do dāre*, to give: *reddĕre*, to give back, to compensate, to render. As in many other words, the French insert a euphonic *n*; hence *rendre*, and the English, *render*. *Rent* is therefore a something rendered or returned, and originally was a return made to the lord of the soil, the return at first consisting mainly of military service, and afterwards of villanage, or even the most menial offices. Still later, corn or other produce was given as rent, and lastly, money became the almost universal form of recompense for the use of land, tenements, or other property, the use of which was given up for a time to the renter, or tenant.

The word has three different meanings, which it is important to distinguish:—

I. In common speech, it signifies the payment periodically made for the use of lands, houses, or property of any kind.

II. In legal phraseology, signifies the *Right to demand* payment for the same, and not the payment itself.

III. In Political Economy the meaning is more restricted, and is applied to the payment annually made for the use of *agricultural* land; not city land, or lands covered by shops or warehouses, but lands employed simply for the production of such wealth as is yielded by tilling it. The produce of such land may be divided into two parts, and one of these may be further analyzed. Thus:—

Value of Produce.
- COST OF PRODUCTION.
  - Expense of Production.
  - Interest on Capital Employed.
  - Farmer's Earnings.
- RENT, the surplus after the above items are discharged.

The costs of production must always be paid out of the value of the produce before any rent can be paid. If they were not, the land would not be tilled at all. If after they are paid, a large surplus remains, a high rent will be paid for such land as yields the surplus; if a small surplus, then only a low rent can be paid; if no surplus, no rent at all. It is in vain that a landowner insists on having a given rent, if the above items in the cost of production are not first discharged. He could get no one to hire or till his land. But if after they are discharged a surplus or profit remains, farmers will compete with each other, and offer a higher rent for it.

Rentes. Italian, *Rendita;* Spanish, *Renta;* from the Latin, *reditus,* a return. (*See Rent.*)

The annual interest payable on French, Austrian, Italian, and some other Government Stocks. Although French, Italian, Spanish, Austrian, and Hungarian Rentes constitute the great National Debts of their respective countries, and so far resembles our Consols, there is notwithstanding a difference in the form of the Bonds or Certificates which ought to be observed. The difference is most plainly marked in the French and Italian Rentes, for these, unlike our Consols have on their face the annual sum payable, that is, the Rente or Interest on the Bond, whereas an English Consol Bond has the Capital or Principal Sum on which interest is to be paid printed thereon. Take, for example, a £100 Consolidated Three per Cent. Bond with its coupons, each *half-yearly* coupon will be seen to have upon it the sum of £1 10*s.* plainly printed, with certain words giving the holder a right to claim that amount every half year—*i.e.*, three pounds a year. It matters not what the holder paid for the Bond; it might be the full £100 or it might be £80, or any other sum; but in any case the holder of it would be entitled to his £1 10*s.* each half year. Now take up a Certificate of French Rente for say 100 francs. It will be called Certificate for "Rente 100 francs," meaning that the holder is entitled to an annual payment of 100 francs, and the coupons, if payable half-yearly will have the sum of 50 francs printed in words or figures upon them, but no *capital* or *principal* will be named. Nevertheless, this *capital* or *principal*, though purely imaginary is always assumed, otherwise there would be no reason in calling them as they are always called, 3 per cent. Rentes, 5 per cent. Rentes, 4½ per cent. Rentes, and so forth. Hence, Rentes and Consols are all alike in this one respect—viz., the holder of the Bond or Certificate is entitled to an *annual sum* in return for what he has given for that Bond or Certificate, but in no case is he entitled to claim the repayment of the principal or capital, whether printed on the Bond, like Consols, or not printed, as in the case of Rentes.

Shortly speaking, the purchaser of Consols or Rentes, purchases the right to claim an annual sum of money for ever, and this right he may sell and re-purchase as often as he likes. For this reason Consols are always mentioned in official documents as "Bank Annuities," as if to fix attention on the fact that these *Annuities*, and these only, are what he is entitled to claim.

Spanish and Hungarian Rentes somewhat more closely resemble English Consols, inasmuch as though the coupons give a claim for Annual Rente, the imaginary Capital Sum on which Interest or Rente is paid is also printed on the Bond itself.

Report. The technical name given by refiners to a statement, after assaying, of the fineness of a bar of gold or silver. (*See Fineness, Betterness, and Worseness.*)

Representative Money. This is merely another name for "token money" and "paper money," both of which are treated of under their respective headings.

Reserve. Latin, *reservare*, to save, keep.

In banking operations, the word "Reserve" is used in three distinct senses: (*a*) The Currency or Issue Reserve, (*b*) the Banking Reserve, (*c*) The Liability Reserve.

(*a*.) The *Currency Reserve.* This is also sometimes called the Issue Reserve, and refers to the gold held in *reserve* at the Bank of England in order to secure the convertibility of the bank note. The amount varies with the quantity of gold in coins or bars deposited with the Bank, and consequently is out of the control of that establishment. £15,000,000 in bank notes are issued on the security of the Government, and no gold is kept in reserve nor is any needed in order to secure the convertibility of that portion of the Note Issue, but all beyond that amount is represented by gold kept in the Bank vaults, and whatever sums the public or other banks may send there with a view to obtain notes for their use, must be kept intact, so that wherever notes are presented gold may always be at hand for their payment. Hence it follows that all the Bank of England Notes in circulation are completely covered by the two items—Government Securities and Reserve.

(*b*) The *Banking Reserve.* When depositors place their money in a bank, it is because they do not want it for immediate use, and wish to put it in a place of safety. If the amount thus deposited is considerable, they desire further to derive some profit or interest upon it, and yet have it in such a position that they can avail themselves of it at a minute's notice when needed. In practice, however, it never happens that all, or nearly all the money deposited with a banker is wanted at once, and hence a custom has arisen of employing a large portion of the money deposited in banks, in discounting bills of exchange, and lending money on good security so as to make a profit upon it. But some money must always be kept on hand to meet the daily and hourly demands made by the bank's customers, and the money thus kept on hand is called the

Reserve. How much ought thus to be kept in reserve is a question that can only be solved by observation and experience. One-third of the sums deposited is considered a tolerably safe proportion, but the circumstances of each bank vary; and much tact and judgment are required in the determination of the proportion of the reserve to the liabilities; in this respect it differs entirely from the *currency reserve* just described. In regard to that, no discrétion or judgment is allowed. In regard to this, the safety and prosperity of a bank depend chiefly on the discretion and judgment shown in deciding how much of the bank's deposits must be kept idle, and how much may be safely employed in making profits.

(c.) For *Liability Reserve.* (*See Liability.*)

Respondentia Bond. (*See Bottomry Bond.*)

Rest. We have here two English words identical in form, but differing in origin and meaning.

(1.) With the meaning to cease from toil, to repose, from the Saxon, *resten, hrestan;* German, *rasten;* Dutch, *rusten,* all signifying rest from action or motion of any kind.

(2.) With the meaning of "remainder," or what is left, from the Latin, *restare* (*re,* and, *stare,* to stand). French, *rester,* to remain; *reste,* a remainder. Italian, *restare,* with the same meaning. We use both these words in colloquial English, thus:—

(1.) Now I will sit down and *rest* (repose).
(2.) Take what you like and leave the *rest* (remainder).

A technical term used in the Bank of England weekly reports, denoting the balance of assets above liabilities. It is of the nature of a reserve against any contingencies that may arise, and dates from the year 1722. At first it was small in amount. In the weekly Report of the Bank published on the 3rd of February, 1881, it was £3,363,161. (*See Bank Return.*)

Retenue. A charge for the expense of coinage made to the importers of gold and silver into certain mints. The French mints charge 6·70 francs per kilogramme for gold, and 1½ francs per kilogramme for silver. (*See Franc.*) In England the charge for the expenses of coinage is called *Seigniorage* (*which see*).

Retire. From French, *tirer,* to draw or pull, and *re,* again, allied to Gothic, *tairan.* Old German, *zeran;* Dutch, *téren;* Spanish and Portuguese, *tirar,* and the English, *tear,* to pull off or to pieces. We have the same root in the Greek, *δειρω, deiro,* to draw off the skin, to flay; and in the Sanscrit, *dar,* all conveying the notion of pulling, pulling off, drawing, &c.

To Retire a Bill or Note is to withdraw it from circulation, which is usually effected by one of the parties to it, who buys it up, and keeps it in his possession till it matures, or cancels it at once.

Revenue Account. An account kept by a trading company showing the income of the company on the one side, and the expenditure argeable against income on the other. It is thus distinguished from the capital account, which shows the subscriptions of the shareholders on the one side, and the charges against capital on the other.

Reversions. Latin, *vertere*, to turn; *re*, again.

A Reversion is an Annuity or some other benefit, the enjoyment of which begins after a given number of years, or after the occurrence of some event, such as the death or the birth of a certain individual. Reversions are bought and sold in the market like any other rights. (*See Right of Action.*)

Right of Action. In Mercantile Law, the right of one man to claim a debt due by another.

An *Action* in law is defined to be "the lawful demand of one's right." But as there are some things to which one has a right, although that right cannot be enforced in a court of law—*e.g.*, the right of parents to the respect and obedience of their children, the right of children to the affection of their parents, the right to an office of the most competent and deserving, it follows that there are some rightful claims which cannot be made the subject of an *action* at law. This is commonly expressed by saying that the person has no "Right of Action" with respect to those claims. On the other hand, there are certain claims so clearly defined, that there is no difficulty in enforcing them by law. Such are claims to houses or lands held under an undisputed title, and notably sums of money due by one person to another. These last, owing to the accuracy with which they may be stated and recorded, and the simplicity of the subject matter of the claims render them pre-eminently amenable to legal treatment, and in the earliest periods of commercial enterprise, the attention of merchants and bankers was occupied in devising the best forms in which money claims could be recorded, so as to make them readily negotiable, and at the same time render the money easily recoverable in a court of law. Out of these efforts grew the now-established form of modern Bills of Exchange, Promissory Notes, Dock Warrants, &c., the usefulness and negotiability of which arise from the fact that they carry with them the right of action so absolutely as to be beyond question, while they may be transferred from one person to another by simple endorsement, without any form of conveyance or registration similar to that required in the transfer of property in houses or land.

Rights. A Right to anything is a claim to that thing protected by legal remedies—*i.e.*, a claim which can be enforced in a court of law. Rights are distinguished by Blackstone as Rights of Possession and Rights of Property.

A Right of Possession is a right to anything hired, borrowed, or received in deposit as security, A banker, for example, has a right of Possession in £1,000 Russian Bonds deposited with him as security for a loan, but he has no right to treat them as if they were his own property; he is not at liberty to lend, or sell them, or appropriate the half-yearly interest on them, but simply to hold them in his *possession* as security for the money lent.

A Right of Property is a right to claim certain things as one's own, which includes the right to use those things, sell, or otherwise dispose of them as he chooses, always with the proviso that he shall not use or dispose of them in such a way as to injure or molest anyone else. £1,000 in Russian Bonds, purchased by a banker out of his own capital, stands in a very different position from the same bonds deposited with him as security. These are his own, he has a Right of Property in them, he may sell them, lend them, take the interest on them, and appropriate it to his own use.

In most banks Commercial Bills are to be found in great numbers, which are held under one or the other of these rights. Some are *deposited* simply as security against money lent; over these the bank has simply the Right of Possession. Others have been *discounted* (that is, *bought* at a discount), and over these the bank has a Right of Property. This distinction is of great importance in banking practice. One of the most painful cases of mal-administration in modern times (with the subsequent prosecution and conviction) arose from the non-observance of it.

Rights are said to originate in this wise. "The necessities of his physical position oblige man to exert his power over the world of things. At first the property is held by the community or tribe, then by the family, and lastly by the individual, and when society has reached this last stage, ... his special interests prompt each man to claim, as against his fellows, an exclusive interest in particular things." *Justinian.*

Rigsdaler or **Riksdaler.** The former unit of value in Denmark. Although the Scandinavian Monetary Union makes the Krone or Crown the new unit of value, the Rigsdaler is still in active circulation, and prices are often quoted in Rigs-dalers.

The Silver Rigsdaler weighs 14·447 grammes ·875 fine. Taking $15\frac{1}{2}$ parts of *fine* silver as equal to 1 of fine gold the value of the Rigsdaler in sterling is 26·730 pence or 2*s.* $2\frac{3}{4}$*d.* It is divided into 96 skilling. Its value is determined by the mint regulation, which requires 3608 Troy grains—the Cologne Mark Weight—of fine silver to be alloyed and coined into $18\frac{1}{2}$ Dalers. (*See Rix Dollar.*)

Riksdaler Riksmynt. The Riksdaler, or Riksmynt Riksdaler was formerly the monetary unit of value in Sweden. It consists of silver ·750 fine, and weighs 8·502 grammes: reckoning $15\frac{1}{2}$ parts of *fine* silver to one of fine gold, its value in sterling is found to be 13·483*d.* or 1*s.* $1\frac{1}{2}$*d.* nearly. It is subdivided into 100 öre. Sweden being one of the kingdoms forming the Scandinavian Monetary Union, the Krone or Crown is now the unit of monetary value. (*See Rix Dollar.*)

Rio or **Kobang.** *See Kobang.*

Rin. The $\frac{1}{1000}$ part of the new Japanese unit of value, the *Yen.* It is represented by a small copper coin weighing $\frac{9}{10}$ of a gramme, and is worth $\frac{1}{20}$ of a penny.

Rixdaler. A silver coin issued in Holland in conformity with the Dutch Monetary Laws of 1847 and 1849. It weighs 25 grammes ·945 fine, and is worth $2\frac{1}{2}$ Dutch florins, or 5 francs 25 centimes, or 4*s.* 2*d.* nearly. (*See Rix Dollar.*)

Rixdaler Species. Formerly the unit of value in Norway, and still in active circulation. Its weight is 28·893 grammes of Silver ·875 fine, and is worth 53·46*d.* sterling. It is divided into 5 Orts or 120 Skilling. Norway being one of the parties to the Scandinavian Union, the Krone is now the unit of value. (*See Rix Dollar.*)

Rix-Dollar. The English way of writing the names of several different coins used on the Continent, and in the dependencies of some European States. The origin of *dollar* is explained under *Dollar*, which see. *Rix* is the German, *Reich*, empire, realm, kingdom, and undergoes changes adapting the syllable to other tongues, as the Danish, Swedish, Norwegian, Dutch, &c. Hence, we have the German, *Reichsthaler;* Danish, *Rigs-daler;* Swedish, *Riks-daler;* Dutch, *Rigs-daler*, all meaning the dollar of the realm—the Royal or Imperial dollar.

(*a.*) A silver coin made at the British mint for use in the island of Ceylon. It is valued at 1*s.* 6*d.*; English sterling money being also current there. It is divided into 12 fanams of $1\frac{1}{2}d.$ each.

(*b.*) Formerly the unit of value in Bremen, worth about 3*s.* $3\frac{2}{5}d.$ English. It is divided into 72 *groten*, each grot into 5 *Schwaren*, but is now being replaced by the new German coinage. It is also called the Frederick d'Or.

(*c.*) A silver coin used at the Cape of Good Hope, divided into 8 *Schillings*, and worth about 1*s.* 6*d.* sterling.

Rose Noble. An old English gold coin, valued at 6*s.* 8*d.*, now only to be found in cabinets.

Rose Royal. A gold coin of the time of James I., valued at 30*s.*

Royalty. French, *royauté;* Italian, *realtà*, from the Latin, *rex*, a king; Italian, *re*, and French, *roi.*

A *royalty* was originally something due to the king, such as a payment on mineral produce, on manufacturers, on imports or exports. The same word is now used to denote a payment made to any person in return for some privilege or concession; as for instance, the payment made by a manufacturer to the inventor of a machine, at a specified rate for every machine made or sold; or that of a coal owner to a landlord for every ton of coal extracted. (*See Seignorage.*)

Rubel, Ruble, or **Rouble.** The Russian unit of monetary value. It is divided into 100 copecks. Its value is best derived from the gold imperial or 10-ruble piece, which weighs 13·088 grammes, and is ·916 fine; giving for the ruble 1·3088 grammes, worth in sterling 39·388*d.* or 3*s.* $3\frac{1}{4}d.$ (*See Imperial.*)

The *Silver Ruble* was for some years valued at 38·02*d.* sterling, but owing to the fluctuations in the value of silver in late years, its precise value cannot be definitely stated. Its weight, according to the mint law of Russia, is 20·735 grammes, ·868 milliemes fine.

The paper ruble, which for many years has formed the legal currency of Russia, stood, before the Russo-Turkish war, at about

30*d.*; during that war it fell in value at one period to 22*d.*, from which depressed state it is now slowly recovering.

Running Policies. The same with open policies, and are so called when they cover the risk attaching to the property on board a ship, *during an entire season*, or up to some specified date, instead of during a single voyage.

Run upon a Bank. When in times of civil commotion, or foreign complications, the masses of the people become alarmed for the safety of their money at the bank, or the convertibility of the notes issued by the bank, it is not unusual for them to rush panic-stricken and withdraw their deposits, or demand gold for their notes. When such a phenomenen occurs, it is technically called a "run" upon the bank.

Rupee. The unit of value in British India. It consists of silver $\frac{11}{12}$ or .9166 fine, and weighs 1 tola Indian weight, 180 troy grains, or 11·664 grammes. Its value in English money necessarily varies with the price of silver, and as this has fluctuated in the course of a few years between 62*d.* and 47*d.* per ounce, its metallic value is not easy to determine. If, however, we take one part of *fine* gold as equivalent to $15\frac{1}{2}$ parts of *fine* silver, the rate adopted throughout this work, we find the rupee worth 22·60*d.* sterling or 1*s.* $10\frac{3}{5}$*d.* In all ordinary retail transactions it is taken at 2*s.* 0*d.*

This coin is known also as the Company's rupee, or the Government rupee, and was first so called in 1835. It is divided into 16 annas, and each anna into 12 pice.

The same rupee is now the monetary unit of Ceylon, and is divided into 100 cents.

There have been several different rupees circulating from time to time in India, of which the following are the most noteworthy:—

The *Arcot Rupee*, formerly circulating in Madras. It consisted of silver ·9166 fine, and weighed 180 troy grains.

The *Bombay Rupee* was the rupee of the Madras Presidency, of the same weight and fineness as the preceding.

The *Furrackabad Rupee*, formerly circulating in the North-Western Provinces. It was ·9166 fine, and weighed 179·16 troy grains.

The *Sicca Rupee* was the unit of value for the lower districts of Bengal. It was ·9166 fine, and weighed 191·9 grains troy.

The *Sonat Rupee* was simply the Sicca rupee abraded and diminished in weight by use. After two years of circulation, it was reckoned as $4\frac{1}{3}$ per cent. lighter than the Sicca.

The current rupee was the same coin still further deteriorated by use. (*See Lac of Rupees, and Crore of Rupees.*)

Rupee Paper. The same with *Enfaced Paper* (*which see*).

Rupee Loan. An Indian Loan issued in 1879, which, although an internal loan, like that represented by rupee paper, yet differs from it in having coupons attached to the bonds, which the enfaced paper has not.

S.

S occurs in the following abbreviations:—

S. G. Salutis Gratiâ (for the sake of safety) = insured.
S. P. Supra Protest.
S. L. or L. S. *Sigilli* or *Sigillo Locus*. (place for the Seal).

Sachib, Sahib, or Keran. The Real of Silver. A silver coin valued at one-fifth of the Persian Toman, or 20 Shahis. It weighs 10·40 grammes ·900 fine, worth Fr. 2·08 centimes, or 1*s.* 7½*d.* The coinage of Persia is very irregular, and some of the coins are much worn. The only way of estimating the value of the silver coins is to take a number of new and old ones and calculate the average.

Sale. A transaction in which a commodity is exchanged for *Money* or *Credit*, and is distinguished from *Barter*, in which one commodity is exchanged *directly* for another commodity. The party giving money or credit for a commodity is said to *buy* or effect a *purchase;* the one who gives a commodity for money or credit is said to *sell* or effect a *sale*. A *Sale* has been aptly termed "the half of an exchange," a phrase implying that the object of an exchange is to give one commodity for another commodity, whereas a Sale signifies the parting with a commodity in exchange for money and necessitating a second operation, called a purchase, before a second commodity can be had in place of the first. Although this view of a *sale* is supported by high authorities, it is deemed by others a fanciful distinction, inasmuch as the exchange is complete whether a dealer exchanges goods for goods or goods for money.

Salung or Miam. A Siamese silver coin equal to one-fourth of the Siamese *Tical*, and is divided into 2 Foangs. The value of the salung in English money is about 7½*d.*

Salvage. Latin, *salvare*, to save.

Goods or property saved from a wreck, or abandoned vessel.

The same term is also applied to the *payment made* to those who assist in saving either the vessel itself, or the cargo taken out of it when abandoned.

Sans Recours. (*See Recourse.*)

Sapeck, *Dong*, or *Cash*. $\frac{1}{100}$ part of the Kivan. A coin used in Cochin China, worth about $\frac{1}{18}$ of a penny.

Satisfaction. From Latin, *satisfacĕre*, to satisfy, to appease, to pay or discharge a debt.

Satisfaction is a term derived from the commercial language of the Romans, to signify the complete discharge and extinguishment of debt. It differs essentially from *payment*, which is often effected by means of a cheque, a bill, a note, or goods delivered. But this is not a complete "satisfaction" of the debt. The cheque must be presented and entered in the bank-book. The bill or note must mature, and be honoured at maturity, and the goods proved to be what they purport to be, before the debt is "satisfied" and extinguished.

It is, however, of great importance to observe that if a receipt or acknowledgment be given for goods, a bill or cheque, in "satisfaction," or "full satisfaction" of a debt, the creditor has no further claim, and he must bear any consequences resulting from his want of caution, should the instrument be dishonoured or the goods prove unsound. (*See Laches.*)

Schedule. From the Greek, σχιδη, a splinter, a piece cut off, or cleft. Hence the Latin forms *scheda* and *scida*, a piece cut off from anything, and especially a leaf cut from the plant *papyrus*, from which the ancient paper was made.

"Ut *scida* ne qua depereat" (that the leaf—or document—on no account may perish).—CICERO.

"Omnes *schedas* excutit" (he examined all the papers).—QUINTILIAN.

From these two words were formed the diminutives *schedula* and *scidula*, a small leaf of paper, and the English, *schedule*.

A *schedule*—which the dictionaries tell us should be pronounced *sed-ul*, and which is so pronounced by some lawyers—is mostly called a *shed-ule* in City circles. It usually signifies a short document appended to, or accompanying some larger work, and is generally expected to be in the form of a list or catalogue, or to consist of some details not essential to the body of the volume or document to which it is attached.

Schilling. (*a.*) A Hamburg silver coin worth about $\frac{5}{8}$ of an English penny.

(*b.*) A Mecklenburg coin worth about $\frac{35}{48}$ of an English penny, or $\frac{1}{48}$ of the thaler.

(*c.*) A Billon coin formerly circulating in the Hanse Towns, worth about one penny English.

(*d.*) A coin used in the Cape of Good Hope equal to 6 stivers, and worth about $2\frac{1}{4}d.$ English.

Schuite. A silver, boat-shaped coin used in Japan, valued at £1 5*s.* 3*d.* English.

Schwaren. A small copper coin used in Bremen, value about $\frac{1}{10}$ of an English penny.

Scrip. A Stock Exchange term contracted from "subscription." When a foreign loan is issued, or a new company is about to borrow capital, the public are invited to "subscribe" to it, that is, in plain language they are asked to say how much money they are willing to lend for either of those purposes. This invitation is presented in the form of a "prospectus." The lender or subscriber "applies" for a share in the loan, or for the privilege of contributing to a company's capital, and in answer receives a "letter of allotment."

This letter of allotment is afterwards exchanged for "scrip," that is a kind of provisional document entitling him to claim definitive bonds or share certificates, indicating how many bonds or shares he has *subscribed*. It further indicates the amount and date of each instalment that is to be paid on the scrip, and when these instalments are all paid, it is exchanged for a definitive Bond or Share Certificate. A piece of "scrip," therefore, expresses the total amount to be paid by the subscribers, and also each of the fractional sums to be paid at the respective dates therein named. A copy of a piece of "Scrip" of the Egyptian State Domain Loan is appended on the opposite page.

Scudo. (*a*) The Scudo or Roman Crown was the former unit of value in the Roman States; divided into 10 Paoli, or 100 Bajocchi, equal to about 4*s*. 3*d*. English. It is now superseded by the new *Scudo* of 10 *Lire*, which assimilates it to the French system.

(*b*) The Scudo of Austria, now disused, was a silver coin worth about 4*s*. 3*d*., English.

(*c*) The Scudo of Naples, also disused, was a silver coin worth about 4*s*. English.

(*d*) The Scudo d'Oro was, as its name implies, a gold coin, circulating in Genoa, and was worth about 4*s*., English.

Sechser. A German copper coin worth about 2*d*. English. It means literally a "sixer," and was so called because it represented 6 Kreutzers, or $\frac{1}{10}$ of the old Florin.

Sechsling, or sixpfennige piece. A small Hamburg coin of very impure silver, value 6 pfennige, or rather more than a farthing, English. It is disappearing now that the new German Monetary System is introduced.

Security. Latin, *securus*, safe, quiet, free from anxiety; *securitas*, safety, assurance, confidence; used by Pliny in the sense of a receipt or acquittance; also synonymous with the Latin, *cautio*, in some of its applications. From *cura*, care, with separative prefix *se*.

A bond, document, or other instrument giving the holder a title. (1) to a sum of money, or (2) to certain specified goods, or (3) to property in land or buildings. (*See Securities.*)

Securities. (*a*) *Securities for Money*. A Security for Money is a written or printed document giving a claim to the holder for the payment of a specified sum of money from some person, and at a time named on the face thereof. Its distinctive characteristic is that it is always a claim *on the person* for a stated sum, and not for any specific money.

(*b*) *Convertible Securities* are so called because they are easily convertible into money, although *no particular person* is bound to pay them. They give the holder a title or claim, sometimes to certain specified goods, as Dock Warrants, or to portions of the State revenues, as Government Bonds. Hence among *Convertible Securities* we find Consols, Railway Shares, Dock Warrants, and Bills of Lading. Among *Securities for Money*, Bank Notes, Bills of Exchange, Exchequer Bills and the like.

£20 **A.** **No.** ....

EGYPTIAN STATE-DOMAIN MORTGAGE BONDS,

1878,

FOR

£8,500,000 STERLING NOMINAL CAPITAL

IN 5 PER CENT. BONDS.

BEARING INTEREST from 1st DECEMBER, 1878,
payable HALF-YEARLY.

Scrip for Twenty Pounds Nominal Capital.

Received the Sum of Four Pounds, being the First Instalment of Twenty per cent. upon **TWENTY POUNDS** Nominal Capital; and on payment of the remaining Instalments, at the period specified, the Bearer will be entitled to receive in exchange for this Scrip a definitive Bond for **TWENTY POUNDS** Nominal Capital, as soon as the same is ready for delivery.

London, 18th November, 1878.

The Instalments are to be paid at our Office, as follows:—

£4 on the 16th January, 1879.
£4 „ 17th April, „
£2 12*s*. „ 19th May, „

Subscribers may pay up the same under a Discount of 5 per Cent. per annum on any Monday or Thursday. In default of payment of any of the Instalments at their proper dates all previous payments will be liable to forfeiture.

London, 16*th January*, 1879.

Received *the further Sum of* **FOUR POUNDS,** *being the Second Instalment of* 20 *per Cent.*

Entered. No...................................

....

London, 17*th April*, 1879.

Received *the further Sum of* **FOUR POUNDS,** *being the Third Instalment of* 20 *per Cent.*

Entered. No...................................

....

London, 19*th May*, 1879.

Received *the further Sum of* **TWO POUNDS TWELVE SHILLINGS,** *being the Final Instalment of* 13 *per Cent.*

Entered. No...................................

....

10s. Egyptian State-Domain Mortgage Bonds. No. ....

On the 1st June, 1879, this Warrant for **TEN SHILLINGS,** Interest for Six Months on **TWENTY POUNDS** Nominal Capital, will be paid at the Office of Messrs. A. B.—— & Co., London.

(c) *Securities to Bearer.* Bonds, Shares, Certificates, Debentures and all Instruments which are freely negotiable, and pass from hand to hand without registration or formal transfer. The vast majority of Foreign Loan Bonds, Railway Debentures, are of this character, and are thus distinguished from Railway Shares, Shares in Joint Stock Companies, Registered Stocks, most of which are encumbered in the transfer by sundry formalities, by the signing of documents, by transfer fees, and stamp duty.

Seigniorage, or Seignorage. Latin, *senex*, old; *senior*, older, an elder. This word dates back to those primitive times when the elder or senior member of a family was lord and king of the clan or tribe, and thus became a title of the highest dignity, as in the case of the Grand Seignior, or Grand Seignieur, which is the title still conferred on some Eastern potentates, and especially those of Turkey. In western Europe it signifies generally a lord, or lord of the manor, and is often applied as a mere title of courtesy, as in the French, *seigneur*; Italian, *signore;* Portuguese, *senhor;* and Spanish, *senor*. In old English, *seignior* was the title applied to the lord of the manor, or to any great landowner, and the dues which he claimed from his dependants and tenants were called *seigniorage or seigniory*. Seniorage was a term applied also to the dues payable to the sovereign lord or king, and especially to that deduction made upon all gold and silver brought to the royal mint, exchange, or "bullion," to be coined into money.

Seigniorage, seigneurage, or seignorage, as used in commerce, signifies the charge or deductions made by the master of the mint to cover the cost of coining gold and silver for the use of the public. In England no charge is made for the coinage of gold. Any person taking to the mint 40 troy pounds of gold $\frac{11}{12}$ or ·916$\frac{2}{3}$ fine, may have in return 1,869 sovereigns, each weighing on an average 123·27447 troy grains. Since there are 480 grains to the troy ounce, we find the value of 1 ounce of standard gold equal to £3 17*s.* 10$\frac{1}{2}$*d.*, and any amount of standard gold whatever may be exchanged at the mint at the rate of £3 17*s.* 10$\frac{1}{2}$*d.* per troy ounce. In practice, however, this is never done. Bullion is invariably taken to the Bank of England to be exchanged for coin; but instead of receiving sovereigns at the rate of £3 17*s.* 10$\frac{1}{2}$*d.* per ounce, he receives £3 17*s.* 9*d.* *there* and *then*, the difference of 1$\frac{1}{2}$*d.* per ounce, which he gives up, being but a very small compensation for the expense and anxiety attending the conveyance of the gold to the mint, and for the interest he saves by having the money paid over to him without delay. This 1$\frac{1}{2}$*d.* per ounce is therefore in no sense a *seigniorage* paid to the Government, but simply a payment for services rendered by the bank.

In the case of silver and bronze coinage these observations do not apply. For the coinage of silver a charge is made, and for bronze a still heavier charge. This charge is, properly speaking, a *seigniorage.*

In France, a seigniorage is paid upon both gold and silver coinage at the rate of 6 francs 70c. per kilogramme of gold ·900 fine, and of 1 franc 50c. per kilogramme of silver of the same degree of fineness.

In most other mints of the world, a seigniorage is levied on the coinage, and in some it is so heavy as to go a long way towards paying the expenses of the establishment.

Selling Out. The converse operation of "buying in" (*which see*). If a broker sells a quantity of stock for delivery on a given day, and the buyer fails to pay for it by half-past two o'clock on that day, the broker may sell the stock again in the market at the price then current; if any loss occurs, it must be paid by the original buyer. Both "buying in" and "selling out" are conducted publicly by one of the officials of the Stock Exchange, and not by the members themselves.

Sequestration. Latin, *sequestrare*, to separate, to deposit, to seize.

A legal process called *sequestrari facias*, in virtue of which a sheriff, or other officer, is empowered to hold goods or property belonging to a person pending the settlement of a dispute or payment of a debt.

Sequin. Variously derived from the Italian, *zecca*, the mint, or the town, *Zecha*, where the coin was first struck. The name has undergone manifold changes, and is written *Sequin, Chequin, Zechin, Zequin, Zechino, Zequin.*

Although the *Sequin* still circulates in some continental States, it is superseded, as a national coin, by others of more recent introduction:—

(*a.*) The *sequin, chequin*, or *sultany*, is a gold coin whose metallic value is about 9*s.* 3*d.*

(*b.*) The Italian *zequin*, or *zechino*, is valued at 22 paoli, or 9*s.* 2*d.*

(*c.*) The *Venetian sequin* circulates in Egypt at a fixed "tariff value" of 46 piastres, 17 paras; or 9s. 6*d.*

(*d.*) The *Austrian sequin* also circulates in Egypt at a "tariff value" of 45 piastres, 26 paras; or 9*s.* 4*d.*

(*e.*) The *Abyssinnian sequin* is valued at 2¼ patakas, or about 9*s.* 4½*d.* sterling.

(*f.*) The *sequin* of Tuscany is a gold coin worth about 9*s.* 5*d.* sterling.

Services. This homely word has of late years been made to do duty as a scientific term in the nomenclature of political economy. Owing to the supposed ambiguity and indefiniteness of certain terms long current in that science, such as wealth, money, commodity, &c., and the difficulty of fixing attention on the essential idea involved in exchanges, it has been suggested, and the suggestion has been largely adopted, that the fundamental fact underlying all our notions of value is that of *service*, or services rendered. Whether you possess a coin, a house, a coat, or a sheet of paper, in so far as it has value at all it is the embodiment of services rendered; and all exchanges of things of value hence become simply an exchange of services. There is certainly one merit in the use of this term which ought not to be overlooked, namely, the *twofold notion* which it keeps constantly before the mind of the person employing it. If a service is rendered, it is rendered *by* someone, and *to* someone; whereas, people are constantly speaking of articles of wealth and value, and in a way which shews they are ignoring the important truth that value depends upon something altogether outside the object of value—*that is, the desire* of someone to obtain it.

A service depends for its magnitude on two things:—(1.) The needs and desires of the recipient of the service, and (2) the amount of labour expended in rendering it. If a man bestow never so much labour, whether of brain or limb, in making and presenting to me a number of harpoons, he renders me a very small service; I do not need harpoons, and do not desire them, nor do my friends. I could do nothing with them, but part with them at considerable trouble and expense. On the other hand, if I am suffering from some painful and dangerous malady, the nature of which I do not understand, and I go to a physician, and he at a glance at the symptoms at once determines their cause, and prescribes a remedy, the service rendered is immense, although effected with so little effort, and in so short a space of time. In general terms it may be said that when equal needs are satisfied, the service is greater when the labour and difficulty of rendering it are greater, and conversely when the difficulty of rendering any two services is equal, that is the greater service which satisfies the most urgent need, or the most intense desire.

This language is justified by those who use it, on the ground that every article having a purchasing power, in other words, every article that is exchangeable is the embodiment of services rendered. If a bootmaker exchanges a pair of boots for a quantity of wine, it is because the services rendered by all the persons who have contributed to the making of the boots are deemed equal to the services of all the persons who have contributed to the making of the wine. If, instead of a direct exchange, the goods pass from one hand to the other, through the intervention of money, the function discharged by this money is, as McLeod says, "to enable persons to obtain the equivalent of the service they have done to one person from some one else."

Hence the inference is that money is simply a *Right* or *Title* on the part of the holder to demand a certain amount of service from someone else.

Set-off. The extinguishment of *debt payable* by means of *debt due.* When the two debts are of equal amount the settlement is complete without the passing of money from one to the other; but when they are unequal, the balance of the greater debt must be paid either in money or by the creation of a new debt equal to the balance. (*See Compensation.*)

Settling-Day. In most markets there is a day appointed for the periodical settlement of bargains. In city circles, the "settling-day" *par excellence* is the settling-day on the Stock Exchange, which occurs twice every month, one as near as may be about the middle, and the second about the end of the month. It is preceded by the

Ticket-day (the day before the settlement) and the *Contango-day* (the day preceding the Ticket-day); so that every fortnightly settlement occupies three days. So vast are the ramifications of Stock Exchange business, that few banks or mercantile offices exist in London in which no transactions of greater or less amount have to be closed on that day.

Sen. The $\frac{1}{100}$ part of the new Japanese unit of value, or Yen. It is made of copper, weighs 7·13 grammes, and is worth almost exactly $\frac{1}{2}$d. English as a token Coin.

The *Silver Sen.* In conformity with the Japanese Monetary Law of 1871, silver pieces of 50, 20, 10, and 5 Sen each have been struck. The 10-sen piece weighs 2·500 grammes ·800 fine, and is worth 45 centimes French, or $4\frac{1}{4}$*d.* English. Hence the single Silver Sen is worth ·4176*d.*, or a trifle more than 4-10ths of a penny.

Sencilla. Another name for the Macuquino Dollar of Columbia. (*See Dollar.*)

Shahee, Shahi or **Schahi.** The $\frac{1}{100}$ part of the Persian Toman. Silver pieces of four Shahis are coined, worth about 4*d.* sterling; from which we find the value of the Shahi almost exactly one penny English. Many of the coins, however, are so inferior as to give a value of not more than one-half of this for the Shahi.

Shares. Saxon, *scear*, a piece cut off; *scearan*, or *scyran*, to cut or divide.

A portion of the capital of a trading company. It is usual for companies of any magnitude to divide their capital into a large number of equal parts, when each part is called a *Share.* The profits accruing to the shareholders are divided annually or semi-annually into as many parts as there are shares, and each shareholder receives as many of these parts as will correspond to the number of shares he holds. Shares of this nature are called *Ordinary* Shares, and are to be distinguished from *Preference* Shares on the one hand, and from *Deferred* Shares on the other. (*See Preference and Deferred.*)

Shilling. From the Saxon, *scill* and *scilling*, which appears to have been the name applied to a sum of money and not to a coin. The scilling consisted sometimes of four pennies, but more commonly of five. At the Norman Conquest, the Saxon scilling passed out of use, and was superseded by the Norman shilling of 12 pence, in which the values recorded in Domesday Book are stated. *Shilling* was also the name of a weight, and stood in the same relation to a *pound of merchandise* as the shilling of monetary value to the *pound of silver*. Thus, "If the corn be at twelvepence a quarter, the farthing loaf shall weigh *six pounds sixteen shillings*" (Statute of Henry II., 1266), that is, 6 pounds and 16-20 of a pound, the pound weight being divided at that time into 20 parts. The word itself is said to be derived from the Hebrew, *shekel*, through the mediæval Latin, *ciclus;* Old French, *cicle*, whence the Anglo-Saxon, *scill*.

Previous to the reign of Henry VII., the *shilling* was a name given to a number of silver pennies, and not to any coin. In the time of the Saxons, it was reckoned sometimes at four pennies, at others five. In the reign of the Conqueror it was fixed at twelve pennies, and so has ever since remained. But although the numerical relation between the penny, the shilling, and the pound has always since the Conquest been the same, the monetary value of each of these coins has undergone great alterations; in other words, the weight of silver they contained has greatly varied. The following table shows that immediately after the Conquest our Norman kings began to make a charge or seigniorage, for the coinage of silver, inasmuch as the pound troy of silver instead of being coined into 240 pennies, was divided into 256, the 16 pennies being a recompense to the king's moneyers for the cost of coining. From this time the *pound in money* was no longer a *pound in weight*, and subsequent kings carried the process of depreciation so far as to reduce the pound *sterling* to less than one-third the pound troy *in weight*.

Date.		The Troy Pound was Coined into—			
William I.	...	256	pennies		
Edward III.,	1349	258	,,		
,, ,,	1356	320	,,		
Edward IV.	...	480	,,		Shillings
Henry VII.	...	480	,,	or	40
Henry VIII.	1527	512	,,	,,	42⅔
Elizabeth	1560			into	60
,,	1600			,,	62
George III.	...			,,	66

The *shilling*, as a coin, was first struck in the reign of Henry VII. It was reckoned equal to 12 silver pennies, and 20 of these shillings went to the monetary pound. The fineness of the silver was that known from time immemorial as "The Ancient Right Standard," that is, 11 oz. 2 dwt. fine silver to 18 dwts. alloy. As the shilling was $\frac{1}{20}$ of the pound, its weight, according to the ancient method of computation, should have been $\frac{5760}{20}$ = 288 grains troy. But since 480 pennies, or 40 shillings, were coined from the pound troy, the weight of each shilling was exactly one half of this, or 144 grains. In 1560 the pound troy was coined into 60 shillings, in 1600 into 62 shillings, and by the Act 56, George III., it was ordered to be coined into 66 shillings, which is the rate at which shillings are now struck.

The modern English shilling is therefore the $\frac{1}{66}$ part. 5760 grains = 87·27272 grains, or 5·65518 grammes of silver ·925 fine, which is the "Ancient Right Standard" expressed decimally.

Short Bills. Bills having less than *ten* days to run are considered *Short Bills*. Hence the name is often applied to *Three Months* Bills, or *Six Months* Bills, when they have nearly matured, as well as to Bills on Demand and Sight Bills.

Short Exchange. The rate of exchange quoted in the market for bills payable ten, twenty, thirty or more days *after* sight. The term "long exchange," as opposed to "short exchange," is seldom used, as it is too indefinite, the number of days or months which bills have to run being an important element in their market value.

Sight Bills. Bills drawn payable *at* Sight, or on Demand, in which case no days of grace are allowed. When bills are made payable *after* sight, the customary days of grace are allowed.

Sighting a Bill. A bill is said to be *sighted*, when, being drawn payable at sight, or so many days *after* sight, it is presented for acceptance to the person on whom it is drawn, so as to bring it under *his sight*. This should be done as soon after receipt as possible.

Signature. The name or *sign* of a party appended to a document. In the case of bills, notes, and some other instruments, the signature may be made by means of a *mark* or by a *stamp*.

Silver Groschen. A billon coin used in Prussia, the $\frac{1}{30}$ part of the thaler. It is now being displaced by the new system of coinage issued by the German Government. Its value is a little less than $1\frac{1}{4}d.$ English.

Silver Standard. (*See Standard of Value.*)

Sinking Fund. When public loans are contracted, it is a common practice for the borrowing State or Company to make such terms with the lenders as will satisfy their demands for interest, and at the same time extinguish the loan by degrees, until it is finally paid off. In order to effect this object, it is usual for the borrowing party to pay a fixed rate per cent. on the whole loan, one portion of which rate is regarded as interest, and the remainder is devoted to the extinction or amortization of the debt. Thus, if a loan be contracted, and the borrower is prepared to pay 6 per cent. on the whole sum borrowed until the loan is extinguished, 5 per cent. might be paid to the lenders as interest, and 1 per cent. might be applied to the paying off the debt. The 1 per cent. in this case, with its accumulations, would constitute what is called a "Sinking Fund," because by its application the original amount of the debt would continue "sinking" until it finally disappeared. It is usual to apply a sinking fund in this manner, because it possesses two distinct advantages: (1) it provides a means of making a fixed charge for the service of the loan, and the borrower knows from the first precisely what that charge will be, and (2) by the paying off of portions of the loan from year to year, the quantity remaining in the market is constantly diminishing, and the bondholders have the satisfaction of seeing their holdings always increasing in value. The Brazilian 1865 loan was issued on these terms, and as the 1 per cent. continues to be paid when the debt has diminished, just the same as at first, and as the amount to be paid in interest is always growing less, this loan will be finally extinguished in rather less than 37 years. In fact, the 1 per cent. is as effective as though it were invested in the Brazilian Loan at 5 per cent. *compound interest*, and it may be easily shown that one pound per annum at 5°/₀ compound interest will amount to £100 in rather less than 37 years.

Sinking Funds are sometimes applied to the purchase in the market of the bonds of the loan to which the sinking fund refers. But this practice offers a temptation to dishonest Governments to depreciate their own stocks. Spain, for a time, bought up bonds at 15, for which her creditors paid her nearly 30 a few years before.

Skilling. A coin still circulating in Denmark, but being gradually superseded by the system of the Scandinavian Monetary Union. It is the 96th part of the Rigsdaler, and worth $\frac{52}{19}$ *d.* English.

The *Skilling* of Norway is the 24th part of the Ort, worth about $\frac{4}{9}$ of a penny English.

Sleeping Partner. A partner in a mercantile firm who puts a certain capital into the business, and receives a proportional share of the profits of the business, but who takes no active part in the management, nor assists in conducting its affairs.

Sol. The unit of value and of account in Peru. By the Monetary Law of February, 1864, it is represented by both gold and silver coins.

The *Gold Sol* weighs 1·613 grammes, ·900 fine, and is worth 5 francs or £·1982 or 3*s.* 11½*d.* sterling.

The *Silver Sol* weighs 25 grammes, ·900 fine, and has the same nominal value as the gold sol, and the French five-franc piece.

Gold pieces of 20, 10, 5, 2, and 1 sols are struck, and silver pieces of 1 sol, ½ sol, and ⅕ sol.

Sola. Latin, *solus*, alone, solitary.

Single, or alone. Applied to a Bill of Exchange it indicates that only one copy of the Bill is in circulation, and is thus distinguished from Bills drawn in groups of *two* or *three*, when each copy is called respectively the *first second*, or *third* of exchange. The object of drawing bills in groups of two or three is to ensure safety in transmission by post or otherwise. As all these copies must come eventually into the hands of the party who has to accept them, the Acceptor signs but one of them, and withdraws the others from circulation as soon as they fall into his hands.

Soldo. (*a.*) The 20th part of the Roman Lira, worth about 9½*d.* sterling.

(*b.*) The 20th part of the Tuscan Lira, worth about 7¾*d.* sterling. (*See Solidus.*)

Solidus. Latin, *solidus*, thick, dense, not loose or in pieces. *Solidus* appears to have been applied by Latin writers to a *single coin*, as distinguished from, though equal to, the total value of *several* smaller coins. In mediæval Latin, the *solidus* was sometimes an imaginary coin like the Saxon *solidus* or *scilling*, which was equal to 5 silver pennies, or the Norman shilling, equal to 12 silver pennies; but no coin called a shilling was struck in England till the reign of Henry VII. *Solidus* was sometimes contracted by the early Latin writers in *soldus*, and this appears to be the origin of the *Soldo* of Rome and Tuscany.

Solidus, the Anglo-Saxon shilling or scilling, equal sometimes to 4 pennies, at others, and more commonly, to 5 pennies. The name was applied to a number of coins and not to any single coin, for no single piece called a solidus or scilling appears to have been struck in Saxon times.

The old Roman *Solidus* was a gold coin worth about twelve shillings of our money, and is frequently mentioned by Latin authors.

Sou. (*a.*) A French coin formerly a part of the national system of currency. It was so near in value to the present five-centime piece, that the common people still adhere to the practice of calling the five-centime piece a *sou*.

(*b.*) A coin used in the Mauritius, 20 to the livre, worth nearly $\frac{1}{4}$*d.* English.

Sovereign. From the Latin root, *super*, over, above, whence *supernus*, high lofty, on high; and in Ovid, celestial. In French it took the form of *souverain*, with the sense of superlative, superior, supreme, and when applied to a person, one of supreme power, a king, a sovereign. Passing into the English language, the *u* of the Latin was dropped, and the *o* of the French retained; but the old French pronunciation still clung to it, and down till within the memory of many persons still living it was called a *suvran* or *suvrin*. It is now always called a *sovrin*, except by those whose education was controlled by the habits of a former generation.

The application of the term *sovereign* to a coin is in accordance with the practice of most nations, of calling their best coins by a name which associates them with the titular dignity of their chief ruler, as *Imperial* from an emperor, *Ducat* from a duke, *Royal* from a king, *Rei* from rex, &c.

By the Coinage Act of 1816, the gold coinage of England consists of gold 22 carats, is $\frac{11}{12}$ or ·916 fine, which is called Standard Gold. The value of the sovereign is deduced from the fact that 40lbs. Troy of standard gold is coined into 1869 sovereigns from which the following useful memoranda are obtained. (*See Price of Gold.*)

40lbs. Troy	=	1869 sovereigns (or pounds sterling).
1lb ,,	=	£46 14*s.* 6*d.*
1 oz. ,,	=	3 17 10$\frac{1}{2}$
123·27447 grains	=	1 0 0

The alloy in our present gold coinage consists mainly of copper, but with a small proportion of silver.

The remedies, or allowances for imperfections of workmanship, are detailed under article *Remedy*.

The wear and tear of the coinage, caused by continued use, does not unfit a sovereign to circulate as legal tender so long as it weighs 122·5 grains. When reduced to that weight or below it, it is reckoned only as bullion.

A coin called a sovereign was first struck in England during the reign of Henry VII. The same coin was sometimes called the Rose Rial, sometimes the Double Rose, names already familiar with the English people, and more comprehensible than the new name of sovereign. Leake, in his "Historical Account of English

Money" says, "they were struck upon extraordinary occasions only, in the nature of medals, and perhaps, were first coined in honour of the king's coronation, as his figure thereon, in the attitude of that solemnity, seems to intimate. . . . . We are told such were distributed at the coronation of Queen Mary, and sovereigns were coined in every reign afterwards to King James I. inclusive."

In the reign of James I., the standard of fineness for gold was fixed at 22 carats; but the number of coins struck from a Troy pound varied considerably, thus:—

In 1604 it was coined into £33 10*s*. Shortly afterwards it was coined into £37 4*s*. 6*d*.; and still later into £40 10*s*. The twenty shilling piece at this time was called the "Unity," but the name did not take root in the English language, and that of "sovereign" was by this time growing more familiar.

In 1612 the pound of gold was coined into £40 18*s*. 4*d*., for "unities," or twenty shilling pieces; or, as they were popularly called, "broad pieces."

In 1626, the second year of Charles I., two kinds of gold were used, one of 23 carats, 3½ grains fine, one pound of which was coined into £44 10*s*., and the other 22 carats fine, one pound being coined into £41. Owing to the exigencies of this reign many irregularities were afterwards introduced into the coinage.

In 1816, after sundry fluctuations, the gold coinage of England was fixed by Act of Parliament both in regard to weight and fineness, and no alteration of importance has since been made.

The *Sovereign* was a name also applied to a coin formerly used in Austria, valued at 3 ducats, and worth about £1 8*s*. sterling.

Special Endorsement. (*See Endorsement.*)

Specie. From Latin, *specio*, I look at, or see. Whence *species*, something seen, a form, appearance. More definitely something seen with the eyes, as distinguished from something imagined, or seen by the mind; *species argenti*, pieces of money, coin.

A general term signifying metallic money, in contradistinction to paper, bills, and other instruments of credit.

Species-Daler or Riksdaler Species.

(*a*) The former unit of value in Norway, divided into 5 Orts or 120 Skilling. It consists of 28·893 grammes of silver, ·875 fine, and is worth 53·46*d*.

(*b*) A Swedish silver coin, now partially superseded by the new coinage. It was worth 4 Swedish Riksdalers, or 4*s*. 5*d*. sterling.

(*c*) A Danish coin, valued at 2 Danish Rigsdalers, and worth about 4*s*. 5*d*. sterling. This also is giving place to the new coinage of the Scandinavian Monetary Union.

Specie Payments. Payments in coin or bullion as distinguished from payments by means of inconvertible paper money.

Specie Point. That point above or below the mint par of exchange, at which it becomes more profitable to export or transmit bullion than to buy commercial bills. The cost of transmitting bullion varies from ½ per cent. to 2 per cent., according to distance, risks, and other circumstances, and hence it is only under exceptional conditions that the price of commercial bills rises above or falls below these limits. The conditions under which these limits are exceeded are notably those of commercial panic or imminent war.

The cost of transmitting gold between London and Paris is less than between any other two commercial centres, and hence the *specie point* is more quickly reached in the exchanges between these two centres than most others. Mr. Ernest Seyd furnishes a minute calculation (*Bullion and Foreign Exchanges*, p. 394), from which it appears that—

"When the French exchange is at 25·10 it pays to send gold from England to France."

"And when the exchange is at 25·35 it pays to send gold from France to England."

"The Mint Par being taken at 25·22½ we have thus a margin of 12½ centimes, or ½ per cent. either way, and 25 centimes or 1 per cent. between the two extreme points."

But as above said, there are conditions under which all ordinary limits are much exceeded, and Mr. Goschen, in his *Theory of Foreign Exchanges*, furnishes a case in point. It was in the early part of the year 1861, when civil war was apprehended in the United States.. At that time large quantities of grain and flour had been exported to London and elsewhere, and few products had been imported. American merchants had therefore large claims against foreign countries, while foreign countries had fewer claims than usual against them, and the rate of exchange fell not only to *specie-point*, but far below it. Mr. Goschen says:—

"The reason must be sought in the peculiarly urgent necessity under which the exporters were labouring of selling their bills immediately at any sacrifice. It was a question of time. Three or four per cent. were sacrificed to secure the proceeds of bills to England at once, instead of waiting for the arrival of gold. The exporter had two courses before him—either to sell his bills at what they would fetch, or send them himself to Europe, with instructions to his correspondents to encash them, and remit the amount in bullion. The latter course was cheaper, but as he required funds immediately (or under the influence of panic, believed he would so require them), he adopted the former."

"In ordinary times, capitalists would have competed with each other in buying up the drafts of urgent sellers. They would then have remitted them to Europe for their own account, so as to secure the profit between the low price paid for the bills and their specie value; that is to say, they would have bought at a heavy discount much below *specie point*, in order subsequently to realize at least specie value. But at a time of commercial panic, such capitalists are seldom willing to launch out into a speculation which deprives them during the weeks which must elapse before the gold arrives of the command over their funds." This cause, however, will not come into operation when commercial transactions are pretty evenly balanced, because there will then be as many purchasers on compulsion as there are sellers, and the exchanges will fluctuate between the two specie points, the limits of which have been above indicated.

Speculation. Latin, *specio*, I look, or the frequentative form, *specto-are*, to keep on looking, hoping, expecting.

Speculation in commerce is a term of rather wide signification, and means primarily the expenditure of capital with a view to profit. The establishment of any new business or the opening of a shop is in this sense a speculation, and is often so called.

The term is, however, employed in a more restricted sense, and is, when so employed, intended to convey the idea of hazard and risk. Enterprises of all kinds are therefore more or less speculative, as for example the opening up of a mine, or the making of railways, for it is always doubtful whether a mine will be productive, or whether a railway will attract traffic enough to make it pay, even when engineering difficulties have all been surmounted. In all such enterprises the speculator "looks forward," "hopes," "expects" to make a profit sufficiently large to compensate not only for his outlay and labour, but also for the risk he runs. These results being uncertain, his mental attitude is "speculative," and the enterprise itself is called a "speculation."

There is another sense still more restricted in which the word is used on the Stock Exchange. Among the members of the body, it is usual to class *bona-fide* purchases as simply investments, however risky may be the stocks or shares taken up, and the term "speculation" is confined to "time bargains" (*See Time Bargain*), that is, buying or selling for the fortnightly account. In these transactions a purchaser buys what he never intends to take up, or sells what he has no intention of delivering. If, when the day of settlement comes, prices have so moved as to yield him a profit, he takes the profit; if, on the contrary, prices have moved so as to entail a loss, he pays the amount of the loss, and closes the bargain. This operation is what is called *speculation*, in its narrow sense, among City men.

Standard Gold. A mixture of metal containing 11 parts of pure gold, with 1 part of alloy—*i. e.*, 22 carats fine, with 2 carats of alloy. It is represented in the *milliemes* system as ·916 ⅔ fine.

Standard of Value. By a *Standard of Value* is meant some substance or commodity with which all other commodities may be compared, when we wish to denote the proportions in which they exchange for each other. Any substance whatever might be chosen for this purpose, and a great number of different substances have been employed in different countries, but the qualities essential to a good standard of value are found in very few substances. These qualities, as enumerated by Professor Jevons, are:—

1. *Utility and Value;* that is, it must be some substance generally desired and esteemed.

2. *Portability;* that is, capable of being carried about or passed readily from hand to hand.

3. *Indestructibility;* that is, it must be some material not liable to rust, decay, or waste.

4. *Homogeneity;* every portion of the substance must be similar in properties to every other portion.

5. *Divisibility;* it must be capable of being cut or moulded into fragments of any size or weight.

6. *Stability of Value;* this is a most important quality, and one very difficult to find.

7. *Cognizability;* that is, easy to be distinguished, in virtue of its colour, specific gravity, hardness, shape, &c.

For these reasons the precious metals have been regarded in all ages as possessing the above properties in the most eminent degree, and in all countries making any pretence to civilization, either gold or silver has been adopted as the standard of monetary value. The following is a list of the most important countries in the world divided into three groups, those using (1) a gold standard, (2) a silver standard, (3) a double or variable standard. Of these last it may be said that the term "variable" is preferable to that of "double," inasmuch as a "double standard" never exists at one and the same time; gold or silver becoming alternately the standard, as the state of the exchanges makes the one or the other the more desirable as the practical medium of exchange.

Gold.	Silver.	Double or Variable.	
Great Britain & Ireland	Russia	France	Latin Monetary Convention.
Australia	Austria	Italy	
New Zealand	Hungary	Belgium	
British Colonies in Africa	India	Switzerland	
Portugal	China	Greece	
Turkey	Cochin China	Spain	
Egypt	East Indian Isles	Roumania	
Chili	West Indies	Peru	
Brazil	Mexico	Ecuador	
Germany	Central American Republics	New Granada	
Denmark	Canada		
Norway			
Sweden			
Japan			
United States			
Holland			

N.B.—At the last moment before going to press, the United States and some European countries are discussing the expediency of resuming the Double or Variable Standard.

It is important to observe that the existence of a double or variable standard in such influential countries as France, United States, and Italy, has a tendency to maintain a fixed relation between the commercial value of the two metals gold and silver. In France, fine gold in virtue of the Mint regulations is always 15½ times the value of silver, and as each is a legal tender payments will always be made in that metal which is most abundant and cheap; a demand for it will hence immediately arise, and will continue till its price is brought up to a par with the dearest metal. This view has been very ably defended by M. Wolowski, but experience has forced upon the French nation a departure from the principle thus maintained. Owing to the cheapness of silver, debts were paid in that metal almost exclusively, and gold was sent abroad. This caused such a drain of gold, that the French Mint refused to coin more than a limited number of the five-franc pieces, always demanded in payment of debts, and thus forced on debtors the obligation to pay in gold. Hence, without professing it, the gold standard alone now prevails in France, and it is doubtful whether that country ought any longer to be classed among those which maintain a double standard.

Standard Money. *Standard money*, as distinguished from *token money*, consists of coin which depends for its value in exchange upon the value of the metal of which it consists. The legend and device stamped upon it merely show that the coin contains the proper quantity of metal of the requisite fineness. If the stamp were defaced, or the coins melted up, the metal would be worth just as much, and would be accepted at its full value in other countries as readily as new coins from the mint. (*See Token Money.*)

Standard Silver. A mixed metal containing 37 parts of pure silver, with 3 parts of alloy, or 11 ozs. 2 dwts. fine, with 18 dwts. of alloy. Decimally expressed, ·925 fine. (*See Ancient Right Standard.*)

Standard Unit of Value. (*See Unit of Value.*)

Standarding. *Standarding* is an arithmetical operation constantly used in finding the value of gold and silver bullion. The process, when reduced to its simplest elements, consists in finding how much *pure* gold is contained in a mass of gold or silver bullion, and then estimating the quantity of *standard* gold or silver it would suffice to make.

It may, however, be differently expressed: thus, to standard gold or silver is to convert the gross weight of either metal, whose fineness differs from the standard, into its equivalent weight of standard metal.

The data on which this operation is based, are found in the "Assay Report," which, in England, is generally expressed in terms of "betterness," or "worseness," that is, it is reported as "better" than standard, or "worse" than standard. (*See Betterness.*)

Examples of the mode of conducting these calculations will be found in *Tate's Counting House Guide*, and in *Seyd's Bullion and Foreign Exchanges*, both of which works may be consulted with great advantage by those who wish for a thorough knowledge of the subject.

State Notes. Notes issued by any State or Government containing a promise to pay to the bearer on demand a certain amount of metallic money. These notes, if the promise to pay is always kept, are as acceptable to most people as money. In Russia, Austria, Italy, and some other European States, they are at a discount. In some others, as Turkey, the discount is very heavy, and the paper is not worth more than one-tenth its nominal value. (*See Caimes, Paper Currency, &c.*)

Sterling. The earliest documents speak of a *sterling* as another name for the English silver *penny*, which for many years was the unit of monetary value in this country. In a Charter of Henry III. we read:—

> "In centum marcis bonorum novorum et legalium *sterlingorum* tredecim solid, et 4 *sterling:* pro quâlibet marcâ computetis." (In one hundred marks; for every mark you shall reckon thirteen shillings and 4 *pence* of good new and lawful *sterlings*.)

The shilling at this time was not a coin, but a number of coins equal to twelve silver pennies.

In a Statute of Edward I.:—

> "Denarius Anglice qui vocatur *Sterlingus*." (A penny which we in English call a *Sterling*.) Here sterling is evidently used as an alternative name for the *denarius* or penny.

In a Statute of David II., King of Scotland, the word was used as synonymous with money in general.

> "Moneta nostra, videlicet *sterlingi* non deferatur extra regnum." (Our money, namely, *sterlings*, shall not be carried out of the kingdom.)

Again, in one of the old chronicles we read:—

> "In this yere (1351) William Edginton made the kyng to make a new coyne—destroying alle the elde *sterlynges* which were of gretter weight!

In all these quotations, it is evident from the context that the word *sterling* was used as the name of a coin, and not in reference to the quality or purity of the coinage. As to the origin of the name many conjectures have been offered. Walter de Pinchbeck, a monk of Bury, in the time of Edward I., says:—

> "Sed moneta Angliæ fertur dicta fuisse a nominibus opificum, ut Floreni a nominibus Florentiorum, ita Sterlingi a nominibus Esterlingorum nomina sua contraxerant, qui hujus modi monetam in Angliæ primitus componebant." (But the coinage of England is said to have derived its name from the name of the craftsmen, as Florens from the Florentines, so Sterlings from the Easterlings, who were the first to fabricate this kind of money in England.)

This, however, reads like one of those "shots," of which the old monkish chroniclers were so fond. It is, nevertheless, almost the only ground for the prevalent opinion as to the origin of the name.

By "sterling" is now meant English money, as distinct as from that of all other nations. The word is often used metaphorically, to indicate purity, or superiority of any kind, as "sterling silver" and "sterling character."

Stiver. (*a.*) The 20th part of the Dutch guilder, value 1*d.*

(*b.*) The 6th part of the Cape of Good Hope schilling, value $\frac{3}{8}$ of a penny, English.

Stock. Anglo-Saxon, *stoc;* Belgian, *stock;* and provincial German, *stuke,* the trunk of a tree, whence the diminutive, *sticca,* and English, *stick,* a branch of a tree, a small piece of wood. *(See Tally.)*

This homely English word found its way into the higher regions of finance, through a practice which prevailed in the Court of Exchequer for many centuries. It was the custom when money was borrowed for State purposes to record the transaction by means of notches on a stick (commonly hazel), and then to split the stick through the notches. The lender took one half as a proof of his claim against the Exchequer, and it was called his *Stock.* The Exchequer kept the other half which was called the *Counter-Stock,* and which answered the same purpose as was served in after-times by the "counterfoil." Hence it appears that the term *Stock* was originally applied to the material sign and proof of money lent. But as the thing signified was of greater importance to both parties than the sign, it was at length transferred to the money itself, or rather to the right to claim it. In this way *Stock* came to be understood as money lent to the Government, and eventually to any public body whatever, and the different funds subscribed from time to time came to be called "*The Stocks.*"

In modern finance, the term is applied to an imaginary sum of money, almost invariably £100, on which interest is paid at a given rate in perpetuity. Hence, a person who buys *Stock,* simply buys a right to receive the said interest; and this right he may sell again, but the principal sum is altogether imaginary, and cannot be claimed. Consols, Railway Stocks, and Stocks in Commercial Companies are examples. In the first of these, any amount of Stock can be purchased and held that does not involve fractions of a penny. In Railway Stocks the limit more commonly stands at one shilling or one pound, and any amount of Stock in quantities, not involving fractions of a shilling or pound, may be obtained. In this respect, *Stock* differs from Bonds, Debentures, Shares, and Obligations, which are invariably for round sums, as £10, £20, £50, £100, and so on; nevertheless, the term *Stocks* is currently used in a loose way, to signify Bonds, Shares, and Financial Securities of any kind whatsoever.

The phrase "an old stocking," which is popularly supposed to mean "old hose," or covering for the foot, is said to have originated in the practice of laying by a private *stock* of money against emergencies, which process was called "stocking;" whence, a sum that had been made up of small savings spread over a great length of time would be called "an old stocking." Mr. Bagehot, in one of his "*Essays on Finance*," uses the phrase freely, and in such a manner as to give countenance to this view.

Stopped. Payment Stopped. It often happens that bank-notes, cheques, bonds, and other instruments are lost or stolen, and with a view to recover them it is customary to go to the bank or other office through which it must or is likely to be passed, and request that a "stop" may be put upon such note, cheque, &c. It must not, however, be inferred that a bank has the power to refuse payment of a note or cheque to Bearer when presented. All that a bank can do lawfully is to tell the person presenting it that it has been lost or stolen. If the person thus presenting it has come by it honestly and in the ordinary way of business, it is to his interest that the matter should be inquired into, and he is hardly likely to refuse time for such inquiry. If he should refuse, that act alone would be *prima facie* evidence that he had some reason best known to himself for stifling inquiry. For the honour of the bank, or of the drawer of the cheque, he might under these circumstances receive payment of the note or cheque, but it is most probable that he would not have left the office long, or proceeded many steps before he found himself in the hands of a detective, and accused of having stolen or lost property in his possession, and for which he would be called upon to give an account in a court of law. Hence, whenever the honest holder of any instrument finds that a "stop" is put upon it, his wisest course is to acquiesce in the arrangement and afford every facility in his power for the clearing up of the matter, and not to stand too pertinaciously on his abstract rights. At the same time, it will be admitted that those rights are in some cases of a most substantial kind. For example, a bank note, a cheque to bearer, a bill endorsed in blank, and many foreign bonds all go by simple delivery, and possession proves property in them in all cases. Nor would this right be invalidated by acquiescing in the "stop," and so giving time for inquiry. It does not, however, follow that either of these instruments need be detained because a "stop" has been put upon it. All that is meant technically by a "stop" is the taking note of some name, number or description of an instrument, so that when it comes into the possession of the proper officer or clerk, attention shall be drawn to it, and steps taken to trace the finder, thief, or other offending party.

Strikes. A *strike* is a combination among workmen with a view to exact a certain rate of wages by a refusal to work unless their terms are complied with. Strikes, like street brawls between individuals, or wars between nations, always entail much loss and suffering to both contending parties, and until both nations and individuals are sufficiently enlightened to see the advantages of conciliation over revenge, revenge will continue to be, as it always has been, the rough and ready instrument by which the aggrieved party seeks to enforce his claims.

Sum Payable. The sum payable on a bill, cheque, draft, or promissory note, is the sum written at full length on the body of it. The sum written in figures on the margin is placed there for convenience, and if through error or inadvertence it differs from the sum stated on the body, the instrument is good for the sum written at length.

Supply and Demand. French equivalent, *l'offre et la demande.* "Supply" is from the Latin, *suppleo*, to fill up, to supply. "Demand," from the French, *demander*, to ask, to ask for.

Supply and *demand* are correlative terms. *Supply* signifies the quantity of the various commodities brought into the market and offered for sale. *Demand* signifies the desire for those commodities on the part of persons who have something to offer in exchange. It should be observed that the word "demand" in commerce, contains two factors, both of which are essential, namely (1), the desire for a thing, and (2), the possession of something to give in exchange. For it is obvious that the mere desire for an article, however strong that desire might be, would not induce the owner of the article to part with it, unless an equivalent were given in return; and, on the other hand, if a man possessed ever so much wealth, that wealth would not create a demand for commodities of any kind for which he had no *desire*. The word "supply," in like manner, contains two factors; it means in economics, (1), the making of an article, and (2), the bringing into the market and offering it for sale.

Supra Protest. (*See Protest.*)

Suspense Account. A private account kept by a merchant or banker of sundry items which at the moment cannot be placed in the regular accounts. Owing to postal irregularities, deaths, oversights, and various causes, moneys have somtimes to be credited, and charges to be debited, but at the time, it is not clear to whom. Such items are temporarily placed in the Suspense Account, to be transferred as soon as the proper creditor or debtor is determined.

Sweating. A fraudulent process practised on coins, by which their weight is reduced. It is effected by attrition or solution.

Sycee or **Sysee.** The English pronounciation of the word *se-tze* or *se-sze*, which primarily means "fine silk." The word is applied to silver, as in the phrase "sycee silver," either on account of the silky appearance presented by the rough blocks of Chinese silver when new and fresh from the refinery, or, as others say, because, when nearly pure, it can be drawn into threads as fine as silk. For pure or fine silver, the Chinese term is *wän-yin*. Sycee silver was first taken at the Bank of England in 1849.

T.

Tael. The unit of value, and the unit of weight in China.

The weight of the Tael is equal to 579·84 grains Troy (commonly taken as 580 grains), and is called Canton weight.

The unit of value, called the *Tael*, consists of 580 grains of Sycee silver (*see Sycee*), and is exchanged at the rate of 720 Taels for 1,000 Mexican Dollars. At this rate—

1 Tael = 1·3885 Mexican dollars.
1 Dollar = ·720 taels.

The Tael, therefore, when of full weight is worth 5*s.* 11¾*d.* English, but allowing for abrasion and other irregularities is rarely worth more than 5*s.* 10*d.*

The Tael is divided into 10 mace of 10 candareens each.

The Tael of Japan is divided into 10 Mas = 100 Candareens = 1000 Leni or cash.

It is giving place to the newly introduced decimal system. (*See Yen* and *Sen.*)

Talent. From the Greek, ταλαντον, a balance; plural, ταλαντα, a pair of scales. Afterwards it came to signify anything weighed, and at length a definite weight. When used in reference to the precious metals, a *talent* of gold or of silver gradually assumed the character of a monetary unit, but was not at first represented by a coin; ingots or bars containing a *talent's weight* of gold or silver formed the primitive money of the Hebrews and ancient Greeks. There is no evidence of coined money among the Hebrews until after the return from Babylon, 530 B.C.; nor among the Greeks till the time of Pheidon, King of Argos and Œgina, about 700 B.C.

The weight called a *Talent*, both among the Hebrews and the Greeks, underwent great changes from time to time, so that it is almost impossible to say what the metallic value of the talent was as measured in our money, unless we know all the circumstances of time and place under which it is mentioned. In general terms it may be said that the *talent* consisted of 60 *mĭnas*, the mina appearing to have had more of the character of a monetary unit than the talent; but as there was a large or heavy mina, and a small mina in circulation at one and the same time, and as they are often used in such a way as to make it quite uncertain which is meant, great obscurity hangs over the whole subject. Nevertheless some two or three *talents*, which acquired greater celebrity than others, are pretty well known, The following values have been determined by Mr. Barclay, V. Head of the British Museum;—

		lbs.	ozs.	dwts.	
The Græco-Asiatic talent	=	119	9	10	
The Æginetic talent	=	101	0	10	
The Euboïc talent	=	67	8	10	
The Attic Solonian talent	=	70	3	15	
The Perso-Babylonic talent	=	90	0	12	12 grs.

These weights were applied, as might be inferred from their magnitude, chiefly to silver; but their value, either in gold or silver, may easily be estimated by recollecting that 40 troy pounds of gold are coined into 1869 sovereigns, and a pound of silver into 66 shillings.

Tally. French, *tailler*, to cut; Portuguese, *talhar;* Spanish, *tallar*, all from the Latin, *tālea*, a piece cut off; a twig, or branch cut from a tree.

Tallies have been adopted in all countries as a rude and primitive method of recording numbers, in the highest offices of the State, through every grade of society, down to the waggoner and fisherman, amongst which latter class they are still extensively used. In the Court of Exchequer they were used for centuries. A hazel stick had notches cut transversely into it, corresponding in number to the pounds or hundreds of pounds to be recorded. It was then split down the middle through all the notches; one half was held by one party to the transaction, and the corresponding half by the other. Buyers and sellers, debtors and creditors, borrowers and lenders, thus held each against the other a proof of the transaction, and when a settlement of claims took place, it was only necessary to bring forward the notched stick and to place it by the side of its companion, when, if the irregularities of the sticks themselves, and the notches upon them, answered precisely to each other, it was accepted as legal proof of the claim on the part of the holder. From the noun "tally," was formed the verb "to tally." Any two sticks which showed perfect agreement, any two slips of paper like the serrated edge of indentures, which exactly corresponded, were said to *tally;* and long after the use of sticks or wooden tallies was abandoned, the custom prevailed of cutting or tearing off tickets, cheques, indentures, and other documents from their counterfoils by an irregular line of separation, with a view to prevent fraud. If the torn or cut edges "tallied," it afforded evidence of the *bona-fides* of the claim made.

These tallies were bought and sold on the Stock Exchange just as bonds or debentures are in the present day. Francis, in his *History of the Bank of England,* referring to the time of William III., remarks:—"Tallies lay bundled up like Bath faggots in the hands of brokers and stock-jobbers." By an Act passed in 1783 the use of them was abolished; certificates printed on paper or parchment having taken their place. In former times they had been multiplied to such an extent that they fell to a discount, which varied from time to time, till in 1696 they were at a discount, of fifty to sixty per cent. Notwithstanding the Act of Parliament above mentioned, the use of exchequer tallies was not finally abandoned in the Government offices till 1826, and from an official report it appears that the destruction of the old Houses of Parliament, in 1832, was caused by the overheating of a flue while the workmen were employed in burning the heaps which had been accumulating for centuries.

Talon. From the French and Spanish, *talon*, the heel; and generally any shoot, protuberance, or extension. It is connected with the Welsh, *tellu*, to stretch; the Spanish, *tallo*, a shoot or projection; the Portuguese, *talo*, a stalk; and with similar roots in several languages, all conveying the notion of extension, projection, sprouting, &c.

A Talon, as most commonly known in commerce, is the last portion of a sheet of coupons. It generally resembles a coupon, but differs somewhat in size, and contains on its face an intimation that if it is presented at the house or office indicated, a new sheet of coupons will be given in exchange for it. In the case of French Rente Certificates or Bonds, the coupons and the letter-press constituting the certificate are all printed on a single sheet. When the coupons are all cut off, the whole of the remainder is called the *Talon*, and must be presented entire at the office named by the Government, when a new certificate, with its complement of coupons, will be given in exchange.

The *Talon* is also a name applied to the marginal appendage of a Spanish coupon, and is of some importance, since payment of the coupon is refused if such talon or appendage happens to have been cut off.

Tare. Taring. From the Latin, *tero*, to rub, to wear away, to lessen, to diminish, to waste. Danish, *tarer*, to waste; German, *zehren*; French, *tare*; Italian and Spanish, *tara*, all denoting waste, or deduction for waste. (See *Tret.*)

Tare is an allowance made for the weight of a box, bag, or other article in which goods are packed.

Taring is the process of calculating and making the Tare, which is done in three different ways, thus giving rise to three technical terms, which should be carefully distinguished.

(*a.*) *Average Tare*, which is found by taking some few out of a number of packages, and from these calculating the average of the entire lot.

(*b.*) *Customary Tare*, which is a stated allowance fixed by the custom of each particular trade.

(*c.*) *Particular or Real Tare*, found by actual weighing of each package, and deducting it from the gross weight of the parcel.

Tariff. From Jibel-el-Tarifa (Gibraltar). The mountain or fort of Tarif, an early Moorish conqueror.

The word *tariff*, or *tarif* (French), is said to be derived from the rock Tarifa, where the Spanish in the days of their power exacted certain dues from all vessels passing through the Straits. These dues were embodied in a schedule called the Tarif dues, and from this circumstance lists and schedules of dues of all kinds came in course of time to be called "tariffs" or "tarifs."

Tariff Value. By Tariff Value is meant a certain value assigned to coins of different countries, somewhat less than their mint par value, on account of irregularities in workmanship, charges for coining, &c.

Under the headings *Allowance* or *Remedy*, *Wear and Tear*, *Retenue*, and *Seigniorage*, explanations of these terms have been given. It is therefore only necessary here to point out their bearing on the process of Tarification, that is, the determination of their Tariff value.

Allowance or *Remedy* is a certain departure from the prescribed weight and fineness of coins permitted by the State, in consequence of the practical difficulty of securing absolute uniformity in their fabrication. Two parts in one thousand above or below the standard are allowed in the gold coinage of England and France. In Russia, however, no allowance is made for either weight or fineness. For the purpose of Tarification a number of coins are selected from heaps of the same denomination, and carefully assayed. The average departure is then calculated, and the result noted.

Wear and Tear, all coins in active circulation are necessarily subject to. To ascertain the average depreciation, a number of coins of the same denomination are selected from different heaps that have been fairly but not excessively worn. The total deficiency divided by the number of coins operated upon, gives the average deficiency of each coin.

Retenue, as it is called in France, and *Seigniorage*, as it is called in the United States, is a charge made by the Government to defray the cost of coining. In England no charge is made for the coining of gold. In other countries the charges vary, and in some the mint regulations are so imperfectly observed that the only way of determining the metallic (or what is sometimes called the *intrinsic*) value of coins is to subject them to the ordeal of weighing and assaying, with a view to Tarification.

The difference between the par value of coins and the tariff value is very small in those countries where no charge is made for coining, but in countries like France, where a *retenue* is deducted, and besides this charge, a further deduction is made for slight irregularities in weight and fineness, the difference is considerable. For example, the par value of the English sovereign is 25 francs, 22 centimes, but the tariff value is only 25 francs, 15 centimes. Or, if you take a heap of sovereigns weighing 1 kilogramme, their par value (that is, their value as coins in circulation) would be 3,157 francs, 40 centimes; but the same sovereigns, if taken to the French mint to be exchanged for French 20 franc pieces, would be treated simply as bullion, and would be valued at 3,148 francs, 29 centimes, which is their tariff value. And as the charge for coining, or the retenue, is 6·70 francs per kilogramme, the mint par value is made up of the following elements, namely:—

Tariff Value	Fr. 3,148·29
Retenue	6·70
Remedies and Abrasion . .	2·41
Mint par Value . .	3,157·40

Annuaire pour l'An 1879, *publié par le Bureau des Longitudes*, p. 201.

Tchetwertak. A Russian silver coin, value 25 copecks. It weighs 5·183 grammes, ·868 fine, and is worth 99 centimes French, or $9\frac{1}{2}d.$ sterling.

Tempo. A Japanese bronze coin, valued at 100 Monseng, or $\frac{1}{25}$ of a penny. (*See Zeni.*)

Terminable Annuities. From the Latin, *terminare*, to limit, to fix bounds to.

A sum of money paid yearly by Government, by an insurance company, or other recognized party, for a stated number of years. These annuities may be bought and sold like any other property. In the case of Government annuities, they are bought by means of lump sums paid down at the time of purchase. In some insurance companies an annuity is purchased by monthly or quarterly contributions during the prime of life, the annuity to commence at a fixed age in the latter period of life, and *terminating* at death. The so-called *Long Annuities* are terminable, but run usually for 99 years. *Terminable Annuities* are for various periods, but always shorter than those properly called *Long*. (*See Annuities Deferred, Perpetual, &c.*)

Testament. Latin, *testor, testari*, to bear witness, to declare, to call to witness, to make a will.

A testament or will is much the same now as defined by the old Roman lawyers. "*Voluntatis nostræ justa sententia, de eo quod quis post mortem suam fieri velit.*" (A declaration in legal form concerning that which anyone wishes to be done after his death.) Wills and testaments are not much required in connection with commercial and banking transactions, copies of probate and letters of administration answering nearly all the purposes of business. (*See Administration, Probate.*)

Testo or **Testoon** (*a*). The tenth part of the Portuguese milreis. It is represented by a silver coin, weighing 2·500 grammes, $·916\frac{2}{3}$ fine, and is worth 51 French centimes, or 4·8*d.* sterling; coins of 5, 2, 1, and $\frac{1}{2}$ testoons, of proportional weight and equal fineness, are struck.

(*b*.) An English coin, date of Henry VII., was called *Testoon*, from the French *teste* or *tête*, a head, which was stamped upon it in profile, instead of the full-faced portrait hitherto used from the time of Stephen.

Thaler. For etymology see *Dollar*.

(*a*.) The *Union Thaler* of Austria is a silver coin, valued in Austria at $1\frac{1}{2}$ florins (or gulden), and weighs 18·5185 grammes, ·900 fine. Its value in sterling is derived at once from the Austrian florin (*see Florin*), thus:—

Value of Silver Florin . .	23·495*d.*
„ Half Florin . . .	11·747*d.*
„ Thaler	35·242*d.* or 2*s.* $11\frac{1}{4}d.$

It is now superseded by the monetary laws of 1867 and 1870, but still continues in circulation as a commercial coin.

(*b*.) The *Maria-Theresa Thaler* of 1870, called also a Levantine, contains 28·075 grammes of silver, ·833 fine. Mint par value 5 fr. 20 cent. = £·2061 or 4*s*. $1\frac{1}{2}$*d*. It is now a commercial coin, and not legal tender even in Austro-Hungary. Of course, in foreign countries it is mere bullion.

(*c*.) The thaler or dollar of Hamburg is a silver coin, valued at $2\frac{1}{2}$ marks courant.

Mark Courant=14·13*d*.
$2\frac{1}{2}$

28·26
7·06

Silver Thaler or Dollar=35·32*d*.

(*d*.) The former unit of value in Lubeck, worth about 3*s*. 4*d*. English, and divided into 3 marks.

(*e*.) The former unit of value in Mecklenburg, worth about 2*s*. 11*d*. English, and divided into 48 schillings.

(*f*.) In North Germany a silver coin, the mint par value of which is 2*s*. $11\frac{1}{4}$*d*. It is divided into 30 new groschen, and weighs 18.5185 grammes, ·900 fine. Although now replaced by the new gold coinage, the old silver coinage is accepted as legal tender at the rate of 3 marks per thaler, the 10 groschen piece being equal to 1 mark or $11\frac{3}{4}$*d*. sterling. (*See Mark*.)

Thilik. A Turkish silver coin, value 2 piastres, or $4\frac{1}{3}$*d*.

Third of a Guinea. A long disused English coin, worth, as the name implies, 7 shillings.

Three Per Cents. The name applied *par eminence* to that portion of the Consolidated Debt, which originated in 1752 in consequence of some annuities granted by George I. being "consolidated" in one fund, with a three per cent. stock formed in 1731. In the year 1880 it amounted to £395,820,861.

Three Per Cents. Reduced. The name applied to that portion of the Consolidated Debt which had borne 4 per cent. interest down to the year 1750, and $3\frac{1}{2}$ per cent. down to 1757, from which date it was "reduced" to 3°/₀. The amount of this stock in existence in the year 1880 was £92,461,985.

Thrift. Thrive. Old Norse, *thrifa*, to seize, lay hold of; Danish, *trives*, to thrive, prosper, flourish; *thrifnadr*, well being, prosperity; *thrif*, good luck, well-being; Swedish, *trifvas*.

The word *thrift* has two meanings in English.

1. *Frugality*, a habit of saving, not wasting; *e.g.*, by his *thrift* he made his own capital, and then employed it in trade.

2. Prosperity, success, well-being, a thriving, as in Shakespeare;

"I have a mind presages me such *thrift*."

Thrimsa. Anglo-Saxon; three-fifths of a shilling.

Tical. The Tical of Burmah is the name of a coin, and also of a weight, sometimes called the kyat. A tical of silver (258 troy grains) is worth about two shillings, but the fineness of the silver is so variable that these coins pass, simply as bullion outside of the country.

With the same reservation, the Tical of Siam is worth 2*s.* 6*d.* It is called the *bat.* (*Which see.*)

Ticket Day. The day before settling day on the Stock Exchange. It is the day for the passing of tickets between brokers and jobbers, by means of which they learn the amount of stocks and shares they have respectively to deliver or receive on the day following. Tickets are passed before eleven o'clock on the ticket day.

Time Bargains. Time bargains are engagements entered into with a view to being closed before or at a given time. The object matter of these bargains may be any commodity whatever, such as cotton, iron, wool, tobacco, corn, &c., and purchases or sales of these commodities against time are often made. But by far the largest number of time bargains are made in Stock Exchange securities; indeed, it may be safely affirmed that an immense preponderence of the business done in the Stock Exchange consists of transactions which fall under this denomination. The essential features of a time bargain, properly so called, may be shewn best by an example (1), of a purchase, and (2), of a sale. Suppose Egyptian United Bonds to have had a drop; this would tempt a speculator to buy, say, £1,000 at 65 (that is, at £65 for a £100 bond). If the price rises before the settling day to the price of £66, there will evidently be a profit of £10 on the transaction. Thus—

Sold £1,000 Egyp. Unif. at	66	=	£660
Bought ,, ,,	65	=	650
	Profit		£10

Suppose, on the other hand, there has been a rise in the market price of Egyptians before the operator begins to deal. This would naturally tempt him to sell. In this case he begins by selling a £1,000 of stock, say, at 68. If before the settling day arrives the stock has fallen to 66½, and he buys back at that price, his account at the settlement would stand thus:—

Sold £1,000 Stock at	68	=	£680
Bought ,,	66½	=	665
	Profit		£15

Of course, it often happens that when a speculator buys in hope of a rise, he realizes a fall; and when he sells in expectation of a fall, a rise occurs, and then instead of profit he makes a loss, but whether he loses or gains, the inexorable settling day fixes the result, if it has not been secured before, and it is this fact which has given to transactions of this description the name of "time bargains." Time bargains originated in the practice of closing the bank for six weeks in each quarter for the preparation of the dividends. As no transfer could be made during that period, it became a practice to buy and sell for the opening. The habit, once formed, was extended to other stocks, and as neither stock nor capital was necessary for the conclusion of bargains, it opened the way for a host of needy adventurers, who were not slow to avail themselves of an opportunity of making a gain, while they had nothing to lose.

Tithes. Saxon, *teotha*, the tenth part.

The tenth part of anything, but applied more particularly to the tenth part of the produce of land, and appropriated to the support of the clergy. McLeod refines on this definition, and points out that in law, the *tithe* is not the tenth part of the produce itself but "the right to demand the tenth part." Tithes are thus distinguished:—

1. Prodial tithes; those arising from the produce of the land itself, as corn, hay, fruits, &c.
2. Personal tithes; those arising from the profit of personal industry, trades, professions, &c.
3. Mixed tithes; those arising from the increase of live stock on the land, as pigs, cattle, sheep, eggs, butter, cheese, &c.

Titre. Titre des Monnaies. The French expression for "Standard Fineness."

Titre is also a general name for a bond, a share certificate, or other financial document.

Tlaco. (*See Claco.*)

Tokens. Old English, *tàken, tôkne.* Anglo-Saxon, *tâcen, tâen.* Old Frisian, *têken.* Old Low German, *tecan.* Old Icelandic, *takn, teikn.* Old H. German, *zeichan.* Gothic, *taikns*—all meaning token, sign, signum.

"In tôkne that pais scholle be bitvext god and manne."

William de Shoreham.

The word *token* is used in the sense of "sign" or "representative," and had this meaning at a very early period. It is often used in Scripture, sometimes in the sense of a "sign," and at others with that of the classical *portentum* or "portent."

In commerce it is applied to coins or substitutes for coins made of inferior metal, or of a quantity of metal of less value than its name would indicate. Owing to the scarcity of small change, and the great loss occasioned to the poor for want of some coin of less value than the silver penny in use down to the time of the Commonwealth, half-penny and farthing tokens were struck in brass, copper, tin, pewter, lead, and even leather, not only by the Government, but by tradespeople, tavernkeepers and others, for circulation in their own neighbourhood. When copper coinage became sufficiently abundant to meet the wants of the population it was made a criminal offence to issue these private tokens, although they continued to circulate in small quantities down to quite recent times. Our modern bronze pennies, half-pennies and farthings are pre-eminently a *token* coinage, as they are not worth more than about one-fourth their nominal value. The silver coinage consists also of tokens, but their metallic value more nearly approaches their nominal value than do the bronze coins. The silver florin, for example, weighs when new 11·31036 grammes, and is $\frac{222}{240}$ fine. The fine silver therefore in the florin is $\frac{222}{240}$ of 11·31036 grammes, and taking fine gold as worth $15\frac{1}{2}$ times as much as fine silver, its metallic value would be 22·1229*d.* But silver at the present moment is worth only about $\frac{1}{16}$ its weight in gold, so that the silver florin is worth much less than here calculated, and varies from 18*d.* to 20*d.* according to the price of silver in the market. In order to prevent loss to traders using these token coins, the law of legal tender was passed, so that no one need, unless he choose, accept more than 40 silver shillings in one payment. For all sums above that value, he may demand gold or Bank of England notes. The silver five-franc piece in France is not a token coin; its metallic value is equal to that of the gold five-franc piece, and these both (owing to the Double Standard prevailing in France) are equal to their nominal value.

"Tokenhouse Yard derived its name from the Mint House, erected for the coinage and issue of farthing tokens, under the patent granted to Henry, Lord Maltravers and Sir Francis Crane in 1635." BEAUFOY's *Tradesmen's Tokens.*

The old Mint House or Token House was on the north side of Lothbury, but the houses on this spot have all been recently rebuilt so that no trace of the ancient structure remains.

Toman. The unit of value in Persia. The mint regulations, if there are any, are not observed. Only by trial essays can any useful inference be drawn. Seyd gives the weight of the Toman of 1839 at 3·5 grammes, about ·970 fine, and calculates the value to be 9·$3\frac{1}{4}$*d.* The Toman is divided into 10 Sahibkirani, Zabkran, or Keran.

More recently, and since the Paris International Conference of 1878, M. Sudre has given in the *Annuaire par le Bureau des Longitudes,* additional data for calculating the metallic value of the Thoman or Toman. He gives as the weight of the gold Thoman 3·76 grammes ·916 fine, and assigns to it a value of Fr. 11.86 centimes, or £·470, say 9*s.* $4\frac{3}{4}$*d.* sterling.

The Thoman is divided into 100 schahis or shahis.

Tontines. A species of annuity devised by an Italian named Lorenzo Tonti. They were adopted in the first place by governments as a means of raising a loan. In return for a sum paid down the government engaged to grant annuities to a certain number of persons. When one died, his share was divided among all the survivors, and this process went on till only one was left, and he enjoyed the benefit of all the annuities himself, until his death, when the transaction ceased. Assurances and other benefits have also been arranged on the Tontin principle, but they have not found much favour in England, or indeed in any country, being based on the principle of profiting by another's death, a thing repugnant to the sentiments of most people.

Tower Pound. (*See Troy Weight.*)

Trade. As in several other instances mentioned in this work, we have again two distinct words confounded into one. One of these is Low Saxon *trade*, a trodden path, whence *wagentrade*, a waggon rut; it is connected with the German, *treten*, to tread. As thus derived *trade* signifies a trodden way, a course; and metaphorically, a way of life, a custom. Hence a tradesman is one who follows a special course of life, as distinguished from husbandmen, and labourers, or serfs.

"Tho would I seek for queen apples unripe
To give my Rosalind, and in summer shade
Dight gaudy girlonds was my common *trade* (custom)
To crown her golden locks."

SHEPHERD'S *Calendar*.

The *trade winds* are winds which follow a certain *trade* or direction, and owe their name to this circumstance, and not as commonly supposed, to the fact of their favouring commerce; for it is obvious that they obstruct and impede commerce in one direction as much as they favour it in the other. The following couplet illustrates the use of the word in the sense of "course" or direction.

"Wyth wind at will the *trad* held thaî
And in England com ryght swyth."

WYNTON.

Trade, in the sense of commerce, is derived from the Latin, *tractare*, to handle, touch; German, *handeln*, to deal, traffic, trade. From *tractare* is derived the Italian, *trattare;* Spanish and Portuguese, *tratar*, and the French, *traiter*, all meaning to handle, treat, trade, &c. *La traite des noirs* is the French expression for the African Slave Trade.

Trade, in the commercial sense of the term, includes all those departments of business which relate to the production and exchange of commodities embodied in some material or *corporeal* product; and excludes those professions whose services result in the production of incorporeal wealth. Thus the merchant, manufacturer, shopkeeper, handicraftsman, are said to be engaged in trade. But we never speak of the trade of a schoolmaster, clergyman, barrister, physician, &c., except, indeed, as a term of contempt. The business of the banker, broker, and some others is usually regarded as on the borderland between a trade and a profession, and hence many persons in those ranks of life where it would be thought degradation to "go into trade," enter these businesses without hesitation.

Trade Dollar. A Silver Dollar issued by the United States. It is of superior weight to the ordinary current dollar and appears to have been struck with the view of creating a market for American silver, by furnishing a medium of exchange for American merchants in their dealings with Eastern countries; and with China especially, that country having no national mint of its own.

The coinage of the Silver *Trade Dollar* was first authorized by the Act of Feb. 12th., 1873. Its weight is 420 grains or 27·215 grammes, ·900 fine, and is worth 5·44 francs, or £·2156 sterling = 4*s.* 3¾*d.*, taking 15½ parts of *fine* silver to one of *fine* gold. But owing to the depreciation of silver, it is no longer a legal tender in America beyond the sum of *five dollars*, and the undue multiplication of them has been checked by the issue of a Treasury order dated October, 1877; of which the following is a clause:—

> "So long as gold continued at a premium and silver bullion commanded a price sufficient to keep the bullion value of 420 grains of standard silver, together with the coinage charge for a trade-dollar, above the gold value of a United States legal tender dollar note, there was no likelihood of trade-dollars finding their way into domestic circulation, at least, not to any embarrassing extent; but when, from the appreciation of United States notes as compared with gold, and the decline in the value of silver, a trade-dollar added to its coinage charge became of less intrinsic value than the gold value of a dollar note, owners of silver bullion deposited the same at the mints for returns in trade-dollars, and placed them in circulation at a profit to themselves. This state of affairs first manifested itself in the latter part of 1877, and in October of that year the Secretary of the Treasury directed that the receipt of deposits of silver for coinage into trade-dollars should be discontinued at the coinage mints, and at the assay office at New York."

As these sheets are passing through the press, the question of adopting or rejecting the Double Standard is being discussed at a Conference called for that purpose, by several influential States. The preliminary correspondence seems to indicate that the long-prevailing ratio between gold and silver of 15½ to 1 will be but little if at all departed from; and for this reason, that proportion has been made the basis of all comparisons throughout this work.

Trades Unions. That groups of individuals having common interests should associate themselves together for the protection of those interests, is one of the most natural things to be expected as resulting from our social instincts. Hence we find in all ages, as society becomes more highly organized, a tendency to form guilds, clubs, and companies for the regulation of the conduct of almost every separate trade or profession, and for the relief of the members in sickness, old age, or misfortune. Out of this same feeling modern Trades Unions took their rise; at first almost wholly occupied in protecting their respective members against the vicissitudes of life, and in this way conferring a great benefit on them. They also conferred great advantages on their members by collecting information relative to the trade, and by establishing a correspondence between the unions in different parts of the country, thus finding out the best markets for their labour, and the most promising fields for employment, and these are the main objects for which they exist even in the present day. But some few Unions have unfortunately been tempted to make experiments in coercion, which have proved very injurious to many members, without yielding any commensurate advantage to the rest. Following the bad example of those who ought to have known better—of those who by Act of Parliament fixed the rate of wages for the artizan and the labourer, as well as the price at which the loaf of bread should be sold—the labourers and artizans in their turn have tried to fix the rate of wages for which they would work, and compel all others of the same craft to work. These attempts have too often been accompanied by intimidation and "ratting," expedients which have always entailed heavy losses on both employers and employed. (*See Strikes.*)

Traffic. Derived by some from Latin, *trans*, over, and *facio*, to make or do. By others from a Celtic root, *tra*, or Welsh, *trafu*, to stir, to agitate. It seems probable that two different words were originally in use, one among the Celtic and other northern nations of Europe, the other among the southern or Latin-speaking nations, and that owing to a similarity in the main features of the two, they became gradually fused into one, whence the Spanish, *trafagar*, *traficar*; Italian, *trafficare*, and French, *trafiquer*.

Traffic is often used in a general way in the sense of "trade," but is more properly restricted in commerce to that kind of trade which involves the carrying and transfer of commodities from one place to another. Thus we speak of the "traffic on a railway," "traffic returns," "the slave traffic," "foreign traffic," &c., but not of the traffic of a shoemaker, house decorator, or carpenter. Foreign trade is nearly always spoken of as traffic, but the home retail trade rarely so.

Transfer. Latin, *trans*, over, across, beyond, and *fero*, to bear or carry away.

Although the verb "to transfer," and the corresponding noun "transfer," are both frequently used in common speech in the sense of handing over anything to another, or the carrying of a material product from place to place, and metaphorically applied to the affections, desires, &c., it is applied in commercial law to a formal surrender of some Right in favour of the party named in the instrument by which it is transferred. Cheques, Bills of Exchange, Promissory Notes, are all "transfers" in this sense, as they all transfer a Right due *to* one party *from* a second *in favour of* a third. But in the money market and Stock Exchange, the term has a more strictly technical meaning, and by *transfer* is understood the surrender by one party in favour of another of the Right to dividends, annuities, &c., derived from the shares of public companies, Government funds, foreign stocks, and the like. For the security of the holder, the operation is attended with certain formalities, and where the rightful owner cannot attend personally to append his signature, a Power of Attorney is commonly required. (*See Power of Attorney.*) The following is a form used for the purpose of transferring shares in a commercial company, and gives a fair idea of the nature of such documents:—

H. C. Y.

Stock forwarded to the Company's Office by

E

in consideration of the Sum of [See Note.]

paid by

hereinafter called the said Transferee ,

Do hereby bargain, sell, assign, and transfer to the said Transferee:—

of and in the undertaking called the

Coupon for £

To hold unto the said Transferee , Executors, Administrators, and Assigns, subject to the several conditions on which held the same immediately before the execution hereof; and the said Transferee , do hereby agree to accept and take the said , subject to the conditions aforesaid.

As Witness our Hands and Seals, this Day of in the Year of our Lord One Thousand Eight Hundred and Eighty

Signed, sealed, and delivered, by the above-named in the Presence of
* Witness's { Signature, Address, Occupation,

Place for Seal.

Signed, sealed, and delivered, by the above-named in the Presence of
* Witness's { Signature, Address, Occupation,

Place for Seal.

Signed, sealed, and delivered, by the above-named in the Presence of
* Witness's { Signature, Address, Occupation,

Place for Seal.

Signed, sealed, and delivered, by the above-named in the Presence of
* Witness's { Signature, Address, Occupation,

Place for Seal.

NOTE.—The Consideration-money set forth in a transfer may differ from that which the first Seller will receive, owing to sub-sales by the original Buyer; the Stamp Act requires that in such cases the Consideration-money paid by the sub-purchaser shall be the one inserted in the Deed, as regulating the *ad valorem* Duty; the following is the *Clause* in question:—

"Where a Person, having contracted for the purchase of any Property, but not having obtained a Conveyance thereof, contracts to sell the same to any other Person, and the property is, in consequence, conveyed immediately to the Sub-purchaser, the Conveyance is to be charged with *ad valorem* Duty in respect of the Consideration for the Sale by the original Purchaser to the Sub-purchaser."

[33 & 34 Vict. cap. 97 (1870), Clause 74, Section 3, of the Schedule.]

* When a Transfer is executed out of Great Britain, it is recommended that the Signatures be attested by H. M. Consul or Vice Consul, a Clergyman, Magistrate, Notary Public, or by some other person holding a public position—as most Companies refuse to recognize Signatures not so attested.

Transfer Days. Days fixed by the Bank of England for the *transfer, free of charge,* of Consols and other Government Stocks. These days are Monday, Tuesday, Wednesday, Thursday, and Friday, *before three o'clock.* On Saturdays transfers may be made, but a transfer fee of 2*s.* 6*d.* is then charged.

Transire. Latin, *trans,* over, beyond; *io, ire,* to go; *transire,* to go away, to go beyond certain limits.

A *Transire* is a document signed by the master, before any coasting vessel can depart from the port of lading. *General Transires* are sometimes issued to save delay in taking fresh transires for each voyage of coasting vessels.

Treasury. A Government Department which has charge of the revenue and expenditure of the *Crown.* The offices of this department are in Whitehall. The First Lord of the Treasury is now invariably the Premier of the House of Commons, and it is under that designation the Premier is officially known. The Chancellor of the Exchequer is Under Treasurer.

In connection with finance, the word "Treasury" has a more restricted meaning. In the Act of May 18, 1866, relating to Exchequer Bills and Bonds, "the Treasury" is defined to mean "the Commissioners of Her Majesty's Treasury for the time being, or any two or more of them," and it is evident from the wording of this Act that the old distinction between the Treasury and the Exchequer has ceased to have any force; for, throughout the Act, all the duties involved in the preparation and issue of Exchequer Bills is thrown upon the Treasury as above defined. (*See Treasury Bill, Exchequer Bill, Exchequer Bond.*)

Treasury Bill. Treasury Bills are Instruments of Credit, whose origin dates back only to 1877, when they were authorized by Act of Parliament. Previous to this it was the custom for the Commissioners of the Treasury to borrow from the Bank of England such sums as were wanted for a short time only, but it was thought advisable on various grounds to offer these loans to public tender, a practice which has continued ever since.

Treasury Bills are drawn for three months, or for six months. *They have no interest,* the holder always receiving them at discount. The discount varies with the rate current in the market. The tenders for a recent issue were as high as £99 16*s.*, for every £100 in Three Months' Bills, thus yielding to the purchaser 4*s.* per quarter, or 16*s.* per annum for interest on £100. This is a trifle over $\frac{3}{4}$ of 1 per cent., but the current rate for the best commercial bills was 1 per cent. at that time, and this shows that government security is preferred to the best commercial paper, and that the moneyed classes are willing to accept lower interest for their capital when the higher class of security can be obtained.

Appended is a copy of a form of tender for Treasury Bills, which may be obtained at the Bank of England, whenever an announcement appears in the *London Gazette* inviting such tenders.

No.

LONDON, *4th December*, 1879.

To the Lords Commissioners
of Her Majesty's Treasury.

My Lords,

In accordance with the terms of the notice in the London Gazette, of the *7th November*, 1879,

We hereby beg to tender for the sum of £20,000 Treasury Bills, per Act 40 Vict., cap. 2, at *Three* months' date, viz., *Five* of £1,000, *One* of £5,000, *One* of £10,000, for which, or for any less amount that may be allotted to *us*, *we* agree to give the sum of £99 12*s.* 6*d.*, say *ninety-nine pounds twelve shillings and sixpence* per cent.

We have the honour to be,
My Lords,
Your Lordships' most obedient Servant.
Signature, *R. S. Burt & Sons.*
Address, *Throgmorton Street, London.*

N.B.—The price per cent. offered must be written in words at length, and in figures.

Tret. From Latin, *tero*, I rub, or wear; *tritus*, rubbed, or worn, according to some writers; but the etymology is doubtful.

An allowance made for wear, damage, or deterioration in goods during transit from one place to another.

Trial of the Pyx. A ceremony instituted for the trial of the weight and purity of the gold and silver coins of the kingdom. Formerly, it was performed at irregular intervals; the trial is now made annually. When the coinage was done by contract, this ceremony was of great importance, as the contractors were not entitled to full payment until a jury of experts had delivered a favourable verdict. The process is now much simplified, but the following is a description of it, as it was conducted before the trial was made annual. It is given in the "*Almanac and Companion for* 1880."

"The pyx is a box to contain the gold coins that are to be tested; and there is another pyx for silver coins. A few coins from every day's mintage are put into the pyx, and these are taken to be a fair average of the whole number. Trial plates are preserved with great care, rigorously made of the exact alloy for sterling or standard; and by these the coins are tested. There are trial plates still preserved, extending over a period of four centuries, showing in what way the standard has varied from time to time. The present plates, made by the Goldsmith's Company, are replicated, one copy being kept at the Mint, another at the Assay Office, a third at the Exchequer, a fourth at Goldsmiths' Hall, and others at the official assay offices; but those at Westminster are deemed to be the authoritative standards, brought forward at the trial of the pyx. The boxes and chests containing the trial pieces are secured with the best locks that Chubb can provide, and the keys are so many that the all important trial-pieces cannot be brought forward to the light of day without a good deal of unlocking by officials. The trial plates were in 1870 transferred from the Exchequer to that of the Warden of the Standards, an officer under the Board of Trade. He also keeps the Imperial standard weights for weighing gold and silver coins.

The trial of the pyx has been shorn of some of its dignity lately; but the following was, in a general way, the mode of procedure before the trials were made annually. All new coins, as minted, were made up into bags or *journeys* of 180 oz. gold, or 720 oz. silver; a journey being a technical name for coins made in any one day. All the coins in each bag were of one denomination only. One coin was taken from each bag, and put into the gold or silver pyx, as the case might be. One coin out of each bag was also handed to the Queen's Assay Master. The pyxes were locked by three officials, after each day's proceedings. When there were about a hundred bags in each pyx, one pound troy was taken from each, to be counted as well as weighed. Then two coins were taken from each pound by the deputy master, and weighed with scrupulous accuracy, any deviation from the proper weight being recorded to a minute fraction of a grain. One of these two coins was sent to the Mint assay room, while the other was placed in the all-important official pyx. On an appointed day the Government, at the instance of the Master of the Mint, invited the Goldsmiths' Company to assist at a trial of the pyx. Many officials assembled at the office of the Queen's Remembrancer, Old Palace Yard; the Pyx Chamber, in the cloisters of Westminster Abbey, was opened, and two trial pieces (gold and silver) taken out; Imperial standard weights of gold and silver were produced also. A jury of goldsmiths, after being sworn, were at work for several hours, melting into an ingot a certain number of gold coins from the one pyx, and of silver coins from the other, rigorously assaying the ingots, assaying small bits of the two trial pieces, and comparing the assays one with another. For convenience most of these operations were conducted at Goldsmiths' Hall, where the necessary assay furnaces, balances, &c., were ready at hand. At a certain hour in the evening, the jury of goldsmiths having announced that their labours were finished, all the officials again assembled, and the foreman of the jury read their verdict. It is invariably the case that the coins in the pyxes are found to be up to the proper standard, both in quality and in weight, within that minute allowance called the remedy. The Queen's Remembrancer, therefore, pronounced a verdict of *acquittal*, implying that the Master of the Mint had duly fulfilled his engagement to Her Majesty the Queen. The proceedings of the day were wound up with a banquet, given by the Goldsmiths' Company to the officials concerned."

Troy Weight. The Tower Pound or Moneyer's Pound, that which was used in the mints of this realm down to the time of Henry VIII. was lighter than the Troy Pound by three-quarters of an ounce Troy. "Henry VIII. in the 18th year of his reign forbade the use of the Tower Pound in his mint, and introduced the Troy Pound in its stead, which has continued to be used there ever since." EARL

OF LIVERPOOL, *Coins of the Realm.* Hence the Tower Pound was to the Troy Pound—

as $11\frac{1}{4}$: 12, or multiplying by 4.
as 45 : 48
as 15 : 16

so that weights expressed in terms of the Tower Pound are reduced to Troy by adding on one-fifteenth. This correction is of importance, whenever the metallic value of coins struck in Norman and Plantagenet times is compared with that of coins subsequent to the reign of Henry VIII. *See Pound (in money).*

> "The silver penny was about twenty-two and a half grains of Troy weight, but called a pennyweight Tower. The shilling was twelve of these pennies, and the pound *Tower* was twenty of these shillings."—WALTER MERREY.

Truck System. French *troc*, exchange of goods without the intervention of money; barter; *troquer* to exchange, to barter; Spanish and Portuguese *trocar*.

At first sight it would seem that the practice of *truck or barter* was more simple than that of purchase and sale, and when it can be done in perfect fairness, it doubtless is so. But the impossibility of always exchanging value for value led to so many abuses that the system was first viewed with great disfavour, and is now forbidden under legal penalties.

Trust. A *Trust* is defined by Stephens to be "the confidence reposed by one man in another when he invested him with the nominal ownership of property, to be dealt with in some particular manner, or held for some particular person or purpose pointed out." This definition of a trust answers pretty well to the nature of the "Trusts" instituted in the City in the course of the last few years, such as the "Foreign and Colonial Securities Trust," "The Government Securities Trust," "The Omnium Trust," and some others; in all these instances, a certain capital is subscribed, say £1,000,000 sterling, which is placed in the hands of trustees to be invested by them in a particular way, and the way prescribed is, to scatter the investments over a considerable number of carefully selected stocks, so as to diminish the risk which necessarily arises when a large sum is all invested in one stock only. The project is thoroughly sound in principle; but experience has shown that in some cases a great want of discretion has been manifest on the part of those entrusted with the selection of stocks; in other cases the rate of interest promised was fixed at too high a figure. The result has been that several of these schemes have fallen into disrepute. It is the opinion of persons well versed in these matters, that the safest mode of conducting these investment trusts would be to fix the rate of interest somewhat lower than the stocks are likely to realize, and to distribute any surplus that accrues by way of bonus at the end of each year. Or, according to another suggestion that has been made, it is recommended that one half-yearly coupon should be *fixed* and the second *variable*. Thus, if the first half-yearly coupon be 3 per cent. (that is, at the rate of 6 per cent. per annum), the second half-yearly coupon might be advertised at 1, 2, 3, or 4 per cent., according to the funds at the disposal of the trustees. In this way no liabilities would be incurred but what might pretty certainly be met, and the confidence which is reposed in the directors and trustees would not be exposed to those rude shocks which unfulfilled engagements are sure to cause.

Turn of the Market. The "turn of the market," or the "jobbers' turn," is the difference between the two prices quoted in the official lists for stocks, shares, &c. Thus, Consols are quoted $99\frac{3}{4}$ to $\frac{7}{8}$, and it means that the jobber, when asked the price of Consols at that moment, was prepared to give $99\frac{3}{4}$ for them, or to sell them at $99\frac{7}{8}$. The difference between the two is the compensation to the jobber for his service in the transaction.

Turnover. The sum total of the money value of goods sold in a shop or warehouse in a given time. In establishments where a large ready-money business is carried on, the turnover is many times greater than the entire capital employed in the concern; and this is the principal reason why prices in markets and crowded thoroughfares are often so much more moderate than in outlying localities, where capital lies idle for months together. Five per cent. on capital turned over once a month, is 60 per cent. per annum. Any tradesman who turned over his capital twice a year would be obliged to put a profit of 30 per cent. on his goods, in order to make 60 per cent. per annum.

Twelvemonth, Twelvemonths. The ambiguity arising from the use of the word month led to a distinction of some importance in former times between "a twelvemonth" and "twelve months."

"A lease," says Blackstone, "for 'twelve months' is only for forty-eight weeks; but if it be for 'a twelvemonth,' in the singular number, it is good for a whole year." By a recent Act, however, it is enacted, "That in all Acts the word *month* shall be deemed and taken to mean *calendar month*, unless words be added showing lunar month to be intended.

U.

U occurs in the following abbreviations:—

U.K., United Kingdom.
Ult., ultimo, in the last.

Underwriter. In marine insurance, an *underwriter* is one who writes his name at the foot of a policy of insurance. On some polices, only one such name appears: on others several names are added, when each party thus entering his name, is said to "take a line." Etymologically, the term "underwriter" signifies the same as "subscriber" (*sub* under, *scribere* to write), but while the Latinized form is used in all kinds of documents, the pure English word is appropriated almost exclusively by the insurance companies and their agents.

Unfunded Debt. The unfunded debt is often called the floating debt, and constitutes in fact the *real debt* of the nation. It arises from arrears in the Government accounts, from exchequer bills, and treasury bills, upon which money has been raised, and which are supposed to be paid out of the supplies of the year following their issue. It is thus distinguished from the funded debt, which is in reality no debt at all, since it is already paid by means of an engagement to grant the holders of it an annuity either in perpetuity, or for a term of years. (*See Funded Debt, Floating Debt.*)

Unilateral Contract. Latin, *unus*, one; *latus, lateris*, a side. (*See Contract.*)

A unilateral contract is a one-sided contract, that is, a contract which binds only one party; the other party, from the nature of the case, not needing to be bound. It consists essentially of a duty or obligation on the one side, and a right to be claimed on the other. Of course, there is no necessity to bind a person to claim his rights; but a duty or obligation is in its essence binding. The relation of debtor and creditor is strictly unilateral in its nature. A policy of insurance is also a unilateral contract, the obligation of the policy-holder being discharged by the payment of the premium, although he is still under an obligation not to do anything that would vitiate his claim. Agreements between landlord and tenant are sometimes unilateral, at others bilateral contracts, according as the landlord agrees to pay certain rates, and execute certain repairs, or not.

Unlimited Liability. (*See Liability.*)

Unit of Account. The unit of value in which accounts are kept. It may, or may not, coincide with any coin in circulation. In England, not only the unit of account (the pound sterling), but its fractional parts, the shilling and the penny, are represented by carefully devised coins. The Anglo-Saxon unit of account was the shilling, or twentieth part of the pound weight of silver; but no coin called a *shilling* was issued before the reign of Henry VII. In France, Belgium, and some other countries, the unit of value and the unit of account, is the *gold franc*; but this coin, if struck, would be so small, weighing only 5 grains, that pieces of 5 francs, or its multiples, only are made. Coins of smaller value are made of silver. Hence, the French unit of account is not represented by any actual coin. In countries less advanced in civilization, the disparity between the moneys of account and the actual coinage is still greater. In Canada the unit of value and the unit of account is the *dollar*, assumed to be equal to 50 English pence, but it is represented by a *bank note* and not by any coin.

Unit of Value. Sometimes called the *standard unit of value.* As it is impossible to name any substance which shall at all times retain the same fixed value in exchange, it has been the aim of Governments and financiers to find some substance which shall experience fewer fluctuations in value than any other substance. The metals have been found to possess this property in a greater degree than most other substances, and amongst the metals gold stands pre-eminent in this respect. The circumstances which affect the exchangeable value of a commodity, are chiefly those of *quantity* and *quality*. Now the quality of pure gold is always one and the same; while the quantity is free from violent fluctuations, from the fact that when once won from the soil, it rarely disappears, except in quantities comparatively small. Whether made into coin, plate, or jewellry, it is always an object of great care; as it neither rusts nor decays, every addition to the already existing stock is nearly permanent. It might be supposed that every addition to our stock of gold would diminish its purchasing power. *Theoretically*, this is true, and, *practically*, this inconvenience has been felt since the mines of California and Australia have been laid open. Nevertheless, the stock of gold that has accumulated in the world during the last two or three thousand years is so great that even the immense amount recently added has not seriously depressed its purchasing power; and as the existing permanent stock increases, the effect of future additions must be felt less and less; inasmuch as the addition of any given amount will always bear a constantly decreasing ratio to the stock already existing. It is therefore probable that the tendency now seen in most civilized States, to substitute a gold standard for those of inferior metals will gradually become more pronounced.

Unproductive Labour. In the early stages of Political Economy, labour which yielded no *profit* after paying the costs of production, was called unproductive labour. But this definition was soon found to include too much. Many kinds of labour, like those of the clergyman, schoolmaster, dramatist, and musician, were classed among the forms of unproductive labour, for no reason apparently except that their labour was not embodied in any *material* product. This was felt to be a very unsatisfactory reason. The services of these men, and of many others, although not capable of being estimated in money, or measured by any material standard, were clearly seen to be extremely useful, and in a high stage of civilization indispensable. In other words, they were productive of *utilities:* they produced something that was desired, and, being desired, possess value. The term unproductive labour is therefore now but little used.

Usance. From the French, *usance;* Italian, *usanza;* Spanish, *uso,* all from the Latin, *usus*, usage, practice, custom.

Usance, in commerce, is the time allowed by *usage* and custom for the payment of a bill of exchange. The length of usance varies in different countries between thirty days for French and Dutch bills to six months on Indian bills. Long usance is felt to be very objectionable, and in view of the fact that intercourse between distant countries is much more rapid than formerly, merchants are making efforts to reduce usance within narrower limits. Indian houses especially, are reducing it by one-third, that is, from six months to four. In England *usance* always means the *usual time*, and must not be confounded with *usury*. (*See next art.*)

Usury. From the Latin, *utor*, to use; whence *usura*, something given for the use of a thing, and especially money given for the use of money.

Usury originally signified nothing more than is now understood by the word *Interest*. But in ancient times, the rates charged for loans were so exorbitant and oppressive, that the very name of *usury* has something odious and repulsive about it. In England, the term is now used only in a reproachful sense. A "usurer" is always understood to be one who takes advantage of the needy to extort excessive interest, which is indeed often called an "usurious rate of interest." Severe laws were enacted in England against usurers, and it was not till 1833 that it became lawful to take more than 5 per cent. on bills of exchange. The Usury Laws were finally abolished in 1854.

Utility. Latin, *utilitas*, from *utor*, to use. French, *utilitè*.

Utility is that quality in things in virtue of which they afford satisfaction and enjoyment to those who possess them, or create a desire in persons to get possession of them.

The words "possess" and "possession" are here used in their widest signification, and this includes the case of those who merely have the right or privilege of looking at a picture, or hearing the voice of a singer. For the time being, and in so far as the requirements of this definition are concerned, all who look at the picture or hear the singer are joint possessors of them.

Utility is the source of value in all valuable things. Anything that is useless for any purpose whatever, is without any value. Nevertheless, utility, like value, is not a quality inherent in things themselves, but arises from the fact that things are desired, and only so far as they are desired. Fire and water are both useful things when supplied in quantities not greater than are wanted, but are useless and destructive when forced upon us in greater quantities than our needs demand.

Utter, To. Saxon, *ut*, out; *uter*, outer, extreme; *utter*, to give out, to issue: to *utter* goods, to sell goods.

Te send out: to put into circulation. To *utter* coin is usually understood to mean the passing off of false coin. Lawful coin is said to be *issued*, not uttered. To utter a bill or note, is to raise money upon it in any way, but the usual practice is by discounting it.

V.

Value. French, *valoir*, to be worth; Italian, *valòre*; Spanish, *valer, avaliar;* all from the Latin, *valēre*, to be well, to be in good health, to be worth, to avail, to be able. The old English form of the word was *valour*, as Sir T. More writes: "the *valour* of a peny;" or *valure*. "The same day ther was offered and given well to the *valure* of three thousand frâkes."

Value is a quality vested in things in consequence of their being esteemed and desired.

By "things," in the above definition, is to be understood (*a*) material things, as gold, silver, timber, houses, land, pictures, air, water, paper, documents, &c. (*b*.) Immaterial things, as friendship, opinion, beauty, skill, character, ease, security, duty, honour, &c.

It must also be observed that the quality of *value* is "vested" in things; by which term attention is directed to the fact, that value is not a quality *inherent in the things themselves,* but is imparted to them by the action of some force from the outside. The force thus indicated is that of human esteem and desire. Some things, as gold, silver, land, and house property, have been esteemed and desired so long and so universally, that they are commonly thought of as possessing some inherent or intrinsic value. There are others so little esteemed or desired that they possess but little or no value, such as chalk. But if, in the progress of invention, some very extensive use should be found for carbonic acid, and lime, our chalk-hills might become mines of wealth to the possessors, owing to the value set upon the chalk as a source of these products, arising from the desire of everybody to possess them.

Economists make a distinction between things that have a value in use, and those which have a value in exchange. There are many things—some material, some immaterial—which are very valuable in use, but of little value in exchange; such as air, water, wild flowers, friendship, love, ease. These things, either on account of their abundance, or because they are not susceptible of measurement and transfer, have little value set upon them in the markets of the world, yet they are much esteemed and universally desired: in other words, they are highly valued for the sake of the enjoyment which the use of them affords. Shortly, it may be said that value in use depends mainly on the *feelings* of those who use the things so valued. Value in exchange, while largely dependent on these feelings, is also greatly affected by qualities in the things themselves; such as scarcity, difficulty of attainment, susceptibility of measurement and transfer, the labour and skill embodied in them.

It has been said that

"The value of a thing
Is just as much as it will bring,"

which is a very fair definition of the term. Mr. McLeod says more precisely, "the value of any Economic Quantity is any other Economic Quantity for which it can be exchanged." Professor JEVONS, in his *Theory of Political Economy*, proposes to reject the term, and to substitute "Ratio of Exchange."

Vellon. Real-Vellon. Reale de Vellon or Vellou. Latin, *vellus*, a lock of wool torn from a sheep: a sheepskin with the wool on it. Old English, *fell*, a skin still retained in the word *fellmonger*. German, *Fell*, a skin, or hide. Spanish, *vellon*, a fleece. The Latin, *vellera*, fleeces, was used in poetry to signify sheep, much in the same way as we use "head of cattle," to signify the cattle themselves.

Vellon, in the Spanish language, appears to possess the same hazy sort of importance that "sterling" does in ours. The Reale de Vellon, the Ducado de Vellon, the Maravedi de Vellon, have taken rank among the most esteemed coins of Spain: and their names seem to point to a time when sheep and cattle, or their skins, formed the currency of the country.

Venezolano. The unit of value and of account in the United States of Venezuela, in conformity with the Monetary Law of May, 1871; and is represented both by gold and silver coins.

The *Gold Venezolano* weighs 1·613 grammes ·900 fine. It is worth 5 francs, or £·1982, or 3*s.* 11½*d.* sterling. Gold pieces of 20, 10, 5 and 1 venezolano are struck.

The *Silver Venezolano* is identical in weight, fineness, and value with the French five-franc piece, and to this extent is conformity with the requirements of the Latin monetary convention.

The Venezolano is also sometimes called the *Bolivar:* but as this latter name is also applied to two other coins, it is important to distinguish them, thus:—

In the carefully constructed tables by M. Sudre, for the *Annuaire par le Bureau des Longitudes*, he gives *Bolivar* as the alternative name for the 20-venezolano piece, which is worth 100 francs.

But in a report issued 21 July, 1881, the Venezuelan Consul, when quoting sums of money in *Bolivares*, makes a definite note—"The value of a Bolivar is equivalent to that of a franc," which is only one-fifth of the venezolano.

Ventem. A Portuguese coin valued at 20 reis.

Via. Under the article *Foreign Bill*, it is said that such bills are drawn in sets of *two* or *three*. Each one of the set is called a "*Via*," and is of equal validity with either of the others, until one is accepted, when all three are fastened together, and become one bill. Of course the drawee takes care, after accepting one via, not to accept another, but simply waits till the others come into his hands, as they are sure to do before they become payable or arrive at maturity. These *vias* differ from mere copies, which are often made when only one *via* has been drawn. A *copy*, it is true, may be negotiated in place of the original, but it derives its value from the original; whereas either via is on a par with the others, and when accepted, renders the others worthless.

Voucher. From the Latin, *vocare*, to call; *vocatio*, a calling: Norman-French, *voucher*, to call, a calling.

This word was formerly used in law to denote the *calling* upon a defendant to answer to a claim or charge about to be made against him. In this sense it continued to be used for some centuries, till it got mixed up in popular speech, when its original meaning was almost entirely lost sight of, and it came to signify almost the opposite of what it first expressed: that is to say, a voucher in its modern acceptation is a document, invoice, or other paper which *answers* to a call, or *bears witness*, or *affords proof* respecting some matter under examination. The transition from one meaning to the other was not violent. The *voucher* was a "calling" upon a defendant: or it might be a "calling" upon witnesses in favour of a defendant: or again it might be a "calling" for documents, title-deeds, accounts, warrants, contracts, or receipts, by way of proof. In commerce, it was papers of this latter kind that were "called" for: and as more importance was attached to the papers than to the person who called for them, the name of *voucher* was in course of time completely transferred to the documents themselves.

Another way of accounting for the application of the name *voucher* to the thing called for is, that it is a corruption of the correlative term *vouchee*. If this derivation could be substantiated by examples, it would be a very natural one; for all the defendants, witnesses, documents, &c., were denominated with strict accuracy *vouchees* (things called), and the corruption of *vouchee* into *voucher*, is not more gross than is found in scores of instances furnished by the hasty and uncritical language prevailing among men of business.

W.

Wager Policies, or Wagering Policies. Policies containing the phrase "interest, or no interest," intended to signify insurance of money when no property is on board the ship. A policy of this nature is a mere bet that a vessel will or will not arrive in port safe and sound within a given time; or that an individual named will or will not live till a certain age. These policies are not recognized in law.

Wages. From French, *gager*; German, *wagen*; Dutch, *waagen*, all meaning to venture, to throw down as a pledge, to hazard. In agricultural communities, where the term was first used, the term, *gage*, *wage*, or venture, expresses very accurately the nature of the pledge between an employer and his labourers. Although he knew there would be no return for what he paid to his labourers, until the in-gathering of his harvest, the employer "ventured" and "pledged" himself to give certain compensation for work done week by week; and as attention was more constantly fixed on what was pledged than on the act of pledging, the name of *gage*, *wage*, was at length completely transferred to the payment made in fulfilment of the pledge.

Wages (plural in form but singular in meaning) is payment given for the right to demand a certain amount of work, labour, or service from the recipient. This definition covers all kinds of recompense for work done under the direction of an employer, such as the *pay* of an officer, the *stipend* of a clergyman, the *fees* of a barrister, or the *salary* of a clerk.

Wages Fund. A fund theoretically assumed to exist, and out of which wages are paid. Practically, also, such a fund is known to exist, from the fact that wages are actually paid out of it. It is made up of two principal items. (1) A portion of the produce of *past* labour; and (2) Credit based on the anticipation of the profits of *future* labour. But the absolute amount of the wages fund is never accurately known, and it is probably never the same for two days together. It fluctuates with the multifarious causes, separately and combined, which go to create a demand for labour or to limit its supply, such as the general state of trade, the weather, fashion, the spirit of enterprise, financial disorganization, accumulation of capital, &c. It is found a convenient term to use when discussing economic questions; but the thing itself is too shadowy and unstable to admit of being employed in precise calculations, or to afford ground for safe inferences.

Waiver. The discharge by the holder of a Bill, or note, of any one or more of the parties to it. This discharge may be given either before or after it has become due, and without any *consideration*. (*See Consideration.*) It may be given by word of mouth, or in writing, but in the former case, it must necessarily be in the presence of witnesses, or it would have no binding force in law.

Watering of Stock. A metaphorical expression signifying the addition of Stock to that already issued by a Company or State, without making any additional provision for the payment of interest on the same. When a Railway Company issues new Stock for the building of a branch railway, the revenues of the new branch are expected to provide the interest on the newly-created stock. But if, instead of making a railway, the new stock were absorbed in paying debts or charges that ought to be disbursed out of the revenue, it is clear that interest has to be paid on a large additional amount of stock, while no provision is made to meet the increased charge. The stock in this latter case is said to be "watered."

Wealth. Latin, *valeo valēre*, to be well, to be worth something; *vale*, farewell French, *valoir*, to be worth, to have value. Saxon, *waleth*, rich; *walan*, happiness or prosperity; *wela*, well-being; *welega* or *welga*, rich. Danish, *vel*, well being. German, *Wohl*, weal, good, benefit, well-being; *das gemeine Wohl*, the public weal. There are a great number of words both in the Latin and Teutonic dialects, which appear to have their origin in some old root word, *wel* or *vel*. all conveying the idea of something good, desirable, or useful. In different lands and under varying circumstances, the root word took various though allied forms; our English words, *weal* and *wealth*, are amongst them, and cannot be traced to any one of them with certainty as its direct progenitor. The Greek word for wealth, goods, property, possessions, &c., was χρημα, *chrema;* plural, χρηματα, *chremata*, and is used by Aristotle in giving the oldest known, and perhaps the best definition, of wealth. χρηματα δε λεγομεν παντα ὁσων ἡ αξια νομισματι μετρειται. (We call wealth all things the value of which can be measured in money.)—*Ethics*, Book iv. chap. i.

This word is used by writers in two very different senses. Under the name of Natural Wealth is often comprehended a fertile soil, mineral deposits, watercourses, and a healthy climate. But Political Wealth, or Wealth Proper, as understood in Economics, signifies something which has an exchangeable or purchasing power, anything that can be bought or sold; and derives its value from the labour and skill employed in finding, making, and protecting it, and from its power of exciting in the minds of human beings a desire to possess it. There are three distinct kinds of Quantities, enumerated by MacLeod under the term Wealth—viz., *Money* which may be taken as the type of all material objects as land, houses, furniture, clothing, timber, metals, &c.; *Labour*, the type of every kind of service, whether physical, intellectual, or moral, and would include skill, ability, integrity, dexterity, &c.; and *Credit*, the type of Rights of every kind, as Rights of Action, Right to the payment of a Debt, Right to a Reversion, the Right to Crops, Vintages, and Goods not at present in existence. These, as they may all be bought or sold, come under the denomination of Political Wealth.

Many writers of eminence refuse to include such things as Credit and Rights in a definition of Wealth, and they advance very plausible reasons for doing so. At the same time, it is rather difficult to understand why a Right should not be included in the definition of Wealth, seeing that a Right to a thousand pounds will exchange for a house as readily as a thousand sovereigns. Probably the objection arises from the defective nature of some Rights, and from the fact that they cannot be enforced. A Right to a thousand pounds payable at the Bank of England would be regarded as a very substantial bit of wealth, but a Right to the same amount against a man on the verge of bankruptcy would be a shadowy form of wealth indeed.

William. A gold coin formerly used in Holland, and valued at 10 guilders. Its metallic value was about 16*s*. 2*d*. sterling.

Winding Up. Wound Up. *Winding Up* is the legal process by which the affairs of a Joint Stock or an Insurance Company are adjusted, and the Company itself dissolved. For details see "The Companies' Act," of 1862 and 1867, and the "Insurance Companies Act," of 1870 and 1872.

Worseness. (*See Betterness.*)

Y.

Yarim. A gold coin used in Turkey, value 9*s.* = half-Medjidie. Also a Silver Yarim, equal to half real or 10 piastres.

Yen. The new unit of value and of account in Japan, in conformity with the Monetary Law of 1871. It is represented both by gold and silver coins.

The *Gold Yen* weighs 1·666 grammes, ·900 fine, and is worth 5 francs, 17 centimes, or £·2049, equal to 49·17 pence English. It is divided into 100 sen, and each sen into 10 rin. The new coinage of Japan is thus assimilated very closely with that of the United States, and like that, is divided into 100ths and 1,000ths, the corresponding nomenclature being—

Yen = Dollar.
Sen = Cent.
Rin = Mil.

The *Silver Yen* weighs 26·956 grammes, ·900 fine. It is worth 5 francs, 39 centimes French, or £·2136, equal to 4*s.* 3*d.* sterling. This value is obtained, like all other values of silver coins mentioned in this work (unless otherwise stated) by reckoning *fine* gold as $15\frac{1}{2}$ times the value of an equal weight of *fine* silver. When absolute accuracy is required, in conformity with the current market price of silver, important corrections have always to be made. (*See Price of Gold and Silver.*)

Yermeebeshlek. A gold coin used in Turkey, value 12*s.* 6*d.*

Z.

Zabkran. The same with Sahib Kiran (*which see*).

Zecchino. A disused Venetian gold coin, worth about 9*s.* 5*d.*, so named from *zecca*, a mint, and the original of the *sequin* (*which see*).

Zehner. From the German, *zehn*, ten.

The Austrian 10 kreutzer piece, silver, and worth about $2\frac{1}{4}$*d.* English.

Zeni or Zheni. A small iron coin, with a hole in the centre, used in Japan, of which 1,600 or 1,700 went to the Itziboo. As the itziboo is worth about 16 or 17 pence, the *zeni* would be worth $\frac{1}{100}$ of a penny.

Zollverein. German, signifying *Toll-Union*, or Customs-Union.

A union of the States of Germany, for the purpose of establishing a uniform rate of customs duties or tolls between the various States joining the union. Since the consolidation of the Empire, the Zollverein has ceased to have any importance.

CPSIA information can be obtained at www.ICGtesting.com
Printed in the USA
LVOW070437301012

305008LV00008B/7/P